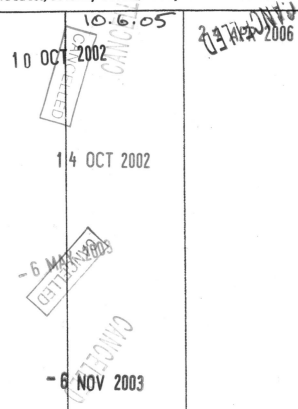

# Basic Readings in Communication Theory

07156 27/4/77

Under the advisory editorship of
J. Jeffery Auer

# Basic Readings in Communication Theory

## C. DAVID MORTENSEN
### University of Wisconsin

**HARPER & ROW, PUBLISHERS**
New York, Evanston,
San Francisco, London

**BASIC READINGS IN COMMUNICATION THEORY**

Copyright © 1973 by C. David Mortensen

Standard Book Number: 06-044625-0

Library of Congress Catalog Card Number: 72-87883

# CONTENTS

# PREFACE

This book is designed for any introductory course that seeks to acquaint students with a basic understanding of the process of human communication. The breadth and scope of subject matter is adaptable to a number of approaches to the first course in communication, whether theoretical, practical, contemporary, or traditional in orientation. Students in performance courses will find the material useful in assessing their own participation in communicative situations; those enrolled in courses built around the insights of communication theory will find much to enrich lectures and discussions on the subject.

The readings do not presuppose any prior background or technical competence. Each blends a lively and interesting style with a well-written, thoughtful consideration of fundamental issues, concepts, and problems in communicating. Parts I, II, and III explore the underlying nature of the communication process and provide a working conception of the forces that help to shape various patterns of human interaction. Parts IV, V, and VI examine the impact of intrapersonal, interpersonal, and cultural environments on the fabric and tenor of communicative behavior.

Appreciation is due many authors, publishers, and professional associations for making this book possible and for contributing to the larger interests of a field increasingly aware of an embarrassment of riches.

C. David Mortensen

# Basic Readings in Communication Theory

# INTRODUCTION

In seeking to understand the nature of human communication, man's most complex and ennobling social achievement, one is hardly at a loss for important subject material. Most of us spend up to 80 percent of our waking hours engaged in some form of communication; listening and responding to the messages of others occupies much of this time; the rest divides among talking, reading, and writing. An added consideration is the rich assortment of nonverbal cues. Taken together, the stream of verbal and nonverbal information bombards our senses and contributes to as many as 2,000 distinguishable units of interaction in a single day. The mix changes momentarily: morning greetings, cereal labels, bus signs, charts, traffic lights, hate stares, graffiti, coffee shop banter, peace gestures, laughter, and head nods. The themes are endless.

We approach the study of communication in the spirit of a search—hopefully a deeply personal and rewarding search—of ways to examine and understand various modes of communicative experience. Our objective is a broad one: It requires a working knowledge of the communication process and an understanding of the underlying forces at work in given social settings; also a certain familiarity with alternative explanations of communicative outcomes.

When one sifts through the fascinating complexities of human conduct, it is generally advisable to consult a number of possible interpretations. Something as complex and elusive as human communication does not lend itself to neat and tidy theories. Hence, it is too much to expect a study of basic theory to yield a single, unified perspective on the subject. The concept of communication theory should be taken as an umbrella term for a host of general principles and orienting statements designed to specify causes and key relationships among given facets of communicative behavior. Underlying this vast range of theoretical ideas is a diverse assortment of concepts, insights, and research findings. Some discoveries emerge from investigations on the psychological factors involved in the creation and interpretation of messages. Others focus on the social influences in communication, particularly the roles and cross-currents of tension and conflict in face-to-face settings. Still others relate to the impact of the physical environment and the larger role of culture in communication.

Given the complex nature of our subject, it will be useful to approach the study of communication from a number of perspectives. The first is organized around the psychological and social forces that seem to operate in all communicative settings. Readings in the first half of the book deal with the key denominators of communicative behavior—the context in which they occur, the varying types of messages, and the channels used to link respective parties. Having developed a better understanding of leading characteristics of our subject, we explore the dynamics of communication from the vantage point of its complexity in *intrapersonal, interpersonal,* and *culturally defined contexts.*

The term intrapersonal refers to the physical and psychological forces at work *within* individual communicators. Of central import is the struggle of the nervous system to impose order on the deluge of incoming sensory activity and to transform it into the language of conscious experience. Equally significant are the larger psychological influences, particularly the impact of self-awareness on attitudes toward signals received from the physical world. The section on interpersonal communication may be regarded as a broadly based study in the social psychology of the subject. Topics include the many influences at work in person perception, credibility, attraction, and the psychological defenses used to maintain social distance and outright avoidance. A final section traces the impact of culture on communication and shows how variations in cultural background alter patterns of personal demeanor, style, speech, nonverbal cues, and reactions to the physical environment of communication.

# PART I
# Perspectives

Nowadays we tend to conceive of complex social events as "happenings" where everything seems to occur randomly and at once, and it is nearly impossible to distinguish any one of countless simultaneous impressions. Communication may well qualify as the most elaborate single element in man's social happenings. In the verbal arena, everything is in a state of flux—the participants, their language, and the nature of their immediate physical surroundings. This quality of elusiveness in the communicative act makes our study more interesting but it also creates a problem. With so much going on at once, it is difficult to know what to study. Since we cannot possibly consider all the subtleties of any given act of communication, we need guidelines—or perspective—on what is significant and what can be ignored. The essays in this section are designed to serve as road maps for our inquiry; each one specifies in broad terms different fundamental elements in the various modes of communicative experience.

Communication occurs in a context of change, and men react differently to the forces of change. For some change is threatening while for others it is seen as necessary for growth. In "Communication: The Context of Change," Dean C. Barnlund examines the strategies people use in their attempts to cope with change. Among the defensive reactions are avoidance, silence, psychic withdrawal, noncommittal replies, verbal cocoons, detours, formulas, doubletalk, and 'insoltation'. Barnlund considers ways to escape these self-imposed defenses and discusses the need for communication based on mutual involvement and responsible self-disclosure. In "How Communication Works," Wilbur Schramm examines how participants in a communicative act can be "tuned" to a particular message. Schramm emphasizes the need for efficient encoding (the process of creating messages) and decoding (the process of interpreting messages), and accurate transmission of signals (through channels and feedback) from one person to another. To illustrate how the entire system works, Schramm uses models to represent the process of communication in general terms. Models are like road maps; they provide orientation and direction but not detail. Remember, too, that models, like road maps, should not be confused with the reality they represent.

To complete our perspective, it is necessary to have a working knowledge of the conditions necessary before communication can occur. In a provocative discussion of "Some Tentative Axioms of Communication," Paul Watzlawick, Janet Beavin, and Don Jackson consider the communicative significance of our interactive behavior with others. It is often said that we can stop talking but we cannot stop behaving. Hence, insofar as our behavior influences others, it becomes impossible *not* to communicate. The authors consider the complex interplay between message content and human relationship and show how the impact of messages depends on the nature of the relationships in which they occur. Finally, they show how individual viewpoints give rise to unexpected ways of defining the ongoing stream of communicative experience. This essay contains many exciting, if difficult, ideas and you may find after examining it carefully that your efforts have led to important self-discoveries.

# COMMUNICATION: THE CONTEXT OF CHANGE
## Dean C. Barnlund

Among the few universals that apply to man is this: That all men—no matter of what time or place, of what talent or temperament, of what race or rank—are continually engaged in making sense out of the world about them. Man, according to Nicholas Hobbs, "has to build defenses against the absurd in the human condition and at the same time find a scheme that will make possible reasonably accurate predictions of his own behavior and of the behavior of his wife, his boss, his professor, his physician, his neighbor, and of the policeman on the corner."[1] Although men may tolerate doubt, few can tolerate meaninglessness.

To survive psychically, man must conceive a world that is fairly stable, relatively free of ambiguity, and reasonably predictable. Some structure must be placed on the flow of impressions; events must be viewed from some perspective. Incoming sensations will be categorized, organized around some theme. Some facts will be noted and others neglected; some features will be emphasized and others minimized; certain relationships will appear reasonable, others unlikely or impossible. Meaning does not arise until experience is placed in some context.

Man is not a passive receptor, but an active agent in giving sense to sensation. The significance that any situation acquires is as much a result of what the perceiver brings to it as it is of the raw materials he finds there. Terms such as "personal constructs," "social schema," or "perceptual sets" have been used to identify the cognitive processes by which men render experience intelligible. As George Kelly notes, "Man looks at this world through transparent patterns or templets which he created and then attempted to fit over the realities of which the world is composed. The fit is not always good. But without such patterns the world appears to be such an undifferentiated homogeneity that man is unable to make any

Reprinted by permission from *Perspectives on Communication*, C. E. Larson and F. E. X. Dance, eds., Madison, Wisc.: Helix Press, 1968, pp. 24-40.

sense out of it. Even a poor fit is more helpful to him than nothing at all."[2]

As the infant matures into adulthood he gradually acquires a picture of the world he inhabits and his place within it. Pervasive orientations—of trust or suspicion, of affection or hostility—are learned early, often at considerable pain, and through communication with significant other people. Every success or failure contributes in some way to his accumulating assumptions about the world and how it operates. Such cognitive predispositions are learned unconsciously, and most people are only vaguely aware of their profound effects. Yet they are, in the view of Roger Harrison, "the most important survival equipment we have."[3] Thus it is not events themselves, but how men construe events, that determines what they will see, how they will feel, what they will think, and how they will respond.

Such perceptual biases, taken together, constitute what has been called the assumptive world of the individual. The world men get inside their heads is the only world they know. It is this symbolic world, not the real world, that they talk about, fight about, argue about, laugh about. It is this world that drives them to cooperate or compete, to love or hate. Unless this symbolic world is kept open and responsive to continuing experience, men are forced to live out their lives imprisoned within the constructs of their own invention.

The worlds men create for themselves are distinctive worlds, not the same world. Out of similar raw materials each fabricates meanings according to the dictates of his own perceptual priorities. It is not surprising that nurtured in different families, informed by different sources, frightened by different dreams, inspired by different teachers, rewarded for different virtues, men should view the world so differently. The way men project private significance into the world can be readily illustrated. Here is a group of people asked to respond to an ordinary photograph showing adults of various ages, standing together, and looking up at a distant object. The experimenter asks, "What do you see?" "What does it mean?" Some of the viewers comment on the mood of the figures, reporting "grief," "hope," "inspiration," or "despair." Others notice the identity of the persons, describing them as "peasants," "members of a minority," "Mexicans," or "Russians." Still others see the "ages of man," a "worshiping family," or "three generations." Even at the objective level there is disagreement; some report three persons, some four, some five. When shown before lunch "hunger" is one of the first interpretations; after lunch this meaning is never assigned. A similar process of projection would seem to fit the varying reactions people have to a peace demonstration, Charles de Gaulle, a labor contract, the Hippies, or the Pill.

Two behavioral scientists, Hastorf and Cantril, studied the conflicting reactions of Princeton and Dartmouth students to a hotly contested game between their football teams. The students seemed not to have attended the same game, their perceptions were subservient to their personal loyalties. The investigators conclude: "It is inaccurate and misleading to say that different people have different attitudes toward the same 'thing.' For the 'thing' is *not* the same for different people whether the 'thing' is a football game, a presidential candidate, Communism, or spinach. . . . We behave according to what we bring to the occasion, and what each of us brings to the occasion is more or less unique. And except for these significances which we bring to the occasion, the happenings around us would be meaningless occurrences, would be 'inconsequential.' "[4]

While we are continually engaged in an effort after meaning, every perception is necessarily a private and incomplete one. No one ever sees all, for each abstracts in accordance with his past experience and emerging needs. Where men construe events similarly, they can expect to understand and agree readily; where they construe events differently, agreement is more difficult. In exploring the impact of cognitive styles upon communication, Triandis found that pairs of subjects who categorized objects similarly communicated more effectively than those who categorized them differently.[5]

Paradoxically, it is these differences in perception that make communication inevitable. If men saw the same facts in the same way, there would be no reason to talk at all. Certain rituals of recognition or flattery might interrupt the silence, but there would be no occasion for serious talk. There would be no experiences to share, no conflicts to negotiate. A simple experiment will demonstrate this idea. At the next conversational opportunity, agree completely, both in fact and feeling, with the person who has just expressed an opinion. (This is more difficult than many people imagine). In a matter of seconds following this restatement, the conversation will grind to a halt, or someone will change the subject. The reason is clear: Where men see and feel alike there is nothing to share. Talk is primarily a means of confronting and exploring differences. Conversation moves from disagreement to disagreement, interrupted only occasionally to note areas of momentary concurrence.

It is not only inevitable that men communicate, but fortunate that they do so. The exposure to differences through communication, painful as it sometimes is, provides the only opportunity to test our private perceptions, to construct a total picture out of our separate visions, and to find new ways of negotiating unresolved problems.

Research on decision-making illustrates how important communication is in improving human performance. Subjects in one of these studies solved a set of problems working alone, then through majority vote, and finally by discussing them in small groups.[6] The problems resembled those in everyday life; that is, they were difficult, emotionally involving, and presented a range of possible solutions. The results indicated that voting did not improve the quality of solutions reached by solitary effort, but group decisions were clearly superior to individual decisions. In some instances, groups of the least competent subjects were, through discussion, able to surpass the decisions made by the most talented person working alone. Subsequent research using executives in labor, government, education, and business confirmed these findings. Even groups composed of persons who were unable to solve *any* of the problems by themselves, made better group decisions than the most effective person working alone. That is, administrators with no ability to solve the test problems by themselves showed superior judgment when allowed to confer. Maximizing communicative opportunity produced superior judgments.

How can we account for these results? Careful study of the recorded conversations revealed a number of contributing factors: Groups had a wider range of information so that each person benefited from the knowledge of others. Every person had his own view of the problem, and sharing these perspectives enlarged the number of possible approaches. More solutions were proposed in the groups, supplying more alternatives from which to choose. The different biases of participants prevented any subject from suffering the consequences of his own prejudices. Finally, sharing opinions led to more critical examination of proposals. Where persons worked alone they could remain blind to their own errors, but groups quickly identified mistakes that would lead to wrong decisions.

After finishing the analysis, one further question arose: Why were the groups not infallible? Although this smacked of asking why men are not perfect, the question led to new findings. Two conditions accounted for most of the group errors. In some cases the groups lacked conflict, and, assuming that unanimity proved they were correct, did not discuss the problem. In others, despite the occurrence of conflict, the subjects lacked the patience or skill to resolve it, and compromised to avoid interpersonal antagonism. The absence of conflict or the inability to explore it prevented communication and thereby diminished the quality of decisions. In the vocabulary of science, communication among mature persons may be a necessary if not a sufficient condition for personal growth and social progress.

What, then, prevents men from transforming their differences into agreements? Why are facts so often distorted and disputed? What inhibits the flow of new ideas? What produces friction? Why is there so often an undercurrent of resistance when men talk? It is, I believe, because communication nearly always implies change. Aside from common social rituals, *men nearly always talk in a context of change.* What prompts communication is the desire for someone else to see our facts, appreciate our values, share our feelings, accept our decisions. Communication is initiated, consciously or unconsciously, to change the other person. If difference is the raw material of conversation, influence is its intent.

For most people, change is threatening. It is the old and familiar that is trusted; the novel and unknown that arouses alarm. "No one," John Dewey once wrote, "discovers a new world without forsaking an old one."[7] To change is to give up cherished values, to be left defenseless and forced to assume responsibility for a new organization of experience. The degree to which fear is aroused is usually proportional to the extent to which core values are placed in question. In some cases the fears may be quite specific, and can be articulated. More commonly, the threatened person is unable to identify the reason for his anxiety. Ordinarily threat arises from the source, the content, or the manner of communicating.

The mere presence of some people produces tension. Persons who are superior in age, power, wealth, appearance, esteem may create apprehension. Secretaries and lathe operators, medical interns and practice teachers are often incapable of accurate work while supervisors are observing their performance. There is evidence that people who control the destiny of others, such as parents, teachers, supervisors, provoke ego defensive reactions, quite apart from what they may say. The same seems to be the case for those who interrupt or reverse the direction of self-growth.[8] Threatening people, Landfield found, are those who perceive us as we once were, or now are and no longer wish to be.[9] Even status signs—the policeman's uniform, the judge's gavel, the executive's desk, the physician's stethoscope, the psychologist's tests—can arouse fear before or during interpersonal encounters. The presence of threat, of course, affects the depth and accuracy of communication. A number of studies demonstrate that where superiors are feared, information is withheld or distorted.[10] Thus where human institutions proliferate status differences or personal habits aggravate them, communication may be more difficult because of the repressive context in which it occurs.

The substance of communication, that is, the subject being discussed, may also trigger defenses. A new fact tests an old fact; a new attitude challenges an existing one. New proposals may provoke fear of an unknown future, fear of possible failure, fear of loss of power or prestige. No matter how frustrating the present, its dangers are palpable and familiar. Time has permitted some adjustment to them. But to turn in new directions is to face a host of uncertainties. Even consideration of a new program implies an attack on those who created or support an existing program. "We tend to maintain our cognitive structures in relatively stable form," writes Joseph Precker, "and select and interact with those who do not attack these structures." When such encounters were unavoidable he found they aroused defensiveness or rejection of the attacker.[11] Any new or unassimilated thought challenges the assumptions on which behavior is based, and no one is so secure that he cannot be aroused at the thought of revising favored values. Thus, even where people are not initially hostile and try to avoid unnecessary friction, the topic, because of its emotional significance, may trigger resistance.

Beyond the source and content lies the manner in which men talk. One cannot separate who is speaking and what is talked about from the way differences are expressed. Matter and manner interact to produce meaning. Although all men have their own rhetoric, preferring some interpersonal strategies to others, a number of techniques that complicate communication can be identified.[12] Since interpersonal attitudes are conveyed both by verbal and nonverbal codes, any discrepancy in these codes may be regarded as a warning signal. Warm words are spoken in a cold voice. Frank statements are offset by calculating glances. Expressions of respect are contradicted with every interruption. Against the deceit that is evident in a confusion of codes, men become apprehensive and guarded in their own messages.

An attitude of infallibility discourages communication. The dogmatic assertion of difference leaves no opportunity for influence to move in both directions. Where men claim, "There is only one conclusion," "It all boils down to," "The only course of action is," there will be negligible exploration of differences. The person who is impervious to the words of others while demanding sympathetic consideration of his own denies his associates any significant role in communication. They are forced to disregard their experience, deny their feelings, censor their thoughts. Since unquestioned statements are untested statements, the dogmatic person appears to be more interested in triumph than in truth.

Messages that convey a manipulative purpose also subvert communication. A calculated use of argument, a carefully phrased idea, a solicitous manner, a restrained reaction, all indicate that someone is being maneuvered into a predetermined position. Sooner or later the manipulated recognizes his manipulator. He begins to feel regarded as an object, not as a person. He becomes suspicious, emotionally tense, and verbally devious himself. That the manipulator is sometimes unaware of his own desires to control others, does not reduce the threat he poses for them.

Information normally flows between communicants in

both directions: The man who speaks also listens. But often, through deliberate design or personal preference, interaction is blocked so that one person sends all the messages, the other only receives them. The captain commands, the soldier obeys; the teacher lectures, the student takes notes. A letter from a friend who is an educational consultant in India illustrates how far it is possible to carry this kind of communicative irresponsibility. His daughter, raised in one of the great cattle provinces of Western Canada, is attending school in India.

Thora came home the other day doggedly repeating to herself, "A cow is a big animal with four legs and two horns. It is the most useful of all animals. The feet of the cow are called hoofs." I asked what she was doing, repeating this over and over again, and she replied that this was nature study and she had to memorize the cow. The teacher will not tolerate improvised replies, but the students must jump up smartly beside their desks and repeat exactly what was copied from the blackboard the day before. It sounds fantastic, but the end of the system is to stifle initiative, destroy creativity and engender a violent dislike for learning.[13]

One-way communication implies, of course, that meanings in the nervous system of one person can be deposited in the nervous system of another. Unfortunately communication is not this simple. Men differ not only in experience, but in their habits of speech as well. The only way to arrive at common meanings is through mutual accommodation. Each must share some responsibility for calibrating his words and intentions with the other.

Limiting communication to the sending of messages impoverishes the process and renders at least one participant impotent. Studies by Leavitt and Mueller illustrate some of the difficulties that attend one-way communication.[14] Persons attempting to give even the simplest instructions found their orders were inaccurately executed, that errors of interpretation could not be corrected, and that this condition produced extremely low morale. It is not difficult to estimate the cause of the low morale: For someone to receive confusing or complicated information and to be unable to clarify it, especially when it affects his performance or status, can be unnerving. Since all messages are ambiguous in some respect, cutting off efforts to confirm their meaning leaves the receiver without protection in a potentially punishing situation.

A threatening atmosphere is probable, also, in encounters in which one of the communicants maintains considerable emotional distance. The person who is coldly objective or who refuses to disclose his own feelings is likely to be viewed with suspicion. To be treated as a set of facts or as a problem to be solved, rather than as a human being, seldom contributes to interpersonal rapport. Such emotional distancing creates, to use a phrase of Martin Buber's, an I-It rather than I-Thou relation. One is not likely to approach or expose himself to an unresponsive facade. It is safer to remain on guard in the company of those who are themselves guarded. Any verbal indiscretion or spontaneous revelation may give an advantage or be used against one. As interaction continues, participants draw farther and farther apart from any real confrontation with their differences.

The most familiar form of threat is found in a highly evaluative communication context. There is continual appraisal. Remarks are judged rather than understood. Conversation becomes cross-examination. Criticism may be given directly through attack, or indirectly through sarcasm or innuendo. (The latter, because of its ambiguity, is far harder to handle.) Compliments seem only slightly less corrupting than insults, for in one case the receiver modifies his behavior to gain further rewards and in the other to avoid further punishments. In either case he is encouraged to distort his judgment. It becomes hazardous to be honest, to be open, to be original. Ideas are suppressed and remarks tailored to fit the expectations of others. The result is to diminish honest contribution to the conversation, and to isolate men from their own experience.

A more subtle form of threat occurs when conversation is converted into a struggle over identity. At one level, talk flows around a common interest or problem; at another, communication becomes a competition for status. Participants present their credentials and challenge those of others. In organizational life these claims relate to the respective power, intelligence, skill, or rank of the communicants. But even in ordinary encounters, men verbally compete to determine who is in better physical condition, who has the more talented children, who can consume more alcohol, or who is more attractive to the opposite sex. Communication becomes an occasion for asserting and validating personal identity rather than for testing what we know. Status-reminding phrases, such as "I've devoted years to this matter," "I've had much more experience," or "You wouldn't be able to appreciate," are likely to invite reaction in kind. "Once the 'proving' syndrome is present," according to Paul Goodman, "the boys are quite out of touch with the simplest realities."[15] People who constantly remind us of who they are and of who we are—especially when who they are is superior, and who we are is inferior—threaten the concept we have of ourselves. When identity is challenged, few have enough insight or strength to resist. What might have become a productive conversation turns into an interaction of roles and of facades. Even the expression of affection can turn into a competitive affair:

"I love you," she said.
"I adore you," he said.
"I love you more," she said.
"More than what?" he said.
"Than you love me," she said.
"Impossible," he said.
"Don't argue," she said.
"I was only . . ." he said.
"Shut up," she said.[16]

In short, the prospect of communication may threaten people for a number of reasons: Because such interactions occur with persons endowed with considerable power and status; because the underlying purpose is to change perceptions that have personal significance; because the communicative approach prevents a full and sympathetic exploration of differences. Any one of these factors alone can produce an undercurrent of tension in human affairs; but in many instances all three combine to arouse deeper anxiety.

Through all there runs a common theme. Though manifested differently, there is always a challenge to the personal integrity and self-respect of the person in communication. To talk to some people is dangerous because they control what it is possible for us to be and do. To talk about some topics is hazardous for it exposes one to differences in attitude and feeling. To talk in some ways is disturbing for one must guard continually against being exposed and attacked. But it is at the intersection of all three that men are most vulnerable:

Where a sensitive topic must be discussed with a powerful person in an emotionally charged atmosphere.

During a lifetime of painful encounters people acquire an extensive repertoire of defensive strategies.[17] At low levels of stress men tend to remain open to new facts, flexible in interpretation, creative in response. As the perceived threat increases, they narrow their vision, resist certain kinds of information, distort details to fit their own biases, even manufacture evidence to bolster their preconceptions. The old, whether appropriate or not, is favored over the new. Anxiety is aroused when a person, in encounters with others, confronts perceptions that are beyond his capacity to assimilate. As Gregory Bateson has suggested, "This is a terrifying moment . . . , you've been climbing up a ladder, you knew it was an unsound ladder and now you're asked to step off it and you don't really know there's going to be another ladder—even if the ladder you were on was a rather unsound one. This is terror."[18] Defenses protect the individual against facts that might otherwise undermine the system of assumptions that give stability and significance to his experience.

Not all defending behavior, of course, is defensive. Most men hold tentative conclusions about many issues. We believe that certain ways of looking at the world and at ourselves have some credibility. At any time we may voice these opinions. If, when confronted with opinions that differ from our own, we can explore these differences quietly, comfortably, thoroughly, and with the aim of testing the validity of our own beliefs, then we are only defending an opinion to reach more reliable conclusions. However, if when confronted with disagreement, we find it difficult to examine that thought or feeling, find the opposing view arousing us emotionally, find our hearts racing and our minds frantically seizing upon arguments, find we cannot reply calmly and without antagonism, the reaction is probably defensive. Words are being used to protect rather than to test private judgment.

Some defensive techniques are conscious; most of them are unconscious. Each person has his own hierarchy of tactics to which he retreats when faced with inadmissable perceptions. These defenses, provoked in a context of change, constitute the major barriers to communication among men. When attacked, as Paul Tournier notes, "Each of us does his best to hide behind a shield."

For one it is a mysterious silence which constitutes an impenetrable retreat. For another it is facile chit-chat so that we never seem to get near him. Or else, it is erudition, quotations, abstractions, theories, academic argument, technical jargon; or ready-made answers, trivialities, or sententious and patronizing advice. One hides behind his timidity, so that we cannot find anything to say to him; another behind a fine self-assurance which renders him less vulnerable. At one moment we have recourse to our intelligence, to help us to juggle with words. Later on we pretend to be stupid so that we cannot reply. . . . It is possible to hide behind one's advanced years, or behind one's university degree, one's political office, or the necessity of nursing one's reputation. A woman can hide behind her startling beauty, or behind her husband's notoriety; just as, indeed, a husband can hide behind his wife.[19]

One of the principal forms of defense is to avoid communicative contact altogether. It is unlikely that anyone reading these words has not, on some occasion, deliberately avoided certain persons. It may have been a teacher, a parent, a supervisor, or, depending on circumstances, anyone with the ability to contradict, to embarrass, to attack us. Selective communication—Whites talking with Whites, Republicans with Republicans, Generation with Generation, Physicians with Physicians—greatly reduces the prospect of having to cope with discrepant or damaging points of view.

Even when contact cannot be avoided, it is possible to resist exposure by remaining silent. If a person does not speak he cannot expose himself or his judgments to public scrutiny. By retreating into his own private world he can remain untouched by the worlds of others. Theodore Newcomb has identified the process of communicative avoidance, whether of persons or topics, as "autistic hostility."[20] Confrontation is avoided to protect prevailing attitudes. In talking together people run the risk of understanding one another, hence of having to alter existing prejudices. Fraternizing with the enemy or socializing with competitors is traditionally avoided lest one become incapable of manipulating and mistreating them on other occasions.

A kind of psychic withdrawal is also possible. In this case the person never really presents himself as he is. According to Ronald Laing, "He never quite says what he means or means what he says. The part he plays is always not quite himself."[21]

Where this withdrawal occurs, there is often an undercurrent of nonverbal signs that express defensive feelings. Recent research shows that people who wish to avoid communication choose to sit at a greater distance from others than those who wish to interact.[22] Tension-reducing body movements and gestures which serve no instrumental purpose increase.[23] Any act, from smoking a cigarette to doodling on a note pad, may reflect developing resistance. Research on mutual glances shows that eye contact is reduced when persons are in competitive, embarrassing, or critical encounters with others.[24] Thus many nonverbal indicators may convey the defensive attitudes of another person.

Just short of the verbal forms of resistance lies the noncommittal reply. Such phrases as "Uh-huh," "I guess so," "Maybe," and "Oh yeah" fill the void left by a preceding question, but reveal little of the thought or feeling of the respondent. They provide an escape route, for at the moment of utterance they convey only an ambiguous neutrality; later, according to the shifting intent of the speaker, they may be given a variety of meanings.

Yet men also talk to protect themselves from confronting differences. Words become a substitute for, rather than a means to, understanding. People spin verbal cocoons around themselves that disquieting ideas cannot penetrate. One person describes it this way: "If, for example, I can talk at such an abstract level that few can determine what I am saying, then I must have high intelligence. This is especially true if no one can understand me. The reason I could not communicate was that I did not want to."[25] Men often talk compulsively, and through long and frequent repetitions leave others no chance to reflect on what was said, to explore their own reactions, or to answer objections. Opponents are overwhelmed and defeated in a rush of words. Sometimes this takes the form of counter-attacks, with the defensive person placing the burden of proof upon the opposition. By turning attention to others and exposing their weakness he hopes to hide his own vulnerability.

Conversational detours around painful topics are not uncommon. This may be done consciously, as in the case of the hostess who steers talk away from religious or political topics. More commonly it is done unconsciously by people who are unaware of the threat they seek to avoid. The essential point of a remark is disregarded, and some tangential or entirely new thought is introduced. Parents who fear discussing sex with their children, or supervisors who prefer not to know about critical failures of their subordinates, often rely upon topical control to neutralize communication. Each time a threatening or sensitive comment is made talk is turned abruptly in a new direction. Men have become so skillful at defensively diverting conversation into painless channels that some are able to avoid meaningful interaction on nearly every vital issue that touches their lives.

Men also hide from each other through communicating by formula. Talk is prompted not by inner necessity, but by social convention. Everyone is familiar with the meaningless phrases used in social greetings. But this same verbal game may be extended to cover more serious encounters. Phrases are uttered and repeated, but when examined turn out to be empty. Flattery substitutes for frankness. There is much moralizing and sloganizing. Instead of examining differences, communicants obscure them in large abstractions that permit a multitude of interpretations. A kind of double-talk preserves the illusion of confrontation while preventing it from ever occurring. There is often an interaction of roles rather than of persons. When people speak as parents, professors, as physicians, or as political candidates, listeners are likely to discount or mistrust much of what is said. Their remarks are seen as a consequence of their position, not of their personal experience. Of all the defenses, this currently seems most disruptive of efforts to reach across races and generations.

There is also the use of indirection. Instead of speaking frankly, men speak in double meanings. At the explicit level, one idea is transmitted; at the implicit level another idea, often the opposite. The most familiar forms include kidding and sarcasm. Humor, despite its high reputation as a form of recreational communication, often serves defensive and destructive ends. Verbal indirection is almost an unassailable stratagem, for anyone who takes the implied meaning seriously may be accused of projecting false interpretations of it. With a few oblique comments, efforts to openly explore differences may be totally blocked.

Defensive behavior is characteristic of some men all of the

time, and of all men some of the time. Everyone must build the house of his own consciousness to interpret events around him. It is this "personal cosmology" that stands between us and the unknown and unacceptable. With such a guidance system events become recognizable and comprehensible. Those who perceive reality in different terms—as everyone does—alarm us because they shake the stability of our system. Defenses, note Kahn and Cannell, "are designed in large part to help us to protect ourselves against making some undesirable revelation or against putting ourselves in an unfavorable light. They are man's methods of defending himself against the possibility of being made to look ridiculous or inadequate. And in most cases we are not content merely to avoid looking inadequate, we also want to appear intelligent, thoughtful, or in possession of whatever other virtues are relevant to the situation from our point of view." [26] Confronted with difference, men may deny it, obscure it, confuse it, or evade it in order to protect their own assumptive world against the meanings of others.

Unfortunately, to the extent that men insulate themselves from the worlds that others know, they are imprisoned within their own defenses. They become blind to the limits of their own knowledge, and incapable of incorporating new experience. They are forced to repeat the same old ways of thinking because they result from the same old ways of seeing. Interaction loses the significance it might have. "This shutup self, being isolated," writes Ronald Laing, "is unable to be enriched by outer experience, and so the whole inner world comes to be more and more impoverished, until the individual may come to feel he is merely a vacuum." [27] Without access to the experience and perceptions of others, the individual deprives himself of the raw material of growth. Defenses corrupt the only process by which we might extend and deepen our experience. Until we can hear what others say, we cannot grow wiser ourselves.

To appreciate the full significance of incomplete communication in organizational life, another factor must be added. It is this: The higher men rise, the fewer the problems with which they have direct contact, and the more they must rely on the words of others. Unfortunately, as men assume greater power their higher status increases the difficulty in obtaining reliable accounts from others, and increases their own capacity to shield themselves from unpleasant information. Given a superior who prefers reassurance and a subordinate who fears to speak out, there is every reason to expect censored and distorted reports. Yet it is imperative that those in high places cope with realities rather than defensive fantasies.

What, then, can be done to create conditions in which men are not afraid to communicate? How can the destructive cycle of threat and defense be broken? Are there conditions that encourage men to respond to each other more creatively, so that differences can widen and deepen human experience? Can self-protective encounters be converted into self-enriching ones?

To reduce defenses, threat must be reduced. Such threats, as suggested earlier, spring from the source, the content, or the manner of communicating. Where it is the person who threatens, it is usually because differences in status exist, are introduced, or accentuated. For this reason groups and organizations ought regularly to review their internal structure to see if differences in authority are essential to or destructive of effective performance. Differences in rank are often multiplied or emphasized without regard for their inhibiting and distorting effects on the flow of information and ideas. Studies of organizational behavior suggest that those marked by severe competition for status often have serious problems of communication.[28] Status barriers, however, may dissolve in the face of facilitating interpersonal attitudes.

Where the threat arises from different perceptions of problems and policies, there are ways of rendering these differences less disruptive. Proposals can be made as specific as possible to counteract fears of an uncertain future; they can be introduced gradually to reduce the amount of risk involved; they can be initiated experimentally so that failure can be remedied; they can include guarantees against the loss of personal prestige and power. Every new idea, since it is an implicit criticism of an old idea, may disturb those responsible for the prevailing view; but it is possible to innovate without attacking unnecessarily those associated with former policies.

Neither the source nor the subject, however, is as critical

as the climate in which interaction occurs. Communication as a physical fact produces no magic: Words can lead toward destructive or productive outcomes depending on the attitudes that surround them. Where the object is to secure as complete, as frank, as creative an interaction of experience as possible, the following attitudes would seem to promote communication in a context of change.

Human understanding is facilitated where there is a willingness to become involved with the other person. It means to treat him as a person, not as an object; to see him as a man, not as a number, a vote, or a factor in production. It is to regard him as a value in himself, rather than a means to some other value. It is to prize his experience and his needs. Most of all, it is to consider and explore his feelings. In practical terms it means one is willing to take time, to avoid interruptions, to be communicatively accessible. Dozens of superficial and fragmentary conversations do not encourage a meeting of minds. There must be as much respect for his experience as we expect for our own. Since it is the loss of self-esteem that men fear most, such respect can do much to reduce the motivation for defensive interaction.

Communication is facilitated when there is a frank and full exposure of self. It is when men interact in role, speaking as they believe they should rather than as they feel, that communication is often corrupted. In the words of Sidney Jourard, "We say that we feel things we do not feel. We say that we did things we did not do. We say that we believe things we do not believe."[29] We present, in short, persons that we are not. As one person retreats behind his false self—performing his lines, weighing his words, calculating his movements—the danger signs are recognized. Rarely does the other person fail to detect them. In an atmosphere of deceit, his suspicion is aroused and defenses go up. He begins to edit his thoughts, censor his feelings, manipulate his responses, and assume the rituals and mask of his office. Not only does communication stop, but mistrust lingers on to corrupt future encounters. Afterwards each says to himself, "I don't believe him," "I don't trust him," "I will avoid him in the future." This pattern accounts for much of the communicative isolation of parent and child, teacher and student, Black and White. It may also be the reason why interaction is so often accompanied by an undercurrent of strain, for it takes considerable energy to sustain both a false and a real self.

In contrast, defenses tend to disintegrate in an atmosphere of honesty. There are no inconsistent messages. What is said is what is known, what is felt, what is thought. Pretenses are dropped and contrivance ceases. Instead the effort is to express, as spontaneously and accurately as possible, the flow of thought and feeling. In the absence of deceit, there is less reason to distort or deny in reply. A genuine interaction of experience can occur. Much of the tension goes out of personal relationships. Communication becomes something to seek rather than something to avoid. Through talk it becomes possible to learn more about ourselves and more about the issues we face as men.

The willingness to be transparent leads to a further condition that promotes healthy interaction. In social encounters men see their purposes in many ways: Some as manipulative, some as dominating, some as competitive, some as impressive, some as protective. People seldom talk for more than a few moments without exposing their underlying communicative strategy. Most of our defenses are designed to prevent damage to the symbolic self that occurs in the face of these depreciating motives. But an attitude of mutuality can also be heard, and heard loud and clear. This attitude is manifest in many ways: Whenever there is patience rather than impatience, whenever there is a tentative rather than dogmatic assertion of opinion, whenever there is curiosity rather than indifference for alternative views, whenever there is a creative rather than inflexible approach to arguments. Where there is a feeling of mutual involvement among communicative equals, defenses are unlikely to interfere with the pursuit of new meanings.

Understanding is also promoted when people assume their full communicative responsibilities. Now what does that mean? Simply that one will listen as well as speak, that he will try to understand as well as try to be understood. There is little doubt among specialists that listening is by far the harder communicative task. Then why is it so often assigned to the younger, the weaker, the less competent? Usually it is the student who must understand the teacher, the employee who must understand the supervisor, the patient who must understand the doctor, the young who must understand the old. In response to an essay "On Being an American Parent," one college student wrote the following lines as part of a "Letter to the Editor."

> Your paragraph under "Listen" very well sums up what I'm trying to say. I could never tell my parents anything, it was always "I'm too busy . . . too tired . . . that's not important . . . that's stupid . . . can't you think of better things. . . ." As a result, I stopped telling my parents anything. All communication ceased.
> I have only one important plea to parents . . . *Listen, listen,* and *listen again.* Please, I know the consequences and I'm in hell.[30]

In instance after instance the heavier communicative burden is forced upon the weaker, and the easier load is assumed by the stronger. It is not surprising that such exploitation should occasionally arouse defensive reactions.

Research in the behavioral sciences gives consistent support to the principle that two-way, as compared with one-way, communication produces more accurate understanding, stimulates a greater flow of ideas, corrects misunderstandings more efficiently, and yields a higher level of morale. Why, then, do men so often block feedback? Partly out of habit. In many interpersonal encounters listening means no more than a passive monitoring of the conversation, a time in which men prepare their next remarks. Partly we prevent feedback because of fear. It is upsetting to find how confusing our instructions have been, how inconsistent our words and deeds, how irritating our actions sometimes are. Where receivers have been given a chance to talk back after long periods of following orders, they usually respond at first with hostility. Yet the easing of communicative restrictions, in most instances, quickly restores a constructive and cooperative relationship.

On the national scene these days we hear much about the need for more dialogue. Many are skeptical of this demand. Has there not always been the right of free speech, free access to the platform for every advocate? True, but freedom to speak is not freedom to influence. For genuine dialogue there must be someone to talk, but also someone to listen. To speak is an empty freedom—as racial clashes and political demonstrations should remind us—unless there is someone willing to hear. And to reply in ways that prove that what was said has made a difference.

Within the intimacy of the therapeutic relationship—where communicative principles are tested at every moment—this premise seems equally valid. Again, it is not the talking that appears to accomplish the cure but association with someone capable of hearing. To be with someone who is truly willing to listen, who concentrates sensitively on all that is said, is no longer to need defenses. Such listening, of course, involves the risk of change. No one can leave the safety and comfort of his own assumptive world and enter that of another without running the risk of having his own commitments questioned. Not only questioned, but perhaps altered. To communicate fully with another human being, since it entails the risk of being changed oneself, is to perform what may be the most courageous of all human acts.

Communication is facilitated when there is a capacity to create a non-evaluative atmosphere. Defenses are provoked not so much by the expectation of difference, as by the expectation of criticism. "The major barrier to interpersonal communication," Carl Rogers has suggested, "is our very natural tendency to judge, to evaluate, to approve, or disapprove the statement of the other person or group." Under the surface of many, if not most, conversations there runs an undercurrent of censure. If we differ, one of us, usually the other fellow, must be wrong, must be stupid, must be incompetent, must be malicious. In so polarized a setting, where conversation becomes cross-examination, it is not surprising that men speak cautiously, incompletely, ambiguously; it is not surprising that with such critical preoccupations they listen suspiciously, partially, vaguely, to what is actually said. "The stronger our feelings," continues Rogers, "the more likely it is there will be no mutual element in the communication. There will be just two ideas, two feelings, two judgments, missing each other in psychological space." [31] When people recognize that they will not be forced beyond their own limits, when they see that their meanings will be respected and understood, when they feel that others will help in exploring difficult or dangerous experiences, they can begin to drop their defenses.

As the atmosphere becomes less evaluative, men are more likely to express and examine a wider range of differences without distortion. Where the intent is to comprehend rather than to attack, communication becomes a source of benefit rather than harm. In a permissive climate people feel comfortable, feel respected, feel secure enough to talk openly. "Conveying assurance of understanding," writes Anatol Rapoport, "is the first step in the removal of threat."[32] Research done on the attributes of helpful people indicates that they are easy to talk with, maximize areas open to discussion, minimize embarrassment, and seldom disapprove.[33]

In such trusting relationships men can develop empathy. They can participate in each other's experience, sharing the assumptions, the perspectives, and the meanings that events hold for them. This is not to insist that evaluation always be avoided, for decisions must be made about facts, theories, policies, even people. It is only to argue that mutual understanding should precede mutual evaluation. Problems cannot be solved until they are understood, and highly critical attitudes inhibit the communication of problems.

It appears that whether communication promotes understanding and affection, or blocks understanding and builds defenses, depends more on the assumptions than on the techniques of the communicator.[34] Or, rather, it is to say that technique cannot be divorced from assumption: As men assume, so will they communicate. Where men presume their knowledge to be complete or infallible, there is no communication or only a manipulative concern for others. Where men presume—as we know to be the case—that their knowledge is fragmentary and uncertain, genuine communication can occur. To recognize the limits of one's own facts and feelings is to become curious about the facts and feelings of others. At such moments men are likely to be open, honest, trusting, empathic, not because of some altruistic motive, but because it is the only way to correct and to extend their own perceptions of the world. Each stands to gain: The speaker because he can test what he believes and because it is rewarding to be understood; the listener because he can broaden his experience and because it is stimulating to understand.

Every significant human crisis begins or ends in a communicative encounter of one kind or another. It is here that differences are voiced. It is here that differences threaten. It is here that defenses are raised, and men embittered. But it is here, too, that differences may be welcomed. It is here that words may be heard. It is here that understanding may be reached, that men may cross the distance that divides them. "In my civilization," wrote Antoine de Saint-Exupéry, "he who is different from me does not impoverish me—he enriches me." [35]

## REFERENCES

1. Hobbs, Nicholas, "Sources of Gain in Psychotherapy," *American Psychologist*, 1962, 17, 74.
2. Kelly, George A., *The Psychology of Personal Constructs*, New York: Norton, 1955, 8-9.
3. Harrison, Roger, "Defenses and the Need to Know," in Paul Lawrence and George V. Seiler, *Organizational Behavior and Administration*, Homewood, Ill.: Irwin and Dorsey, 267.
4. Hastorf, Albert, and Cantril, Hadley, "They Saw a Game: A Case Study," *Journal of Abnormal and Social Psychology*, 1954, 49, 129-134.
5. Triandis, Harry, "Cognitive Similarity and Communication in a Dyad," *Human Relations*, 1960, 13, 175-183.
6. Barnlund, Dean C., "A Comparative Study of Individual, Majority and Group Judgment," *Journal of Abnormal and Social Psychology*, 1959, 58, 55-60.
7. Dewey, John, *Experience and Nature*, Chicago: Open Court, 1925, 246.
8. Hurwitz, Jacob, Zander, Alvin, and Hymovitch, Bernard, "Some Effects of Power on the Relations Among Group Members," in D. Cartwright and A. Zander, *Group Dynamics: Research and Theory*, New York: Harper & Row, 1960.
9. Landfield, A., "A Movement Interpretation of Threat," *Journal of Abnormal and Social Psychology*, 1954, 49, 529-532.
10. See, for example, John Thibaut and Henry Riecken, "Authoritarianism, Status, and the Communication of Aggression," *Human Relations*, 1955, 8, 113-133; Arthur Cohen, "Upward Communication in Experimentally Created Hierarchies," *Human Relations*, 1958, 11, 41-53; William Read, "Upward Communication in Industrial Hierarchies," *Human Relations*, 1962, 15, 3-16.
11. Precker, Joseph, "The Automorphic Process and the Attribution of Values," *Journal of Personality*, 1953, 21, 356-363.
12. Efforts to identify nonfacilitating techniques may be found in Jack Gibb, "Defensive Communication," *Journal of Communication*, 1961, 11, 141-148; in Frank Miyamoto, Laura Crowell, and Allan Katcher, "Communicant Behavior in Small Groups," *Journal of Communication*, 1957, 7, 151-160; and in Phillip Lichtenberg, "Emotional Maturity as Manifest in Ideational Interaction," *Journal of Abnormal and Social Psychology*, 1955, 51, 298-301.

13. Personal correspondence.
14. Leavitt, Harold, and Mueller, Ronald, "Some Effects of Feedback on Communication," *Human Relations*, 1951, 4, 401-410.
15. Goodman, Paul, *Growing Up Absurd*, New York: Random House, 1960, 206.
16. Ciardi, John, "Manner of Speaking," *Saturday Review*, December 23, 1967.
17. Men defend themselves intrapersonally as well as interpersonally. The principal forms of such inner defense—introjection, identification, repression, denial, regression, reaction-formation, displacement—will not be treated here. It is the character of defensive behavior in interpersonal relationships that is our major concern.
18. Bateson, Gregory, lecture at San Francisco State College, 1959.
19. Tournier, Paul, *The Meaning of Persons*, New York: Harper & Row, 1957, 219.
20. Newcomb, Theodore, "Autistic Hostility and Social Reality," *Human Relations*, 1947, 1, 69-86.
21. Laing, Ronald, *The Divided Self*, Chicago: Quadrangle, 1960.
22. Rosenfeld, Howard, "Effect of Approval-Seeking Induction on Interpersonal Proximity," *Psychological Reports*, 1965, 17, 120-122.
23. Krout, Maurice, "An Experimental Attempt to Determine the Significance of Unconscious Manual Symbolic Movements," *Journal of General Psychology*, 1954, 51, 121-152.
24. Exline, Ralph, and Winters, Lewis, "Affective Relations and Mutual Glances in Dyads," in S. Tomkins and C. Izard (eds.), *Affect, Cognition, and Personality*, New York: Springer, 1965.
25. Personal correspondence.
26. Kahn, Robert, and Cannell, Charles, *The Dynamics of Interviewing*, New York: Wiley, 1967, 6.
27. Laing, *op. cit.*, 75.
28. Read, *op. cit.*
29. Jourard, Sidney, *The Transparent Self*, New York: Van Nostrand Reinhold, 1964.
30. *Time*, December 22, 1967, 7.
31. Rogers, Carl, *On Becoming a Person*, Boston: Houghton Mifflin, 1961, 54.
32. Rapoport, Anatol, *Fights, Games and Debates*, Ann Arbor: University of Michigan Press, 1960.
33. Thomas, Edwin, Polansky, Norman, and Kounin, Jacob, "The Expected Behavior of a Potentially Helpful Person," *Human Relations*, 1955, 8, 165-174.
34. Barnlund, Dean C., *Interpersonal Communication*, Boston: Houghton Mifflin, 1968, 613-641.
35. Saint Exupéry, Antoine de, *Airman's Odyssey*, New York: Reynal, 1939, 420.

# HOW COMMUNICATION WORKS
## Wilbur Schramm

*Communication* comes from the latin *communis*, common.
When we communicate we are trying to establish a "commonness" with someone. That is, we are trying to share information, an idea, or an attitude. At this moment I am trying to
communicate to you the idea that the essence of communication is getting the receiver and the sender "tuned" together
for a particular message. At this same moment, someone
somewhere is excitedly phoning the fire department that the
house is on fire. Somewhere else a young man in a parked
automobile is trying to convey the understanding that he is
moon-eyed because he loves the young lady. Somewhere else
a newspaper is trying to persuade its readers to believe as it
does about the Republican Party. All these are forms of communication, and the process in each case is essentially the
same.

Communication always requires at least three elements—the
source, the message, and the destination. A *source* may be an
individual (speaking, writing, drawing, gesturing) or a communication organization (like a newspaper, publishing house,
television station, or motion picture studio). The *message*
may be in the form of ink on paper, sound waves in the air,
impulses in an electric current, a wave of the hand, a flag in
the air, or any other signal capable of being interpreted mean-
ingfully. The *destination* may be an *individual* listening,
watching, or reading; or a member of a *group*, such as a discussion group, a lecture audience, a football crowd, or a mob;
or an individual member of the particular group we call the
*mass audience*, such as the reader of a newspaper or a viewer
of television.

Now what happens when the source tries to build up this
"commonness" with his intended receiver? First, the source en-
codes his message. That is, he takes the information or feeling
he wants to share and puts it into a form that can be transmitted. The "pictures in our heads" can't be transmitted until
they are coded. When they are coded into spoken words, they

Reprinted by permission from *The Process and Effects of Mass Communication* by Wilbur Schramm, Urbana: University of Illinois Press,
1954, pp. 3-10.

Perspectives

can be transmitted easily and effectively, but they can't travel very far unless radio carries them. If they are coded into written words, they go more slowly than spoken words, but they go farther and last longer. Indeed, some messages long outlive their senders—the *Iliad*, for instance; the Gettysburg address; Chartres cathedral. Once coded and sent, a message is quite free of its sender, and what it does is beyond the power of the sender to change. Every writer feels a sense of helplessness when he finally commits his story or his poem to print; you doubtless feel the same way when you mail an important letter. Will it reach the right person? Will he understand it as you intend him to? Will he respond as you want him to? For in order to complete the act of communication the message must be decoded. And there is good reason, as we shall see, for the sender to wonder whether his receiver will really be in tune with him, whether the message will be interpreted without distortion, whether the "picture in the head" of the receiver will bear any resemblance to that in the head of the sender.

We are talking about something very like a radio or telephone circuit. In fact, it is perfectly possible to draw a picture of the human communication system that way:

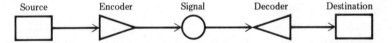

Substitute "microphone" for encoder, and "earphone" for decoder and you are talking about electronic communication. Consider that the "source" and "encoder" are one person, "decoder" and "destination" are another, and the signal is language, and you are talking about human communication.

Now it is perfectly possible by looking at those diagrams to predict how such a system will work. For one thing, such a system can be no stronger than its weakest link. In engineering terms, there may be filtering or distortion at any stage. In human terms, if the source does not have adequate or clear information; if the message is not encoded fully, accurately, effectively in transmittable signs; if these are not transmitted fast enough and accurately enough, despite interference and competition, to the desired receiver; if the message is not decoded in a pattern that corresponds to the encoding; and finally, if the destination is unable to handle the decoded message so as to produce the desired response—then, obviously, the system is working at less than top efficiency. When we realize that *all* these steps must be accomplished with relatively high efficiency if any communication is to be successful, the everyday act of explaining something to a stranger, or writing a letter, seems a minor miracle.

A system like this will have a maximum capacity for handling information and this will depend on the separate capacities of each unit on the chain—for example, the capacity of the channel (how fast can one talk?) or the capacity of the encoder (can your student understand something explained quickly?). If the coding is good (for example, no unnecessary words) the capacity of the channel can be approached, but it can never be exceeded. You can readily see that one of the great skills of communication will lie in knowing how near capacity to operate a channel.

This is partly determined for us by the nature of the language. English, like every other language, has its sequences of words and sounds governed by certain probabilities. If it were organized so that no set of probabilities governed the likelihood that certain words would follow certain other words (for example, that a noun would follow an adjective, or that "States" or "Nations" would follow "United") then we would have nonsense. As a matter of fact, we can calculate the relative amount of freedom open to us in writing any language. For English, the freedom is about 50 percent. (Incidentally, this is about the required amount of freedom to enable us to construct interesting crossword puzzles. Shannon has estimated that if we had about 70 percent freedom, we could construct three-dimensional crossword puzzles. If we had only 20 percent, crossword puzzle making would not be worth while).

So much for language *redundancy*, as communication theorists call it, meaning the percentage of the message which is not open to free choice. But there is also the communicator's redundancy, and this is an important aspect of constructing a message. For if we think our audience may have a hard time understanding the message, we can deliberately introduce more redundancy; we can repeat (just as the radio operator on a ship may send "SOS" over and over again to make sure it is heard and decoded), or we can give examples and analogies. In other words, we always have to choose between transmitting more information in a given time, or transmitting less and repeating more in the hope of being better understood. And as you know, it is often a delicate choice, because too slow a rate will bore an audience, whereas too fast a rate may confuse them.

Perhaps the most important thing about such a system is one we have been talking about all too glibly—the fact that receiver and sender must be in tune. This is clear enough in the case of a radio transmitter and receiver, but somewhat more complicated when it means that a human receiver must be able to understand a human sender.

Let us redraw our diagram in very simple form, like this:

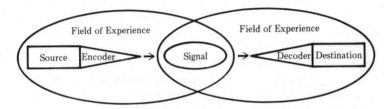

Think of those circles as the accumulated experience of the two individuals trying to communicate. The source can encode, and the destination can decode, only in terms of the experience each has had. If we have never learned any Russian, we can neither code nor decode in that language. If an African tribesman has never seen or heard of an airplane, he can only decode the sight of a plane in terms of whatever experience he has had. The plane may seem to him to be a bird, and the aviator a god borne on wings. If the circles have a large area in common, then communication is easy. If the circles do not meet—if there has been no common experience—then communication is impossible. If the circles have only a small area in common—that is, if the experiences of source and destination have been strikingly unlike—then it is going to be very difficult to get an intended meaning across from one to the other. This is the difficulty we face when a non-science-trained person tries to read Einstein, or when we try to communicate with another culture much different from ours.

The source, then, tries to encode in such a way as to make

it easy for the destination to tune in the message—to relate it to parts of his experience which are much like those of the source. What does he have to work with?

Messages are made up of signs. A sign is a signal that stands for something in experience. The word "dog" is a sign that stands for our generalized experience with dogs. The word would be meaningless to a person who came from a dog-less island and had never read of or heard of a dog. But most of us have learned that word by association, just as we learn most signs. Someone called our attention to an animal, and said "dog." When we learned the word, it produced in us much the same response as the object it stood for. That is, when we heard "dog" we could recall the appearance of dogs, their sound, their feel, perhaps their smell. But there is an important difference between the sign and the object: The sign always represents the object at a reduced level of cues. By this we mean simply that the sign will not call forth all the responses that the object itself will call forth. The sign "dog," for example, will probably not call forth in us the same wariness or attention a strange dog might attract if it wandered into our presence. This is the price we pay for portability in language. We have a sign system that we can use in place of the less portable originals (for example, Margaret Mitchell could re-create the burning of Atlanta in a novel, and a photograph could transport world-wide the appearance of a bursting atomic bomb), but our sign system is merely a kind of shorthand. The coder has to be able to write the shorthand, the decoder to read it. And no two persons have learned exactly the same system. For example, a person who has known only Arctic huskies will not have learned exactly the same meaning for the shorthand sign "dog" as will a person who comes from a city where he has known only pekes and poms.

We have come now to a point where we need to tinker a little more with our diagram of the communication process. It is obvious that each person in the communication process is both an encoder and a decoder. He receives and transmits. He must be able to write a readable shorthand, and to read other people's shorthand. Therefore, it is possible to describe either sender or receiver in a human communication system thus:

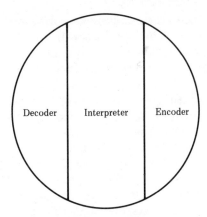

Decoder    Interpreter    Encoder

What happens when a signal comes to you? Remember that it comes in the form of a sign. If you have learned the sign, you have learned certain responses with it. We can call these mediatory responses, because they mediate what happens to the message in your nervous system. These responses are the *meaning* the sign has for you. They are learned from experience, as we said, but they are affected by the state of your organism at the moment. For example, if you are hungry, a picture of a steak may not arouse exactly the same response in you as when you are overfed.

But subject to these effects, the mediatory responses will then determine what you do about the sign. For you have learned other sets of reactions connected to the mediatory responses. A sign that means a certain thing to you will start certain other processes in your nerves and muscles. A sign that means "fire," for example, will certainly trigger off some activity in you. A sign that means you are in danger may start the process in your nerves and muscles that makes you say "help!" In other words, the meaning that results from your decoding of a sign will start you *en*coding. Exactly *what* you encode will depend on your choice of the responses, available in the situation and connected with the meaning.

Whether this encoding actually results in some overt communication or action depends partly on the barriers in the way. You may think it better to keep silent. And if an action does occur, the nature of the action will also depend on the avenues for action available to you and the barriers in your way. The code of your group may not sanction the action you want to take. The meaning of a sign may make you want to hit the person who has said it, but he may be too big, or you may be in the wrong social situation. You may merely ignore him, or "look murder at him," or say something nasty about him to someone else.

But whatever the exact result, this is the process in which you are constantly engaged. You are constantly decoding signs from your environment, interpreting these signs, and encoding something as a result. In fact, it is misleading to think of the communication process as starting somewhere and ending somewhere. It is really endless. We are little switchboard centers handling and rerouting the great endless current of communication. We can accurately think of communication as passing through us—changed, to be sure, by our interpretations, our habits, our abilities and capabilities, but the input still being reflected in the output.

We need now to add another element to our description of the communication process. Consider what happens in a conversation between two people. One is constantly communicating back to the other, thus:

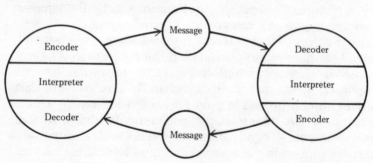

The return process is called feedback, and plays a very important part in communication because it tells us how our messages are being interpreted. Does the hearer say, "Yes, yes, that's right," as we try to persuade him? Does he nod his head in agreement? Does a puzzled frown appear on his forehead? Does he look away as though he were losing interest? All these are feedback. So is a letter to the editor of a newspaper, protesting an editorial. So is an answer to a letter. So is the applause of a lecture audience. An experienced communicator is attentive to feedback, and constantly modifies his messages in light of what he observes in or hears from his audience.

At least one other example of feedback, also, is familiar to all of us. We get feedback from our own messages. That is, we hear our own voices and can correct mispronunciations. We see the words we have written on paper, and can correct misspellings or change the style. When we do that, here is what is happening:

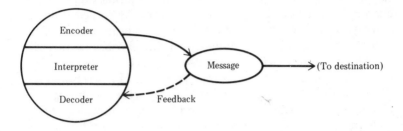

It is clear that in any kind of communication we rarely send out messages in a single channel, and this is the final element we must add to our account of the communication process. When you speak to me, the sound waves from your voice are the primary message. But there are others: The expression on your face, your gestures, the relation of a given message to past messages. Even the primary message conveys information on several levels. It gives me words to decode. It emphasizes certain words above others. It presents the words in a pattern of intonation and timing which contribute to the total meaning. The quality of your voice (deep, high, shrill, rasping, rich, thin, loud, soft) itself carries information about you and what you are saying.

This multiple channel situation exists even in printed mass communication, where the channels are perhaps most restricted. Meaning is conveyed, not only by the words in a news item, but also by the size of the headline, the position on the page and the page in the paper, the association with pictures, the use of boldface and other typographical devices. All these tell us something about the item. Thus we can visualize the typical channel of communication, not as a simple telegraph circuit, in which current does or does not flow, but rather as a sort of coaxial cable in which many signals flow in parallel from source toward the destination.

These parallel relationships are complex, but you can see their general pattern. A communicator can emphasize a point by adding as many parallel messages as he feels are deserved. If he is communicating by speaking, he can stress a word, pause just before it, say it with a rising inflection, gesture while he says it, look earnestly at his audience. Or he can keep all the signals parallel—except *one.* He can speak solemnly, but wink, as Lowell Thomas sometimes does. He can stress a word in a way that makes it mean something else—for example, "That's a *fine* job you did!" And by so doing he conveys secondary meanings of sarcasm or humor or doubt.

The same thing can be done with printed prose, with broadcast, with television or films. The secondary channels of the sight-sound media are especially rich. I am reminded of a skillful but deadly job done entirely with secondary channels on a certain political candidate. A sidewalk interview program was filmed to run in local theaters. Ostensibly it was a completely impartial program. An equal number of followers of each candidate were interviewed—first, one who favored Candidate A, then one who favored Candidate B, and so on. They were asked exactly the same questions, and said about the same things, although on opposite sides of the political fence, of course. But there was one interesting difference. Whereas the supporters of Candidate A were ordinary folks, not outstandingly attractive or impressive, the followers of Candidate B who were chosen to be interviewed invariably had something slightly wrong with them. They looked wildeyed, or they stuttered, or they wore unpressed suits. The extra meaning was communicated. Need I way which candidate won?

But this is the process by which communication works, whether it is mass communication, or communication in a group, or communication between individuals.

# SOME TENTATIVE AXIOMS OF COMMUNICATION
# Paul Watzlawick, Janet Beavin, and Don Jackson

## THE IMPOSSIBILITY OF NOT COMMUNICATING

First of all, there is a property of behavior that could hardly be more basic and is, therefore, often overlooked: Behavior has no opposite. In other words, there is no such thing as nonbehavior or, to put it even more simply: One cannot *not* behave. Now, if it is accepted that all behavior in an inter-actional situation[1] has message value, i.e., is communication, it follows that no matter how one may try, one cannot *not* communicate. Activity or inactivity, words or silence all have message value: They influence others and these others, in turn, cannot *not* respond to these communications and are thus themselves communicating. It should be clearly under-stood that the mere absence of talking or of taking notice of each other is no exception to what has just been asserted. The man at a crowded lunch counter who looks straight ahead, or the airplane passenger who sits with his eyes closed, are both communicating that they do not want to speak to anybody or be spoken to, and their neighbors usually "get the message" and respond appropriately by leaving them alone. This, obviously, is just as much an interchange of com-munication as an animated discussion.[2]

Neither can we say that "communication" only takes place when it is intentional, conscious, or successful, that is, when mutual understanding occurs. Whether message sent equals message received is an important but different order of analy-sis, as it must rest ultimately on evaluations of specific, intro-spective, subject-reported data, which we choose to neglect for the exposition of a behavioral theory of communication. On the question of misunderstanding, our concern, given cer-tain formal properties of communication, is with the develop-ment of related pathologies, aside from, indeed in spite of, the motivations or intentions of the communicants.

From *Pragmatics of Human Communication* by Paul Watzlawick, Janet H. Beavin, and Don D. Jackson, pp. 48-50, 51, 54-58, 59. Reprinted by permission of W. W. Norton & Company, Inc. Copyright © 1967 by W. W. Norton & Company, Inc.

To summarize, a metacommunicational axiom of the pragmatics of communication can be postulated: *One cannot* not *communicate.*

## THE CONTENT AND RELATIONSHIP LEVELS
## OF COMMUNICATION

Another axiom was hinted at in the foregoing when it was suggested that any communication implies a commitment and thereby defines the relationship. This is another way of saying that a communication not only conveys information, but that at the same time it imposes behavior. Following Bateson (2), these two operations have come to be known as the "report" and the "command" aspects, respectively, of any communication. Bateson exemplifies these two aspects by means of a physiological analogy: Let $A$, $B$, and $C$ be a linear chain of neurons. Then the firing of neuron $B$ is both a "report" that neuron $A$ has fired and a "command" for neuron $C$ to fire.

The report aspect of a message conveys information and is, therefore, synonymous in human communication with the *content* of the message. It may be about anything that is communicable regardless of whether the particular information is true or false, valid, invalid, or undecidable. The command aspect, on the other hand, refers to what sort of a message it is to be taken as, and, therefore, ultimately to the *relationship* between the communicants. All such relationship statements are about one or several of the following assertions: "This is how I see myself . . . this is how I see you . . . this is how I see you seeing me . . ." and so forth in theoretically infinite regress. Thus, for instance, the messages "It is important to release the clutch gradually and smoothly" and "Just let the clutch go, it'll ruin the transmission in no time" have approximately the same information content (report aspect), but they obviously define very different relationships. To avoid any misunderstanding about the foregoing, we want to make it clear that relationships are only rarely defined deliberately or with full awareness. In fact, it seems that the more spontaneous and "healthy" a relationship, the more the relationship aspect of communication recedes into the background. Conversely, "sick" relationships are characterized by a constant struggle about the nature of the relationship, with the content aspect of communication becoming less and less important.

Perspectives

For the time being let us merely summarize the foregoing into another axiom of our tentative calculus: *Every communication has a content and a relationship aspect such that the latter classifies the former and is therefore a metacommunication.* [3]

## THE PUNCTUATION OF THE SEQUENCE OF EVENTS

The next basic characteristic of communication we wish to explore regards interaction—exchanges of messages—between communicants. To an outside observer, *a series of communications can be viewed as an uninterrupted sequence of interchanges.* However, the participants in the interaction always introduce what, following Whorf (3), Bateson and Jackson (1) have termed the "punctuation of the sequence of events." They state:

The stimulus-response psychologist typically confines his attention to sequences of interchange so short that it is possible to label one item of input as "stimulus" and another item as "reinforcement" while labelling what the subject does between these two events as "response." Within the short sequence so excised, it is possible to talk about the "psychology" of the subject. In contrast, the sequences of interchange which we are here discussing are very much longer and therefore have the characteristic that every item in the sequence is simultaneously stimulus, response and reinforcement. A given item of A's behavior is a stimulus insofar as it is followed by an item contributed by B and that by another item contributed by A. But insofar as A's item is sandwiched between two items contributed by B, it is a response. Similarly A's item is a reinforcement insofar as it follows an item contributed by B. The ongoing interchanges, then, which we are here discussing, constitute a chain of overlapping triadic links, each of which is comparable to a stimulus-response-reinforcement sequence. We can take any triad of our interchange and see it as a single trial in a stimulus-response learning experiment.

If we look at the conventional learning experiments from this point of view, we observe at once that repeated trials amount to a differentiation of relationship between the two organisms concerned—the experimenter and his subject. The sequence of trials is so punctuated that it is always the experimenter who seems to provide the "stimuli" and the "reinforcements," while the subject provides the "responses." These words are here deliberately put in quotation marks because the role definitions are in fact only created by the willingness of the organisms to accept the system of punctuation. The "reality" of the role definitions is only of the same order as the reality of a bat on a Rorschach card—a more or less over-determined creation of the perceptive process. The rat who said "I have got my experimenter trained. Each time I press the lever he gives me food" was declining to accept the punctuation of the sequence which the experimenter was seeking to impose.

It is still true, however, that in a long sequence of interchange, the organisms concerned—especially if these be people—will in fact punctuate the sequence so that it will appear that one or the other has initiative, dominance, dependency or the like. That is, they will set up between them patterns of interchange (about which they may or may not be in agreement) and these patterns will in fact be rules of contingency regarding the exchange of reinforcement. While rats are too nice to re-label, some psychiatric patients are not, and provide psychological trauma for the therapist!

It is not the issue here whether punctuation of communicational sequence is, in general, good or bad, as it should be immediately obvious that punctuation *organizes* behavioral events and is therefore vital to ongoing interactions. Culturally, we share many conventions of punctuation which, while no more or less accurate than other views of the same events, serve to organize common and important interactional sequences. For example, we call a person in a group behaving in one way the "leader" and another the "follower," although on reflection it is difficult to say which comes first or where one would be without the other.

Disagreement about how to punctuate the sequence of events is at the root of countless relationship struggles. Suppose a couple have a marital problem to which he contributes passive withdrawal, while her 50 percent is nagging criticism. In explaining their frustrations, the husband will state that withdrawal is his only *defense against* her nagging, while she will label this explanation a gross and willful distortion of what "really" happens in their marriage: Namely, that she is critical of him *because of* his passivity. Stripped of all ephemeral and fortuitous elements, their fights consist in a monotonous exchange of the messages "I withdraw because you nag" and "I nag because you withdraw." Represented graphically, with an arbitrary beginning point, their interaction looks somewhat as shown on the next page.

It can be seen that the husband only perceives triads 2—3—4, 4—5—6, 6—7—8, etc., where his behavior (solid arrows) is "merely" a response to her behavior (the broken arrows). With her it is exactly the other way around; she punctuates the sequence of events into the triads 1—2—3, 3—4—5, 5—6—7, etc., and sees herself as only reacting to, but not determining, her husband's behavior. In conjoint psychotherapy with couples one is frequently struck by the intensity of what in traditional psychotherapy would be

Perspectives

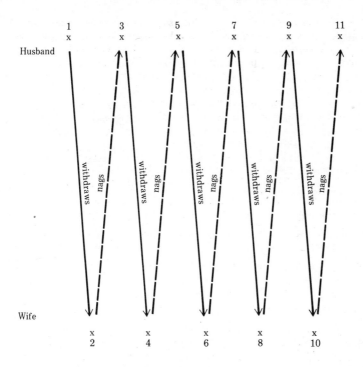

referred to as "reality distortion" on the part of both parties. It is often hard to believe that two individuals could have such divergent views on many elements of joint experience. And yet the problem lies primarily in an area already frequently mentioned: their inability to metacommunicate about their respective patterning of their interaction. This interaction is of an oscillatory yes-no-yes-no-yes nature which theoretically can go on ad infinitum and almost invariably is accompanied, as we shall see later, by the typical charges of badness or madness.

Thus we add a third metacommunicational axiom: *The nature of a relationship is contingent upon the punctuation of the communicational sequences between the communicants.*

## NOTES

1. It might be added that, even alone, it is possible to have dialogues in fantasy, with one's hallucinations, or with life. Perhaps such internal "communication" follows some of the same rules which govern interpersonal communication; such unobservable phenomena, however, are outside the scope of our meaning of the term.

2. Very interesting research in this field has been carried out by Luft, who studied what he calls "social stimulus deprivation." He brought two strangers together in a room, made them sit across from each other and instructed them "not to talk or communicate in any way." Subsequent interviews revealed the highly stressful nature of this situation. To quote the author:

   He has before him the other unique individual with his ongoing, though muted, behavior. At this point, it is postulated, that true interpersonal testing takes place, and only part of this testing may be done consciously. For example, how does the other subject respond to him and to the small nonverbal cues which he sends out? Is there an attempt at understanding his enquiring glance, or is it coldly ignored? Does the other subject display postural cues of tension, indicating some distress at confronting him? Does he grow increasingly comfortable, indicating some kind of acceptance, or will the other treat him as if he were a thing which did not exist? These and many other kinds of readily discernible behavior appear to take place.

3. We have chosen, somewhat arbitrarily, to say that the relationship classifies, or subsumes, the content aspect, although it is equally accurate in logical analysis to say that the class is defined by its members and therefore the content aspect can be said to define the relationship aspect. Since our primary interest is not information exchange but the pragmatics of communication, we will use the former approach.

## REFERENCES

1. Bateson, Gregory, and Jackson, Don D., "Some Varieties of Pathogenic Organization." In David McRioch, ed., *Disorders of Communication*, Vol. 42, Research Publications, Association for Research in Nervous and Mental Disease, 1964, pp. 270-283.
2. Ruesch, Jurgen, and Bateson, Gregory, *Communication: The Social Matrix of Psychiatry*. New York: W. W. Norton, 1951.
3. Whorf, Benjamin Lee, "Science and Linguistics" from *Language, Thought, and Reality* in John B. Carroll, ed., *Selected Writings of Benjamin Lee Whorf*. New York: Wiley, 1956, pp. 207-219.

# PART II
# Messages

When people engage in social interaction, they do so mainly, though not exclusively, through messages. In fact, the concept of message—broadly conceived as any form of decoded or interpreted information—is implicit in the very fabric of social conduct. Behavior has potential message value insofar as it conveys information that alters the interpretations attributed to the course of whatever is said and done. The act of ascribing significance to behavior occurs simultaneously at verbal and nonverbal levels. Generally speaking, we associate verbal interaction with a linguistic code and nonverbal with paralinguistic or extralinguistic units of behavior. This section explores the fundamental and complex interplay between verbal and nonverbal constituents of messages.

Given the staggering complexity of language, there is no limit to the number of ways of classifying and interpreting what happens when persons interact through the spoken or written word. Of import is the fascination of sound itself, the psychological significance of word meanings, syntax, and the effect of speech on relationships. Also, one may cut through the particulars and focus on the larger functional importance of what is said and done. The term function refers to the utility or use that words play in human affairs, particularly their impact on the respective notions of what is occurring between the respective parties of communication. In the essay "When People Talk with People" John Condon offers an absorbing account of the functional uses of language and shows how patterns of human talk reflect particular psychological wants, emotions, inner defenses, and needs for information, magic, ritual, and understanding of the subtext or "metacommunication" of messages.

In studying the dynamics of personal encounters, it is important to discover the sense in which the most powerful messages are often silent. Communication cannot be equated solely with the impact of spoken or written words. Feelings, emotions, moods, expectations, and biases do not necessarily lend themselves to verbal expression. In "Communication Without Words" Albert Mehrabian discusses the communicative import of facial expression, tone of voice, gesture, and other nonverbal aspects of messages. He concludes with an engaging discussion of the complex interplay that goes on between verbal and nonverbal modes of interaction.

When judging the import of human talk, we naturally rely on the accompanying facial expression for cues. The face is the primary expressor of emotional meaning. It is visible, transparent, and quite accessible for inspection. In the essay on "Facial Engagements" Erving Goffman explores the complex rules that govern the various readings human beings give to certain facial expressions. The themes vary from looks of nonrecognition, indifference, and other modes of "civil inattention" to phases of visual activity that change from opening moves and clearance signs to later moments of focused visual interest and eventually to leave-taking and other signs of impending separation from the implicit communicative contract.

With the broad perspectives of Mehrabian and Goffman in mind, it is useful to explore some representative aspects of nonverbal interaction in detail. Of particular relevance are the topics of looking behavior and touch. Michael Argyle in "Eye-Contact" examines what Simmel has termed ". . . the most direct and purest reciprocity that exists anywhere." Even when the necessary allowances are made for individual differences, human beings are known to share certain common nonverbal signals of their attitudes toward each other and the topic at hand. Also significant is the role of the subconscious in looking behavior, namely the expressions conveyed beyond awareness and conscious intent. Finally, the essay on "Tactile Communication" by Lawrence Frank affords a unique classic statement on the interplay among the human senses in various social settings. Frank examines the close tie between various modes of sensory experience and physical interaction between men, objects, and social surroundings.

# WHEN PEOPLE TALK WITH PEOPLE
## John C. Condon, Jr.

Years ago, a popular phonograph record produced by Stan
Freberg presented a short conversation between two persons,
Marsha and John. The conversation began like this:

"John . . ."
"Marsha . . ."
"John . . ."
"Marsha . . ."
"John . . ."
"Marsha . . ."

(Using the above dialogue as a basis, the clever reader can
extrapolate the entire three-minute conversation.)

The printed form does not convey what the recording
artists did with only two words. They were able to indicate
differences in meaning by speaking the words with varied
inflections and in different tones of voice. In fact, so skillful
was the performance that several radio stations banned the
harmless record from the air as "too suggestive."

The vocal variations on a theme of two words illustrate a
simple but important point about communication: That one
word or sentence may serve many purposes and have many
meanings, depending on its context and on how it is said. The
sensitive conversant, the diplomat, the therapist are well
aware of the many purposes of communication that any word
or phrase may serve, functions our language serves for us
each day. In this chapter we will very briefly look at eight of
these functions of communication.

### PHATIC COMMUNION

Small talk, uninspired greetings, and idle chatter are among
the descriptions of a fundamental type of communication
that Bronislaw Malinowski called *phatic communion*. To
show that we welcome communication, that we are friendly,
or that we at least acknowledge the presence of another

Reprinted with permission of The Macmillan Company from *Semantics
and Communication* by John C. Condon, Jr. pp. 87-107. Copyright ©
by John C. Condon, Jr., 1966.

person, we exchange words. In English we do not have special words for this function of communication, though phatic communion tends to be rather unimaginative. We say, "How are You?" or "Hello," or "Nice day." There may be variations based on geography ("Howdy!") or familiarity ("Hi ya, Baby!") or specific conditions ("Cold enough for ya?"). Whatever the words, the speaker is saying, in effect, "I see you and I am friendly." The channels of communication are opened.

In phatic communion, the specific words exchanged are not important. This is illustrated in the story of a U.S. businessman who, while traveling to Europe for the first time, finds himself seated across from a Frenchman at lunch. Neither speaks the other's language, but each smiles a greeting. As the wine is served, the Frenchman raises his glass and gesturing to the American says, *"Bon appétit!"* The American does not understand and replies, "Ginzberg." No other words are exchanged at lunch. That evening at dinner, the two again sit at the same table and again the Frenchman greets the American with the wine, saying, *"Bon appétit!"* to which the American replies, "Ginzberg." The waiter notices this peculiar exchange and, after dinner, calls the American aside to explain that "the Frenchman is not giving his name—he is wishing you a good appetite; he is saying that he hopes you enjoy your meal." The following day the American seeks out the Frenchman at lunch, wishing to correct his error. At the first opportunity the American raises his glass and says, *"Bon appétit!"* To which the Frenchman proudly replies, "Ginzberg."

Although in this story the ignorance of a common language made more significant communication impossible, it was the exchange of simple words like *bon appétit* (and Ginzberg) that broke the tension of silence and expressed friendship. Without the small talk first there can be no "big talk" later.

The only rule that seems to apply to phatic communion is that the "subject" of the communication be such that each party can say something about it. That is why everybody talks about the weather. The important thing is to talk—and this is why so much of phatic communion begins with a question, for a question requires a reply.

We do not request specific information in phatic communion and we are not expected to reply with precision or accuracy. If we are greeted with a "How are you?" we do not reply as we might if our doctor asked the question. When we are precise the result is likely to be humorous, as when James Thurber was once asked, "How's your wife?" and replied, "Compared to *what*?"

Specific information is sought in one kind of greeting, however. Members of secret organizations sometimes speak in code when they meet to determine whether each knows the password, special handshake, or other symbol. If the answer to the secret question is not precise, then the other is not regarded as a brother Mason or sister Theta or whatever, and subsequent communication will be prevented. Such coded phatic communion dates from times when members of such organizations might be persecuted if discovered. Among some "secret organizations" today, the reverse seems to be true. The coded greeting is often expressed loudly, more for the benefit of the outsiders than for the "secret" members. Phatic communion is usually the most casual, even careless, form of communication. The stories of persons passing through receiving lines and saying something like "I just killed my mother-in-law," which is met with a smile and a "Fine, I hope you're enjoying yourself" are well known. They illustrate what little significance is attached to phatic communion, so little that the speaker is not even listened to. In such extreme cases, however, we may wonder to what extent the channels of communication have been opened after that exchange of noises. In any case, it seems that we prefer some noise to no noise.

### PREVENTION OF COMMUNICATION

A second function of communication is the opposite of the first. Just as we rarely open a conversation with "I see you and I am friendly," when this may be the real "message" of our greeting, we rarely prevent further communication by saying directly, "I don't want to talk to you anymore." This is said sometimes, to be sure. But there are more sophisticated ways that we have mastered.

There are the dismissal reactions "Ha!" "That's crazy!" "Yeah, I'll bet!" and so forth. Whether the speaker intends these to stop communication or whether they merely function in this way is often difficult to determine. In either case it takes but a few well chosen reactions to end a conversation—and a few more to end a friendship.

Then there are the guarded utterances or verbal grunts that seem to show a lack of interest in speaker or subject: "Oh, really?" "I see—," "Indeed," or "Hmm."

These brief snips of uninterested responses will end a conversation, and often large hunks of verbiage will achieve the same end. Either the language seems to say nothing or it is so difficult to decipher that it does not seem worth the effort. A favorite technique of naughty children, students taking examinations, and some U.S. Senators is to talk on and on about anything irrelevant to the subject at hand.

## RECORD-TRANSMITTING FUNCTIONS

One definition of teaching goes something like this: "Teaching is the transmission of the professor's notes into the students' notebooks without their having passed through the minds of either." A few years ago it was reported that a professor at a large mid-western college put his lectures on tape and had the tape recorder sent into his classroom and played every day. Weeks later, when he stopped into the room to see if all was going well, he found, on each student's desk, another machine recording the lectures. Allowing for the hyperboles here, these stories illustrate a basic function of communication, where the individual performs like a precise and self-contained transmitting and recording machine.

In one sense, all communication is a process of transmitting some information that is received by another. This is one definition of communication. But as we note the variety of ways in which we can describe the kind and purpose of a message sent, the category of transmitting-recording seems insufficient. The category is useful only for the most neutral exchanges of information, messages without intent to be instrumental, compliment the listener, let off steam, and so on. Thus, asking when the next bus leaves and being told; asking what time it is, and being told; reporting or hearing the news, weather, classroom lectures, and so on, all might be examples of this function of communication.

## INSTRUMENTAL COMMUNICATION

When we say something and something happens as the result of our speaking, then our comments have been instrumental in causing that event to happen. The instrumental function of communication is one of its most common purposes. We request a secretary to type three copies of a letter. We ask a friend at dinner to pass the butter. We order a salesman out of the house.

The category of instrumental communication is loose enough to allow for several kinds of statements. There are statements that are clearly instrumental in their wording, for which the result correlates with the language. If we say "Shut the door" and the door is then shut, we may assume that the noise we made was influential in the shutting of the door. There are also statements for which the results cannot be so easily attributed to our utterances. If on a day planned for a picnic it is raining and so we sing, "Rain, rain go away"—and the rain does stop—it would be immodest to assume that our words caused that action. Much of prayer has been tradition-ally instrumental, and if the faithful believe that some pray-ers "have been answered," we could say that for these people the prayer was an instrumental communication. We will touch on this subject again when we discuss ritual and the magic function of communication.

Some statements are instrumental in intent or effect, but are not phrased as such. For example, if you want the salt passed to you, you may request it directly (instrumental) or you might comment that the food needs salt (transmitting information). If a wife wants a new fur coat, she may request it directly or she may comment on how well dressed her husband seems, especially when compared to her (apparently an effective technique). One instrumental request may result in a different instrumental action, as when commercial airlines do not ask passengers to stop smoking but to "observe the no smoking sign."

One characteristic of some instrumental statements is a faint resemblance between manner of speaking and the requested action itself. One sometimes speaks as if his words *were* instruments, as a belaying pin or rawhide whip are instruments. The voice (see metacommunication) does its best to imitate the desired action, as do voices instrumentally cheering at a football game, "Push 'em back, push 'em back, w-a-a-a-y back!"

## AFFECTIVE COMMUNICATION
Communication in which the message is the emotional feelings of the speaker toward a listener is known as *affective communication*. Compliments, praise and flattery, and also snide and cutting remarks may be so classified.

There are affective elements in many of the functions of communication. Phatic communion may contain praise, as when old friends greet by saying, "You're looking great!" As noted in the previous section, instrumental purposes are often best served through affective communication, too.

It seems to be part of the woman's role in our society to use more affective communication than does the opposite sex. Where tradition has not given women authority in all situations, women have had to achieve their goals indirectly. And this indirection may be reflected in instrumental desires disguised in affective language. The wife who says to her husband, "You look so handsome all dressed up," might be requesting a new wardrobe for herself or be asking to go out to dinner, rather than just complimenting her husband.

The nonaffective language of fact and description or the language of clear and explicit requests need not be any more desirable than it is common in interpersonal communications. We admire and respect the clarity of the scientist in writing his report, but we may find him less explicit during his courtship. Perhaps the reason is that whereas the scientist communicates to himself and to others pursuing one goal, the diplomats or the lovers may not be sure they are pursuing the same goal.

A study of the social gestures of dating, which I once made in an attempt to discover what was "meant" when a man held the door for his date or failed to open the door, and so on, certainly indicated this. Each sex had its own mythology for the purpose of the gesture. To the woman, the man performed the task out of respect for Woman. To the man, he performed the task because he "had to" if he was going to get anywhere. Again, the man's purpose even in the nonverbal language was far more instrumental than the woman's.

If the words and actions were more specific, it would not be possible for the sexes to maintain their mutual self-delusion.

Affective language is also *convincing* language. In many cases a person would not do something if asked to do it directly; he would be too aware of reasons that he might not be able to accept. We seem to prefer to do things we think we want to do, not things we are told to do. There is a story of an experiment performed by a university class on its professor. The class set out as a group to apply simple learning theory (reward-punishment) on the professor in order to force him to do something he would not ordinarily do and certainly not do if requested. The emotional rewards and "punishments," though nonverbal in this case, are comparable to the use of affective language for instrumental purposes. The class decided it would try to move the professor into a corner from which he would deliver his lectures. The reinforcement was of the kind professors like best, interested expressions on student faces, passionate note taking at his every word, smiles at his whimsy and laughter at his wit. These responses, when appropriate, were made whenever the professor moved in the direction of the desired corner. When he moved in the other direction the class responded with looks of boredom, gazing out the windows, shuffling of feet, and the other academic behaviors one has rehearsed since childhood. As the story goes, by the end of the semester the professor was, indeed, giving his lectures from the corner of the room.

Although this story may be apocryphal, affective communication in a variety of situations does "move" the listener in a way that direct requests would not. The salesman knows it ("I'll make a special deal just for you"), the professor knows it ("I'm sure that your studies of Artaud and Beckett have led you to ask . . ."), the lover knows it. Most persons recognize the influence of words on the ego. (I'm sure that *you*, dear reader, are very sensitive to the communication process. . . .) To make another person feel good (or bad) through language is a rather common and vital function of communication.

It is possible to characterize attitudes of speakers toward their listeners on the basis of instrumental-affective content. One unpublished study[1] of Mexican attitudes toward male and female members of the Holy Family discovered that the language used toward male statues in a church was almost entirely instrumental in content, whereas the language used before the statue of the Virgin was highly affective. This distinction mirrored the differences in language used by children toward their parents in the average Mexican home. It is possible that degrees of anger, hostility, authority, and so on, can be measured by the comparative content of instrumental and affective language in our everyday expressions.

Many criticisms of the U.S. visitor or resident abroad have their basis in a lack of affective communication and a preponderance of instrumental communication. As a pragmatic people, we may have a cultural tendency to "get down to business," to be impersonal. Former Secretary of State John Foster Dulles is often quoted in Latin America as having said with some pride that "the U.S. does not have friends; it has interests." If others are treated as "interests" when they are more accustomed to being treated as "brothers" or at least "cousins," surely they will resent the change. The nonaffective communication may be honest, fair, sincere. But to one who does not expect it, the communication is cold, unfeeling, mechanical.

"Better understanding through communication" is a popular slogan. Too often what is meant is an improvement in semantics, an increase in the clarity of what we *mean*. We must not forget the affective aspects of communication, and must strive for an increase in the interpersonal attraction that we *feel*.

## CATHARSIS

When you are angry or disturbed or hurt, physically or mentally, probably you give expression to your feelings. It is curious that expressions, which could be as personal as the feelings that evoke them, are rather stylized and predictable within a language. Words like *ouch!* or *oh!* are spoken by a people who speak English, whereas our neighbors who speak Spanish will say *ay!* when they express a comparable feeling. Grunts may be the only universal expression of catharsis.

When pain or frustration is sufficient, our cathartic expression becomes more obviously symbolic. We move from the "ouch!" to words that might be used in other ways, most often words that are socially disapproved of. We swear or curse or substitute words that sound something like the popular curses we long ago learned were "adult" and special. We find that different kinds of expressions for releasing tension are appropriate among different ages and occupations. A sailor who is angry is not expected to say "Oh, goodness me!" and an angry nun is not expected to sound like a sailor.

The physical stimulus finds expression in a symbol. This symbol eventually ceases to stand for, directly, anything in the outside world except an attitude toward whatever produced it. We move from physical sensation to verbal assault on that sensation ("Damn it!") to mere release of tension.

The idea of cursing a situation dates to times when the belief in magic language was more common. There was a time when "God damn you" was meant as a magic curse to bring about suffering. The transference into such symbols was a step above the infantile reaction of actually attacking the offending person or object. Children may be observed to run into a wall and then physically retaliate against the wall, kicking it and saying "you mean old wall." But when the child's father runs into the wall and says "damn it!" (or, if the child is there, "darn it!") he probably is not talking to the wall. He is simply relieving his tension in symbols that have long evolved from their literal meaning.

Because expressions of catharsis have no referential meaning, any word may serve the cathartic function. Probably each person has some favorite expressions for releasing anger. If you were to prepare a list of cathartic expressions, ranking them according to the degree of tension to be released, you might find it an easy task, too, which indicates that there are personal favorites for a hierarchy of catharsis. The meaning of any of these expressions is to be found in what they do for us, not in a dictionary or in what they do for anybody else. Through repetition we give our select swear words added significance, so that with each new experience and repeated expression we may recall the release of tension from past experiences.

If you have studied another language, you may have learned the kinds of swear words that are most common in that language. In the literal translation they may not seem to "do much for you." Obviously, they cannot, for they have not yet come to be associated with the experiences that give them meaning. This same observation might be made for all words, but the language of catharsis, associated with the strongest of emotions, is the most extreme example of the general principle.

## MAGIC[2]

The belief in the magic power of words exists in all cultures and takes the form of superstitions, instrumental curses, aspects of most religions, and minor forms of wishful thinking. At the root of the attitude of magic is the assumption that words are part of the thing to which they refer and, often, that words precede the "thing" (such as expressed in the Bible, "In the beginning was the Word"). Another quality of the magic attitude of words is that words "stand for things" in the sense that a friend "stands for" a bride or groom in a marriage by proxy. With this belief it follows that one can alter a thing by altering its word. If I write your name on a piece of paper and burn it, you, too, will burn, or at least suffer pain. Words, in the magical interpretation, must be treated with the same care as one would treat what the words stand for.

A common example of the belief in word-magic is the hesitancy to speak of possible dangers. If, on an airplane, you remark about the possibility of crashing, fellow passengers may turn on you as if your utterance of the possibility might just cause that to happen. In some cases, of course, it may be simply that others do not wish to think of unpleasant things; but the manner and intensity of the reply often indicates a very real fear of the words. If the belief in a magic function of communication seems immature (that is, not at all what *you* would think or do), ask yourself whether in a plane you ever avoided such "thoughts" or whether you ever thought "we will not crash, we will not crash." For better or for worse, the belief that thinking or saying words will have some effect on what the words stand for is an example of the magic function of communication.

In many religions the magic function of language is still present. One would expect this of any institution that is centuries old and seeks to conserve the language and ritual of the past. The distinction between transubstantiation and consubstantiation of the Roman Catholic and Protestant sects is, in part, the difference in attitude toward the magic function of language. Do the bread and wine *become* the body and blood of Christ, or do they merely symbolize the body and blood? There are other examples in religions. The Anglican and Roman Catholic Faiths retain rituals for the exorcising of spirits from a haunted house. One may wish to make a distinction between these examples and examples of words that call for the intercession of a divine spirit (such as prayers of petition) where the effect is produced not by the utterance of the words but by the action upon the words by another being. The difference is the difference between Ali Baba saying "Open Sesame!" (and having the cave door open because of the magic in the words) and having the words heard by a god who then opens the door. In the latter case we have an example of instrumental communication.[3]

Symbols associated with persons have long been recognized for their magical associations. Personal names have been regarded as "part of the person," so that what is done to the name results in affecting the person. (Elements of this attitude are still very common today, as when parents give their child the name of somebody important to them so that the child will be like his namesake.) The magical attitude toward personal names requires that these names not be taken in vain or, on some cases, not even uttered.

Here the name is never a mere symbol, but is part of the personal property of its bearer; property which is exclusively and jealously reserved to him. . . . Georg von der Gabelentz, in his book on the science of language, mentions the edict of a Chinese emperor of the third century B.C. whereby a pronoun in the first person, that had been legitimately in popular use, was henceforth reserved to him alone. . . . It is said of the Eskimos that for them man consists of three elements—body, soul, and name. And in Egypt, too, we find a similar conception, for there the physical body of man was thought to be accompanied, on the one hand by his Ka, or double, and on the other, by his name, as a sort of spiritual double. . . . Under Roman law a slave had no legal name, because he could not function as a legal person.[4]

Cassirer points out, too, that this attitude toward personal names was held by the early Christians, and hence today Christians still say "In Jesus' name" instead of "In Christ."

The belief in the magic function of language is based on assumptions that are quite opposed to the discipline of semantics, which regards words as conventional and convenient and without necessary associations with persons or objects in themselves. There is a sense, however, in which words do have "power." Words have the "power" to limit our thought, for example, though this is a different sense of the word "power." With rumor, with labels that evoke signal reactions, and with labels we try to live up to, we see some effects of the "power" of words. Such powers, however, are not magical, for they are not to be found *in* the words. Rather, the powers are social, and thus they are effective only to the degree that we accept our language without evaluation and respond to words without evaluation. When we understand and evaluate our language habits this social magic spell of words is broken.

## RITUAL

The scene is a Senate Subcommittee hearingroom on October 1, 1963. A 60-year-old convicted murderer, Joseph M. Valachi, calmly reports to the investigators some of the history and methods of the crime organization known as Cosa Nostra. According to the press reports, the witness appeared comfortable throughout his testimony until he described his induction into the organization. Emanuel Perlmutter[5] of the *New York Times* reports:

Valachi said he had been taken into a large room, where 30 or 35 men were sitting at a long table.

"There was a gun and a knife on the table," Valachi testified. "I sat at the edge. They sat me down next to Maranzaro. I repeated some words in Sicilian after him." . . .

"You live by the gun and knife, and die by the gun and knife." . . .

The witness said Maranzaro had then given him a piece of paper that was set afire in his hand.

"I repeated in Sicilian, 'This is the way I burn if I betray the organization.'" . . .

Valachi said the men at the table then "threw out a number," with each man holding up any number of fingers from one to five. The total was taken. Starting with Maranzaro, the sum was then counted off around the table. The man on whom the final number fell was designated as Valachi's "godfather" in the family. Valachi said the lot had fallen to Bonanno.

The witness said that he had then had his finger pricked by a needle held by Bonanno to show he was united to Bonanno by blood. Afterward, Valachi continued, all those present joined hands in a bond to the organization.

> Valachi said he was given two rules in Cosa Nostra that might—one concerning allegiance to it and another a promise not to possess another member's wife, sister or daughter.
>
> For the first time, the witness grew grim. "This is the worst thing I can do, to tell about the ceremony," he said. "This is my doom, telling it to you and the press."

If the ceremony Valachi described seems strange to us, stranger still is the fear of his "doom" caused by revealing that secret. For a tough-minded criminal who reported that for him "killing was like breathing," who gave evidence about the methods and men of the Cosa Nostra, why should the most fearful disclosure be his report of some remote and grisly rite performed years ago? The answer to that question is part of the answer to why some rituals affect almost all of us.

Few organizations or institutions have rituals quite like the Cosa Nostra. The language of the rituals of secret organizations, social fraternities, lodges, and some religious or political organizations is kept secret, known only to their members. But the language of other rituals—patriotic, religious, academic, and so on—is not kept private. Nevertheless, an oath of allegiance or a communal prayer can affect the nervous system as no statement of fact or judgment can.

Ritual is sometimes described as the behavioral part of a mythology. The mythology may be for almost any purpose, but consistently it emphasizes a sense of community among its members and a sense of permanence. To participate in a ritual is to participate in a community, often one that claims a tradition of centuries. The sense of timelessness is quite important. When the anthropologist asks the primitive why he performs a certain ritual, the answer might be, "because our ancestors have always done this." If in the modern-day United States our sense of tradition is a short one, we may find the same comfort in rituals realizing that we as individuals have always said the pledge or sung the hymn.

There appears to be little that is instrumental in the performance of a ritual, with some notable exceptions. Sociologist Robert Merton has noted that activities originally conceived as instrumental often become transmuted into ends in themselves. What was originally obtained through certain words or acts is no longer needed or desired. If at one time meat had to be prepared in a certain way to avoid contamination, meat may still be prepared in such a way because "that's the way our ancestors have always done it." If certain prayers were recited with the hope of rewards, the same prayers may be repeated even though a congregation no longer expects those rewards. In many, perhaps most, cases, a new mythology will develop to explain certain words and actions of a ritual. It is not clear whether rituals continue to exist by virtue of constant repetition or whether the participants in a ritual feel that some ends are being served.

Three characteristics of most rituals are most important: The rituals must be performed with others (immediately or symbolically present); they must be performed on some occasion; and they must be performed with special care to details.

This last characteristic makes ritual somewhat different from other forms of communication. Many children have difficulty with the high-level abstractions and archaic language often present in ritual. The usual vocabulary of children contains few high-level abstractions. But a child will learn to imitate or approximate the sounds of the rituals in which he finds himself participating. Frequently these words become translated in his own vocabulary without conflict. My niece and nephew, when very young, sang their favorite Christmas carol in church. The boy concluded "Silent Night" with the words "Sleep in heavenly beans." "No," his sister corrected, "not beans, peas."

Most of us have associations with aspects of some rituals from our earliest memories. Perhaps you have had the sudden awareness of what some words you have been saying all your life were really supposed to be. It can be both a startling and amusing realization. But it is one that characterizes a form of communication in which repetition of certain words over an expanse of time is most important.

For some persons, part of the appeal of ritual may be the pleasure of solemnly repeating words that seem to have no referent; this may evoke a mood of mystery for such persons. Other persons may find a deep satisfaction in discovering the meaning of what they have been saying for years. Such attitudes, if they exist, would seem to be unhealthy, not only as regards an understanding of the purpose of language but also for the significance of the ritual itself.

There are other characteristics of ritual that make it distinct from other functions of language in communication. One of these is the sublimation function of ritual. Through ritual, a person may symbolically take part in an event that would exclude his actual participation. During wartime, rituals tend to become more common and more significant. The displaying of the flag, the reciting of the pledge of allegiance, even the rationing of food and gasoline are ways of symbolically participating in the war effort. Or, to take a happier example, during a football game the fans who wish to help their team may better do so by cheering than by assisting on the field. It is common, for example, that at the kick-off the fans will go "ssssssspoooom!" as if their noise will help to carry the ball farther down field.

Some rituals last longer than their mythologies. At a time when some persons begin to question religious beliefs, they may find it relatively easier to "lose the faith" than to lose the habit of prayer or church attendance on certain holy days. A sense of compulsiveness frequently attends ritual, and a sense of guilt may enter when ritual has gone. As a nation becomes what is called a "nontraditional society" the rituals that are a part of the tradition die. This finds expression as "alienation," the subject of many books, dramas, and films of recent years. It may also explain, in part, the current attraction for many philosophies of the "absurd." If a society's stability has been largely dependent on ritual and the rituals fall, it is an easy out to label the world as "absurd."

A final point should be made and emphasized. That is that what was intended for some purpose other than ritual can take on a ritual function. This may be a healthy addition to some other instrumental purpose, or it may be unhealthy if it substitutes for that other purpose. An example of the former might be the lasting effect of the Negro Civil Rights March on Washington of 1963. No legislation was passed as a direct result of the march, but there was produced an important sense of community among white and black that had not been exhibited so dramatically before.

Conventions of many kinds, political, social, and academic, many times serve more of a ritual function than the function of exchanging information or achieving some instrumental goal. To see the participants cheer or clap as the speaker speaks the holy jargon and drops the right names at the right time is amusing and a little sad at the same time. What is called a report may better serve as an incantation. No group can maintain itself without strong cohesiveness, it is true. But if the main result of the group's effort is only cohesiveness then surely we have the origins of a new ritual.

## METACOMMUNICATION

In communication there are always more than words that pass between persons. There are also cues that indicate to the persons how the spoken words are to be interpreted. These communications about communication are called *metacommunication cues.* These may be vocal inflections (as in the spoken John-Marsha dialogue) or nonverbal indicators, such as gestures and expressions (pounding the table or frowning). Even clothing and the distance between speakers may provide clues for interpreting the message correctly and thus may also be classified as metacommunication.

These cues may reinforce the meaning of the words, may sometimes distract from the words spoken, or may even contradict what the words seem to mean. When the cues are different from the words, a listener has difficulty in accepting the spoken message. Sometimes, for example, the words sound like phatic communion, but the way in which they are spoken sounds more like the straight transmission of information with, perhaps, a vague hint of some ulterior instrumental purpose. If you have ever answered the telephone and found yourself in what sounded like a friendly conversation until you began to realize you were being solicited for magazine subscriptions, you know the feeling. A friend once found himself in such a conversation. The words were familiar but the metacommunication was mechanical. When he asked the anonymous voice, "Are you *reading* that?" the woman became so startled, she hung up.

Not only may a message be interpreted differently because of metacommunication cues, some messages may be greatly altered or even not spoken because the speaker has received such cues from the listener. A friend who is a priest in Brazil says that one definition of the priest there might be "the person you lie to." When the Roman collar and clerical garb is seen the communication changes completely. For some persons in the United States, unfortunately, a person's skin color serves as a cue to others. John Howard Griffin's *Black Like Me* is an excellent account of the change in communication that was forced on the white author when he traveled in the South disguised as a Negro.

One other function served by metacommunication is that of feedback. Feedback, a term borrowed from the field of cybernetics, refers to signals sent from the listener to the speaker in order to tell the speaker how he is being understood. Upon receiving such signals, which are usually nonverbal, the speaker alters his message accordingly. If a listener wrinkles his brow, the speaker explains more carefully; if a listener nods knowingly, the speaker may speed up or skip over parts of his message, assuming that the listener understands clearly. As with all metacommunication cues, those associated with feedback may conflict or be confusing. One smiles as if he is friendly to the message, while at the same time he taps his foot impatiently.

## ON SAYING WHAT YOU MEAN, AND MEANING WHAT YOU SAY

Semanticists are sometimes thought to desire complete honesty of expression, directness, and "no beating around the bush." An understanding of the many purposes of communication should dispel that view. We use language for too many purposes and find ourselves forced to make some comment in too many difficult situations to hold to such a goal. Simple friendship, not to mention diplomacy and tact, prohibits us from always saying what we are thinking.

Suppose, for example, some friends are in a drama. You attend the opening-night performance, which is, as accurately as you can judge it, a real turkey. Then, as you leave the theater you encounter your friends and the director. Do you say what you are thinking and maybe hurt a friendship? Do you betray your critical integrity? No. Assuming that you cannot avoid comment, you equivocate, you speak in ambiguities. The popular expressions for this moment of untruth are many: (to the director): "Well, you've done it again!"; (to the actors): "You should have been in the audience!"; (to the elderly bystander who may be the dean, the director's father, or the playwright): "It was an unforgettable evening!"

If you feel that the potential ridicule of these expressions is too strong, you may equivocate further with the always safe "Congratulations!"

One may protest that these comments, however deft, are still lies and should not be excused. I think, however, that to so regard them is to confuse standards of different functions of communication. Affective communication directed to the emotional responses of the listener does not require the accuracy, even of judgments, that the transmission of specific information does. The purpose is often friendship, not a critical evaluation. Often it is much more important to tell a person that you like his tie, coat, smile, voice, and so on, than to be bound by some standards of judgment which would severely limit your affective communications. A kind or friendly remark often does more for human understanding than a diplomatic silence or a hundred "honest" judgments.

To be aware of the many functions of communication is to be alive and sensitive to the most basic of human needs. As our needs for bodily health and comfort are met, we become more aware of (and create new) needs for symbolic health and comfort. To be loved or respected, to help others, to feel trust—the list could be elaborated greatly—becomes extremely important. Each communication situation both reveals our frailty and offers some promise for support.

NOTES

1. Cynthia Nelson, "Saints and Sinners: Parallels in the Sex-Role Differentiation in the Family of Saints and in the Family of Man in a Mexican Peasant Village" (mimeographed, N.D.).
2. Susanne Langer includes the magic function of language as part of "ritual." She writes, "Magic . . . is not a method, but a language; it is part and parcel of that greater phenomenon, ritual, which is the language of religion." (*Philosophy in a New Key* [Cambridge, Mass.: Harvard University Press, 1942], p. 39.) Although this may have a historical basis, and although magic and ritual are also clearly related today, I find it useful to make a distinction between the two.
3. Some students are unimpressed by the distinction.
4. Ernst Cassirer, *Language and Myth* (New York: Dover, N.D.), pp. 50-51.
5. Emanuel Perlmutter, "Valachi Names 5 as Crime Chiefs in New York Area," *New York Times*, October 2, 1963, p. 28.

# RECOMMENDED READING

Barnlund, Dean C., and Haiman, Franklyn S., *The Dynamics of Discussion*, Boston: Houghton Mifflin, 1960.

Berlo, David K., *The Process of Communication: An Introduction to the Theory and Practice*, New York: Holt, Rinehart and Winston, 1960.

Cassirer, Ernst, "Word Magic," in *Language and Myth*, New York: Dover, 44-62.

Goffman, Erving, *The Presentation of Self in Everyday Life*, Garden City, N.Y.: Doubleday (Anchor Books), 1959.

Hayakawa, S. I., *Language in Thought and Action*, 2nd ed., New York: Harcourt Brace Jovanovich, 1964, chapters six through nine, especially.

Hayakawa, S. I. (ed.), *The Use and Misuse of Language*, Greenwich, Conn.: Fawcett (Premier Books), 1962.

Johnson, Wendell, *Your Most Enchanted Listener*, New York: Harper & Row, 1956.

Malinowski, Bronislaw, "The Problem of Meaning in Primitive Languages," Supplement I in C. K. Ogden and I. A. Richards, *The Meaning of Meaning*, New York: Harcourt Brace Jovanovich (Harvest Books), 1923, 296-336.

Ruesch, Jurgen, and Bateson, Gregory, *Communication: The Social Matrix of Psychiatry*, New York: Norton, 1951.

# FACIAL ENGAGEMENTS
## Erving Goffman

### 1. CIVIL INATTENTION

When persons are mutually present and not involved together
in conversation or other focused interaction, it is possible for
one person to stare openly and fixedly at others, gleaning
what he can about them while frankly expressing on his face
his response to what he sees—for example, the "hate stare"
that a Southern white sometimes gratuitously gives to Negroes
walking past him.[1] It is also possible for one person to treat
others as if they were not there at all, as objects not worthy
of a glance, let alone close scrutiny. Moreover, it is possible
for the individual, by his staring or his "not seeing," to alter
his own appearance hardly at all in consequence of the presence of the others. Here we have "nonperson" treatment; it
may be seen in our society in the way we sometimes treat
children, servants, Negroes, and mental patients.[2]

Currently, in our society, this kind of treatment is to be
contrasted with the kind generally felt to be more proper in
most situations, which will here be called "civil inattention."
What seems to be involved is that one gives to another enough
visual notice to demonstrate that one appreciates that the
other is present (and that one admits openly to having seen
him), while at the next moment withdrawing one's attention
from him so as to express that he does not constitute a target
of special curiosity or design.

In performing this courtesy the eyes of the looker may pass
over the eyes of the other, but no "recognition" is typically
allowed. Where the courtesy is performed between two persons passing on the street, civil inattention may take the
special form of eyeing the other up to approximately eight
feet, during which time sides of the street are apportioned by
gesture, and then casting the eyes down as the other passes—a
kind of dimming of lights. In any case, we have here what is
perhaps the slightest of interpersonal rituals, yet one that constantly regulates the social intercourse of persons in our
society.

By according civil inattention, the individual implies that he has no reason to suspect the intentions of the others present and no reason to fear the others, be hostile to them, or wish to avoid them. (At the same time, in extending this courtesy he automatically opens himself up to a like treatment from others present.) This demonstrates that he has nothing to fear or avoid in being seen and being seen seeing, and that he is not ashamed of himself or of the place and company in which he finds himself. It will therefore be necessary for him to have a certain "directness" of eye expression. As one student suggests, the individual's gaze ought not to be guarded or averted or absent or defensively dramatic, as if "something were going on." Indeed, the exhibition of such deflected eye expressions may be taken as a symptom of some kind of mental disturbance.[3]

Civil inattention is so delicate an adjustment that we may expect constant evasion of the rules regarding it. Dark glasses, for example, allow the wearer to stare at another person without that other being sure that he is being stared at.[4] One person can look at another out of the corner of his eyes. The fan and parasol once served as similar aids in stealing glances, and in polite Western society the decline in use of these instruments in the last fifty years has lessened the elasticity of communication arrangements.[5] It should be added, too, that the closer the onlookers are to the individual who interests them, the more exposed his position (and theirs), and the more obligation they will feel to ensure him civil inattention. The further they are from him, the more license they will feel to stare at him a little.

In addition to these evasions of rules we also may expect frequent infractions of them. Here, of course, social class subculture and ethnic subculture introduce differences in patterns, and differences, too, in the age at which patterns are first employed.

The morale of a group in regard to this minimal courtesy of civil inattention—a courtesy that tends to treat those present merely as participants in the gathering and not in terms of other social characteristics—is tested whenever someone of very divergent social status or very divergent physical appearance is present. English middle-class society, for example, prides itself in giving famous and infamous persons the

privilege of being c̶a̶l̶m̶l̶y̶ a̶t̶t̶e̶nded in public, as when the
Royal children man̶a̶g̶e̶ t̶o̶ w̶a̶lk through a park with few persons turning around t̶o̶ s̶t̶a̶re. And in our own American
society, currently, we k̶n̶o̶w that one of the great trials of the
physically handicapped is that in public places they will be
openly stared at, thereby having their privacy invaded, while,
at the same time, the invasion exposes their undesirable attributes.[6]

The act of staring is a thing which one does not ordinarily do to another
human being; it seems to put the object stared at in a class apart. One
does not talk to a monkey in a zoo, or to a freak in a sideshow—one
only stares.[7]

An injury, as a characteristic and inseparable part of the body, may be
felt to be a personal matter which the man would like to keep private.
However, the fact of its visibility makes it known to anyone whom the
injured man meets, including the stranger. A visible injury differs from
most other personal matters in that anyone can deal with it regardless
of the wish of the injured person; anyone can stare at the injury or ask
questions about it, and in both cases communicate to and impose upon
the injured person his feelings and evaluations. His action is then felt
as an intrusion into privacy. It is the visibility of the injury which makes
intrusion into privacy so easy. The men are likely to feel that they have
to meet again and again people who will question and stare, and to feel
powerless because they cannot change the general state of affairs . . .[8]

Perhaps the clearest illustration both of civil inattention
and of the infraction of this ruling occurs when a person
takes advantage of another's not looking to look at him, and
then finds that the object of his gaze has suddenly turned
and caught the illicit looker looking. The individual caught
out may then shift his gaze, often with embarrassment and a
little shame, or he may carefully act as if he had merely been
seen in the moment of observation that is permissible; in
either case we see evidence of the propriety that should have
been maintained.

To behave properly and to have the *right* to civil inattention are related: Propriety on the individual's part tends to
ensure his being accorded civil inattention; extreme impropriety on his part is likely to result in his being stared at or
studiously not seen. Improper conduct, however, does not
automatically release others from the obligation of extending
civil inattention to the offender, although it often weakens
it. In any case, civil inattention may be extended in the face
of offensiveness simply as an act of tactfulness, to keep an

orderly appearance in the situation in spite of what is happening.

Ordinarily, in middle-class society, failure to extend civil inattention to others is not negatively sanctioned in a direct and open fashion, except in the social training of servants and children, the latter especially in connection with according civil inattention to the physically handicapped and deformed. For examples of such direct sanctions among adults one must turn to despotic societies where glancing at the emperor or his agents may be a punishable offense,[9] or to the rather refined rules prevailing in some of our Southern states concerning how much of a look a colored male can give to a white female, over how much distance, before it is interpreted as a punishable sexual advance.[10]

Given the pain of being stared at, it is understandable that staring itself is widely used as a means of negative sanction, socially controlling all kinds of improper public conduct. Indeed it often constitutes the first warning an individual receives that he is "out of line" and the last warning that it is necessary to give him. In fact, in the case of those whose appearance tests to the limit the capacity of a gathering to proffer civil inattention, staring itself may become a sanction against staring. The autobiography of an ex-dwarf provides an illustration:

There were the thick-skinned ones, who stared like hill people come down to see a traveling show. There were the paper-peekers, the furtive kind who would withdraw blushing if you caught them at it. There were the pitying ones, whose tongue clickings could almost be heard after they had passed you. But even worse, there were the chatterers, whose every remark might as well have been "How do you do, poor boy?" They said it with their eyes and their manners and their tone of voice.

I had a standard defense—a cold stare. Thus anesthetized against my fellow man, I could contend with the basic problem—getting in and out of the subway alive.[11]

## 2. THE STRUCTURE OF FACE ENGAGEMENTS

When two persons are mutually present and hence engaged together in some degree of unfocused interaction, the mutual proffering of civil inattention—a significant form of unfocused interaction—is not the only way they can relate to one another. They can proceed from there to engage one another in focused interaction, the unit of which I shall refer to as a *face engagement* or an *encounter*.[12] Face engagements comprise all those instances of two or more participants in a situation joining each other openly in maintaining a single focus of cognitive and visual attention—what is sensed as a single *mutual activity*, entailing preferential communication rights. As a simple example—and one of the most common— when persons are present together in the same situation they may engage each other in a talk. This accreditation for mutual activity is one of the broadest of all statuses. Even persons of extremely disparate social positions can find themselves in circumstances where it is fitting to impute it to one another. Ordinarily the status does not have a "latent phase" but obliges the incumbents to be engaged at that very moment in exercising their status.

Mutual activities and the face engagements in which they are embedded comprise instances of small talk, commensalism, love-making, gaming, formal discussion, and personal servicing (treating, selling, waitressing, and so forth). In some cases, as with sociable chats, the coming together does not seem to have a ready instrumental rationale. In other cases, as when a teacher pauses at a pupil's desk to help him for a moment with a problem he is involved in, and will be involved in after she moves on, the encounter is clearly a setting for a mutual instrumental activity, and this joint work is merely a phase of what is primarily an individual task.[13] It should be noted that while many face engagements seem to be made up largely of the exchange of verbal statements, so that conversational encounters can in fact be used as the model, there are still other kinds of encounters where no word is spoken. This becomes very apparent, of course, in the study of engagements among children who have not yet mastered talk, and where, incidentally, it is possible to see the gradual transformation of a mere physical contacting of another into an act that establishes the social relationship of jointly accrediting a face-to-face encounter.[14] Among adults, too, however, nonverbal encounters can be observed: The significant acts exchanged can be gestures[15] or even, as in board and card games, moves. Also, there are certain close comings-together over work tasks which give rise to a single focus of visual and cognitive attention and to intimately coordinated contributions, the order and kind of contribution being determined by shared appreciation of what the task-at-the-moment requires as the next act. Here, while no word of direction or sociability may be spoken, it will be understood that lack of attention or coordinated response constitutes a breach in the mutual commitment of the participants.[16]

Where there are only two participants in a situation, an encounter, if there is to be one, will *exhaust* the situation, giving us a *fully-focused gathering*. With more than two participants, there may be persons officially present in the situation who are officially excluded from the encounter and not themselves so engaged. These unengaged[17] participants change the gathering into a *partly-focused* one. If more than three persons are present, there may be more than one encounter carried on in the same situation— a *multifocused* gathering. I will use the term *participation unit* to refer both to encounters and to unengaged participants; the term *bystander* will be used to refer to any individual present who is not a ratified member of the particular encounter in question, whether or not he is currently a member of some other encounter.

In our society, face engagements seem to share a complex of properties, so that this class of social unit can be defined analytically, as well as by example.

An encounter is initiated by someone making an opening move, typically by means of a special expression of the eyes but sometimes by a statement or a special tone of voice at the beginning of a statement.[18] The engagement proper begins when this overture is acknowledged by the other, who signals back with his eyes, voice, or stance that he has placed himself at the disposal of the other for purposes of a mutual eye-to-eye activity—even if only to ask the initiator to postpone his request for an audience.

There is a tendency for the initial move and the responding "clearance" sign to be exchanged almost simultaneously, with all participants employing both signs, perhaps in order to prevent an initiator from placing himself in a position of being denied by others. Glances, in particular, make possible this effective simultaneity. In fact, when eyes are joined, the initiator's first glance can be sufficiently tentative and ambiguous to allow him to act as if no initiation has been intended, if it appears that his overture is not desired.

Eye-to-eye looks, then, play a special role in the communication life of the community, ritually establishing an avowed openness to verbal statements and a rightfully heightened mutual relevance of acts.[19] In Simmel's words:

Of the special sense-organs, the eye has a uniquely sociological function. The union and interaction of individuals is based upon mutual glances. This is perhaps the most direct and purest reciprocity which exists anywhere. This highest psychic reaction, however, in which the glances of eye to eye unite men, crystallizes into no objective structure; the unity which momentarily arises between two persons is present in the occasion and is dissolved in the function. So tenacious and subtle is this union that it can only be maintained by the shortest and straightest line between the eyes, and the smallest deviation from it, the slightest glance aside, completely destroys the unique character of this union. No objective trace of this relationship is left behind, as is universally found, directly or indirectly, in all other types of associations between men, as, for example, in interchange of words. The interaction of eye and eye dies in the moment in which directness of the function is lost. But the totality of social relations of human beings, their self-assertion and self-abnegation, their intimacies and estrangements, would be changed in unpredictable ways if there occurred no glance of eye to eye. This mutual glance between persons, in distinction from the simple sight or observation of the other, signifies a wholly new and unique union between them.[20]

It is understandable, then, that an individual who feels he has cause to be alienated from those around him will express this through some "abnormality of the gaze," especially averting of the eyes.[21] And it is understandable, too, that an individual who wants to control others' access to him and the information he receives may avoid looking toward the person who is seeking him out. A waitress, for example, may prevent a waiting customer from "catching her eye" to prevent his initiating an order. Similarly, if a pedestrian wants to ensure a particular allocation of the street relative to a fellow pedestrian, or if a motorist wants to ensure priority of his line of proposed action over that of a fellow motorist or a pedestrian, one strategy is to avoid meeting the other's eyes and thus avoid cooperative claims.[22] And where the initiator is in a social position requiring him to give the other the formal right to initiate all encounters, hostile and teasing possibilities may occur, of which Melville's *White Jacket* gives us an example:

But sometimes the captain feels out of sorts, or in ill-humour, or is pleased to be somewhat capricious, or has a fancy to show a touch of his omnipotent supremacy; or, peradventure, it has so happened that the first lieutenant has, in some way, piqued or offended him, and he is not unwilling to show a slight specimen of his dominion over him, even before the eyes of all hands; at all events, only by some one of these suppositions can the singular circumstance be accounted for, that frequently Captain Claret would pertinaciously promenade up and down the poop, purposely averting his eye from the first lieutenant, who would stand below in the most awkward suspense, waiting the first wink from his superior's eye.

"Now I have him!" he must have said to himself, as the captain would turn toward him in his walk; "now's my time!" and up would go his hand to his cap; but, alas! the captain was off again; and the men at the guns would cast sly winks at each other as the embarrassed lieutenant would bite his lips with suppressed vexation.

Upon some occasions this scene would be repeated several times, till at last Captain Claret, thinking that in the eyes of all hands his dignity must by this time be pretty well bolstered, would stalk toward his subordinate, looking him full in the eyes; whereupon up goes his hand to the cap front, and the captain, nodding his acceptance of the report, descends from his perch to the quarter-deck.[23]

As these various examples suggest, mutual glances ordinarily must be withheld if an encounter is to be avoided, for eye contact opens one up for face engagement. I would like to add, finally, that there is a relationship between the use of eye-to-eye glances as a means of communicating a request for initiation of an encounter, and other communication practices. The more clearly individuals are obliged to refrain from staring directly at others, the more effectively will they be able to attach special significance to a stare, in this case, a request for an encounter. The rule of civil inattention thus makes possible, and "fits" with, the clearance function given to looks into others' eyes. The rule similarly makes possible the giving of a special function to "prolonged" holding of a stranger's glance, as when unacquainted persons who had arranged to meet each other manage to discover one another in this way.[24]

Once a set of participants have avowedly opened themselves up to one another for an engagement, an eye-to-eye ecological huddle tends to be carefully maintained, maximizing the opportunity for participants to monitor one another's mutual perceivings.[25] The participants turn their minds to the same subject matter and (in the case of talk) their eyes to the same speaker, although of course this single *focus* of attention can shift within limits from one topic to another and from one speaker or target to another.[26] A shared definition of the situation comes to prevail. This includes agreement concerning perceptual relevancies and irrelevancies, and a "working consensus," involving a degree of mutual considerateness, sympathy, and a muting of opinion differences.[27] Often a group atmosphere develops—what Bateson has called ethos.[28] At the same time, a heightened sense of moral responsibility for one's acts also seems to develop.[29] A "we-rationale" develops, being a sense of the single thing that we the participants are avowedly doing together at the time. Further, minor ceremonies are likely to be employed to mark the termination of the engagement and the entrance and departure of particular participants (should the encounter have more than two members). These ceremonies, along with the social control exerted during the encounter to keep participants "in line," give a kind of ritual closure to the mutual activity sustained in the encounter. An individual will therefore tend to be brought all the way into an ongoing encounter or kept altogether out of it.[30]

Engagements of the conversational kind appear to have, at least in our society, some spatial conventions. A set of individuals caused to sit more than a few feet apart because of furniture arrangements will find difficulty in maintaining informal talk;[31] those brought within less than a foot and a half of each other will find difficulty in speaking directly to each other, and may talk at an off angle to compensate for the closeness.[32]

In brief, then, encounters are organized by means of a special set of acts and gestures comprising communication about communicating. As a linguist suggests:

There are messages primarily serving to establish, to prolong, or to discontinue communication, to check whether the channel works ("Hello, do you hear me?"), to attract the attention of the interlocutor or to confirm his continued attention ("Are you listening?" or in Shakespearean diction, "Lend me your ears!"—and on the other end of the wire "Um-hum!").[33]

Everyday terms refer to different aspects of encounters. "Cluster," "knot," "conversational circle"—all highlight the physical aspects, namely, a set of persons physically close together and facially oriented to one another, their backs toward those who are not participants. "Personal encounter" refers to the unit in terms of the opportunity it provides or enforces for some kind of social intimacy. In the literature, the term "the interaction" is sometimes used to designate either the activity occurring within the cluster at any one moment or the total activity occurring from the moment the cluster forms to the moment at which it officially disbands. And, of course, where spoken messages are exchanged, especially under informal circumstances, the terms "chat," "a conversation," or "a talk" are employed.

It may be noted that while all participants share equally in the rights and obligations described, there are some rights that may be differentially distributed within an encounter. Thus, in spoken encounters, the right to listen is one shared by all, but the right to be a speaker may be narrowly restricted, as, for example, in stage performances and large public meetings. Similarly, children at the dinner table are sometimes allowed to listen but forbidden to talk;[34] if not forbidden to talk, they may be "helped out" and in this way denied the communication courtesy of being allowed to finish a message for themselves.[35] And in other engagements, one category of participant may be allowed to say only "Yes, sir," or "No, sir," or restricted to the limited signalling that a modulation of applause allows. The differential rights of players vis-à-vis kibitzers in games provide another example.

When the communion of a face engagement has been established between two or more individuals, the resulting state of ratified mutual participation can last for varying periods. When a clearly defined task is involved, the engagement may last for hours. When no apparent work or recreational task is involved, and what is perceived as sociability alone holds the participants, certain durations seem to be favored. The contact may be very brief, as brief, in fact, as the opening meeting of eyes itself. In our own middle-class society there are "chats," where two individuals pause in their separate lines of action for what both recognize to be a necessarily brief period of time; there are greetings, whereby communion is established and maintained long enough for the participants to exchange brief interpersonal rituals; and, briefest of all, there are recognitional or "friendly" glances. (Of course, a recognitional glance may be merely the first interchange in an extended greeting, and a greeting merely the opening phase of a chat, but these extensions of coparticipation are not always found.) Except for the ritual of civil inattention, the mere exchange of friendly glances is perhaps the most frequent of our interpersonal rituals.

Encounters of an obligatory kind are linked to the world of domestic convivial occasions. In some social circles, a guest entering a party has a right to be greeted by the host or hostess and convoyed into the proceedings in visible contact with the authorizing person, this encounter thereby legitimating and celebrating the newcomer's participation in the occasion. His departure may be marked with the same kind of ceremony, officially bringing his participation to an end.[36] The occasion then closes in and over the place he has left, and if he should have to return for something he has forgotten, embarrassment is likely to be felt, especially if the ethos of the occasion has changed, and especially if marked ceremonial attention had been given his leave-taking.[37]

Encounters, of course, tend to be taken as an expression of the state of a social relationship. And, as will be considered later, to the degree that contact is practical, it may have to be made so as not to deny the relationship.[38] Further, each engagement tends to be initiated with an amount of fuss appropriate to the period of lapsed contact, and terminated with the amount appropriate to the assumed period of separation. There results a kind of tiding over, and a compensation for the diminishing effects of separation.[39] At a party, then, a version of Mrs. Post's ruling is likely to prevail:

In meeting the same person many times within an hour or so, one does not continue to bow after the second, or at most third meeting. After that one either looks away or merely smiles.[40]

The same mere smile between the same two persons newly coming within range of each other in a foreign country may constitute a grievous affront to their relationship.

I have suggested that a face engagement is a sufficiently clear-cut unit that an individual typically must either be entirely within it or entirely outside it. This is nicely borne out by the trouble caused when a person attempts to be half-in and half-out. Nonetheless, there are communication arrangements that seem to lie halfway between mere copresence and full scale coparticipation, one of which should be mentioned here. When two persons walk silently together down the street or doze next to each other at the beach, they may be treated by others as "being together," and are likely to have the right to break rather abruptly into spoken or gestured communication, although they can hardly be said to sustain continuously a mutual activity. This sense of being together constitutes a kind of lapsed verbal encounter, functioning more as a means of excluding nonmembers than as a support for sustained focused interaction among the participants.[41]

Persons who can sustain lapsed encounters with one another are in a position to avoid the problem of "safe supplies" during spoken encounters—the need to find a sufficient supply of inoffensive things to talk about during the period when an official state of talk prevails. Thus, in Shetland Isle, when three or four women were knitting together, one knitter would say a word, it would be allowed to rest for a minute or two, and then another knitter would provide an additional comment. In the same manner a family sitting around its kitchen fire would look into the flames and intersperse replies to statements with periods of observation of the fire. Shetland men used for the same purpose the lengthy pauses required for the proper management of their pipes.

To these comments on the structure of engagements I would like to add a brief remark on the information that encounters convey to the situation as a whole. In an earlier section, it was suggested that an individual divulges things about himself by his mere presence in a situation. In the same way, he gives off information about himself by virtue of the encounters in which others do or do not see him. Involvement in focused interaction therefore inevitably contributes to unfocused interaction conveying something to all who are present in the situation at large.

In public places in our society, what is conveyed by being in or out of encounters differs appreciably according to sex and the periods of the week. Morning and lunchtime are times when anyone can appear alone almost anywhere without this giving evidence of how the person is faring in the social world; dinner and other evening activities, however, provide unfavorable information about unaccompanied participants, especially damaging in the case of female participants. Weekend nights, and ceremonial occasions such as Thanksgiving, Christmas, and, especially, New Year's Eve, are given special weight in this connection, being times when an unengaged individual in a semipublic place may feel very much out of place.

It should be added, finally, that in so far as others judge the individual socially by the company he is seen in, for him to be brought into an engagement with another is to be placed in the position of being socially identified as the other is identified.

## 3. ACCESSIBILITY

In every situation, those present will be obliged to retain some readiness for potential face engagements. (This readiness has already been suggested as one way in which situational presence is expressed.) There are many important reasons why the individual is usually obliged to respond to requests for face engagements. In the first place, he owes this to himself because often it will be through such communication that his own interests can be served, as when a stranger accosts him to tell him he has dropped something, or that the bridge is out. For similar reasons he owes this accessibility to others present, and to persons not present for whom those present may serve as a relay. (The need for this collective solidarity is heightened in urban living, which brings individuals of great social distance within range of one another.) Further, as previously suggested, participation in a face engagement can be a sign of social closeness and relatedness; when this opportunity to participate is proffered by another, it ought not to be refused, for to decline such a request is to reject someone who has committed himself to a sign of desiring contact. More than this, refusal of an offer implies that the refuser rejects the other's claim to membership in the gathering and the social occasion in which the gathering occurs. It is therefore uncommon for persons to deny these obligations to respond.

Although there are good reasons why an individual should keep himself available for face engagements, there are also good reasons for him to be cautious of this.

In allowing another to approach him for talk, the individual may find that he has been inveigled into a position to be attacked and assaulted physically. In societies where public safety is not firmly established, especially in places such as the desert, where the traveler is for long periods of time remote from any source of help, the danger that a face engagement may be a prelude to assault becomes appreciable, and extensive avoidance practices or greetings at a distance tend to be employed.[42] Here, of course, the "physical safety" component of civic order and the communication component overlap. But apart from this extreme, we should see that when an individual opens himself up to talk with another, he opens himself up to pleadings, commands, threats, insult, and false information. The mutual considerateness characteristic of face engagements reinforces these dangers, subjecting the individual to the possibility of having his sympathy and tactfulness exploited, and causing him to act against his own interests.

Further, words can act as a "relationship wedge"; that is, once an individual has extended to another enough consideration to hear him out for a moment, some kind of bond of mutual obligation is established, which the initiator can use in turn as a basis for still further claims; once this new extended bond is granted, grudgingly or willingly, still further claims for social or material indulgence can be made. Hence, in one important example, a man and a woman can start out as strangers and, if conditions are right, progress from an incidental encounter to matrimony. We need only trace back the history of many close relationships between adults to find that something was made of face engagements when it need not have been. Of course, persons usually form "suitable" relationships, not allowing casual encounters to be a wedge to something else. But there is sufficient slippage in systems of conviviality segregation to give mothers concern about their daughters and to provide one of the basic romantic themes of light fiction.

I have suggested some reasons why individuals, at least in our own society, are obliged to keep themselves available for face engagements, and I have also suggested some of the dangers persons open themselves up to in so doing. These two opposing tendencies are reconciled in society, apparently, by a kind of implicit contract or gentleman's agreement that persons sustain: Given the fact that the other will be under some obligation, often unpleasant, to respond to overtures, potential initiators are under obligation to stay their own desires. A person can thus make himself available to others in the expectation that they will restrain their calls on his availability and not make him pay too great a price for his being accessible. Their right to initiate contact is checked by their duty to take his point of view and initiate contact with him only under circumstances that he will easily see to be justified; in short, they must not "abuse" their privileges.

This implicit communication contract (and the consequence of breaking it) receive wide mythological representation, as in our own "cry wolf" tale. Understandably, infractions of the rule against undesired overture do cause some anxiety, for the recipient must either accede to the request or demonstrate to himself and the others present that his availability for face engagements was not part of his character but a false pose, to be maintained only when no price was involved in maintaining it.

In noting the implicit contract that makes persons present delicately accessible and inaccessible to each other, we can go on to note a basic margin of appetite and distaste to be found in social situations. The reasons why individuals are obliged to restrain themselves from making encounter overtures provide many of the reasons why they might want to do so. And the obligation to be properly accessible often covers a desire to be selectively quite unavailable. Hence, many public and semipublic places, such as cocktail lounges and club cars, acquire a special tone and temper, a special piquancy, that blurs the communication lines, giving each participant some desire to encroach where perhaps he does not have a right to go, and to keep from being engaged with others who perhaps have a right to engage him. Each individual, then, is not only involved in maintaining the basic communication contract, but is also likely to be involved in hopes, fears, and actions that bend the rules if they do not actually break them.

It has been suggested, then, that as a general rule the individual is obliged to make himself available for encounters even though he may have something to lose by entering them, and that he may well be ambivalent about this arrangement. Here mental patients provide a lesson in reverse, for they can show us the price that is paid for declining to make oneself available and force us to see that there are reasons why someone able to be accessible should be willing to pay the price of remaining inaccessible.

In brief, a patient who declines to respond to overtures is said to be "out of contact," and this state is often felt to be full evidence that he is very sick indeed, that he is, in fact, cut off from all contact with the world around him. In the case of some "organic" patients, this generalization from inaccessibility appears quite valid, as it does with certain "functionals." There are patients, for example, who, before admission, had progressively withdrawn from responding to such things as the telephone and doorbell, and, once in the hospital, decline all staff overtures for engagement, this being but one instance of a general withdrawal of concern for the life about them.

In the case of other patients, however, refusal to enter proffered engagements cannot be taken as a sign of unconcern for the gathering, but rather as a sign of alienation based on active feelings such as fear, hate, and contempt, each of which can be understandable in the circumstances, and each of which can allow the patient to show a nice regard for other situational proprieties.

Thus, there are patients who coldly stare through direct efforts to bring them into a state of talk, declining all staff overtures, however seductive, teasing, or intensive, who will nonetheless allow themselves face engagements carefully initiated and terminated by themselves without the usual courtesies. Still other patients who are out of contact to most persons on the ward will engage in self-initiated encounters with a small select number of others, by means of coded messages, foreign language, whispering, or the exchange of written statements. Some patients, unwilling to engage in spoken encounters with anyone, will be ready to engage in other types of encounters, such as dancing or card playing. Similarly, I knew a patient who often blankly declined greetings extended him by fellow-patients on the grounds, but who could be completely relied upon not to miss a cue when performing the lead in a patient dramatic production.

As might then be expected, a patient declining to conduct himself properly in regard to face engagements might be well conducted in regard to unfocused interaction.[43] One illustration was provided by a patient I observed, a young woman of thirty-two, who at one point in her "illness" was ready to handle her dress and deportment with all the structured modesty that is required of her sex, while at the same time her language was foul. During another phase of her illness, this patient, in the company of a friendly nurse, enjoyed shopping trips to the neighboring town, during which she and her keeper got wry pleasure from the fact that the patient was "passing" as a "normal" person. Had anyone made an opening statement to the patient, however, the masquerade would have been destroyed, for this was a time when the patient was mute in all verbal interaction or, at best, spoke with very great pressure.

A touching illustration of the same difference in capacity for focused and unfocused interaction was provided at Central Hospital by patients who were fearful and anxious of their whole setting, but who nonetheless made elaborate efforts to show that they were still what they had been before coming to the hospital and that they were in poised, business-like control of the situation. One middle-aged man walked busily on the grounds with the morning newspaper folded under one arm and a rolled umbrella hooked over the other, wearing an expression of being late for an appointment. A young man, having carefully preserved his worn grey flannel suit, bustled similarly from one place he was not going to another. Yet both men stepped out of the path of any approaching staff person, and painfully turned their heads away whenever someone proffered an exchange or greeting of some kind, for both employed the tack of being mute with many of the persons whom they met. The management of a front of middle-class orientation in the situation, in these circumstances, was so precarious and difficult that (for these men) it apparently represented the day's major undertaking.[44] In other cases, of course, it is not fear that seems to account for the inaccessibility of otherwise properly mannered persons, but rather hostility: To acknowledge a staff overture is partly to acknowledge the legitimacy of the staff person making the overture, and if he is a serious worthy person then so must be his implied contention that the individual with whom he is initiating contact, namely, oneself, is a mental patient properly confined to a mental ward. To strengthen one's feeling that one is really sane, it may thus seem reasonable to disdain encounters in which the opposite will be assumed—even though this results in exactly the kind of conduct, namely, inaccessibility, that confirms the hospital's view that one is mentally ill.

A final point about accessibility should be mentioned. As previously suggested, conversational engagements are often carried out as involvements subordinated to some other business at hand, just as side involvements, such as smoking, are often carried out as activities subordinated to a conversational main involvement. The question arises as to the limits placed upon this coexistence in middle-class society. There are, for example, records of middle-class Navy personnel postponing a visit to the "head" until others have left so as not to have to defecate while being accessible to others for talk. I have also been told by a middle-class informant that she was always uneasy about painting her toenails while in the presence of her husband, since the painting involved too much attention to leave her sufficiently respectful of the talk.

## 4. LEAVE-TAKING RIGHTS

Just as the individual is obliged not to exploit the accessibility of others (else they have to pay too large a price for their obligation to be accessible), so he is obliged to release those with whom he is engaged, should it appear, through conventional cues, that they desire to be released (else they have to pay too great a price for their tact in not openly taking leave of him). A reminder of these rules of leave-taking can be found in elementary school classrooms where leave-taking practices are still being learned, as, for example, when a teacher, having called a student to her desk in order to correct his exercise book, may have to turn him around and gently propel him back to his seat in order to terminate the interview.

The rights of departure owed the individual, and the rule of tactful leave-taking owed the remaining participants, can be in conflict with each other. This conflict is often resolved, in a way very characteristic of communication life, by persons active in different roles tacitly cooperating to ease leave-taking. Thus, business etiquette provides the following lesson:

*On when to go*—your exit cues are many. They range from clear-cut closing remarks, usually in the form of a "thank you for coming in," to a vacant and preoccupied stare. But in any case they should come from the interviewer. It should not be necessary for him to stand, abruptly; you should have been able to feel the goodbye in the air far enough in advance to gather up your gear, slide forward to the edge of your chair and launch into a thank-you speech of your own. Nor should it be necessary to ask that embarrassing question, "Am I taking too much of your time?"; if that thought crosses your mind, it's time to go.[45]

In fact, persons can become so accustomed to being helped out by the very person who creates the need for help, that when cooperation is not forthcoming they may find they have no way of handling the incident. Thus, some mental patients may characteristically hold a staff person in an encounter regardless of how many hints the latter provides that termination ought now to occur. As the staff person begins to walk away, the patient may follow along until the locked door is reached, and even then the patient may try to accompany him. At such times the staff person may have to hold back the patient forcibly, or precipitously tear himself away, demonstrating not merely that the patient is being left in the lurch, but also that the staff show of concern for the patient is, in some sense, only a show. Pitchmen and street stemmers initiate a similar process; they rely on the fact that the accosted person will be willing to agree to a purchase in order not to have to face being the sort of person who walks away from an encounter without being officially released.

NOTES

1. Griffin, J. H., *Black Like Me*, Boston: Houghton Mifflin, 1961, 54, 128.
2. Goffman, Erving, *The Presentation of Self*, 151-153.
3. Riemer, M. D., "Abnormalities of the Gaze—A Classification," *Psychiatric Quarterly*, 1955, 29, 659-672.
4. A notable observer of face-to-face conduct, the novelist William Sansom, disputes this point in "Happy Holiday Abroad," in *A Contest of Ladies*, London: Hogarth Press, 1956, 228:
   Slowly he walked the length of the beach, pretending to saunter, studying each bather sideways from behind his black spectacles. One would think such dark glasses might conceal the inquisitive eye: but Preedy knew better, he knew they do the opposite, as soon as they are swivelled anywhere near the object it looks like a direct hit. You cannot appear to glance just beyond with your dark guns on.
5. See P. Binder, *Muffs and Morals*, New York: Morrow, n.d., chap. 9, "Umbrellas, Walking Sticks, and Fans," 178-196. The author suggests, p. 193:
   Another quizzing fan [in eighteenth-century England] had an inset of mica or gauze, so that a lady might cunningly use her fan as a lorgnette while her

face appeared to be screened from view. This type of fan was intended for use at a risqué play, where modesty required some equivalent to the earlier face-mask.

Successful devices of this kind must incorporate three features: The user must be able to look at the other, be able to give the appearance of not being ashamed of being seen by the other, and be able to conceal that he is in fact spying. Children in Shetland Isle primary schools handle visiting strangers with something like a fan—but one that fails in the last two counts—by shyly hiding their faces behind their two hands while peeking out at the visitor from a crack between two fingers.

6. See the very useful paper by R. K. White, B. A. Wright, and T. Dembo, "Studies in Adjustment to Visible Injuries: Evaluation of Curiosity by the Injured," *Journal of Abnormal and Social Psychology*, 1948, 43, 13-28.

7. *Ibid.*, 22.

8. *Ibid.*, 16-17.

9. Douglas, R. K. *Society in China*, London: Innes, 1894, 11.

10. See, for example, the notable Webster-Ingram case reported November 12-13, 1952 (AP). In many societies in Africa and Asia, a similar taboo exists regarding glances that males cast females.

11. Viscardi, H., Jr., *A Man's Stature*, New York: Day, 1952, 70, as cited in B. A. Wright, *Physical Disability—A Psychological Approach*, New York: Harper & Row, 1960, 214.

12. The term "encounter," which is much the easier of the two to use, has some common-sense connotations that ought here to be ruled out. First, the term is sometimes used to refer to mediated, as well as to direct, contact between two persons, as when persons have correspondence with each other. Secondly, the term is sometimes used with an implication of there having been difficulty or trouble during the interaction, as in the phrase "a run-in." Finally, the term is sometimes used to cover occasions which bring two persons into easy access to each other, regardless of how many times they may come together in a joint conversation during this time, as in the phrase, "I next encountered him at the Jones's party." I have attempted to consider the internal dynamics of encounters in "Fun in Games" in *Encounters*, 17-81.

13. Suggested by Arthur Stinchcombe.

14. See, for example, the early study by A. Beaver, *The Initiation of Social Contacts by Preschool Children*, New York: Bureau of Publications, Teachers College, Columbia University, Child Development Monographs, No. 7, 1932, 1-14.

15. Efron, D., *Gesture and Environment*, New York: King's Crown, 1941, 38.

16. The kind of intimate coordination consequent on involvement in the same task is nicely described in F. B. Miller, " 'Situational' Interactions—A Worthwhile Concept?" *Human Organization*, Winter, 1958-1959, 17, 37-47. After pointing out the differences between this kind of focused interaction and the kind necessarily involving speech or gestures, the writer does not, however, go on to

consider the similarities, such as the fact that withdrawal of attention, or ineptness, can give rise to the same kind of corrective social control in both cases. A well-described illustration of a task activity as an engagement may be found in T. Burling, *Essays on Human Aspects of Administration*, New York State School of Industrial and Labor Relations, Cornell University, Bulletin 25, August, 1953, 10-11:

> What is actually happening is that the changing needs of the patient, as they develop in the course of the operation, determine what everybody does. When a surgical team has worked long enough together to have developed true teamwork, each member has such a grasp of the total situation and of his role in it that the needs of the patient give unequivocal orders. A small artery is cut and begins to spurt. In a chain-of-command organization the surgeon would note this and say to the assistant, "Stop that bleeder." The assistant, in turn, would say to the surgical nurse, "Give me a hemostat," and thus, coordinated effort would be achieved. What actually happens is that the bleeder gives a simultaneous command to all three members of the team, all of whom have been watching the progress of the operation with equal attention. It says to the surgeon, "Get your hand out of the way until this is controlled." It says to the instrument nurse, "Get a hemostat ready," and it says to the assistant, "Clamp that off." This is the highest and most efficient type of cooperation known. It is so efficient that it looks simple and even primitive. It is possible only where every member of the team knows not only his own job thoroughly, but enough about the total job and that of each of the other members to see the relationship of what he does to everything else that goes on.

17. An "unengaged" participant may of course be involved in a task or other main focus of attention and hence not be "disengaged" in the situation.

18. When the individual is socially subordinated to the one to whom he is about to initiate an encounter overture, he may be required to use a minimal sign so that the superior can easily continue to overlook it, or can respond to it at his own convenience. For example, *Esquire Etiquette*, New York: Lippincott, 1953, 24, in listing the habits of a good secretary, includes "waiting to be recognized, when she has stepped in to speak to you, before interrupting whatever you are doing." In such cases the fiction is maintained that the superordinate alone can initiate an engagement. The classic case here is the mythical butler who coughs discreetly so that his master will take note of his presence and allow him to deliver a message.

19. In face engagements embodying a formal sports activity, opening moves may take other forms, as when boxers touch gloves, or swordsmen touch foils, in order to establish a sporting bracket or frame, as it were, around the oncoming encounter. Where participants know each other well, clearance signs may be taken for granted, and the initiator may pause slightly or in other ways modify his opening action, as a courtesy, and then proceed as if clearance had been granted.

Interestingly enough, some face engagements are of the kind in which coordination of activity is typically embodied in the usual ritual brackets of eye-recognition and exchange of words, but which, under special circumstances, are carefully initiated, maintained, and terminated *without* usual verbal or gestural overlay. Thus, in many mental hospitals, patients expect to be able to call on *any* patient who is smoking for a light, regardless of how withdrawn or regressed the smoker may appear to be. The gestured request for a light seems to be invariably complied with, but very often the complier addresses himself to the technical task alone, declining any other kind of negotiation or business. A similar kind of deritualized encounter is found where a man holds a door open for a woman he does not know, under circumstances that could imply an overture or could bring home undesirable facts about the woman for being in the region; under such circumstances the male may be careful to proffer civil inattention even while nicely adjusting his physical behavior to the movements of the woman. Emily Post, *Etiquette*, New York: Funk & Wagnalls, 1937, 26, suggests a similar courtesy:

Lifting the hat is a conventional gesture of politeness shown to strangers only, not to be confused with bowing, which is a gesture used to acquaintances and friends. In lifting his hat, a gentleman merely lifts it slightly off his forehead—by the brim of a stiff hat or by the crown of a soft one—and replaces it; he does not smile or bow, nor does he even look at the object of his courtesy. No gentleman ever subjects a lady to his scrutiny or his apparent observation if she is a stranger.

20. From his *Soziologie*, cited in R. E. Park and E. W. Burgess, *Introduction to the Science of Sociology*, 2nd. ed., Chicago: University of Chicago Press, 1924, 358. An interesting statement of some of the things that can be conveyed through eye-to-eye contact alone is given by Ortega y Gasset in his *Man and People*, New York: Norton, 1957, 115-117. He implies that there is a whole vocabulary of glances, describing several of them.

21. Riemer, M. D., "The Averted Gaze," *Psychiatric Quarterly*, 1949, 23, 108-115. It would be very interesting to examine techniques employed by the blind and the dumb to provide functional substitutes for clearance cues and other eye contributions to the structure of face-to-face communication.

22. The general point behind this example has been made by T. C. Schelling in his analysis of the bargaining power of the individual who can convincingly commit himself to a line of action, in this case by communicating his inability to receive demands and threats through messages. See Schelling's "An Essay on Bargaining," *The American Economic Review*, 1956, 46, 281-306, esp. 294-295.

23. Melville, Herman, *White Jacket*, New York: Grove Press, n.d., 276.

24. Evelyn Hooker, in an unpublished Copenhagen address, August 14, 1961, titled "The Homosexual Community," suggests: "It is said by homosexuals that if another catches and holds the glance, one need know nothing more about him to know that he is one of them."

25. This may not be a universal practice. According to an early report on the Northwest Coast Amazons:

When an Indian talks he sits down, no conversation is ever carried on when the speakers are standing unless it be a serious difference of opinion under discussion; nor, when he speaks, does the Indian look at the person addressed, any more than the latter watches the speaker. Both look at some outside objects. This is the attitude also of the Indian when addressing more than one listener, so that he appears to be talking to some one not visibly present.

Whiffen, T., *The North-West Amazons*, London: Constable, 1915, 254. In our own society, however, we can readily understand that when convicts are forbidden to talk to one another but desire to do so, they can effectively shield their joint involvement by talking without moving their lips and without looking at each other. See, for example, J. Phelan, *The Underworld*, London: Harrap, 1953, 7-8 and 13. We can also understand that when technical considerations prevent eye-to-eye accessibility (as in the case of a surgical nurse receiving orders from a surgeon who must not take his eyes from the surgical field), considerable discipline will be required of the recipient if communication is to be maintained. Finally, we can appreciate that the blind will have to learn to act as if the speaker is being watched, even though in fact the blind recipient could as well direct his sightless gaze anywhere. In the latter connection see H. Chevigny, *My Eyes Have a Cold Nose*, New Haven, Conn.: Yale University Press, 1962, 51.

26. Cf. R. F. Bales et al., "Channels of Communication in Small Groups," *American Sociological Review*, 1951, 16, 461-468, p. 461:

The conversation generally proceeded so that one person talked at a time, and all members in the particular group were attending the same conversation. In this sense, these groups might be said to have a "single focus," that is, they did not involve a number of conversations proceeding at the same time, as one finds at a cocktail party or in a hotel lobby. The single focus is probably a limiting condition of fundamental importance in the generalizations reported here.

To this the caution should be added that the multiple focuses found in places like hotel lobbies would occur simultaneously with unfocused interaction.

27. Hence, as Oswald Hall has suggested to me, when closeness and sympathy are to be held to a minimum, as when a butler talks to a house guest, or an enlisted man is disciplined by an officer, eye-to-eye communion may be avoided by the subordinate holding his eyes stiffly to the front. An echo of the same factor is to be found even in mediated conversation, where servants are obliged to answer the telephone by saying "Mrs. So-and-So's residence" instead of "Hello."

This tendency for eye-to-eye looks to involve sympathetic accommodation is nicely suggested in Trotsky's description of street disturbances during the "five days" in *The History of the Russian Revolution*, trans. Max Eastman, New York: Simon and Schuster, 1936, 1, 109:

In spite of the auspicious rumors about the Cossacks, perhaps slightly exaggerated, the crowd's attitude toward the mounted men remains cautious. A horseman sits high above the crowd; his soul is separated from the soul of the demonstrator by the four legs of his beast. A figure at which one must gaze from below always seems more significant, more threatening. The infantry are beside one on the pavement—closer, more accessible. The masses try to get near them, look into their eyes, surround them with their hot breath. A great role is played by women workers in the relation between workers and soldiers. They go up to the cordons more boldly than men, take hold of the rifles, beseech, almost command: "Put down your bayonets—join us." The soldiers are excited, ashamed, exchange anxious glances, waver; someone makes up his mind first, and the bayonets rise guiltily above the shoulders of the advancing crowd. The barrier is opened, a joyouse and grateful "Hurah!" shakes the air.

A more formalized version of the same tendency is described as obtaining among the Bedouins. See A. Musil, *The Manners and Customs of the Rwala Bedouins*, New York: American Geographical Society, Oriental Explorations and Studies No. 6, 1928, 455:

A salutation, if returned, is a guarantee of safety in the desert, *as-salâm salâme*. If a stranger travels unaccompanied by a *ḫawi* through the territory of a tribe unknown to him and salutes someone—be it only a little girl—and is saluted in return, he may be reasonably certain that he will be neither attacked nor robbed, for even a little girl with all her kin will protect him. Should the fellow tribesmen of the girl attack and rob him, *mâhûd* he has only to ask the help of her kinsfolk, who must take his part. The girl is the best witness: "A traveler saluted me at such and such a place, of about such and such an age, dressed thus and so, riding on a she-camel," of which she also gives a description. Frequently even an enemy saves himself in this manner when hotly pursued. Realizing that he cannot escape, he suddenly changes his course, returns by a roundabout way to the camp of his pursuers, salutes a child, and, taking its hand, allows himself to be led to the tent of the parents. The adult Bedouins, being more cautious, do not answer at once when saluted by a man they do not know. Especially if two or three are riding together and approach a camp at night, the guard replies to their salute thus:

"Ye are outlawed; I shall not return your salutation; *tarâkom mwaṣṣedin w-lâ 'alejkom radd as-salâm*. For an outlawed one, *mwaṣṣed*, is treated like an enemy to whom a salutation is of no use whatever.

Because of the obligation of considerateness among members of an engagement, and especially between a speaker and the particular member to whom he addresses his remarks, individuals sometimes "talk into the air" or mutter, pointedly addressing their remarks to no one, or to a child or pet. The person for whose benefit the remarks are intended may thus be half forced into the role of overhearer, allowing greater liberties to be taken with him than could be comfortably managed in direct address.

28. Bateson, G., *Naven*, Cambridge: Cambridge University Press, 1936, 119-120:

When a group of young intellectual English men or women are talking and joking together wittily and with a touch of light cynicism, there is established among them for the time being a definite tone of appropriate behavior. Such specific tones of behavior are in all cases indicative of an ethos. They are expressions of a standardized system of emotional attitudes. In this case the men have temporarily adopted a definite set of sentiments towards the rest of the world, a definite attitude towards reality, and they will joke about subjects which at another time they would treat with seriousness. If one of the men suddenly intrudes a sincere or realist remark it will be received with no enthusiasm—perhaps with a moment's silence and a slight feeling that the sincere person has committed a solecism. On another occasion the same group of persons may adopt a different ethos; they may talk realistically and sincerely. Then if the blunderer makes a flippant joke it will fall flat and feel like a solecism.

29. And so we find that bringing someone into a face engagement can be used by the initiator as a form of social control, as when a teacher stops a student's *sotto voce* comments by looking him in

the eye and saying, "What did you say?" or when failure to accord civil inattention is handled as Norman Mailer describes in his novel *The Deer Park*, New York: Signet Books, 1957, 212:

Beda [a celebrity] looked at a woman who had been staring at him curiously, and when he winked, she turned away in embarrassment. "Oh God, the tourists," he said.

Interestingly enough, since joint participation in an encounter allows participants to look fully at each other—in fact, enjoins this to a degree—we find that one strategy employed by an individual when he is caught out by the person he is staring at is to act as if this staring were the first move in an overture to engagement, thereby ratifying and legitimating the failure to accord civil inattention.

30.  One well-established way of confirming and consolidating a leave-taking is for the leave-taker to move away physically from the other or others. In places like Shetland Isle this can cause a problem when two persons pause for a moment's sociability and then find that their directions of movement do not diverge sharply. If the two persons walk at a normal pace, they find themselves attempting to close out the encounter while still having easy physical access to each other. Sometimes one individual offers an excuse to break into a run; sometimes, even if it takes him out of his way, he may take a path diverging sharply from that taken by his erstwhile coparticipant.

31.  Sommer, R., "The Distance for Comfortable Conversation: A Further Study," *Sociometry*, 1962, 25, 111-116. See also his "Studies in Personal Space," *Sociometry*, 1959, 22, 247-260.

32.  See E. T. Hall, *The Silent Language*, New York: Doubleday, 1959, 204-206. In B. Schaffner (ed.), *Group Processes*, Transactions of the Fourth (1957) Conference, New York: Josiah Macy, Jr. Foundation, 1959, 184, R. Birdwhistell comments as follows in a symposium discussion:

It appears that Americans, when standing face to face, stand about arm's length from each other. When they stand side by side, the distance demanded is much less. When "middle majority Americans" stand closer than this in a face-to-face position they will either gradually separate or come toward each other and begin to emit signs of irritation. However, if they are put in a situation in which they are not required to interact—say on a streetcar—they can stand quite close, even to the point of making complete contact.

The amount of this territory seems to vary culturally. So, there can be a situation where two or three ethnic groups occupy different territories, that is, varying amounts of personal space. For example, put together a Southeastern European Jew (who occupies about half the area of personal space) and a middle-class American and a high degree of irritation results, particularly if the middle-class American keeps drifting around to the side, in order not to be insulting, and the Southeastern European Jewish man tries to move around to get face-to-face relationship. You get an actual dance, which very often turns into what is practically a fight.

From all of this it follows that among persons arranged in a discussion circle, persons adjacent to each other may tend not to address remarks to each other, except to pass side comments, since a voice full enough to embrace the circle would be too full for the distance between them. For experimental evidence, see B. Steinzor, "The Spatial Factor in Face to Face Discussion Groups," *Journal of Abnormal and Social Psychology*, 1950, **45**, 552-555.

33. Jakobson, R., "Closing Statement: Linguistics and Poetics," in T. A. Sebeok (ed.), *Style in Language*, New York: Wiley, 1960, 355. Cf. the concept of metacommunication in J. Ruesch and G. Bateson, *Communication*, New York: Norton, 1951.

34. Bossard, J. H. S., "Family Modes of Expression," *American Sociological Review*, 1945, **10**, 226-237, p. 229.

35. *Ibid.*

36. Here there is an interesting difference between Anglo-American and French custom; in France, the entering or departing person ratifies his entrance or departure not only through contact with the person managing the occasion but often also by a hand-shaking engagement with some or all of the other guests present.

37. The same sort of embarrassment occurs when a member of an organization, who has been given a farewell party and gift to mark a termination of his membership and to set the stage for the group's developing a new relation to a substitute, then finds that he must remain with or return to the organization. He finds that the group has "worked through" his membership, leaving him present but socially not there.

38. Face engagements, of course, are not the only kinds of contact carrying ceremonial functions. Gifts, greeting cards, and salutatory telegrams and telephone calls also serve in this way. Each social circle seems to develop norms as to how frequently and extensively these ought to be employed to affirm relationships among geographically separated people, depending on the costs faced by each group in using these several devices. Just as friends at the same social party are obliged to spend at least a few moments chatting together, so a husband out of town on business may be considered "in range" and be obliged to telephone home in the evening.

39. Goffman, E., "On Face-Work," *Psychiatry*, 1955, **18**, 229.

40. Post, Emily, *Etiquette, op. cit.*, 29.

41. Being "with" someone at a given moment is to be distinguished from the party relationship of having "come with" someone to the occasion, the latter representing a preferential claim as to whom one will leave with, be loyal to, and the like.

42. The case of desert contacts is vividly described in a short story by Paul Bowles, "The Delicate Prey," in *The Delicate Prey and Other Stories*, New York: Random House, 1950, 277-289, esp. 279-280.

43. Manner books contain the same suggestion. See, for example, *Good Manners*, New York: Garrity, 1929, 31:

Many people whose "acting" manners are good have poor "talking" manners. They may be gossipy or they may tell off-color stories; or say things that hurt people's feelings, or they may chatter on so continuously that no one else can get a word in "edgewise."

44. Just as it is evident that the individual may comply with rules regarding unfocused interaction while failing to comply with regulations regarding focused interaction, so cases can be found of men-

tal patients who dress in a spectacularly improper manner but who are none the less ready to be socially tractable as conversationalists. Here are two pieces of evidence in favor of distinguishing conceptually between focused and unfocused interaction.

45. *Esquire Etiquette, op. cit.*, 59.

# COMMUNICATION WITHOUT WORDS
## Albert Mehrabian

Suppose you are sitting in my office listening to me describe some research I have done on communication. I tell you that feelings are communicated less by the words a person uses than by certain nonverbal means—that, for example, the verbal part of a spoken message has considerably less effect on whether a listener feels liked or disliked than a speaker's facial expression or tone of voice.

So far so good. But suppose I add, "In fact, we've worked out a formula that shows exactly how much each of these components contributes to the effect of the message as a whole. It goes like this: Total Impact = .07 verbal + .38 vocal + .55 facial."

What would you say to *that*? Perhaps you would smile good-naturedly and say, with some feeling, "Baloney!" or perhaps you would frown and remark acidly, "Isn't science grand." My own response to the first answer would probably be to smile back: The facial part of your message, at least, was positive (55 percent of the total). The second answer might make me uncomfortable: Only the verbal part was positive (eleven percent).

The point here is not only that my reactions would lend credence to the formula but that most listeners would have mixed feelings about my statement. People like to see science march on, but they tend to resent its intrusion into an "art" like the communication of feelings, just as they find analytical and quantitative approaches to the study of personality cold, mechanistic, and unacceptable.

The psychologist himself is sometimes plagued by the feeling that he is trying to put a rainbow into a bottle. Fascinated by a complicated and emotionally rich human situation, he begins to study it only to find in the course of his research that he has destroyed part of the mystique that originally intrigued and involved him. But despite a certain nostalgia for earlier, more intuitive approaches, one must acknowledge that concrete experimental data have added a great deal to our understanding of how feelings are communicated. In fact, as I hope to show, analytical and intuitive findings do not so much conflict as complement each other.

It is indeed difficult to know what another person really feels. He says one thing and does another; he seems to mean something but we have an uneasy feeling it isn't true. The early psychoanalysts, facing this problem of inconsistencies and ambiguities in a person's communications, attempted to resolve it through the concepts of the conscious and the unconscious. They assumed that contradictory messages meant a conflict between superficial, deceitful, or erroneous feelings on the one hand and true attitudes and feelings on the other. Their role, then, was to help the client separate the wheat from the chaff.

The question was, how could this be done? Some analysts insisted that inferring the client's unconscious wishes was a completely intuitive process. Others thought that some non-verbal behavior, such as posture, position, and movement, could be used in a more objective way to discover the client's feelings. A favorite technique of Frieda Fromm-Reichmann, for example, was to imitate a client's posture herself in order to obtain some feeling for what he was experiencing.

Thus began the gradual shift away from the idea that communication is primarily verbal, and that the verbal message includes distortions or ambiguities due to unobservable motives that only experts can discover.

Language, though, can be used to cummunicate almost anything. By comparison, nonverbal behavior is very limited in range. Usually, it is used to communicate feelings, likings, and preferences, and it customarily reinforces or contradicts the feelings that are communicated verbally. Less often, it adds a new dimension of sorts to a verbal message, as when a salesman describes his product to a client and simultaneously conveys, nonverbally, the impression that he likes the client.

A great many forms of nonverbal behavior can communicate feelings: Touching, facial expression, tone of voice, spatial distance from the addressee, relaxation of posture, rate of speech, number of errors in speech. Some of these are generally recognized as informative. Untrained adults and children easily infer that they are liked or disliked from certain facial expressions, from whether (and how) someone touches them, and from a speaker's tone of voice. Other behavior, such as posture, has a more subtle effect. A listener may sense how someone feels about him from the way the person sits while talking to him, but he may have trouble identifying precisely what his impression comes from.

Correct intuitive judgments of the feelings or attitudes of others are especially difficult when different degrees of feeling, or contradictory kinds of feeling, are expressed simultaneously through different forms of behavior. As I have pointed out, there is a distinction between verbal and vocal information (vocal information being what is lost when speech is written down—intonation, tone, stress, length and frequency of pauses, and so on), and the two kinds of information do not always communicate the same feeling. This distinction, which has been recognized for some time, has shed new light on certain types of communication. Sarcasm, for example, can be defined as a message in which the information transmitted vocally contradicts the information transmitted verbally. Usually the verbal information is positive and the vocal is negative, as in "Isn't science grand."

Through the use of an electronic filter, it is possible to measure the degree of liking communicated vocally. What the filter does is eliminate the higher frequencies of recorded speech, so that words are unintelligible but most vocal qualities remain. (For women's speech, we eliminate frequencies higher than about 200 cycles per second; for men, frequencies over about 100 cycles per second.) When people are asked to judge the degree of liking conveyed by the filtered speech, they perform the task rather easily and with a significant amount of agreement.

This method allows us to find out, in a given message, just how inconsistent the information communicated in words and the information communicated vocally really are. We ask one group to judge the amount of liking conveyed by a transcription of what was said, the verbal part of the message. A second group judges the vocal component, and a third group judges the impact of the complete recorded message. In one study of this sort we found that, when the verbal and vocal components of a message agree (both positive or both negative), the message as a whole is judged a little more positive or a little more negative than either component by itself. But when vocal information contradicts verbal, vocal wins out. If someone calls you "honey" in a nasty tone of voice, you are likely to feel disliked; it is also possible to say "I hate you" in a way that conveys exactly the opposite feeling.

Besides the verbal and vocal characteristics of speech, there are other, more subtle, signals of meaning in a spoken message. For example, everyone makes mistakes when he talks—unnecessary repetitions, stutterings, the omission of parts of words, incomplete sentences, "ums" and "ahs." In a number of studies of speech errors, George Mahl of Yale University has found that errors become more frequent as the speaker's discomfort or anxiety increases. It might be interesting to apply this index in an attempt to detect deceit (though on some occasions it might be risky: Confidence men are notoriously smooth talkers).

Timing is also highly informative. How long does a speaker allow silent periods to last, and how long does he wait before he answers his partner? How long do his utterances tend to be? How often does he interrupt his partner, or wait an inappropriately long time before speaking? Joseph Matarazzo and his colleagues at the University of Oregon have found that each of these speech habits is stable from person to person, and each tells something about the speaker's personality and about his feelings toward and status in relation to his partner.

Utterance duration, for example, is a very stable quality in a person's speech; about 30 seconds long on the average. But when someone talks to a partner whose status is higher than his own, the more the high-status person nods his head the longer the speaker's utterances become. If the high-status person changes his own customary speech pattern toward longer or shorter utterances, the lower-status person will change his own speech in the same direction. If the high-status person often interrupts the speaker, or creates long silences, the speaker is likely to become quite uncomfortable. These are things that can be observed outside the laboratory as well as under experimental conditions. If you have an employee who makes you uneasy and seems not to respect you, watch him the next time you talk to him—perhaps he is failing to follow the customary low-status pattern.

Immediacy or directness is another good source of information about feelings. We use more distant forms of communication when the act of communicating is undesirable or uncomfortable. For example, some people would rather transmit discontent with an employee's work through a third party than do it themselves, and some find it easier to communicate negative feelings in writing than by telephone or face to face.

Distance can show a negative attitude toward the message itself, as well as toward the act of delivering it. Certain forms of speech are more distant than others, and they show fewer positive feelings for the subject referred to. A speaker might say "Those people need help," which is more distant than "These people need help," which is in turn even more distant than "These people need our help." Or he might say "Sam and I have been having dinner," which has less immediacy than "Sam and I are having dinner."

Facial expression, touching, gestures, self-manipulation (such as scratching), changes in body position, and head movements—all these express a person's positive and negative attitudes, both at the moment and in general, and many reflect status relationships as well. Movements of the limbs and head, for example, not only indicate one's attitude toward a specific set of circumstances but relate to how dominant, and how anxious, one generally tends to be in social situations. Gross changes in body position, such as shifting in the chair, may show negative feelings toward the person one is talking to. They may also be cues: "It's your turn to talk," or "I'm about to get out of here, so finish what you're saying."

Posture is used to indicate both liking and status. The more a person leans toward his addressee, the more positively he feels about him. Relaxation of posture is a good indicator of both attitude and status, and one that we have been able to measure quite precisely. Three categories have been established for relaxation in a seated position: Least relaxation is indicated by muscular tension in the hands and rigidity of posture; moderate relaxation is indicated by a forward lean of about 20 degrees and a sideways lean of less than 10 degrees, a curved back, and, for women, an open arm position; and extreme relaxation is indicated by a reclining angle greater than 20 degrees and a sideways lean greater than 10 degrees.

Our findings suggest that a speaker relaxes either very little or a great deal when he dislikes the person he is talking to, and to a moderate degree when he likes his companion. It seems that extreme tension occurs with threatening addressees, and extreme relaxation with nonthreatening, disliked addressees. In particular, men tend to become tense when talking to other men whom they dislike; on the other hand, women talking to men *or* women and men talking to women show dislike through extreme relaxation. As for status, people relax most with a low-status addressee, second-most with a peer, and least with someone of higher status than their own. Body orientation also shows status: In both sexes, it is least direct toward women with low status and most direct toward disliked men of high status. In part, body orientation seems to be determined by whether one regards one's partner as threatening.

The more you like a person, the more time you are likely to spend looking into his eyes as you talk to him. Standing close to your partner and facing him directly (which makes eye contact easier) also indicate positive feelings. And you are likely to stand or sit closer to your peers than you do to addressees whose status is either lower or higher than yours.

What I have said so far has been based on research studies performed, for the most part, with college students from the middle and upper-middle classes. One interesting question about communication, however, concerns young children from lower socioeconomic levels. Are these children, as some have suggested, more responsive to implicit channels of communication than middle- and upper-class children are?

Morton Wiener and his colleagues at Clark University had a group of middle- and lower-class children play learning games in which the reward for learning was praise. The child's responsiveness to the verbal and vocal parts of the praise-reward was measured by how much he learned. Praise came in two forms: The objective words "right" and "correct"; and the more affective or evaluative words "good" and "fine." All four words were spoken sometimes in a positive tone of voice and sometimes neutrally.

Positive intonation proved to have a dramatic effect on the learning rate of the lower-class group. They learned much faster when the vocal part of the message was positive than when it was neutral. Positive intonation affected the middle-class group as well, but not nearly as much.

If children of lower socioeconomic groups are more responsive to facial expression, posture and touch as well as to vocal communication, that fact could have interesting applications to elementary education. For example, teachers could be explicitly trained to be aware of, and to use, the forms of praise (nonverbal or verbal) that would be likely to have the greatest effect on their particular students.

Another application of experimental data on communication is to the interpretation and treatment of schizophrenia. The literature on schizophrenia has for some time emphasized that parents of schizophrenic children give off contradictory signals simultaneously. Perhaps the parent tells the child in words that he loves him, but his posture conveys a negative attitude. According to the "double-bind" theory of schizophrenia, the child who perceives simultaneous contradictory feelings in his parent does not know how to react: Should he respond to the positive part of the message, or to the negative? If he is frequently placed in this paralyzing situation, he may learn to respond with contradictory communications of his own. The boy who sends a birthday card to his mother and signs it "Napoleon" says that he likes his mother and yet denies that he is the one who likes her.

In an attempt to determine whether parents of disturbed children really do emit more inconsistent messages about their feelings than other parents do, my colleagues and I have compared what these parents communicate verbally and vocally with what they show through posture. We interviewed parents of moderately and quite severely disturbed children, in the presence of the child, about the child's problem. The interview was video-recorded without the parents' knowledge, so that we could analyze their behavior later on. Our measurements supplied both the amount of inconsistency between the parents' verbal-vocal and postural communications, and the total amount of liking that the parents communicated.

According to the double-bind theory, the parents of the more disturbed children should have behaved more inconsistently than the parents of the less disturbed children. This was not confirmed: There was no significant difference between the two groups. However, the *total amount* of positive feeling communicated by parents of the more disturbed children was less than that communicated by the other group.

This suggests that (1) negative communications toward disturbed children occur because the child is a problem and therefore elicits them, or (2) the negative attitude precedes the child's disturbance. It may also be that both factors operate together, in a vicious circle.

If so, one way to break the cycle is for the therapist to create situations in which the parent can have better feelings toward the child. A more positive attitude from the parent may make the child more responsive to his directives, and the spiral may begin to move up instead of down. In our own work with disturbed children, this kind of procedure has been used to good effect.

If one puts one's mind to it, one can think of a great many other applications for the findings I have described, though not all of them concern serious problems. Politicians, for example, are careful to maintain eye contact with the television camera when they speak, but they are not always careful about how they sit when they debate another candidate of, presumably, equal status.

Public relations men might find a use for some of the subtler signals of feeling. So might Don Juans. And so might ordinary people, who could try watching other people's signals and changing their own, for fun at a party or in a spirit of experimentation at home. I trust that does not strike you as a cold, manipulative suggestion, indicating dislike for the human race. I assure you that, if you had more than a transcription of words to judge from (seven percent of total message), it would not.

# EYE-CONTACT
## Michael Argyle

The movements of the eyes perform a number of important, essential functions in social interaction. During interaction A looks at B in the region of the eyes, intermittently and for short periods—this will be referred to as "Looking" (with a Capital L). For some of this time B is Looking back at A in the region of the eyes—this will be called "eye-contact" (EC). Figure 1 shows how these phenomena can be studied.

B is a confederate who has been instructed to gaze continuously at A. A is a real subject, and his EC with B is recorded by observers who are looking directly into A's eyes from behind a one-way screen behind B's back. The subjects are placed to one side of the one-way vision screen so that A does not see his own reflection in the mirror. The total amount of EC is the same as the time A Looks at B, and can be easily recorded on a cumulative stop watch. Another arrangement is to use two genuine subjects and to take ciné films or videotape recordings of both simultaneously by means of mirrors. The detailed analysis of when people Look, how long their glances meet, and how these are related to speech and listening, needs an event-recorder which is operated by observers, who press different buttons when the subjects they are watching are Looking or speaking.

### THE NORMAL PATTERN OF EYE-CONTACT
When two people are engaged in conversation they Look each other in the eye intermittently. The percentage of the time each Looks is usually between 30 and 60 percent of the time, though the full range from nought to 100 percent has been seen in our laboratory. The glances vary in length from about one to seven seconds, which is much longer than the fixations of $\cdot25$–$\cdot35$ seconds common for visual scanning. Other parts of the face are scanned, deaf people look at the mouth for example, but it is the eyes which are chiefly focused on; the rest of the time people look right away from the other. While

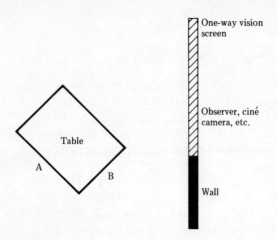

One-way vision screen

Observer, ciné camera, etc.

Table

A

B

Wall

**FIGURE 1.** Laboratory arrangements for studying gaze-direction.

A is Looking at B, B will Look back part of the time, producing EC, typically for 10 to 30 percent of the total interaction time, in periods of about one second on average.

The direction of gaze is closely related to the pattern of speech. People Look more while listening than while speaking, their glances are longer, and their away-glances are shorter. When A is just about to start speaking he looks away from B; at the ends of sentences or phrases he Looks up briefly, and at the end of his utterance he gives B a more prolonged gaze. He does not Look at hesitations or pauses in the middle of sentences, but only at natural breaks. B, who is listening, will at the same time be giving rather longer glances, and may respond to A's short glances by signals of various kinds. Part of this general pattern can be seen in Figure 2, which is based on data collected by Dr. Adam Kendon from conversations between pairs of students who were asked "to get acquainted."

### LOOKING AS A SIGNAL OR SOCIAL TECHNIQUE
When A Looks at B, this conveys information of various sorts to B, and can therefore be regarded as a kind of signal. A may or may not consciously intend to send B such a signal, but nevertheless B is likely to act upon it. What precisely the signal is depends on A's facial expression, the sequence of interaction, and the situation they are in. The main alternatives are as follows:

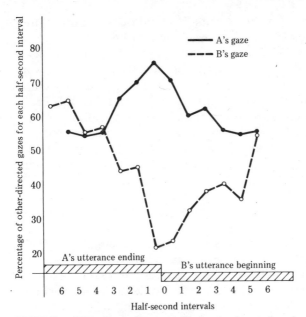

**FIGURE 2.** Direction of gaze at the beginning and end of long utterance (Kendon, 1965)

1. A wants to initiate interaction with B, for example at a party, or in a situation where a number of other people are present. If B Looks back it means that he is willing to engage in interaction. In some cases, if B lets A catch his eye, he is under some obligation to enter the relationship, as is the case with waiters and chairmen. It is interesting that these people are rather good at not letting their eye be caught, presumably by skillful peripheral vision. Conversely, if B Looks away while A is speaking, A realizes that B is no longer attending to what he has to say.

2. A shows B the attitude or emotions which he feels towards B. The most common is that of friendliness; there is more EC towards people that are liked. If B is an attractive member of the opposite sex, Looking combined with a friendly expression conveys A's sexual attraction to B—he is "making eyes at" B—especially if EC is prolonged. Looking combined with a hostile expression means that A dislikes B, or wishes to dominate him.

3. If, after A has Looked at him in one of these ways, B

wishes to show that he accepts this kind of relationship, he will Look back in the appropriate way. If he wishes to reject A's definition of the situation he will first Look angrily at A and then look away entirely. If, on the other hand, B lowers his eyes, this is a signal of submission to A's wishes or admission of defeat in some way. Exline has found that if B is arbitrarily given more power than A, then A will look away—he is rejecting the relationship which he is being offered.

4. At the end of each speech A is likely to Look at B. This is taken as a signal that A has finished and that B may speak. Kendon has found that if A does not Look, B either does not answer at all, or delays longer before doing so. This happened in 71 percent of cases, compared with 29 percent when A did look up.

5. If A accompanies his speech with Looking, B will feel that A is more believable, more confident, and more favorable in his attitude to B. As we shall see, these impressions are to some extent justified, since people Look more when they like the person they are talking to, and when they are telling the truth.

6. Much interaction is accompanied by a series of fairly short glances. If A gives B rather longer glances than are normal, B will interpret this as meaning that A is concerned primarily with B as a person, or with the relationship between A and B, rather than with whatever it is they are talking about. This can be seen in the case of young lovers who are ostensibly talking about politics, religion, or mathematics. It can also be seen in the rather impassive gaze used by some psychiatrists—which signals an interest in the patient as a patient as opposed to what he is saying.

## LOOKING AS INFORMATION-SEEKING

As was shown above, there are a number of ways of getting feedback on another person's reactions, but one of the most important is watching his facial expression. The upper half of the face shows more than the bottom, and once one looks in this area it is difficult not to focus on the other's eyes; the reason for this is probably the instinctive attraction of eyes. The main reason why people Look at the end of their utterances is that they need feedback on the other's response. This may be of various kinds. A wants to know whether B is still attending—his direction of gaze shows if he is asleep, or looking at someone else. A also wants to know how his last message was received—whether B understood, agreed, thought it was funny. At pauses in the middle of long speeches, A will Look for continued permission to carry on speaking, and B will nod or grunt if he is agreeable to this. The reason that A looks away when about to make a fairly long utterance is that he does not want to be distracted by extra inputs of information while he is planning and organizing his message. Similarly, Kendon found that A looks away during hesitating and unfluent passages; if A Looks while speaking he speaks faster— these are the fluent, well-rehearsed parts of his utterance. When the material itself is more complex and difficult, there is less EC for the same reason, as Exline has found.

In an experiment by Argyle, Lalljee, Cook, and Latané, strong support was obtained for the hypothesis that Looking is used to gain information on the other's response. Vision between A and B was interfered with in various ways, e.g., B wore (1) dark glasses, (2) a mask with only eyes showing, (3) both mask and dark glasses. In these conditions A was increasingly uncomfortable, was increasingly less clear about how B was reacting, and expressed a desire for more information about B's responses. The experiment shows that it is more useful to see the face than the eyes. There was one totally unexpected finding here. Females preferred to see the other even when invisible themselves, i.e., behind a one-way screen. Males however did not: When invisible they preferred not to see the other. This was interpreted earlier by saying that for males vision is used in the coordination of bodily movements in a 'kinesic dance.' Females clearly make more use of visual information for feedback purposes.

## THE MOTIVATIONAL BASIS OF LOOKING

There are positive motivations which lead people to Look, and to seek EC, and negative ones which lead them to avoid it. The search for feedback is important in connection with the pursuit of professional goals—interviewers, salesmen, and others need to know how their clients are responding. There are also pure affiliative motivations which seem to be satisfied by EC. In addition, Looking may become rewarded, if a child finds that he is usually responded to by a smiling face, which in turn is associated with rewards of other kinds, such as food or bodily contact. It is probably for this reason that being Looked at is experienced as rewarding—for example, in operant verbal conditioning experiments. It is also emotionally arousing—it has been found that electrical activity in the brainstem of rhesus monkeys increases when humans Look at them.

While short periods of Looking may simply be part of the signaling and information-gathering process, longer periods signify a heightened interest in the other person—either in an affiliative, sexual, or aggressive-competitive sense. When under the sway of one of these motivations, if the situation is appropriate, there will be more Looking. For example, if A is high in affiliative motivation, and likes B, he will engage in more Looking (Exline & Winters, 1965).

Although EC is satisfying, it is unpleasant and embarrassing if there is too much of it, and if mutual glances are too long. This may be because long glances carry a special meaning, as suggested above. Or it may be because there are also avoidance components connected with EC. We have mentioned one of these already—the avoidance of distraction at certain points of the conversation. However, there is no doubt that it is more comfortable watching others from behind a one-way vision screen than watching others who can Look back. This suggests that being aware of being observed by another is disturbing. There are several possible ways in which this could be so:

1. A may expect to see rejecting, negative facial expressions on B's face, as a result of past experiences A has had with parents or others. Laing (1960a) reports on a number of patients who suffered from aversion of gaze for this reason— they were 'overwhelmed by a feeling of rejection.'

2. Another possibility is that people are disturbed by becoming an object for another's perception. Laing (1960b) reports on other patients who felt that they were turned to stone by being gazed at by another, that they lost their spontaneity. Another version of this is that A may feel that he is under the power or control of B when B is watching him—as in the case of the waiter. This feeling may derive from the child's experience of being watched over and supervised by adults. In any case, when there is EC, B is equally under the control of A,

but some people may feel that it is the other who has the control.

3. Another possible source of avoidance of EC is that people wish to conceal either their emotional states or aspects of their personality. Following a 'head-in-the-sand' mechanism, A thinks that if he can't see B, B can't see him. Exline found that if subjects are induced to cheat in an experiment, and later interviewed, they showed less eye-contact (1961). This suggests that the intimacy produced by EC is incompatible with deception, and acts as a source of pressure towards making embarrassing disclosures. It follows that social situations are probably a source of stress for people who are concealing large areas of their self-images.

If there are forces both to engage in EC and also to avoid it, there will be a state of conflict. It follows that there is an equilibrium level of EC for any two people, and that when the approach forces are relatively strong there will be more EC. We will now consider some implications of this equilibrium when the positive forces for EC are mainly affiliative or sexual, as opposed to dominative or aggressive. It was suggested earlier that EC is one of several components of "intimacy," along with physical proximity, intimacy of topic, smiling and tone of voice. If we suppose that there is an overall equilibrium for intimacy, it follows that when one of the component elements is disturbed there will be some complementary change among the others to restore the equilibrium. Several examples of this have been observed.

Exline, Gray, and Schuette (1965) found that if subjects are interviewed by a continuously gazing interviewer there is less EC when more personal questions are asked. Kendon found an inverse relationship between smiling and EC when different points in conversations were compared. If A smiles, B is also likely to smile, and thus the level of intimacy is raised. At these points in the conversation EC is reduced— which is what would be expected from the equilibrium model. In another experiment the author asked subjects to stand "as close as it is comfortable to see well" to a series of objects in what was disguised as an experiment on vision. The objects included the author with eyes shut, and the author with eyes open. In each case a neutral-to-pleasant expression was adopted. Subjects came eight inches less close when the author's eyes were open than when they were shut. More EC caused less proximity.

Argyle and Dean (1965) tested the complementary hypothesis that greater proximity would result in less EC. Subjects took part in three three-minute discussions with stooges trained to stare, at distances of two, six, and ten feet. The amount of EC was recorded by observers in the usual way (Figure 3).

It was thought that this principle might be used to reduce audience anxiety or 'stage fright.' The subjects were American students, and they were asked to give a one-minute talk in

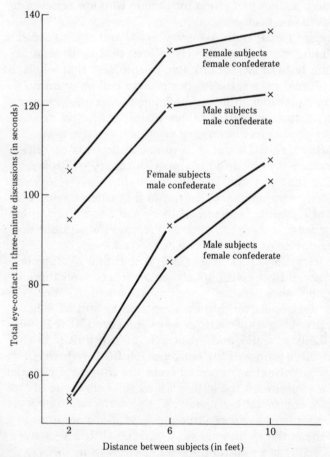

FIGURE 3. Relation between eye-contact and distance apart of subjects.

front of an audience (of 25) about different American states. The conditions of speaking were varied: Subjects spoke from the normal position, from ten feet further away, from behind the audience, wearing dark glasses, and wearing a mask (which concealed their facial expression). Subjective feelings of comfort in these conditions were as shown in Figure 4: Audience ratings of comfort and number of speech errors show the same pattern (i.e., *fewer* speech errors go with greater comfort).[2]

It can be seen that comfort is greatest when there is no EC at all—when the speaker is behind the audience. This cuts out all three kinds of avoidance mentioned above, while dark glasses and distance simply change the balance of approach and avoidance forces. This experiment suggests several ways of overcoming stage fright, and indeed social anxiety in any situation. The price that is paid is that there is less informational feedback from the others. Subjects in the audience experiment were less clear about how the audience was reacting when EC was reduced. It is a strategical question whether loss of feedback or social anxiety will disrupt performance more.

## INDIVIDUAL DIFFERENCES IN LOOKING

There are great variations between individuals in the amount of Looking they habitually engage in and how they do it. Kendon finds that subjects show similar amounts of EC when interacting with different people—though it is also a function of the other person. EC is thus a joint function of personality and situation, like other aspects of interaction.

Women engage in more EC than men, especially when talking to other women. Typical results, from the Argyle and Dean experiment, are shown in Figure 3. Women Look more than men, and same-sex pairs Look more than opposite-sex pairs. The reason for this is probably that Looking is a signal for sexual attraction, and this is something that has to be kept in check under laboratory conditions. In other situations, of course, there is a great deal of EC between opposite-sex pairs. Women also differ from men in their pattern of looking. Exline and Winters (1965) found that women will Look at the other more while speaking, if they like him, while men look more when listening, if the other is liked. The explana-

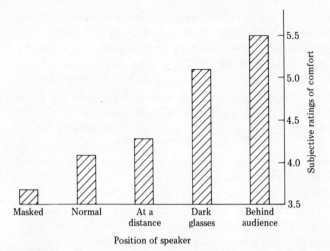

FIGURE 4. The comfort of public speakers in different positions.

tion of this result is so far obscure.

In the experiment by Argyle, Lalljee, Cook and Latané, it was found that when the other is concealed males talk more, females less; furthermore these shifts in quantity of speech were of the order of 40 percent in each direction. The explanation may be that females depend on visual cues giving permission to continue or to break in, while males carry on until receiving visual signals that the other wants to speak.

People high in the need for affiliation Look more, but only when the situation is a friendly or cooperative one. If the situation is competitive, these subjects Look less, and subjects high in dominative needs Look more. The effect is particularly marked in women. This finding can be used to explain the greater EC of women: Females are higher in affiliative motivation and lower in dominative, so that in the friendly setting of most of these experiments they should Look more (Exline, 1963).

Kendon has some preliminary data which show that subjects who produce long utterances in the Chapple standard interview Look less at the interviewer. Exline has some data showing that people who are "field-dependent" engage in more Looking. They are people who are more affected by the immediate environment, and presumably need to keep a close eye on people in it. These findings may be related: People more concerned about the reactions of others will make shorter speeches and look up more. Exline has also found that people who think in an abstract way Look more than people who think in a concrete way. Abstract thinkers have greater powers of integrating incoming data, and are probably less affected by the distracting aspects of EC. A very low rate, or a total absence of Looking is found in autistic children and some schizophrenics. The cause is probably a failure of early imprinting by the mother, or a long experience of rejection. "Machiavellians" have a different pattern of EC from normals. They are people who are motivated to control others with cynical disregard for their welfare. Where others will reduce EC when they have a guilty secret to conceal, Machiavellians contrive to stare unabashed, as Exline found in the experiment on deceit reported above.

## NOTES

1. I am indebted to Dr. Ralph Exline and Dr. Adam Kendon for some of the ideas in this chapter.
2. I am indebted to Jane Davis, Louise Taubitz, Peter Miller, and Robert Robinson, graduate students at the University of Delaware, for conducting this experiment.

## REFERENCES

Argyle, M., and Dean, J. "Eye-Contact, Distance and Affiliation," *Sociometry*, 1965, 28, 289-304.

Argyle, M., Lalljee, M., and Cook, M., "The Effects of Visibility on Interaction in a Dyad," *Human Relations*, 1963, 21, 3-17.

Exline, R. V., "Explorations in the Process of Person Perception: Visual Interaction in Relation to Competition, Sex and Need for Affiliation," *Journal of Personality*, 1963, 31, 1-20.

Exline, R. V., Gray, D., and Schuette, D., "Visual Behavior in a Dyad as Affected by Interview Content, and Sex of Respondent," *Journal of Personality and Social Psychology*, 1965, 1, 201-204.

Exline, R. V., and Winter, L. C., "Affective Relations and Mutual Glances in Dyads," in S. Tomkins and C. Izard (eds.), *Affect, Cognition and Personality*, New York: Springer, 1965.

Kendon, A., "Some Functions of Gaze-Direction in Social Interaction," unpublished report to Science Research Council, 1965.

Laing, R. D., *The Self and Others*, London: Tavistock, 1960a.

Laing, R. D., *The Divided Self*, London: Tavistock, 1960b.

# TACTILE COMMUNICATION
# Lawrence K. Frank

**TACTILE EXPERIENCES IN PERSONALITY DEVELOPMENT**
Personality development will be discussed in terms of the
ways an infant organism relates himself to the world, learning
to transform his organic needs and functional capacities into
the patterned, purposive conduct and prescribed relationships
of his group while continuing to be and to act in his idiosyncratic fashion. This approach enables us to focus upon the
circular, reciprocal processes in and through which the individual carries on his incessant intercourse with the world,
relating himself transactionally as an organism in a geographical, cultural, social *field* (17). Thus the personality process
may be viewed as communication in which we may observe
more closely how tactile experiences provide primary modes
of communication which seemingly are essential to the development of the many forms of symbolic recognition and
response for later learning and maturation.

Tactual sensitivity appears early in fetal life as probably the
first sensory process to become functional (8, 28). During
uterine life the fetus more or less floats in a liquid medium, the
amniotic fluid, cushioned against impacts and the atmosphere,
but continually stimulated by the events of his small world.

During the nine months of gestation, the embryo and fetus
is continuously receiving the rhythmic impacts of the maternal heart beat, transmitted through the amniotic fluid (and
therefore magnified), impinging upon the skin of his whole
body. His own heart beats will later synchronize or be out of
tune with the maternal heart beats and so provide either a
series of coordinated or dissimilar impacts upon his skin to
which he develops a continuous response, as a physiological
resonance. Thus at birth the infant comes from a rhythmically
pulsating environment into an atmosphere where he has to
exist as a discrete organism and relate himself through a
variety of modes of communication (46). Probably the infants

Reprinted by permission of The Journal Press and Mary H. Perry from
"Tactile Communications" by Lawrence K. Frank in *Genetic Psychology
Monographs*, 1957, vol. 56, pp. 209-225.

Messages

who are carried close to the mother on her back or hip receive some continuation of these rhythmic impacts upon the skin.

At birth the fetus passing through the birth canal undergoes a series of pressures and constrictions which involve sometimes intense tactual experiences. Moreover, the newborn is more or less suddenly exposed to the atmospheric pressures and altered temperature, evoking respiratory activity and presumably a number of tactile responses. The skin of the newborn is covered with a creamy substance which, if not interfered with, will be absorbed like a vanishing cream. Usually the newborn is bathed, dried, and often oiled, greased, or powdered.

The infant's need for contacts, for nuzzling, cuddling, patting, and his usually quick and accepting response to these tactile messages may be largely derived from his uterine experiences which have exercised his tactuality. Each infant differs in his "needs," his susceptibility and response and in the time when he will relinquish these infantile experiences and accept alienation from close contact with the mother. Putting fingers, thumb, food, objects or parts of another person's body in the mouth is a tactual experience. It may lead to chewing and swallowing or it may be retained and used as a source of gratification. Parental care and love may be largely tactual contacts and comforting, reassuring tactile experiences which give the infant encouragement and the confidence in the world as well as physiological assistance in achieving a more effective homeostasis, especially when under stress. Thus the kind and duration of early tactile experiences wherein the infant can send and receive messages outside his body have a large significance in early personality development as his first so-called "object-relations" (13). "No new external element gives rise to perceptive, motor or intelligent adaptation without being related to earlier activities" (49).

It is well recognized that the newborn mammal "needs" to be nuzzled, and licked, by the mother who, among infra-human species, performs these functions after biting the cord and often eating the placenta. The young remain close to the mother's body, receiving warmth and close tactual contacts, plus frequent licking and nursing. The human infant may receive a variety of treatments that conforms to this mammalian pattern or departs drastically therefrom. Some infants are kept close to the mother, may be given the colostrum (as do infra-human babies), allowed to nurse freely and as long as desired. Other infants may be isolated from the mother, as in most hospitals, fed at intervals and given a minimum of bodily contacts. The opossum young are extreme cases of pups born prematurely who can survive only by attaching themselves to a teat and remaining there close to the mother for the time necessary for maturation. Tactile experience is immediate, and transitory, operating only as long as contact is maintained. It is also a reciprocal experience in the sense that what a person touches also touches him, and often evokes emotional reactions of greater or less magnitude (56). Tactile experience is ordinarily limited to two persons, a means to intimacy and expression of affection or hostility and anger.

In his earliest experiences, the infant has a number of tactile experiences: Close bodily contacts, being cuddled or patted rhythmically, touching the lips to the mother's body and more specifically to the nipple, increasingly fingering or handling the mother, especially the breast. These experiences may be viewed as early tactile communications which are carried on as transactional processes. The infant evokes from the mother the tactile stimulation which he "needs" and to which he responds in his own individual fashion as in sucking; the mother solicits from the infant this touching and sucking, which evokes milk from the breast (12). Babies seem to differ widely in their "needs" for tactile experiences and in their acceptance and response to tactile ministrations. They are dependent upon the mother person who may provide these generously or may deny or largely deprive the infant of these experiences. A baby may become attached to a blanket, soft cuddly animal, a rattle and begin to enjoy the tactile contacts, especially of textures. These early-found sources of satisfaction may serve as surrogates for contact with the mother's person.

It may not be unwarranted to assume that the infant initially has a primitive tactual sensitivity and capacity for response which is acute at birth in varying degrees in individual infants and which needs to be functionally operative and fulfilled as an essential stage in his development. Denial or deprivation of these early tactile experiences may compromise his future learning, such as speech, cognition, and symbolic recognition, and his capacity for more mature tactile communication, as we will discuss later. This initial or primary tactual sensitivity and need for tactile experiences may then diminish, or be incorporated in larger patterns as do the early reflexes.

In these early tactile experiences we may see more clearly how the infant begins to communicate tactually and gradually enlarges his communications as he develops his capacities for other sensory awareness and perception and for other forms of response. Here the suggestion made earlier about signals, signs, and symbols finds application since in infant development, and indeed in personality development generally, we may observe this progression from signal to sign to symbol.

The baby begins to communicate with himself by feeling his own body, exploring its shape and textures, discovering its orifices and thereby begins to establish his body image which, of course, is reinforced or often negated by pleasurable or painful tactile experiences with other human beings. It seems highly probable that the continual physiological alterations internally, some of which he has such as colic or stomach ache or a full bladder or rectum, also enter into this evolving image of the body. Later on various visual cues may be established as he focuses his vision upon his fingers and feet and so begins to build up a visual image to supplement and to reinforce his tactile experiences.

The newborn infant with underdeveloped, inadequate capacity for homeostasis apparently requires these tactile experiences for maintaining his internal equilibrium. Thus, he keeps warm through bodily contacts. He maintains, or recovers, his internal equilibrium when disturbed by fear or pain (including digestive upsets—stomach ache, gas, etc.), hunger, cold, through close contacts with the mother person and rhythmic tactual stimulation, as in patting, stroking, caressing. It cannot be too strongly emphasized that the infant when disturbed emotionally usually responds to patting or even vigorous, but rhythmic, slapping on the back with increasing composure. In an older child this patting may awaken or keep him awake, but it puts an infant to sleep; this age difference offers some support for the assumption of an early infantile sensitivity or need for rhythmic tactual stimulation which fades out or is incorporated into other patterns or becomes quiescent until puberty.

The baby responds to the signal(s) given by the nipple and the tactile contacts involved in nursing, by sucking, which is a message to the mother; thereby he allays his hunger as she responds by lactation. The combination of two or more signals thus established a sign so that sooner or later the infant recognizes the mother and begins to respond to her with the set or expectation for consummation through feeding (27).

Likewise, the infant is cuddled and patted by the mother when disturbed, frightened, or in pain. Usually she speaks or hums or sings to him at the same time. Thus he learns to recognize the sound of mother's voice as a sign, or surrogate for her touch. Later he may respond to her voice at a distance as a surrogate for her actual physical contact. This becomes clear when he has learned to recognize words (although he may not be able to talk) and her reassuring words are accepted, although she is not present and touchable, as symbolic equivalents of tactile experience. Likewise, the child learns to recognize the mother's voice as a sign of her disappointment and may cringe at her harsh voice as to physical punishment which he has experienced previously when scolded or spanked. It seems clear that the child's reception of verbal messages is predicated in large measure upon his prior tactile experience so that facial expressions and gestures become signs and symbols for certain kinds of tactile communications and interpersonal relations. A person, who is emotionally disturbed while holding or carrying an infant, may communicate that disturbance to the infant through tactile contacts just as a calm, relaxed person may soothe a disturbed child by holding him, with or without patting. The close, tactual contact of being held firmly apparently reassures a child.

What seems to be involved in the infant's maturation is that the primary mode of tactile communication is replaced by auditory and kinesic messages (5) which are no longer signals but become signs which later become or are replaced by symbols to which the infant responds, both physiologically and symbolically (40).

If the human child were limited to purely tactual communications, he could not fully develop his capacity for fantasy and imagination, and for building the conceptual framework required for living in a cultural world. Thus the learning of abstractions means literally developing the capacity to recognize and respond to various symbols as in words or designs which serve as surrogates for the concrete actuality of events, for the most part initially perceived tactually (62).

The baby's initial orientation to the spatial dimensions of the world occurs through tactile explorations—feeling with hands and fingers, often with the lips, manipulating and testing out the qualities, size, shape, texture, density, etc., of whatever the infant can touch. The manipulations involve motor activities and increasingly skillful neuromuscular coordinations which are established through tactile messages that are gradually supplanted and replaced by visual cues in most children. Thus the baby's perception of the world is built upon and initially shaped by tactile experiences (19). It is to be remembered that as in all symbolic processes, the meaning of the symbol derives from prior direct sensory awareness which may or may not be reinstated at a later time. However, as Margaret Lowenfeld has suggested, these early primary sensory experiences are increasingly overlaid by cognitive patterns of symbolic recognition and response so that they may become more or less inaccessible except through such experiences as in the World Game, finger painting, clay modeling, water play, etc., and certain esthetic experiences (36).

The potency of music, with its rhythmical patterning and varying intensities of sounds, depends in large measure upon the provision of an auditory surrogate for the primary tactile experiences in which, as discussed earlier, rhythmic patting is peculiarly effective in soothing the baby, while tickling, a recurrent, more or less rhythmic, tactile message, may evoke a cumulative response of considerable intensity, as in sex orgasm, which comes as a climax to repeated tactile messages. It has been remarked that Wagner's *Liebestod* is a musical version of intercourse leading to orgasm and post-coital subsidence.

The way the blind learn through tactile explorations to build up a series of schemas, if not visual images, of the world, and to develop concepts and symbol recognition and response indicates that while visual symbols often become the surrogates for tactile, nevertheless the tactile may, as in finger language, become a symbolic process for complicated and subtle communications of concepts and highly-differentiated meanings (37). This is illustrated by the account of Helen Keller's initial learning of names, such as water, from tactile experience of running water, and the communication of that word by finger language. As Cassirer has pointed out (p. 56, Anchor Edition), learning names and meanings immediately enlarges the child's world and gives him new modes of communication, even when limited to tactile communication, as with Helen Keller and Laura Bridgman.

As indicated in the section on "Cultural Patterning of Tactile Processes," one of the basic experiences of a child is learning to respect the inviolability of things, animals, places, and persons which occurs when the child becomes mobile and explores the world. This involves the curtailment and prohibition of tactile experiences, forbidding the child to touch whatever is defined by adults as inviolable (property, sacred places, forbidden objects, persons). His naïve approach to these inviting object-persons is blocked and prohibited, often with painful punishment, until they are perceived as not-touchable except when he has permission or has performed the necessary rituals, negotiations, buying, etc. Not only are these tactile experiences of crucial significance for social order, but the transformation of the child's naïve impulsive response to the world into the learned observance of inviolability, usually involves emotional disturbances, conflicts with parents and often over-learning, so that the child may become inhibited and less capable of making tactile contacts, even those which he or she may seek as occasions for interpersonal relations, as in intercourse.

Here we see how tactile experiences undergo a second critical phase. Early, he has experienced primary tactile fulfillment or denial as a baby, and developed his idiosyncratic mode of tactile communication and its elaboration into other modes. Now he must undergo an often severe restriction upon tactile experiences in which the world around him is alienated from his touch so that he must learn to recognize almost everything visually (53) and auditorially, as a symbol of inviolability which he must recognize, inhibiting his spontaneous impulse to touch or strike. His own body, especially the genitals, may be defined as inviolable, not to be touched under penalty of punishment. This means the child must learn to impute inviolability to what was previously accessible and thereby he is inducted into the social world of respect for property and persons and of sex morals, according to the often highly elaborate codes of custom and law. Needless to say, children may learn to observe these inviolabilities through punishment, and exhibit law-abiding conduct when watched or fearful of detection and punishment, but not develop the self-administered inhibitions for social order. Or, they undergo continual conflicts between the impulsive response to forbidden things and persons and the partially learned, but not fully accepted, prohibitions. A recognition of the basic tactile experiences in learning socially-prescribed conduct and respect for the law offers clues to the genetic study of socialization and its vicissitudes.

Tactile experiences and recognition of symbols for tactily accessible and nonaccessible things and persons therefore are highly significant in the development of personality. Thus we may say that initial tactile experiences provide the basic orientation to the world and especially the physiological signals which evoke the child's naïve spontaneous responses. These are transformed, elaborated, refined, and increasingly discriminated through gestures, facial expressions, tones of voice and through language, into the most subtle modes of interpersonal communication. Indeed, the transactional processes of reciprocal, circular relations can become operative only as the child learns how to evoke, as well as to respond, through kinesics and language, and the amazing variety of ritual, ceremonies, and symbols of his group.

Tactile communications are also involved in interpersonal relations in a more direct manner, as we may observe in the infant and child. Through the earliest bodily contacts and other tactile experiences, the baby communicates in a reciprocal way, mother to baby, and baby to mother, one evoking from the other what will in turn evoke his or her response in a tactile dialectic. These experiences establish the individual's early pattern of intimacy and affection, his first interpersonal relations which apparently persist as a sort of template by which he establishes and conducts his subsequent interpersonal relations, using verbal and kinesic patterns, especially in more intimate sexual relations. The baby develops confidence in the world, trust in people, through these early tactile relations which reciprocally establish the meaning of the world for him and also his expectations and feelings toward that world.

Thus, how the baby is treated, what tactual experiences he has being bathed, clothed, tucked in bed, or in sleeping bag, how he is mothered and handled by others governs his initial tactual responses and by so much guides his subsequent learning and relationships. How the baby feels in his own skin, as treated according to the cultural patterns of his group, gives him an image of his body with feelings about it which reflect and express such experiences (32). He may learn to expect, to evoke, tactual contacts or be passive or anesthetic, with little or no such contacts. When one remembers the diversity of patterns of infant care, being kept close to mother's body, or isolated and left alone, being free to kick and squirm and wave his arms, to play with objects, or parts of his own body, or to be tightly swaddled or bound to a cradle board, it is evident that babies can survive under a variety of treatments. But it also seems clear that their early tactile experiences enter into and largely govern their subsequent learning and their use of patterns of communication (16).

If the baby is limited in his tactile experiences, denied much opportunity to send or receive tactile communications, he presumably must wait until his capacity for visual and auditory recognition and reception have developed sufficiently to permit him to enter into communication with others. Thus, such a child will not only have little of the primary tactile experiences upon which to develop his sign and symbolic communication, but will be expected to rely upon more or less arbitrary visual and auditory symbols and to accept their meanings, not as experientially learned, but as prescribed by others. This suggests that while children so reared can and do learn sign and symbol recognition and response, they may be more dependent than other children upon the authority of parents who define and impose these signs and symbols. These children, also being limited in early motor activities and manipulation, therefore may be more willing to abide by authoritative pronouncements or more ready to rebel.

Symbols, lacking primary tactile validation, may be less clearly and less effectively established as basic codes for communication later. This offers one approach to the schizoid and schizophrenic personalities who have been unable to enter fully and effectively into the symbolic, cognitive world of ideas as accepted by others, and who are reported to be frequently rejected babies, or deprived of mothering. Also this may throw light upon the impairment of abstract thinking observed in children who have been separated from the mother (20). Since living in a symbolic world of ideas and concepts is a most difficult and subtle achievement, denial or deprivation of primary tactile experiences may be revealed as crucial in the development of personalities and character structure, and also in the configuration of a culture.

One of the significant events in the development of personality has long been recognized in terms of the child's learning to distinguish between "me" and "not-me," often stated as his first "facing of reality." It seems more probable that the child's first recognition of "not-me," is of a highly specific, idiosyncratic "not-me" as contrasted with the consensual world of actuality ("reality"). The baby apparently quite early recognizes the "not-me" as *my* mother, *my* bottle, *my* crib, *my* rattle, etc., each being tactually experienced and accepted and responded to idiomatically. Only later does the child replace this idiosyncratic "not-me" with the more generalized concepts and symbols of the public consensual world of "reality." This transition occurs and is facilitated with the use of language and the acceptance of visual and auditory surrogates or signs and symbols.

The baby's initial communication with the world being largely tactile, the early recognition of the "not-me" probably comes as these tactual signals become signs of specific meanings, namely, of "my" familiar, reassuring, comforting mother, bottle, bed, etc., from which he receives the familiar, customary tactile messages, plus the reassuring auditory and visual cues (mother's voice and face and hands) which further distinguish and establish these as signs of "my" world. Language, first as recognizable signs and then as symbols and then as verbal messages he can send, provides the conceptual framework of ideas, concepts, and expectations for living in the common public world ("reality"). This requires the gradual replacement of the idiosyncratic "not-me" by the consensual "not-me," a transition from the largely tactile to linguistic and kinesic and symbolic communications. This transition to the symbolic world and acceptance of adult concepts is not always easy for children. Some may only partially give up their idiosyncratic "not-me" and try to live on two levels of communication, while others may be unable to attain even this degree of participation in the consensual world, continuing to rely upon signals.

It seems clear that only as the baby achieves some degree of internal stability (homeostasis) and develops more awareness of the external world, can he begin to shift from dependence upon tactual to linguistic communication and thereby orient himself in the symbolic-cultural world. If we view learning as essentially a process of developing new ways of relating to the world (*knowing* as a transactional relationship as Dewey and Bentley have proposed), then learning to live in a symbolic world requires a firm base of physiological functioning and an initially adequate tactile orientation to the world that can be stabilized through patterned perception guided by concepts (22).

While babies differ in their initial threshold to tactual stimulation, the provision of tactile experiences or their denial undoubtedly will accentuate or modify these individual differences. Thus, deprivation of early tactual experiences may evoke exploratory searches for surrogates such as masturbation, finger and thumb sucking, pulling or fingering the ears, nose, hair, a variety of auto-tactilism, or as indicated, reliance upon other modes of communication. The tactily-responsive baby, despite indulgence by parents, may seek further auto-tactile experiences to provide fulfillments. Each seeks to communicate with the world and especially people, through tactile modes if allowed (the haptic type as V. Lowenfeld has described it), and also to communicate with the self through tactual manipulations if permitted. Here it is difficult to separate the motor, kinesic patterns from the tactile except to say that these motor activities seem to be guided by a tactile orientation, the hands and fingers acting like antennae or feelers which probe the surroundings for ensuing motor activities (38).

This offers a clue to the schizoid and the schizophrenic personalities who quite early in life exhibit this partial or extensive resistance to accepting the ideas and concepts of their culture, which in turn may be viewed as arising from inadequate or distorted tactile experiences early in life, such as denial of tactile experiences or inability to establish and maintain tactile communication upon which conceptualization can be built (7). There is some evidence that speech retardation and difficulties (9, 61) and also reading disabilities may arise from early deprivation of or confusion in tactile experiences, since such children often exhibit peculiarities of tactual sensitivity and response (11). Also it has been found that babies separated from their mothers frequently exhibit limited capacity for abstract thinking or conceptual formulation (7, 20). Hence it seems probable that in the genesis of these various kinds of personalities, there may be basic tactile deprivations and confusions, and also the emotional and affective disturbances arising from lack of adequate or effective tactile reassurance and comforting in early life.

Recently Bateson (1) has suggested that the schizophrenic is unable to distinguish between different kinds of verbal messages, literal and figurative, confusing what is metaphor with what is factual. This he attributes to the ambivalent relations and especially communication with the mother who cannot genuinely love her child but cannot accept her own rejection of the child. The role of tactual communications in early infancy may be highly significant therefore in this suggested development.

The tactile stimulation of the genitals, as in masturbation (or their manipulation by adults, siblings, etc.), seems to be almost universal, but may be curbed by parents, just as the infant and child's approaches and seeking of tactual contacts may be limited or denied. The child is often alienated from the mother around five or six (regarded as the peak of the Oedipus situation) when apparently this seeking and giving of tactual contacts begins to diminish in our culture. Thus we see boys increasingly evading or being denied such tactual contacts and tactual comforting, although girls may continue to enjoy it. If there is a diminution in tactual sensitivity and experiences in middle childhood, the so-called latency period, it abruptly ceases at puberty when the pubertal boy and girl usually become avid for tactual contacts, seeking to touch and to be touched. It may be found fruitful to consider the latency period as primarily a change in tactile sensitivity

which, of course, includes the genitals. However, it should
not be assumed that in this latency period there is no interest
or concern for sex since curiosity about sex and intercourse
may be intense, while mutual and self-masturbation often
takes place, and boys and girls exhibit their nude bodies to
each other to satisfy their curiosity about the other sex.

In adolescence we see the increasing frequency of tactile
communication, at first between members of the same sex,
as boys walk together with arms on each others' shoulders,
girls with arms around each others' waists, and then the first
tentative heterosexual explorations of caressing, petting,
"necking" and frequently attempts at intercourse. Tactile
communication in adult mating, both as foreplay and in
intercourse, has been elaborated and refined by some cultures
into the most amazing array of erotic patterns which through
a variety of tactual stimulation of various parts of the body
serve to arouse, prolong, intensify, and evoke communication.
Here we see tactile communication, reinforced and elaborated
by motor activities and language, by concomitant stimulation,
visual, auditory, olfactory, gustatory, and the deeper muscle
senses, combined to provide an organic-personality relationship which may be one of the most intense human experiences.
It is, or can be, considered an esthetic experience in that there
may be little or no instrumental, purposive or cognitive elements, with greater or less loss of space-time orientation. But
the elementary sexual processes of the human organism may
be transformed and focused into an interpersonal love relationship with an identified person to whom each is seeking
to communicate, using sex not for procreation, as in the mating of a female in heat ready to be fertilized, but as "another
language" (50), for interpersonal communication. Here we
see how the primary tactile mode of communication, which
has been largely overlaid and superseded by auditory and
visual signs and symbols, is reinstated to function with elementary organic intensity, provided the individuals have not
lost the capacity for communication with the self through
tactile experiences.

In the development of the individual personality beginning
in childhood and accelerated in adolescence, we may observe
how the recognition and response to signs, as previously discussed, is elaborated into the symbolic process. But it should

be emphasized that learning symbolic recognition and response for communication occurs only as the child or adolescent is indoctrinated and practiced in this by more experienced individuals who, as culture agents, define the meaning of symbols and direct the less experienced in performing the prescribed conduct responsive to those symbols.

Thus we can see the individual learning to respond, with patterns of various kinds and in different modes, tactual, kinesic, language (which are not naïve organic responses), to biological signals or their learned surrogates; further, the individual develops responses, which are uniquely human, to symbols which have been created and established as the occasions for such learned symbolic responses.

For example, the individual may withdraw his hand when he touches fire or a hot object that serves as a *signal* to that withdrawal response, often a reflex withdrawal to pain. He may learn then to recognize the color of a hot object or its customary shape as a *sign* of its hazardous nature and thereafter avoid touching it. But when he learns to respond to the word "hot," he is acting symbolically, since his recognition of and response to that word, "hot," are not naïve biological responses but recognition of a *symbol* with appropriate response to that symbol according to what others have taught him.

This emphasis upon the cultural patterning of symbolic processes seems justified because we have recognized that symbols are cultural, but have not given equal recognition to the necessity of learning these symbols from others. Thus, various infra-human organisms can be trained to recognize and respond to symbols of a fairly wide range, but no animal ever teaches its young to recognize and respond to symbols, although they do help the young to recognize signals and some signs. This points to the uniquely human capacity for maintaining its basic organic processes, including recognition of many signals, and also for superseding and replacing these primary modes of communication with signs and symbols, thereby enormously enlarging the range and subtlety of human communications, and providing for the development of the highly individualized, idiosyncratic personality processes. We can observe how each person learns to use these processes in his own way for his own purposes as he relates himself to the world and other persons. The elementary, primary modes of communication may be overlaid, superseded, and incorporated in symbolic communication, but under stress may again become regnant.

There is little systematic observation of how tactile experiences and modes of communication function in the development of personality (37) and how the tactile are interrelated with the linguistic and kinesic modes where any one of the three may become a surrogate for one or two others, and all three may be partially or wholly superseded by visual symbols, as in the arts, especially graphical plastic art (30). We can begin to realize the complexity when we gain more understanding of human communication (60). For this we need to recognize that the human child has immense potentialities which give rise to his idiosyncratic awareness and perception of the world (life space-private world), always patterned by his tradition, with a highly idiomatic personal code for communicating and receiving and interpreting messages from the world and from other persons.

## CULTURAL PATTERNING OF TACTILE EXPERIENCES

As pointed out in the discussion of personality development, cultures differ in the kind, amount, and duration of tactile experiences people give the infant. Thus the parents in each culture activate or limit initial tactile communication with the infant and provide such tactile communication in and through the patterns and relationships which are prescribed or permitted by tradition (45).

Since it is impossible to give an adequate statement of this cultural patterning of tactile experiences in this paper, the focus will be upon those tactile approaches and responses which seem to be more significant in human communication, remembering that at every moment the individual is communicating with the environment, receiving tactile stimuli and responding thereto more or less automatically or without awareness (e.g., pressure on sole of feet, on buttocks, changing atmospheric pressures, wind, etc.).

Thus we should note that color of skin is highly significant as a message which serves as a visual identification. While skin color is visual, it elicits responses which are often tactile, in the sense of avoiding contacts or in evoking approaches and contacts which would be inappropriate or prohibited to a person of another skin color. Insofar as an infant may have a nurse of another skin color, and young children apparently play together with little or no awareness of differences in skin color, these discriminatory responses to skin color may be considered as patterned. But within a group of people with similar skin color, there may be degrees of acceptance and rejection, of approval and dislike, as in the light-dark skin of Negroes, the blonde versus brunette, etc.

The skin has many potentialities, some of which are actively recognized, cultivated, refined or coarsened, and selectively utilized by each culture. The exposure of the skin is the most obvious patterning of tactile experiences since the amount and kind of clothing, the covering of specific parts, genitals, breasts, face, and exposure of hands, legs, navel, etc., differ widely and may alter according to the time, place, and occasion, e.g., ceremonial appearance, masks and headgear may also be used to disguise the skin and provide a different kind of communication according to role.

The body arts, which include all the varied kinds of ornamenting, painting, tattooing, incising, use of cosmetics generally, are significant as ways of enhancing the appearance of the skin or intensifying tactile communication where the skin and its decorations serve as messages which are then perceived visually as a sign or symbol, or sometimes as a signal to evoke a direct physiological response.

Grooming the skin, bathing of all kinds, anointing, oiling, perfuming the skin, plucking hair, shaving, are patterns for modifying communication by the skin, again relying upon visual cues to indicate tactual readiness for communication (actual or symbolic). Such grooming and decorating may also serve as signs of rank, caste, prestige, authority which others recognize and respond to with appropriate conduct. Indeed, these skin decorations and coverings are of large significance in the assumption and performance of the various roles when not only the individual assuming a role must act in a prescribed manner, but others must respond appropriately if the role performance is to be completed. Here the skin serves like a carrier wave upon which the particular message is imposed as a modification or patterning of that wave, as in telephoning.

Thus admiring glances, indicating approval of the individual's clothing, body arts, and grooming, serve as surrogates for invitations to actual tactile contacts. This is often elaborated in the customary public exhibition of the self through which courtship is conducted openly and directly, or indirectly as in public strolling or dancing.

The masculine and feminine roles are defined in large part by these different patterns of exposure of skin, body arts, clothing, grooming, and the kinds of tactile approaches and contacts allowed or forbidden to the male and female. Since masculinity and femininity are more or less polarized positions and relations which the boy and girl must learn, each may develop a kind of complementary tactile communication in which the intent may be not primarily to transmit a message but to evoke a response by a variety of tactual approaches or exhibition of signs and symbols of tactile significance. If these responses are evoked, then the initiator may offer more direct tactile communication as in flirting or seduction. There is usually a well-established code for these communications, with degree of intimacy of direct tactual contacts.

It is significant, too, that the dead may be decorated and anointed (sacramental oils), and that bathing the feet has been a traditional ceremony of hospitality to the strangers.

Each cultural group has a conception of the skin and of tactile experiences which may not be explicitly recognized or stated, but is implied in its prescriptions for covering, exposing, decorating, making and avoiding tactile communication. Thus, modesty, in the sense of covering certain portions of the body and prohibiting or approving even symbolic tactile communication, with shame for violation of these prescriptions, blushing or pallor when discovered, are forms of tactile communications which serve to maintain the social order by regulating human conduct and especially interpersonal communication.

The patterning of direct tactile communication may be considered as one of the early and most significant social inventions (14). Among most infra-human species (apart from social insects), the individual can have and can keep his own food, lair, nesting place, etc., only by incessant vigilance, warding off intruders by force, or show of violence or by auditory signals like bird calls. Likewise, the individual organism may enjoy little or no personal safety and freedom from attack or invasion except by continual defensive-offensive activity to repel attackers. This exposure to other approach may be limited in herds or other animal aggregations where the individual is merged in the group and acts as a constituent member of the aggregate.

The establishment of inviolability of things and the person under penalties for unsanctioned approach made social order possible since each member of the group became the guardian of all others' property and person. Each child learns to respect these inviolabilities by refraining from approaching, touching, striking, taking or otherwise invading the private property or the person of others, or the sacred places or objects, always as defined by his culture. Since these inviolabilities are barriers to tactile contacts as well as motor approaches, we may consider private property and the sanctity or integrity of the person as forms of patterned tactile communication. Each object, animal, place, and person gives off a variety of cues, visual, auditory, which have become established initially through tactile contacts, or signs and symbols to which each member of the group exhibits the learned conduct of avoidance.

These lessons in recognizing and respecting the inviolability of objects and persons occur early in life when the child first explores the world, touching, taking, handling whatever he can reach. While learning this space-time orientation, he is blocked, diverted, often punished, with verbal admonitions to stop, "don't touch," etc. Gradually the child transforms these parental prohibitions into self-administered inhibitions by learning to perceive things and persons as signs or symbols for avoidance. His formerly eager exploratory touching is relinquished and he now responds with the prescribed conduct of avoidance when no adult is present to stop him or caution him. As he grows older, he learns to employ the group-sanctioned ceremonies, rituals, symbols for approaching persons, relying upon negotiating, barter, sale, contract, courtship, seduction, marriage for setting aside the inviolability of the object, animal, or person with which he seeks to make direct tactual contacts or to establish tactual communication of intimacy.

Probably the most widely occurring and most rigidly maintained culture inviolability is the incest taboo which again may be violated, as we know, but is usually accepted and upheld not only by the law and threats of punishment, but by the learned conduct of avoidance that is established in the child. This incest taboo is a uniquely human cultural pattern since among infra-human mammals it does not seem to appear and in human breeding of domestic animals this taboo is deliberately violated in order to maintain certain hereditary strains.

Here we see very clearly how early tactile experiences provide the bases for transformation into learned symbolic conduct and participating in social order. It is as if the child who naïvely responds to the tactile communication received from objects and persons learns to recognize these provocative objects or persons as emitting a communication to negative action or inhibition. Instead of "come on," their message is now "don't touch me," which indicates that the child has a new awareness or altered perception of the world and has developed a pattern of conduct which is relevant and appropriate to that new perception. This is usually called repression, as if it were wholly "internalized," but obviously involves communications from things and persons. The wide array of property rights and of inviolability of persons according to kinship, rank, caste, age, marital, occupational, and professional status may be seen as transformations or elaborations of the basic tactile communications which each culture has utilized in its own way for maintaining its traditional way of life (24).

It would take too much time and space to do more than mention the cultural patterning of person-to-person tactile communications, such as handshake, with removal of glove, close contacts in social dancing which are not permitted elsewhere, rubbing of noses or foreheads or cheeks, clasping of arms around shoulders or waist, embracing the knees, and all the varied other tactile-motor contacts which have been established as signs or symbols for interpersonal communication. Kissing among some people has a special significance of intimacy and affection but it is prohibited by others. The laying on of hands as a ceremonial ritual for transmission of authority or of special powers and healing, such as the shaman touching the body, the king's touch as a cure of skin diseases, are also to be noted. Then too each culture sets certain patterns of what kinds of tactile experiences, especially pain, individuals must learn to accept, such as spanking a child, slapping the face or toleration of pain in fire walking, lying on a bed of nails, gashing and scarifying the skin and genitals in initiation ceremonies or ritual performances, stoical acceptance of sharpened objects in the skin (Plains Indians) and the exposure of the skin to heat and extreme cold (Indian all face!).

Likewise it is to be remembered that the elaboration and refinement of erotic arts, as portrayed, for example, in the Kama Sutra and similar manuals, provide a variety of practices for tactile stimulation of various parts of the body, especially the genitals and erogenous zones, but also of concomitant stimuli, pressure, often painful, with rhythmic patterns designed to build up to an intense climax of orgasm, or prolonged nonconsummating intercourse, such as the Karezza of the original Oneida community. Caressing and manual, digital manipulation is usually associated with intercourse.

The stimulation of the genitals either by the individual or by others may be accepted and encouraged by some groups who manipulate the infant's genitals, and prohibited by others who may punish even a baby for such activity. Communication with the self by masturbation is probably universal, but sanctioned only by some. Other forms of tactile communication with the self are exhibited in various tics, and rubbing or patting areas of skin or hair, scratching, pressing against objects and utilizing various forms of bathing. In medicine the physician usually examines the patient by touching him, exploring for tender spots, for painful areas, for the various signs of neurological disorders such as disturbed reflexes, e.g., patellar, Babinski. Therapy may involve tactile manipulation as in osteopathic treatment and physical medicine. Massage or other manipulation of the body involving tactile contacts are also frequent and may be the focus of professional practices.

Each culture fosters or specifically trains its young as children and as adolescents to develop different kinds of thresholds to tactile contacts and stimulation so that their organic, constitutional, temperamental characteristics are accentuated or reduced. As adults they are more susceptible and vulnerable, or are anesthetic and indifferent to various kinds of tactile communications, as is evidenced by the clinical material on the number and variety of tactual idiosyncrasies, including sexual. Moreover, each culture builds upon the early tactile experience of the infant and child a more or less elaborate series of patterns of adult conduct in which tactile surrogates and symbolic fulfillments are provided.

We may say, therefore, that tactile experiences seem to be basic to many of the crucially important patterns of a culture, that tactile communication takes place on the level of signals, direct tactual stimulation, and on the level of signs and symbols which have been established as surrogates for tactile communications, both for sending and receiving. As in other forms of communication, tactile communication is highly susceptible to interference by noise (any kind of disturbance in transmission, or confusion and conflict in sender or receiver), is peculiarly ambiguous, often redundant and liable to frequent errors in coding and decoding. Without tactile communication, interpersonal relations would be bare and largely meaningless, with a minimum of affective coloring or emotional provocation, since linguistic and much of kinesic communication are signs and symbols which become operative only by evoking some of the responses which were initially stimulated by the tactile stimuli for which these signs and symbols are surrogates. Tactile communications are largely reciprocal transactions between two persons, each of whom in responding to the other, provides the stimulus for a response to him that will in turn initiate his response in a tactile dialectic of greater or less duration. These interpersonal communications may become increasingly symbolic as individuals learn to use words and gestures for sending and receiving such messages as culturally patterned (3).

Severing tactile communications, especially those which have involved intimacy, often creates a crisis for one or both participants for which some cultures provide rituals, ceremonies, and special sanctions (such as legal separation or divorce), or puberty rites. Likewise, as indicated earlier, specific rituals, like betrothal and marriage, are provided in some cultures as public sanction for establishing tactile communications, while others permit premarital relations which eventually lead to marriage.

In ritual and ceremonial activities, the tactile communications play a large role, but often on a symbolic level where there is no actual tactile contact, but every action implies or indicates as in the dance some tactile communication, a threat or invitation, and its patterned response. This is apparent in much of the kinesic activity and communication and in linguistic communication where the message may originate in a tactile context, be coded in verbal symbols, and decoded into tactile experiences.

The elaboration and refinement of cultures may be interpreted in part as the provision of signs and symbols as surrogates for tactile communications which, being more elementary and ambiguous, are superseded by more discriminatory symbols, just as writing offers more scope and subtlety than hieroglyphics or a rebus. Abstractions, concepts, generalizations would seem to be impossible through tactile communication, but tactile experiences transformed into signs and symbols may become abstracted and conceptualized as in finger language used by the blind, as Helen Keller has shown.

It should be emphasized that the establishment of signs and symbols has been a very difficult and often precarious undertaking. Every culture has been dependent upon gifted individuals who could perceive the world in new ways and imaginatively create the symbols which then were accepted and utilized by others. Since this is the kind of world in which many events are occurring more or less simultaneously, and every event, object, and animal appears in a context of greater or less complexity (66) that is, with many other existents, it is not at all easy or simple to recognize which particular signal belongs to or is emitted by a specific event, object, or animal to be identified. We speak of data, which literally means that which is given, but the whole history of science shows that these so-called data or signals are rarely or ever given; they must be laboriously and often painfully discovered, isolated, and established as unequivocal indicators of whatever is the focus of inquiry. Indeed, we might say that the progress of science takes place in large part through the recognition that what have been considered as valid data are not reliable and unequivocal indicators and must be replaced by other indicators that seem to be more nearly reliable signals.

# REFERENCES

1. Bateson, G., *A Theory of Play and Fantasy*, New York: Psychiatry Research Reports 2, December, 1955, American Psychiatry Association.
2. Bateson, G., "Social Planning and the Concept of Deutero-Learning," Conf. on Science, Phil. and Religion, 2nd Symposium, New York: Harper & Row, 1942, 81-97.
3. Bateson, G., and Mead, M., *Balinese Character*, New York: Academy of Sciences, 1941.
4. Birch, H. G., *Personal communication*.
5. Birdwhistell, R., *Introduction to Kinesics*, Lousiville, Ky.: University of Louisville, 1954.
6. Bovard, E. W., Jr., "A Theory to Account for the Effects of Early Handling on Viability of the Albino Rat," *Science*, 1954, July, 187.
7. Bowlby, J., *Maternal Care and Mental Health*, Geneva: World Health Organization, 1951.
8. Carmichael, L., "Behavior During Fetal Life," in *Encyclopedia of Psychology*, New York: Citadel, 1951.
9. Despert, J. L., "Emotional Aspects of Speech and Language Development," *International Journal of Psychiatry & Neurology*, 1941, **105**, 193-222.
10. Dewey, J., and Bentley, A., *Knowing and the Known*, Boston: Beacon, 1949.
11. Douglas, E., Personal communication.
12. Ericson, E., *Childhood and Society*, New York: Norton, 1950.
13. Fairbairn, W. R., *An Object-Relations Theory of the Personality*, New York: Basic Books, 1954.
14. Frank, L. K., "Concept of Inviolability in Culture," *American Journal of Sociology*, 1931, **36**, 607-615.
15. Frank, L. K., *Feelings and Emotions*, Pamphlet, New York: Random House, 1953.
16. Frank, L. K., "Genetic Psychology and Its Prospects," *American Journal of Orthopsychiatry*, 1951, **21**, 506-522.
17. Frank, L. K., *Nature and Human: Man's New Image of Himself*, New Brunswick, N.J.: Rutgers University Press, 1951.
18. Frank, L. K., *Individual Development*, Pamphlet, New York: Random House, 1954.
19. Frank, L. K., "Role of Play in Personality Development," *American Journal of Orthopsychiatry*, 1955, **25**.
20. Goldfarb, W., *American Journal of Orthopsychiatry*, 14, 441.
21. Goldstein, K., *Human Nature in the Light of Psychopathology*, Cambridge, Mass.: Harvard University Press, 1940.
22. Goldstein, K., *The Organism*, New York: American Book, 1939.
23. Goldstein, K., "The Sign of Babinski," *Journal of Nervous & Mental Disease*, 1941, **93**, 281-296.
24. Hallowell, I., "The Self and the Behavioral Environment," in *Cul-

*ture and Experience*, Philadelphia: University of Pennsylvania Press, 1955.

25. Hardy, J. D., Goodsell, H., and Wolff, H. G., *Pain, Sensation, and Reactions*, Baltimore: Williams & Wilkins, 1952.

26. Hammett, F. S., "Studies of the Thyroid Apparatus," *Endocrinology*, 1922, 4, 221-229.

27. Hendrick, I., "Early Development of the Ego: Identification in Infancy," Psychoanalytic Quarterly, 1951, 20, 44-61.

28. Hooker, D., *The Prenatal Origin of Behavior*, Lawrence: University of Kansas Press, 1952.

29. Kahn, T. C., "Theoretical Foundations of Audio-Visual-Tactile Rhythm Induction Therapy Experiments," *Science*, 1954, July, 103-104.

30. Kepes, G., *Language of Vision*, Chicago: Theobold, 1951.

31. Kinsey, A. C., et. al., *Sexual Behavior in the Human Female*, Philadelphia: Saunders, 1953.

32. Kubie, L. S., "Body Symbolization and Development of Language," *Psychoanalytic Quarterly*, 1934, 3, 1-15.

33. Kuntz, A., and Haselwood, L. A., "Circulatory Reactions in the Gastro-Intestinal Tract Elicited by Local Cutaneous Stimulation," *American Heart Journal*, 1940, 20, 743-749.

34. Kuntz, A., "Anatomic and Physiologic Properties of Cutaneo-Visceral Vasomotor Reflex Arcs," *Journal of Neurophysiology*, 1945, 8, 421-430.

35. Lloyd, D. P. C., "Reflex Action in Relation to the Pattern and Peripheral Source of Afferent Stimulation," *Journal of Neurophysiology*, 1943, 6, 111-119.

36. Lowenfeld, M., "World Pictures of Childhood," *British Journal of Medical Psychology*, 1939, 18, 65-101.

37. Lowenfeld, V., *Nature of Creative Activity*, New York: Harcourt Brace Jovanovich, 1939.

38. Lowenfeld, V., *Creative and Mental Growth*, New York: Macmillan, 1947.

39. Martin, A. R., "The Body's Participation in Dilemma and Anxiety Phenomena," *American Journal of Psychoanalysis*, 1945, 5.

40. Maslow, A. H., "The Expressive Component in Behavior," *Psychological Review*, 1949, 56, 261-272.

41. Mead, G. H., *Mind, Self, and Society*, Chicago: University of Chicago Press, 1934.

42. Mead, G. H., "A Behavioristic Account of the Significant Symbol." *Journal of Philosophy*, 1922, 19, 161.

43. Mead, M., *Male and Female*, New York: Morrow, 1949.

44. Mead, M., "The Swaddling Hypothesis: Its Reception." *American Anthropologist*, 1954, 56, 395-409.

45. Mead, M., and MacGregor, F. C., *Growth and Culture*, New York: Putnam, 1951.

46. Meerloo, J. A., "Archaic Behavior and the Communicative Act," *Psychiatric Quarterly*, 1955, **29**, 60-73.
47. Montagu, M. F. A., "Sensory Influences of the Skin," *Texas Reports on Biology & Medicine*, 1953, **2**, 291-301.
48. Montague, W., *The Structure and Function of Skin*, New York: Academic, 1956.
49. Piaget, J., *Play, Dreams, and Imitation in Childhood*, New York: Norton, 1951.
50. Plant, J. S., *The Envelope*, New York: Commonwealth, 1950.
51. Reyniers, J. A., *Germ-Free Life Studies*, Lobund Reports 1-2, 1948-1949.
52. Richins, C. A., and Brizzee, K., "Effect of Localized Cutaneous Stimulation of Circulation in Duodenal Arterioles with Capillary Beds," *Journal of Neurophysiology*, 1949, **12**, 131-136.
53. Ruesch, J., and Kees, W., *Non-Verbal Communication*, New York: Basic Books, 1956.
54. Sechehaye, M. A., *Symbolic Realization*, New York: International Universities, 1951.
55. Sulzberger, M. B., and Zaidens, S. H., "Psychogenic Factors in Dermatological Disorders," *Medical Clinics of North America*, 1948, **32**, 669.
56. Straus, E. W., "Aesthesiology: Its Significance for the Understanding of Hallucination," in *A New Orientation in Psychotherapy*, New York: Basic Books, 1957.
57. Tompkins, H. J., "Veterans' Administration," *New York Times*, July 21, 1953.
58. Travell, J., and Bigelow, N. H., "Role of Somatic Trigger Areas in Pattern of Hysteria," *Psychosomatic Medicine*, 1947, **9**, 353-363.
59. Travell, J., and Ringler, S. H., "Relief of Cardiac Pain by Local Block of Somatic Trigger Areas," *Proceedings of the Society of Experimental Biology*, **63**, 480-482.
60. Vigotsky, L. S., "Thought and Speech," *Psychiatry*, 1939, **2**, 29-54.
61. Wyatt, G., "The Role of Interpersonal Relations in the Acquisition of Language," unpublished manuscript.
62. Werner, H., *Comparative Psychology of Mental Development*, New York: Harper & Row, 1940.
63. Waal, N., "Special Technique of Psychotherapy with an Autistic Child," in *Emotional Problems of Early Childhood*, G. Kaplan (ed.), New York: Basic Books, 1955.
64. Walter, G., *The Living Brain*, New York: Norton, 1953.
65. Weiss, S., and Davis, D., "Significance of Afferent Impulses from the Skin in Mechanisms of Visceral Pain; Skin Infiltration as Useful Therapeutic Procedures," *American Journal of Medical Science*, 1928, **176**, 517-532.
66. Weaver, W., "Science and Complexity," *American Scientist*, 1948, **36**, 536-544.

67. Wolfe, C., *The Hand in Psychological Diagnosis*, New York: Philosophical Library, 1952.
68. Zaidens, S. H., "Dermatological Hypochondriasis," *Psychosomatic Medicine*, 1950, 12, No. 4.

# PART III
# Channels

The concept of a channel refers to the medium used to transmit messages from source to destination. We tend to associate channels with technical apparatus—telephone switchboards, microphones, bull horns, radio transmitters, and teletype machines. Yet there are many other types of channels. Blackboards and writing paper may serve as channels of information. So also are seating arrangements and architecture channels that influence the flow of information from person to person.

The study of communication channels until quite recently has been approached in the manner of a telephone repairman assigned to correct a faulty telephone line. His goal is to restore efficiency, to locate and repair the fault, to minimize distortion and noise. Conceived in such mechanistic terms, a channel merely makes communication possible without altering it. Even more misleading is the tendency to regard the influence of channels in passive or neutral terms. Marshall McLuhan, probably more than any other person, has been responsible for advancing a radically different view of the role of channels in communicative experience. In his landmark essay, "The Medium Is the Message," McLuhan shows why the meaning of message content cannot be understood apart from the impact of the medium itself. What he says about the technical media—that they shape and control what we associate as the content of messages—holds for any channel, particularly those used in face-to-face encounters.

Channels of communication operate at all levels of society; access to a channel facilitates interaction between men, machines, groups, organizations, and mass audiences. From a simple morning greeting to the activities of a sensitivity group and larger intercultural affiliations, channels are necessary to assure continuous access and response. In the essay on "Feedback" Theodore Clevenger, Jr. and Jack Matthews analyze the web of personal contacts from the standpoint of feedback. The concept of feedback underscores the dynamic and evolving aspects of the communication process. Whether it is positive, negative, or indifferent, feedback has a profound impact on the flow of information. In ways that differ as widely as individual personalities, feedback alters the fabric of communicative behavior and the stream of our reactions to it.

In "Communication: The Flow of Information" Daniel Katz and Robert Kahn examine the pervasive role of channels in complex organizations. All organizations require the use of many different types of channels. Yet the very idea of a social system implies ". . . a selectivity of channels and communicative acts—a mandate to avoid some and utilize others." So contrary to the prevailing stereotype, the decision to "open all channels of information" does not itself assure efficiency in organizational activity; a full and free flow of information solves some problems and creates others. Hence, more important then the sheer number of available channels is the way given channels are used within the larger context of what Katz and Kahn term the "coding activity" of organizations.

The notion of selectivity is central to an understanding of the role of channels in communicative systems. The use of a given channel implies decision and choice; one selects one medium to the exclusion of others. So the crucial issue is *why* persons decide to use one channel over another. Elihu Katz examines the issue of selectivity in the article "On Reopening the Question of Selectivity in Exposure to Mass Communications." Katz contends that man has a psychological urge to use those channels of information that promise to shield his most cherished attitudes and beliefs from attack. He also suggests how the factors of human interest and the needs for gratification relate to the problem of exposure to mass communication.

The mass media complicate the flow of information from person to person in two major ways. One is by negation. Attention to one medium often rules out exposure to any other. For example, the frequency of contact between neighbors has much to do with the average number of hours spent watching TV. Yet media often define the flow of information by making many different channels available at once. To return to the instance of TV viewing and neighborly conversation, it is quite probable that old acquaintances will be renewed soon after the word is out that someone bought the latest in color TV just in time for the Superbowl. In the essay on "The Social Effects of Mass Communication" Joseph Klapper shows how the complex links among people and media tend to follow predictable and selective lines.

# THE MEDIUM IS THE MESSAGE
## Marshall McLuhan

In a culture like ours, long accustomed to splitting and dividing all things as a means of control, it is sometimes a bit of a shock to be reminded that, in operational and practical fact, the medium is the message. This is merely to say that the personal and social consequences of any medium—that is, of any extension of ourselves—result from the new scale that is introduced into our affairs by each extension of ourselves, or by any new technology. Thus, with automation, for example, the new patterns of human association tend to eliminate jobs, it is true. That is the negative result. Positively, automation creates roles for people, which is to say depth of involvement in their work and human association that our preceding mechanical technology had destroyed. Many people would be disposed to say that it was not the machine, but what one did with the machine, that was its meaning or message. In terms of the ways in which the machine altered our relations to one another and to ourselves, it mattered not in the least whether it turned out cornflakes or Cadillacs. The restructuring of human work and association was shaped by the technique of fragmentation that is the essence of machine technology. The essence of automation technology is the opposite. It is integral and decentralist in depth, just as the machine was fragmentary, centralist, and superficial in its patterning of human relationships.

The instance of the electric light may prove illuminating in this connection. The electric light is pure information. It is a medium without a message, as it were, unless it is used to spell out some verbal ad or name. This fact, characteristic of all media, means that the "content" of any medium is always another medium. The content of writing is speech, just as the written word is the content of print, and print is the content of the telegraph. If it is asked, "What is the content of speech?" it is necessary to say, "It is an actual process of thought, which is in itself nonverbal." An abstract painting represents direct manifestation of creative thought processes as they might appear in computer designs. What we are considering here, however, are the psychic and social consequences of the designs or patterns as they amplify or accelerate existing processes. For the "message" of any medium or technology is the change of scale or pace or pattern that it introduces into human affairs. The railway did not introduce movement or transportation or wheel or road into human society, but it accelerated and enlarged the scale of previous human functions, creating totally new kinds of cities and new kinds of work and leisure. This happened whether the railway functioned in a tropical or a northern environment, and is quite independent of the freight or content of the railway medium. The airplane, on the other hand, by accelerating the rate of transportation, tends to dissolve the railway form of city, politics, and association, quite independently of what the airplane is used for.

Let us return to the electric light. Whether the light is being used for brain surgery or night baseball is a matter of indifference. It could be argued that these activities are in some way the "content" of the electric light, since they could not exist without the electric light. This fact merely underlines the point that "the medium is the message" because it is the medium that shapes and controls the scale and form of human association and action. The content or uses of such media are as diverse as they are ineffectual in shaping the form of human association. Indeed, it is only too typical that the "content" of any medium blinds us to the character of the medium. It is only today that industries have become aware of the various kinds of business in which they are engaged. When IBM discovered that it was not in the business of making office equipment or business machines, but that it was in the business of processing information, then it began to navigate with clear vision. The General Electric Company makes a considerable portion of its profits from electric light bulbs and lighting systems. It has not yet discovered that, quite as much as A.T.&T., it is in the business of moving information.

The electric light escapes attention as a communication medium just because it has no "content." And this makes it an invaluable instance of how people fail to study media at all. For it is not till the electric light is used to spell out some brand name that it is noticed as a medium. Then it is not the light but the "content" (or what is really another medium) that is noticed. The message of the electric light is like the message of electric power in industry, totally radical, pervasive, and decentralized. For electric light and power are separate from their uses, yet they eliminate time and space factors in human association exactly as do radio, telegraph, telephone, and TV, creating involvement in depth.

A fairly complete handbook for studying the extensions of man could be made up from selections from Shakespeare. Some might quibble about whether or not he was referring to TV in these familiar lines from *Romeo and Juliet:*

But soft! what light through yonder window breaks?
It speaks, and yet says nothing.

In *Othello,* which, as much as *King Lear,* is concerned with the torment of people transformed by illusions, there are these lines that bespeak Shakespeare's intuition of the transforming powers of new media:

Is there not charms
By which the property of youth and maidhood
May be abus'd? Have you not read Roderigo,
Of some such thing?

In Shakespeare's *Troilus and Cressida,* which is almost completely devoted to both a psychic and social study of communication, Shakespeare states his awareness that true social and political navigation depend upon anticipating the consequences of innovation:

The providence that's in a watchful state
Knows almost every grain of Plutus' gold,
Finds bottom in the uncomprehensive deeps,
Keeps place with thought, and almost like the gods
Does thoughts unveil in their dumb cradles.

The increasing awareness of the action of media, quite independently of their "content" or programing, was indicated in the annoyed and anonymous stanza:

In Modern thought, (if not in fact)
Nothing is that doesn't act,
So that is reckoned wisdom which
Describes the scratch but not the itch.

The same kind of total, configurational awareness that reveals why the medium is socially the message has occurred in the most recent and radical medical theories. In his *Stress of Life*, Hans Selye tells of the dismay of a research colleague on hearing of Selye's theory:

When he saw me thus launched on yet another enraptured description of what I had observed in animals treated with this or that impure, toxic material, he looked at me with desperately sad eyes and said in obvious despair: "But Selye, try to realize what you are doing before it is too late! You have now decided to spend your entire life studying the pharmacology of dirt!"

(Hans Selye, *The Stress of Life*)

As Selye deals with the total environmental situation in his "stress" theory of disease, so the latest approach to media study considers not only the "content" but the medium and the cultural matrix within which the particular medium operates. The older unawareness of the psychic and social effects of media can be illustrated from almost any of the conventional pronouncements.

In accepting an honorary degree from the University of Notre Dame a few years ago, General David Sarnoff made this statement: "We are too prone to make technological instruments the scapegoats for the sins of those who wield them. The products of modern science are not in themselves good or bad; it is the way they are used that determines their value." That is the voice of the current somnambulism. Suppose we were to say, "Apple pie is in itself neither good nor bad; it is the way it is used that determines its value." Or, "The smallpox virus is in itself neither good nor bad; it is the way it is used that determines its value." Again, "Firearms are in themselves neither good nor bad; it is the way they are used that determines their value." That is, if the slugs reach the right people firearms are good. If the TV tube fires the right ammunition at the right people it is good. I am not being perverse. There is simply nothing in the Sarnoff statement that will bear scrutiny, for it ignores the nature of the medium, of any and all media, in the true Narcissus style of one hypnotized by the amputation and extension of his own being in a new technical form. General Sarnoff went on to explain his attitude to the technology of print, saying that it was true that print caused much trash to circulate, but it had also disseminated the Bible and the thoughts of seers and philosophers. It has never occurred to General Sarnoff that any technology could do anything but *add* itself on to what we already are.

Such economists as Robert Theobald, W. W. Rostow, and John Kenneth Galbraith have been explaining for years how it is that "classical economics" cannot explain change or growth. And the paradox of mechanization is that although it is itself the cause of maximal growth and change, the principle of mechanization excludes the very possibility of growth or the understanding of change. For mechanization is achieved by fragmentation of any process and by putting the fragmented parts in a series. Yet, as David Hume showed in the eighteenth century, there is no principle of causality in a mere sequence. That one thing follows another accounts for nothing. Nothing follows from following, except change. So the greatest of all reversals occurred with electricity, that ended sequence by making things instant. With instant speed the causes of things began to emerge to awareness again, as they had not done with things in sequence and in concatenation accordingly. Instead of asking which came first, the chicken or the egg, it suddenly seemed that a chicken was an egg's idea for getting more eggs.

Just before an airplane breaks the sound barrier, sound waves become visible on the wings of the plane. The sudden visibility of sound just as sound ends is an apt instance of that great pattern of being that reveals new and opposite forms just as the earlier forms reach their peak performance. Mechanization was never so vividly fragmented or sequential as in the birth of the movies, the moment that translated us beyond mechanism into the world of growth and organic interrelation. The movie, by sheer speeding up the mechanical, carried us from the world of sequence and connections into the world of creative configuration and structure. The message of the movie medium is that of transition from lineal connections to configurations. It is the transition that produced the now quite correct observation: "If it works, it's obsolete." When electric speed further takes over from mechanical movie sequences, then the lines of force in structures and in media become loud and clear. We return to the inclusive form of the icon.

To a highly literate and mechanized culture the movie appeared as a world of triumphant illusions and dreams that money could buy. It was at this moment of the movie that cubism occurred, and it has been described by E. H. Gombrich (*Art and Illusion*) as "the most radical attempt to stamp out ambiguity and to enforce one reading of the picture—that of a man-made construction, a colored canvas." For cubism substitutes all facets of an object simultaneously for the "point of view" or facet of perspective illusion. Instead of the specialized illusion of the third dimension on canvas, cubism sets up an interplay of planes and contradiction or dramatic conflict of patterns, lights, textures that "drives home the message" by involvement. This is held by many to be an exercise in painting, not in illusion.

In other words, cubism, by giving the inside and outside, the top, bottom, back, and front and the rest, in two dimensions drops the illusion of perspective in favor of instant sensory awareness of the whole. Cubism, by seizing on instant total awareness, suddenly announced that *the medium is the message.* Is it not evident that the moment that sequence yields to the simultaneous, one is in the world of the structure and of configuration? Is that not what has happened in physics as in painting, poetry, and in communication? Specialized segments of attention have shifted to total field, and we can now say, "The medium is the message" quite naturally. Before the electric speed and total field, it was not obvious that the medium is the message. The message, it seemed, was the "content," as people used to ask what a painting was *about.* Yet they never thought to ask what a melody was about, nor what a house or a dress was about. In such matters, people retained some sense of the whole pattern, of form and function as a unity. But in the electric age this integral idea of structure and configuration has become so prevalent that educational theory has taken up the matter. Instead of working with specialized "problems" in arithmetic, the structural approach now follows the lines of force in the field of number and has small children meditating about number theory and "sets."

Cardinal Newman said of Napoleon, "He understood the grammar of gunpowder." Napoleon had paid some attention to other media as well, especially the semaphore telegraph that gave him a great advantage over his enemies. He is on record for saying that "Three hostile newspapers are more to be feared than a thousand bayonets."

Alexis de Tocqueville was the first to master the grammar of print and typography. He was thus able to read off the message of coming change in France and America as if he were reading aloud from a text that had been handed to him. In fact, the nineteenth century in France and in America was just such an open book to de Tocqueville because he had learned the grammar of print. So he, also, knew when that grammar did not apply. He was asked why he did not write a book on England, since he knew and admired England. He replied:

One would have to have an unusual degree of philosophical folly to believe oneself able to judge England in six months. A year always seemed to me too short a time in which to appreciate the United States properly, and it is much easier to acquire clear and precise notions about the American Union than about Great Britain. In America all laws derive in a sense from the same line of thought. The whole of society, so to speak, is founded upon a single fact; everything springs from a simple principle. One could compare America to a forest pierced by a multitude of straight roads all converging on the same point. One has only to find the center and everything is revealed at a glance. But in England the paths run criss-cross, and it is only by travelling down each one of them that one can build up a picture of the whole.

De Tocqueville, in earlier work on the French Revolution, had explained how it was the printed word that, achieving cultural saturation in the eighteenth century, had homogenized the French nation. Frenchmen were the same kind of people from north to south. The typographic principles of uniformity, continuity, and lineality had overlaid the complexities of ancient feudal and oral society. The Revolution was carried out by the new literati and lawyers.

In England, however, such was the power of the ancient oral traditions of common law, backed by the medieval institution of Parliament, that no uniformity or continuity of the new visual print culture could take complete hold. The result was that the most important event in English history has never taken place; namely, the English Revolution on the lines of the French Revolution. The American Revolution had no medieval legal institutions to discard or to root, out, apart from monarchy. And many have held that the American Presidency has become very much more personal and monarchical than any European monarch ever could be.

De Tocqueville's contrast between England and America is clearly based on the fact of typography and of print culture creating uniformity and continuity. England, he says, has rejected this principle and clung to the dynamic or oral common-law tradition. Hence the discontinuity and unpredictable quality of English culture. The grammar of print cannot help to construe the message of oral and nonwritten culture and institutions. The English aristocracy was properly classified as barbarian by Matthew Arnold because its power and status had nothing to do with literacy or with the cultural forms of typography. Said the Duke of Gloucester to Edward Gibbon upon the publication of his *Decline and Fall:* "Another damned fat book, eh, Mr. Gibbon? Scribble, scribble, scribble, eh, Mr. Gibbon?" De Tocqueville was a highly literate aristocrat who was quite able to be detached from the values and assumptions of typography. That is why he alone understood the grammar of typography. And it is only on those terms, standing aside from any structure or medium, that its principles and lines of force can be discerned. For any medium has the power of imposing its own assumption on the unwary. Prediction and control consist in avoiding this subliminal state of Narcissus trance. But the greatest aid to this end is simply in knowing that the spell can occur immediately upon contact, as in the first bars of a melody.

*A Passage to India* by E. M. Forster is a dramatic study of the inability of oral and intuitive oriental culture to meet with the rational, visual European patterns of experience. "Rational," of course, has for the West long meant "uniform and continuous and sequential." In other words, we have confused reason with literacy, and rationalism with a single technology. Thus in the electric age man seems to the conventional West to become irrational. In Forster's novel the moment of truth and dislocation from the typographic trance of the West comes in the Marabar Caves. Adela Quested's reasoning powers cannot cope with the total inclusive field of resonance that is India. After the Caves: "Life went on as usual, but had no consequences, that is to say, sounds did not echo nor thought develop. Everything seemed cut off at its root and therefore infected with illusion."

*A Passage to India* (the phrase is from Whitman, who saw

America headed Eastward) is a parable of Western man in the electric age, and is only incidentally related to Europe or the Orient. The ultimate conflict between sight and sound, between written and oral kinds of perception and organization of existence is upon us. Since understanding stops action, as Nietzsche observed, we can moderate the fierceness of this conflict by understanding the media that extend us and raise these wars within and without us.

Detribalization by literacy and its traumatic effects on tribal man is the theme of a book by the psychiatrist J. C. Carothers, *The African Mind in Health and Disease* (World Health Organization, Geneva, 1953). Much of his material appeared in an article in *Psychiatry* magazine, November, 1959: "The Culture, Psychiatry, and the Written Word." Again, it is electric speed that has revealed the lines of force operating from Western technology in the remotest areas of bush, savannah, and desert. One example is the Bedouin with his battery radio on board the camel. Submerging natives with floods of concepts for which nothing has prepared them is the normal action of all of our technology. But with electric media Western man himself experiences exactly the same inundation as the remote native. We are no more prepared to encounter radio and TV in our literate milieu than the native of Ghana is able to cope with the literacy that takes him out of his collective tribal world and beaches him in individual isolation. We are as numb in our new electric world as the native involved in our literate and mechanical culture.

Electric speed mingles the cultures of prehistory with the dregs of industrial marketeers, the nonliterate with the semiliterate and the postliterate. Mental breakdown of varying degrees is the very common result of uprooting and inundation with new information and endless new patterns of information. Wyndham Lewis made this a theme of his group of novels called *The Human Age*. The first of these, *The Childermass*, is concerned precisely with accelerated media change as a kind of massacre of the innocents. In our own world as we become more aware of the effects of technology on psychic formation and manifestation, we are losing all confidence in our right to assign guilt. Ancient prehistoric societies regard violent crime as pathetic. The killer is regarded as we do a cancer victim. "How terrible it must be to feel like that," they say. J. M. Synge took up this idea very effectively in his *Playboy of the Western World.*

If the criminal appears as a nonconformist who is unable to meet the demand of technology that we behave in uniform and continuous patterns, literate man is quite inclined to see others who cannot conform as somewhat pathetic. Especially the child, the cripple, the woman, and the colored person appear in a world of visual and typographic technology as victims of injustice. On the other hand, in a culture that assigns roles instead of jobs to people—the dwarf, the skew, the child create their own spaces. They are not expected to fit into some uniform and repeatable niche that is not their size anyway. Consider the phrase "It's a man's world." As a quantitative observation endlessly repeated from within a homogenized culture, this phrase refers to the men in such a culture who have to be homogenized Dagwoods in order to belong at all. It is in our I.Q. testing that we have produced the greatest flood of misbegotten standards. Unaware of our typographic cultural bias, our testers assume that uniform and continuous habits are a sign of intelligence, thus eliminating the ear man and the tactile man.

C. P. Snow, reviewing a book of A. L. Rowse (*The New York Times Book Review,* December 24, 1961) on *Appeasement* and the road to Munich, describes the top level of British brains and experience in the 1930s. "Their I.Q.'s were much higher than usual among political bosses. Why were they such a disaster?" The view of Rowse, Snow approves: "They would not listen to warnings because they did not wish to hear." Being anti-Red made it impossible for them to read the message of Hitler. But their failure was as nothing compared to our present one. The American stake in literacy as a technology or uniformity applied to every level of education, government, industry, and social life is totally threatened by the electric technology. The threat of Stalin or Hitler was external. The electric technology is within the gates, and we are numb, deaf, blind, and mute about its encounter with the Gutenberg technology, on and through which the American way of life was formed. It is, however, no time to suggest strategies when the threat has not even been acknowledged to exist. I am in the position of Louis Pasteur telling doctors that their greatest enemy was quite invisible, and quite unrecognized by them. Our conventional response to all media, namely that it is how they are used that counts, is the numb stance of the technological idiot. For the "content" of a medium is like the juicy piece of meat carried by the burglar to distract the watchdog of the mind. The effect of the medium is made strong and intense just because it is given another medium as "content." The content of a movie is a novel or a play or an opera. The effect of the movie form is not related to its program content. The "content" of writing or print is speech, but the reader is almost entirely unaware either of print or of speech.

Arnold Toynbee is innocent of any understanding of media as they have shaped history, but he is full of examples that the student of media can use. At one moment he can seriously suggest that adult education, such as the Workers Educational Association in Britain, is a useful counterforce to the popular press. Toynbee considers that although all of the oriental societies have in our time accepted the industrial technology and its political consequences: "On the cultural plane, however, there is no uniform corresponding tendency." (Somervell, I, 267) This is like the voice of the literate man, floundering in a milieu of ads, who boasts, "Personally, I pay no attention to ads." The spiritual and cultural reservations that the oriental peoples may have toward our technology will avail them not at all. The effects of technology do not occur at the level of opinions or concepts, but alter sense ratios or patterns of perception steadily and without any resistance. The serious artist is the only person able to encounter technology with impunity, just because he is an expert aware of the changes in sense perception.

The operation of the money medium in seventeenth-century Japan had effects not unlike the operation of typography in the West. The penetration of the money economy, wrote G. B. Sansom (in *Japan*, Cresset Press, London, 1931) "caused a slow but irresistible revolution, culminating in the breakdown of feudal government and the resumption of intercourse with foreign countries after more than two hundred years of seclusion." Money has reorganized the sense life of peoples just because it is an *extension* of our sense lives. This change does not depend upon approval or disapproval of those living in the society.

Arnold Toynbee made one approach to the transforming power of media in his concept of "etherialization," which he holds to be the principle of progressive simplification and efficiency in any organization or technology. Typically, he is ignoring the *effect* of the challenge of these forms upon the response of our senses. He imagines that it is the response of our opinions that is relevant to the effect of media and technology in society, a "point of view" that is plainly the result of the typographic spell. For the man in a literate and homogenized society ceases to be sensitive to the diverse and discontinuous life of forms. He acquires the illusion of the third dimension and the "private point of view" as part of his Narcissus fixation, and is quite shut off from Blake's awareness or that of the Psalmist, that we become what we behold.

Today when we want to get our bearings in our own culture, and have need to stand aside from the bias and pressure exerted by any technical form of human expression, we have only to visit a society where that particular form has not been felt, or a historical period in which it was unknown. Professor Wilbur Schramm made such a tactical move in studying *Television in the Lives of Our Children*. He found areas where TV had not penetrated at all and ran some tests. Since he had made no study of the peculiar nature of the TV image, his tests were of "content" preferences, viewing time, and vocabulary counts. In a word, his approach to the problem was a literary one, albeit unconsciously so. Consequently, he had nothing to report. Had his methods been employed in 1500 A.D. to discover the effects of the printed book in the lives of children or adults, he could have found out nothing of the changes in human and social psychology resulting from typography. Print created individualism and nationalism in the sixteenth century. Program and "content" analysis offer no clues to the magic of these media or to their subliminal charge.

Leonard Doob, in his report *Communication in Africa*, tells of one African who took great pains to listen each evening to the BBC news, even though he could understand nothing of it. Just to be in the presence of those sounds at 7 P.M. each day was important for him. His attitude to speech was like ours to melody—the resonant intonation was meaning enough. In the seventeenth century our ancestors still shared this native's attitude to the forms of media, as is plain in the following sentiment of the Frenchman Bernard Lam expressed in *The Art of Speaking* (London, 1696):

> 'Tis an effect of the Wisdom of God, who created Man to be happy, that whatever is useful to his conversation (way of life) is agreeable to him . . . because all victual that conduces to nourishment is relishable, whereas other things that cannot be assimilated and be turned into our substance are insipid. A Discourse cannot be pleasant to the Hearer that is not easie to the Speaker; nor can it be easily pronounced unless it be heard with delight.

Here is an equilibrium theory of human diet and expression such as even now we are only striving to work out again for media after centuries of fragmentation and specialism.

Pope Pius XII was deeply concerned that there be serious study of the media today. On February 17, 1950, he said:

> It is not an exaggeration to say that the future of modern society and the stability of its inner life depend in large part on the maintenance of an equilibrium between the strength of the techniques of communication and the capacity of the individual's own reaction.

Failure in this respect has for centuries been typical and total for mankind. Subliminal and docile acceptance of media impact has made them prisons without walls for their human users. As A. J. Liebling remarked in his book *The Press*, a man is not free if he cannot see where he is going, even if he has a gun to help him get there. For each of the media is also a powerful weapon with which to clobber other media and other groups. The result is that the present age has been one of multiple civil wars that are not limited to the world of art and entertainment. In *War and Human Progress*, Professor J. U. Nef declared: "The total wars of our time have been the result of a series of intellectual mistakes . . ."

If the formative power in the media are the media themselves, that raises a host of large matters that can only be mentioned here, although they deserve volumes. Namely, that technological media are staples or natural resources, exactly as are coal and cotton and oil. Anybody will concede that society whose economy is dependent upon one or two major staples like cotton, or grain, or lumber, or fish, or cattle is going to have some obvious social patterns of organization as a result. Stress on a few major staples creates extreme instability in the economy but great endurance in the population. The pathos and humor of the American South are embedded in such an economy of limited staples. For a society configured by reliance on a few commodities accepts them as a social bond quite as much as the metropolis does the press. Cotton and oil, like radio and TV, become "fixed charges" on the entire psychic life of the community. And this pervasive fact creates the unique cultural flavor of any society. It pays through the nose and all its other senses for each staple that shapes its life.

That our human senses, of which all media are extensions, are also fixed charges on our personal energies, and that they also configure the awareness and experience of each one of us, may be perceived in another connection mentioned by the psychologist C. G. Jung:

Every Roman was surrounded by slaves. The slave and his psychology flooded ancient Italy, and every Roman became inwardly, and of course unwittingly, a slave. Because living constantly in the atmosphere of slaves, he became infected through the unconscious with their psychology. No one can shield himself from such an influence (*Contributions to Analytical Psychology*, London, 1928).

Gilliard, E., "The Evolution of Bowerbirds," *Scientific American*, 1963, **209**(2), 38-46.

Goffman, E., "Alienation from Interaction." *Human Relations*, 1957, **10**(1); 47-60.

Goffman, E., *The Presentation of Self in Everyday Life*, Garden City, L.I.: Doubleday, 1959.

Greenberg, J., "Language and Evolution," in *Evolution and Anthropology*, Betty Meggers (ed.), Washington, D.C., The Anthropological Society of Washington, 1959a.

Greenberg, J., "Current Trends in Linguistics," *Science*, 1959b, **130**(No. 3383), 1165-1170.

Hall, E. T., "The Anthropology of Manners," *Scientific American*, 1955, **192**, 85-89.

Hall, E. T., *The Silent Language*, Garden City, L.I.: Doubleday, 1959.

Hall, E. T., "Proxemics—the Study of Man's Spatial Relations," in *Man's Image in Medicine and Anthropology*, Iago Gladston (ed.), New York: International Universities Press, 1963a.

Hall, E. T., "A System for the Notation of Proxemic Behavior," *American Anthropologist*, 1963b, **65**, 1003-1026.

Hall, E. T., and Trager, G. L., *The Analysis of Culture*, Washington, D.C.: American Council of Learned Societies, 1953.

Hediger, H., *Studies of the Psychology and Behavior of Captive Animals in Zoos and Circuses*, London: Butterworths Scientific Publications, 1955.

Hinde, R., and Tinbergen, N., "The Comparative Study of Species' Specific Behavior," in *Behavior and Evolution*, Anne Roe and G. G. Simpson (eds.), New Haven, Conn.: Yale University Press, 1958.

Hockett, C. F., *A Course in Modern Linguistics*, New York: Macmillan, 1958.

Hymes, D., "The Ethnography of Speaking," in *Anthropology and Human Behavior*, T. G. Gladwin and W. C. Sturtevant (eds.), Washington D.C.: The Anthropological Society of Washington, 1962, 15-53.

Joos, M., *The Five Clocks*, Supplement to International Journal of American Linguistics, 1962, **28**, part V, Bloomington, Ind.

Kluckhohn, C., 1943, "Covert Culture and Administrative Problems," *American Anthropologist*, 1943, **45**, 213-227.

Linton, R., *The Study of Man*, New York: Appleton-Century-Crofts, 1936.

Pierce, T., *Electrons, Waves, and Messages*, New York: Hanover House, 1956.

Ruesch, J., *Therapeutic Communication*, New York: Norton, 1961.

Ruesch, J., and Kees, W., *Nonverbal Communication*, Berkeley and Los Angeles: University of California Press, 1956.

Sapir, Edward, *Language*, New York: Harcourt Brace Jovanovich, 1921.

Sapir, Edward, "Sound Patterns in Language," *Language*, 1925, 1, 37-51.

Sapir, Edward, "The Unconscious Patterning of Behavior in Society," in *The Unconscious: A Symposium*, E. S. Dummer (ed.), New York, 1927.

Schaller, G. B., *The Mountain Gorilla*, Chicago: University of Chicago Press, 1963.

Sebeok, T. A., "Coding in the Evolution of Signaling Behavior," *Behavioral Science*, 1962, 7, 430-442.

Shannon, C. A., and Weaver, W., *The Mathematical Theory of Communication*, Urbana: University of Illinois Press, 1949.

Sivadon, P., Ms. "Techniques of Sociotherapy."

Sullivan, H. S., *Conceptions of Modern Psychiatry*, Washington, D.C., William Alanson White Foundation, 1947.

Tinbergen, N., "The Origins and Evolution of Courtship and Threat Display," in *Evolution as a Process*, A. C. Hardy, T. S. Huxley, and E. B. Ford (eds.), London: Allen & Unwin, 1954.

Wiener, N., *Cybernetics*, New York: Wiley, 1948.

# THE REVERSE TRANSMISSION OF CULTURE
## Richard E. Farson

I would like to state a rather simple but very disturbing hypothesis: Maybe young people today really do know more than older people.

I am coming to believe that we are undergoing a reversal in the transmission of culture. In every society it is traditionally the job of the older person to transmit the culture of his society to the young—the ritual, the myth, the magic, the wisdom, the rules and mores. Everything known about the world has always been transmitted from the older to the younger. Now the direction is changing. For the first time in history, we may have more to learn from young people than they have to learn from us. Young people used to want to be like their elders. Today it's the other way around.

Of course, the older generation has always learned some things from the younger generation. We have learned about fashion and dance, for example. The best professors have always learned from their students. The *enfant terrible* has always taught us things we haven't wanted to learn. But now something much deeper is taking place. We are now learning from youth about the nature of society and world affairs, about the conduct of human relationships, about ethics and morals, about matters of taste and judgment, about war and peace, about science and sex, and about politics and religion. Youth is teaching us about our potentialities as human beings—about dimensions of humanness of which our generation has little understanding. Paradoxical as it may seem, we are learning about *life* from young people now. Futurists, advertising executives, artists, designers, and social scientists are all looking to youth these days as the leading edge of our culture. There are more of them; they are better educated; they have fewer prejudices; they are more worldly, more confident, more articulate; they have learned things (for

From "The Reverse Transmission of Culture" by Richard E. Farson. In *Experiences in Being*, Bernice Marshall, ed., pp. 214-219. Copyright © 1971 by Wadsworth Publishing Company, Inc. Reprinted by permission of the author and the publisher, Brooks/Cole Publishing Company, Monterey, Calif.

example, new math and science) that simply were not taught when we were in school, and they have learned them by methods (for example, television) that are more powerful than those with which we grew up.

It is small wonder that our institutions are so unstable now. Every institution you can name—family, church, school, community, military, business—is based on a power hierarchy from old to young. Older people are regularly found at the top, where the wisdom and information and skill have always been located. Now these qualities are distributed differently, making such a hierarchy painfully anachronistic.

I suppose we are in this bind because of the acceleration of change in our world. If we were to plot a curve of all the inventions of man, we would find that the curve doesn't merely increase; it accelerates so rapidly that change has become almost a way of life. There are no more plateaus where we can just coast for a while and catch our breath. And it seems to be in the biology of the human animal that the young person is better able to embrace change than is the older person. In describing our current predicament, Margaret Mead suggests that the people in the over-30 generation are like visitors to an alien country: They have all the problems that plague foreigners who try to learn about another culture, except this culture is supposedly their own.

Against the backdrop of this profound problem of the reverse transmission of culture, I would like to discuss what I think is happening, why we are so frightened by it, how things got this way, and what we might do about it. What is it about this generation that really gets to us? Why do we apologize (and there is a lot of apologizing these days) for being in the older generation? In the same way that many have said in regard to the black revolution, "I apologize, I'm a honky," others are now saying, "I apologize, I'm over 30." We're embarrassed, somewhat ashamed, and deeply threatened.

Let me suggest seven reasons why. First of all, we are caught in a crisis of incongruity. Hypocrisy is the word that is often used for it. Time after time we are nailed to the wall by young people on issues for which we have no adequate defense. Take Vietnam, for example: Our most eloquent and thoughtful leaders have not been able to persuade most young people—or many of the rest of us, for that matter—that we should be there. In fact, just the opposite seems to have happened: Young people have been able to persuade some of them that we certainly should not be there. We are similarly caught on the questions of drugs. Members of my generation, the most drugged generation in history, are hopelessly outgunned when we say to the young, "We want our martinis and tranquilizers, but you can't have your pot."

The young continually point to our superficialities and incongruities. We almost never say what we are really feeling. In this connection, I'm reminded of an experiment conducted by Alex Bavelas of Stanford, which illustrates how much we censor what we are saying. Bavelas asks the people he interviews to wear earphones that feed them "white noise"—something like radio static combined with the sound of a jet plane getting ready to take off. The noise in the earphones is activated by the subject's voice, so he can't hear himself talking. In this situation—where the interviewer can both talk to the subject and hear what he says, but the subject can only hear the interviewer—some interesting phenomena turn up. One of them is that people lose some of their ability to control and censor their speech. For example, a man who is asked, "How do you and your wife get along?" might reply, "We get along just fine," and then add very quietly, "That's a lot of crap." When a tape recording of his comments is played back to him, he doesn't remember making the second statement.

The young people, who have been called the open generation, the honest generation, may not be all that honest; but, compared to us, they do seem very honest, don't they? We're uncomfortable when we discover that the name of the game is "truth." We want them to play *our* game. After all, who wants to be around honesty all the time? It makes it difficult to maintain our treasured double standards—our discriminatory practices between men and women, between blacks and whites, between youth and adults.

Second, young people trouble us because they have discovered some powerful new ways of disrupting the system, of getting to us, of forcing change. They do it in ways that we have never tried before, ways that seem to break the rules. One technique, the creation of instant futures, they learned from the civil rights movement. While our sociopolitical style has been gradual and indirect, relying on "legitimate" means for the achievement of social progress (for example, writing letters to the editor, signing petitions, reasoning with authorities, and using other methods with similarly limited power), their style is the new, direct technique of creating the future they want *now*. The civil rights movement taught them a lesson in sociopolitical action: If you want to integrate a restaurant, you don't reason with the restaurant owner; you move a black person into that restaurant, create the future you want instantly, and expect to take your lumps for it. That is perhaps the most powerful tool to emerge from the movement. And so the young have created their instant futures—the experimental college, for example. There are now more than 125 of these colleges—designed and run by students—existing on and off campuses all over the country, and they are forcing changes in the curriculum of the university that is their parent.

What has changed is the whole idea of the legitimacy of breaking rules. Let me give you an example. Often, when speaking to audiences, I have noticed that during the question period adults usually rise, ask their questions, and obediently sit down when asked to do so by the moderator. Many students don't do that. They break the rules. I doubt that they feel much guilt about it, either. They may even feel a sense of pleasure. They are comfortable with that new disruptive style.

Those who saw the television coverage of Dr. Hayakawa's responses during an incident at San Francisco State College in 1969 know that he, too, broke some rules. It doesn't fit our idea of a college president to see him punching kids, ripping out wires, etc., and yet it may be that one reason he is credited with some success in controlling the situation is that he violated his role expectations. For a time he became as unpredictable and unmanageable as the students. Hundreds of underground newspapers in colleges, high schools, and even junior high schools are a constant source of trouble to the people who are trying to maintain campus life as it has been. They understandably wish the students would write in the official school paper about who ought to win the homecoming queen contest or the upcoming football games instead of jabbing at the inadequacies of our present educational system or at the hypocrisy they find in this country.

Third, their sexuality threatens us. Not their actual sexual behavior—that doesn't seem to have changed much through the years. It's their attitudes that disturb us. They don't seem to value the importance of chastity in the way that we do. In talking about sex, they are much too open and free to suit us. They don't even help maintain the traditional role-differences between the sexes. They don't seem to share our concepts of masculinity and *femininity:* Boys are not all devoted to football and other so-called masculine activities, and girls are not all trying to appear chaste, demure, and naïve. Mike Murphy of the Esalen Institute told me recently that what he had been anticipating had finally happened: He had spent about half an hour talking to someone without knowing whether the person was a boy or girl. "I knew it was bound to happen, and it finally did."

The fourth reason youngsters frighten us is that they simply no longer share our deepest values. They don't seem to understand the importance of work as an end in itself. They have the idea that good things should happen to them now, not later. They aren't good at waiting. I find it almost impossible to explain to someone in the younger generation why he should wait for gratification.

They don't understand the glory of military combat. As a matter of fact, they seem to demand the right to live without war. I guess that during the First World War there was some glory attached to military service. During the Second World War there was still some romance and excitement in "serving one's country," but most people just felt dutiful. In regard to the Vietnam war, young people don't even feel dutiful. The war has changed the whole social structure on campuses. It used to be that high social status went to the star athletes, the fraternity and sorority presidents, the homecoming queens, and so forth. But, according to a Berkeley student with whom I spoke recently, the high-status people today are conscientious objectors. Actually, he told me, the people with the highest status on campus are not even on campus; they are in jail for draft resistance.

Young people are valuing education in different terms than we did. They seem to be concerned with more than just the education of the intellect; they seem to be interested in the education of the emotions, the senses, and the affective life.

They are interested in gaining skill in interpersonal relations and in developing a sense of community. They seem to think that education somehow ought to be fun, interesting, and—though the term has become a cliché—"relevant." The idea of education as only "preparation for something" doesn't make sense to them; in their view, it ought to be an experience of value in and of itself.

Fifth, we are disturbed because we have lost control of our young people to outsiders—to the peer group, to mass media, to the school, and to other community institutions. Nowadays, after the first few years of life, the major influence is no longer the parent. Interestingly, parents have not lost this control to the church. The church has virtually no influence over people between the ages of 15 and 30. Of course that is one of the most serious crises facing the church today.

A sixth reason we feel frightened, threatened by what is happening, is that young people seem to be able to live more comfortably—better than we, at least—with temporary systems. They don't seem to be basing their personal sense of security on the reliable sameness of things. Most of us seem to have built our sense of security on the idea that things are going to be the same tomorrow as they were yesterday, on the existence of fundamental truths, on familiar neighborhoods, on lifelong friendships, and on permanent careers. We want to know where we will be in 10 years. They don't. They seem to be able to enjoy the temporary quality of life which characterizes society today.

This flexible attitude shows up in their ability to accept racial and cultural differences. While we haven't succeeded, we have been committed to the idea that we should homogenize society. But young people are apparently quite prepared to accept the possibility of a pluralistic society. They want to appreciate, even celebrate, the differences that exist between us rather than try to minimize them. Maybe their ability, their willingness, to live with differences and with temporary systems has contributed to their ability to handle the thought of anarchy. I am distressed by the thought of anarchy; perhaps most of you are, too. But it just doesn't distress young people.

The seventh, and perhaps the most fundamental, problem we are facing is that young people may actually see the world differently than we do. If McLuhan is right about the differences brought on by the electric age, young people who have grown up with TV may simply be sensing the environment differently. We now must at least question the whole idea of intergeneration communication. The cherished hope that communication will inevitably lead to understanding may prove to be entirely empty, a futile effort.

So what do we do about all this? My first answer has to be "maybe nothing." Maybe there is nothing we should do; maybe there is nothing that we can do. As with most social problems, it may be still too early to recognize the problem and already too late to do anything about it.

It's interesting that today the theme "Let's sit down and listen to each other" seems a bit naïve—necessary perhaps, but not sufficient. We now see that it isn't that simple. Listening and understanding aren't enough. As a matter of fact, I have come to believe that we must have the courage to act *without* understanding, *without* communication. We may have to proceed with decisions and actions without all the facts and without lengthy conferences. We may have to act more on the basis of ideas, personal styles, cogent arguments, and fundamental principles.

It will be difficult to co-opt youth. We can't continually take what they are doing and make an adult thing out of it the way we did rock 'n' roll. Remember how we adults took over the twist? I don't think such take-overs will work when it comes to the things that matter most. We can't simply be influenced by the young without yielding some power to them. And we can't just imitate them. I was sitting with some friends at lunch recently, and next to us was a very much "with-it" woman who said, "My son warned me, 'Mother, if you bring home pot, I am going to call the police.'"

If the idea of the reverse transmission of culture has substance, it means that we have two very difficult jobs ahead of us. The first is to come to terms with our feelings about control and influence and authority. This will be painful as we come to see that our experience and wisdom is less and less valuable and that young people really don't need us, except because they love us. The second job is the monumental task of redesigning every institution of society to give youth a measure of control commensurate with their new capabilities:

We have to redress the balance. These long overdue changes must take place first of all in our educational institutions, but eventually everywhere.

Most of the educators who are battling the students now are quick to admit that the students have been out of things too long. Most feel that there should be some changes made. But how? Gradually? Are we really going to let the students help determine whether or not a professor gets tenure? Are we really going to let them participate in discussions about how the dormitories should be built? Are we really going to let them decide on what courses should be taught in social science? Are we really going to let them have a voice in determining the schools' admission policies? Will we let them have voting membership on all the committees that influence the nature of the learning community and thereby influence their own destinies as learners? And, if we do it in colleges, are we going to do it in high schools and junior high schools and elementary schools? In any event, we have to remember this: We are not going to "give" control to students, because we have substantially lost the power to give it. They have taken it. Their pressures for change have, I think, made one rather permanent difference in higher education: Nobody is going to make unilateral or top-down decisions anymore in any major university in this country.

Changes in schools will not be sufficient. We have to provide access to media, to government, to financial institutions, and to every other basic institution in our society. We have to give young people the vote. We have to abandon the traditional hierarchical organizations in favor of organizations with distributed leadership organized on the basis of temporary systems.

What all this points to, I think, is the necessity of re-inventing all our social institutions. A corollary is that youth participate in the re-invention. If we are to avoid the apocalypse,[1] we must act quickly and with every resource at our disposal. We need to apply newly developed social technology so that people who are components of the system can also be the designers of that system. In this we could not only avoid catastrophe but actually celebrate the renewal of our systems.

Before I close, let me raise the possibility that I am all wet about this; maybe I am dead wrong. You can certainly take some comfort in that. Also, let me make it clear that adults certainly don't have any corner on the market when it comes to hypocrisy, stupidity, immorality, and dullness. Some of the most tiresome and foolish people I know are youngsters. So let's not forget that there is some balance in this—it's not all one way. Maybe you can also take comfort in realizing the problem that the 20-year-old has. He now seems to be riding high, but the generation gap he will have to face is with the 14-year-old. I wish him good luck. Let us also take some comfort in the idea that the present level of discontent in our society is a measure not of its problems but of its success. We have these problems because we have been so tremendously successful as a society. Things were never better than they are today. Let's not kid ourselves—those good old days never were. What we have now is the best situation we have ever had in society, and if we ask the question, "Compared to what?" (which, by the way, is a very good question to ask), we will see that what we have isn't so bad. Compared to the way life used to be, this is pretty good. But compared to the way it *might* be, it's pretty bad.

The discrepancy between what we have and what we might have is what causes our discontent. But that is high-order discontent, and it is certainly okay to have that. We don't ever want to be a society that is satisfied; we want to be a society that is discontented about the right things. And the discontent runs highest in places where things are best. San Francisco State College is not the worst school for blacks in this country; it is one of the best. One reason the discontent there is so high is that blacks have come to expect something decent from that school. Nobody is protesting down at Bob Jones University, because there they don't expect anything.

Paradoxically, with all its problems, this generation is the best one we have ever had. You may not believe this, but our communication with youth is better than it has ever been. Maybe that is why they seem so difficult.

## NOTES

1. I chose this term with the realization that the entire system could collapse. Organizations, after all, are really quite fragile.

# Index

74 75 76   9 8 7 6 5 4 3

# FEEDBACK
# Theodore Clevenger, Jr., and
# Jack Matthews

## INTERACTION WITH FEEDBACK

Whenever a speaker alters his speaking behavior by adapting
in some way to response from his listener, he may be said to
be responding to feedback. Neither the foregoing statement
nor the process to which it refers is nearly as simple as it
seems, but the feedback function is so important in human
communication that it is worth taking time to understand it.

The term *feedback* comes from cybernetics, the branch of
engineering science dealing with control systems.[1] Such systems control operations by using information about effects.
The now-classic example of a simple cybernetic system is
the thermostat on a furnace. When the temperature in a room
drops below a minimal level, the thermostat closes a switch,
sending a signal that turns on the furnace. The thermostat
continuously monitors the room temperature; and when it
reaches the desired maximum, the thermostat opens the
switch, sending a signal that turns the furnace off. Engineers
would refer to the signal that turns the furnace off as "negative feedback"; it causes the furnace to discontinue what it
has been doing. Positive feedback has no place in a thermostat system because furnaces burn at a more or less constant
temperature, and the effect of positive feedback would be to
cause the furnace to burn hotter and hotter. In both cases,
information about the effects of the operation (in this case,
the effect upon room temperature of the firing of the furnace) is used to control the operation (turning it off or causing it to burn hotter). Positive feedback says, in effect, "Do
even more of the same," while negative feedback says, "Stop
what you have been doing."

### Positive and Negative Feedback

Because people use information about the effects of their
communication in controlling how they communicate, it is

natural to extend the concept of feedback into human inter-action. If, for example, one's initial greeting to a stranger meets with a pleasant response, one is likely to continue the conversation, often with a more extended message than the first. This is positive feedback at work. However, if the first message meets with indifference or grouchiness, one is likely to terminate the conversation at that point; here we see the operation of negative feedback. Now, because the words "positive" and "negative" have—in addition to their technical meanings in cybernetics—evaluative meanings for people, it is easy to confuse the two when talking about feedback. In the above example it is not the pleasantness of the listener's response that makes it positive feedback nor the aversiveness of his response that makes it negative feedback. It is simply a question of whether his response causes an increase or a de-crease in some aspect of the speaker's behavior. In this case, the question is whether it causes the speaker to enlarge the conversation or terminate it.

As a matter of fact, favorable responses from the listener often signify negative feedback, and unfavorable responses may signify positive feedback. If I am explaining something to you and observe nonverbal cues that tell me you don't understand what I am saying, your response may be charac-terized as negative; but the feedback it gives to me is positive if it causes me to repeat or enlarge my explanation. On the other hand, if you show that you understand, your response can be said to be positive; but its effect on my behavior will be negative feedback if it signals that I should stop explaining.

### Variable Influence of Feedback

From this, it should be clear that the term *feedback* refers not to any catalog of listener behavior, but to a *relationship* between the behavior of the speaker, the response of the lis-tener, and the effect of that response on the further behavior of the speaker. Thus, a response of the listener is not feed-back if it has no effect on the speaker's subsequent behavior. I may shake my head, frown, even speak out in an effort to generate feedback signals that will influence your communi-cation behavior to me; but if you fail to note my response, or—noting it—refuse to adapt your message in light of it, then my behavior is not feedback. In a sense, then, we may say that feedback, in order to *be* feedback, must be *used as* feedback.

Just as no listener behavior can automatically be classified as feedback if it does not influence the behavior of the speaker, there is no behavior that cannot serve as feedback if it does influence the further behavior of the speaker. In particular, we need to bear in mind that feedback messages need not be transmitted *deliberately* or consciously by the listener. Indeed, most people seeing a film or videotape of their listening behavior in a group discussion or an audience are appalled at the transparency of their reactions. They thought they were sitting in poker-faced inscrutability, but the tape shows many reactions that can be read clearly by an alert observer. They did not intentionally transmit feedback messages to the speaker, but those messages were there to be used as feedback if the speaker was willing and able to perceive and respond to them.

### Using Feedback to Enrich Interaction

To introduce possibilities for feedback into human interaction is to enrich the quality of human contact enormously; for now each partner in the interaction can not only influence and be influenced by the other, but the behavior of each will be conditioned by the behavior of the other. In the alternating monologue we see two people talking in one another's presence. In the stimulus-response interaction pattern, at least one of the people is responding to what the other says. In interaction with feedback, the further behavior of the speaker is conditional upon the nature of the listener's response.

We should note that in order to make use of feedback, the speaker must retain some flexibility in his own behavior. At any given moment several options must be open to him; otherwise, the listener's response cannot influence his behavior, and thus cannot serve as feedback. For example, the public speaker who has written out a manuscript and attempts to present it orally is able to make very limited use of feedback from his audience. He can observe their reactions and adjust features of his delivery to comfortable levels by speaking loudly enough and at a rate that is comfortable for them to listen to. He can pause for laughs, applause, or jeers; he can repeat a passage that did not seem to sink in. But beyond these relatively mechanical matters he cannot adjust without scrapping or ignoring the manuscript. Sometimes it is more important to be precise than to be flexible, and then a manuscript is useful. Most people, however, do not learn how to interact with an audience until they give up the practice of reading speeches from prepared texts.

## INTERACTION WITH FEEDBACK AND FEEDFORWARD

Feedback, as we have seen, is the process whereby a system modified its operations so as to adjust to the known consequences of those operations. In the case of human communication, this refers to the process of adjusting one's communication behavior so as to take account of the observed influence of that behavior on the listener. But how does the speaker know what behaviors to use as feedback from his interaction partner, and how does he decide what alternatives to follow in the event of a particular listener response?

Some feedback adjustments amount to automatic social habits, such as adjusting one's loudness level when the listener displays signs of difficulty in hearing, or asking him a question when he seems bored. But other adjustments seem to result not from habit but from forethought. It is as if the speaker had anticipated certain listener behaviors at specific points in the interaction, and had laid out alternative courses of action depending on whether the expected reactions occurred or not. The setting up of such expectancies and contingencies is called *feedforward*.

Like feedback, feedforward is a term that originated in cybernetic theory. In the same sense that the operation of a thermostat is the simplest example of feedback, setting the thermostat is the simplest example of feedforward. By setting the thermostat to a desired temperature range, the operator may be said to "feed forward" the maximum and/or minimum temperature to the point in the heat cycle where these temperature values will be needed. A more interesting and representative example of feedforward would be an attachment to keep track of both the inside and the outside temperature and to pour into a storage tank ahead of time just the amount of fuel needed to bring the temperature back into the desired range. Such a device could be said to "anticipate" fuel needs. Although there are many significant differences between thermostats and human beings, there are also some intriguing analogies which, if not taken too literally, provide insights into the ways in which we as human beings react and interact.

In human interaction, feedforward most often takes one of three forms: (1) *Goal-setting*, (2) *establishing expectancies*, and (3) *planning contingencies*.

### Goal-Setting

In some ways, setting a specific goal that we hope to achieve with a listener operates much like feedforward: When that goal is reached, our goal-seeking behavior will cease. If the goal is vague or ill-defined, our behavior will be as unreliable as a furnace without a thermostat, and somebody else will have to turn us off. If we are not sensitive to potential feedback signals that tell us the goal has been reached, we will operate like a furnace whose control circuit from the thermostat has been broken.

We should also note that goals are often revised during interaction, and such revision also qualifies as feedforward. Suppose, for example, that you are trying to sell a subscription to the college humor magazine to a student you have just met, and in the process you discover that he seems to know a good deal about magazine writing and publishing. You may now decide that you want more from him than a subscription. If, for example, you now want him to donate some time to the magazine, you will have fed forward a revised goal into the continuing interaction.

### Establishing Expectancies

Marshall McLuhan,[2] along with many contemporary psychologists, would argue that except for the simplest reflex behaviors, human beings seldom communicate without some kind of expectancy. This form of feedforward may occur at many levels, from the linguistic to the social. You will recall, for example, that ... we said that one of the most reasonable theories of language decoding (speech recognition) holds that we use a few clues to "synthesize" or "generate" a best guess as to what the speaker is saying, then check that guess against what we can hear of the utterance. The synthesis of the "best guess" is a kind of feedforward. If we are led to synthesize an estimate of what the speaker will say before he says it, then the synthesis represents the kind of feedforward we call *expectancy*.

As we move from the linguistic to the interactional level, we can find still more examples of feedforward. The "canned" sales pitch is a study in feedforward. Far from being the rigid "speech outlines" that they once were, such interaction plans are now adapted to a variety of listeners, moods, and circumstances. The planner who organizes the pitch will try to anticipate points in the presentation where a listener will ask questions or raise objections, and at each such point will construct appropriate answers. Thus, anticipation of the questions has been fed forward into the interaction plan.

Not all anticipatory feedforward is the result of preplanning. Indeed, much of it arises during the course of interaction with others. For example, suppose that your hobby is shortwave radio. In talking to me you discover very early in the conversation that I know none of the technical terminology. You may very well feed forward the anticipation that I would think it foolish of you to spend so much time and money on the hobby; for unless I know at least some of the terminology, I am not likely to have experienced the satisfactions arising from operating an amateur station, and I certainly will not have dreamed of the amount of money involved. Having encountered such novices in the past, you may predict that I would be amazed to find out how much your hobby costs. Consequently, you will be anticipating this response and will be either marshalling your arguments in defense of such spending or planning ways to dodge the issue.

Whenever anybody says something to us or reacts to something we have said to him in such a way as to increase our awareness of his attitudes or predispositions, we are likely to feed forward new anticipations regarding that person. Since new insights into others happen frequently in interaction, this type of feedforward is a very common occurrence.

Of course, the fact that such feedforward is common is no guarantee of its accuracy or dependability. In the foregoing example, for instance, your prediction about my reaction might be entirely wrong. By avoiding further conversation about a topic you think might become embarrassing, you may deprive both of us of a satisfying encounter. Or, if you were in a more aggressive mood, you might increase the likelihood of an interpersonal crisis between us. By anticipating negative reactions, you might behave in such a way as to increase the likelihood of obtaining one. Thus, you might perversely exaggerate the amount of time and money you spent on your ham station. To such exaggeration I might respond with genuine surprise, which you might interpret as mild disapproval, which might lead you to become defensive, which I might interpret as belligerence, which might lead me to respond coolly, which you might interpret as an escalation of the hostilities, and so on to an interpersonal breakdown—all of which started with your anticipating a negative response. This behavior leads to paranoia, which can be characterized as a condition of distorted feedforward.

### Planning Contingencies
In an earlier example, we said that the prepared sales talk is a study in feedforward, and illustrated it with examples of anticipating the customer's questions and objections. A still more sophisticated approach to the prepared sales talk involves contingency planning. The person organizing the talk may go further than anticipating questions or objections from the customer; the sales strategist may, in fact, introduce questions into the talk that demand the customer give some response. By anticipating the different possible responses at each of these points in the talk, the sales person may plan a highly flexible program of information and persuasion capable of being adapted to a very great variety of different customers. The essence of such a plan is the feedforward of contingencies to the crucial choice-points in the discussion, and the preparation of appropriate plans for meeting each imagined contingency. Most experienced salesmen have in effect programed themselves to such a contingency plan. Through long experience of success and failure in marketing a particular product, they have come to know the critical choice-points in a sales interaction, and have developed appropriate means of dealing with each.

Just as goals may be revised and expectancies changed during interaction, so may contingency plans arise or be modified during the course of interaction. Perhaps the most primitive, everyday example is the desperate thought: "If he says that again, I'm going to let him have it." This is a simple contingency plan arising during the course of interaction. More constructive examples occur also:

"If she smiles, I'll ask her to the game."

"If he likes the IBM deal, I'll show him the entire portfolio; otherwise, I'll switch to the chemical stocks."

"If he seems friendly, I'll ask him to join today."

"The question of salary is bound to come up sooner or later. If he mentions a specific figure below $12,000, we'll agree to it immediately; but if he asks what we're offering, we'll mention $10,000."

"We escalate our demands until the president can no longer say 'yes.' Then, if he says 'no,' we occupy the administration building; if he refers it to the faculty senate, we move in and take over the senate meeting. Charlie, you start to work on the speeches and signs for the ad-building bash; Annette, you get the stuff ready for the senate."

"By this point, they ought to have a pretty good idea of what I'm talking about. If they seem to understand, I'll drop out the third example."

All of the foregoing are examples of feedforward of the type we call contingency planning. An ability to develop and execute plans of this sort is a necessary skill in effective social interaction, and most people develop at least some of this ability at an early age. It is obvious that the more one knows about people in general, about his listener in particular, and about the topic under discussion, the more effective can be his planning in this regard.

We have seen three kinds of feedforward in social interaction: (1) Goal setting, (2) expectancy, and (3) contingency planning. It should have occurred to you that these three levels of feedforward are not in fact strictly separable from each other. Where one leaves off and the other begins is often difficult to determine. But together the three terms describe a continuum of feedforward activities that clearly play a vital role in human communication. Without feedforward, feedback would be a static and sterile affair; and without flexible feedback, interaction could scarcely be human.

## NOTES

1. See Norbert Wiener, *Cybernetics*, Cambridge, Mass.: M.I.T. Press, 1948.
2. McLuhan, Marshall, *Understanding Media: The Extensions of Man*, New York: McGraw-Hill, 1964.

# ON REOPENING THE QUESTION OF SELECTIVITY IN EXPOSURE TO MASS COMMUNICATIONS
## Elihu Katz

The notion of selective exposure is basic to theory and research on the flow of mass communications. It appears as a major explanatory factor in attempts to account for the repeatedly observed fact that the mass media do not easily persuade people to change their attitudes or practices. Communications campaigns—this argument holds—reach the already-converted; others simply tune out. Hence the generalization that the mass media typically reinforce people in their attitudes and practices, but rarely convert them.

In this sense, selectivity is one of a series of ideas that have led to a reformulation of the image of the relationship between the mass media and their audiences. Whereas the media had been thought capable of impressing their message on the defenseless masses, it now appears as if the audience has quite a lot of power of its own. Indeed, the fashion in research nowadays is not to ask "What the media *do to* people" but "What people *do with* the media," or at least to be sure to ask the second question before the first. This shift in emphasis represents a shift of interest away from the study of mass media "campaigns" in favor of the study of the "uses" or the "gratifications" which people derive from exposure to the media. This shift makes the concept of selectivity all the more important, insofar as the attempt now is to explain selectivity in terms of the functional contribution of exposure to some social or psychological need, of which selectivity for the purpose of attitude-reinforcement may be only a particular case.

It is more than a little dissonance-producing, therefore, to read Freedman and Sears' (1965) conclusion that neither experimental nor field studies provide convincing evidence of the operation of this sort of motivated selectivity. There is no question that selectivity exists—i.e., that individuals are disproportionately exposed to communications which are congenial to their attitudes. The question is whether there is a motivated choice involved, one that is specifically associated with the quest for reinforcement, as distinct from the expression of "interest" or the search for "utility," or the like, and as distinct from de facto selectivity whereby circumstances, rather than motives, conspire to expose people to congenial communications.

The objective of what follows is to look again, in the light of the question raised by Freedman and Sears, at the evidence from mass communications studies. We shall try, at the same time, to respond to the Freedman-Sears call to go beyond the specific notion of selectivity-for-the-purpose-of-obtaining-support and to examine other bases of selective exposure. It is probably correct that some of these are considerably more important than "supportive selectivity" and may set the conditions under which the latter does or does not take place. Nevertheless, we shall argue that "supportive selectivity"—at least as far as field studies of mass communications bear witness—is still a factor to be reckoned with.

## SUPPORTIVE SELECTIVITY AMONG MASS MEDIA AUDIENCES

To restate the argument somewhat more carefully, we will be concerned with the hypotheses (a) that an individual self-censors his intake of communications so as to shield his beliefs and practices from attack; (b) that an individual seeks out communications which support his beliefs and practices; and (c) that the latter is particularly true when the beliefs or practices in question have undergone attack or the individual has otherwise been made less confident of them. Propositions (a) and (c) derive from Festinger's (1957) theory of dissonance. But, say Freedman and Sears, the "experimental evidence does not demonstrate that there is a general psychological tendency to avoid nonsupportive and to seek out supportive information" (p. 69), "nor the more specific hypothesis that whatever preference there is for supportive information will be greater under high than under low dissonance" (p. 75).

When Freedman and Sears turn from the laboratory evidence to the evidence from the (mostly nonexperimental) field studies of mass media campaigns, their argument necessarily changes. They do not say that these studies disprove the hypothesis of selectivity-for-the-purpose-of-obtaining-support but rather that other, more parsimonious, explanations have not been ruled out. Thus, they warn that field studies must take account of the relative availability of different kinds of information before concluding that supportive selectivity has taken place. Equally cogently, they insist that socioeconomic status be controlled before inferring supportive selectivity from findings such as that persons favorable to the United Nations were disproportionately exposed to a UN information campaign. This kind of finding, they rightly maintain, may reflect nothing more than the well-known fact that better-educated individuals are more likely to be in the audience for any communication in the field of public affairs and that better-educated individuals are probably more internationally minded.

While the criticism is sobering, a second look at the admittedly far-from-adequate evidence leaves one wondering whether it is really necessary to change one's bet.

The voting studies are the first to come to mind. Even after Freedman and Sears weight the selective exposure by Democrats and Republicans by the greater availability of Republican information in Erie County, Ohio (Lazarsfeld, Berelson, & Gaudet, 1948), there remains very clear evidence of selectivity on the part of the minority party. The same thing holds true—if one weights selectivity by availability in the later Elmira study (Berelson, Lazarsfeld, & McPhee, 1954, p. 245), though the authors do not make the claim themselves. A similar finding turns up in an English election study (Trenaman & McQuail, 1961, p. 87).

The latter, it should be pointed out, presents a stronger case for de facto than for "motivated" selectivity inasmuch as the correlation between partisanship and selective exposure to party *broadcasts* is only very weak while the relationship between partisanship and choice of partisan *newspapers* is strong. Our inference that this makes a better case for de facto selectivity is based on the assumption that the newspaper can be selected for a large variety of reasons other than political compatibility while the choice of a political broadcast is much more likely to reflect a desire to hear what one of the political parties has to say. Still, it is quite possible—and an interesting subject for comparative study—that Britons seek partisanship in print but fair-play and neutrality in radio and television. It is possible, in other words, that certain arenas are expected to be partisan while others are defined in terms of the expectation of "equal time."

Altogether, one must beware of the bias introduced in the search for selectivity in precisely those arenas where fair play and the hearing of both sides is a fundamental norm, such as in elections, jury trials, debates, and the like. Indeed, these institutions were virtually created to ensure exposure to both sides. Perhaps we should be surprised, therefore, to find any selective exposure at all.

The televised series of Kennedy-Nixon debates is a good example of this. The evidence from several studies (summarized in Katz & Feldman, 1962) indicates that an equally high proportion of members of both parties were in the audience—at least for the first debate. (Subsequent debates tended to include greater numbers of Nixon supporters, probably by virtue of their higher education.) It is particularly interesting, therefore, that there were proportionately more Catholics than Protestants in the audience, despite the generally higher educational and occupational status of the Protestants. Indeed, one of the studies (Deutschmann, 1962) found that those Protestants who mentioned religion as "the most important issue of the campaign" were far less likely to be in the viewing audience. This seems to be a real example of selective avoidance, though the number of cases involved is very small. Moreover, this same study demonstrates that after listening to the debate, listeners sought out somebody to talk with, and, overwhelmingly, this was somebody who shared the listener's initial political predisposition. While it is quite likely that this is another case of "de facto" selectivity, it is interesting to see how people move back and forth—within the same substantive realm—between partisan and non- or bipartisan exposures.

But if the audiences for political communications tend to be affected by norms of fair-play and de facto selectivity, neither of these factors seems important in the area of religious communications. It is almost too obvious to point out that not only do people attend the church of their choice, they also attend, very selectively, the religious broadcasts of their choice. In a study of the audience for religious broadcasting in New Haven, Parker, Barry, and Smythe (1955, p. 207) found that the audience for 5 Catholic programs was predominantly Catholic while the audience for 11 Protestant programs was mostly Protestant.[1] Or, to tell the story more exactly, the Catholics are strongly oriented to religious radio broadcasts, the Protestants are not. To the extent that Protestants listen at all (14 percent do), they listen in equal numbers to Protestant and to Catholic programs while a very large proportion of Catholics (41 percent) listen to Catholic programs, and only a small proportion (4 percent) to Protestant programs. Yet, since the total audience of the Protestant programs is small, and the number of religious listeners among the Catholics is very large, the small proportion of Catholics which listens to Protestant programs is enough to constitute a sizable minority. Note that the religious listeners among the Protestants act something like the Republicans in Erie County and Elmira, exposing themselves almost equally to both "parties," while the Catholics, like the Democrats, are much more strongly selective. There is a suggestion here that the "minority group" (in terms of the availability of supporting messages, not in terms of numbers in the population) exercises greater selectivity.

Are these people seeking support for their beliefs? It is difficult to imagine why else they are listening and, in the case of the Catholics, why they focus their attention on their own programs. Freedman and Sears say that church attendance may be motivated by factors other than the desire for reinforcement of belief, but even if this is so, the latent functions of attending to religious broadcasts are surely fewer. It is quite likely that such listening partakes of the feeling that one is in touch with one's "own" and that the mass media are duly recognizing one's belief culture, but these notions are very difficult to separate from the notion of seeking reinforcement.

Another of the studies on which the evidence for selective exposure rests is the classic field experiment reported by Hyman and Sheatsley (1947) in "Some Reasons Why Information Campaigns Fail." Respondents on a national survey were asked whether they had heard a given piece of news (the joint English-French-American announcement denouncing the Franco regime, and the proposal of an Anglo-American

Committee that the United States aid in keeping order in Palestine). All respondents—whether they said they had heard or not—were given the substance of the news items by the interviewer (preceded by "As you remember . . ." in the case of those who claimed they had heard). Respondents were then asked whether or not they favored each of the proposals. The finding that those who had heard previously were more favorable than those who had not is presented in support of the selective exposure hypothesis. It may be rightly objected that educational level should have been controlled since it is possible that persons of higher education would have been more likely both to have heard the news and to agree with these two policies. But assuming—and it is not unreasonable—that the finding would stand up under controls, it represents rather strong evidence in support of the "supportive" hypothesis whether one chooses to regard it as selective exposure or selective retention.

But the notion of selectively seeking support does not appear only in studies of the diffusion of information; it appears in studies of other uses of the mass media as well. A well-known example, though it is based on impressionistic evidence, is Warner's (1948) study of the soap opera, *Big Sister*. Warner argues that the program was so successful among its housewife listeners because it offered them reinforcement for their status in the person of an effective and influential housewife-heroine. In a world in which the housewifely role is challenged as uncreative and unworthy, these programs—so the argument goes—help to reduce the dissonance.

The evidence presented to this point is full of shortcomings and is certainly not conclusive, but it does seem to offer good reason for keeping the hypothesis alive. These studies and the ones criticized by Freedman and Sears (Star & Hughes, 1950; Cartwright, 1949; and others) were not designed, in general, to test the hypothesis that support is sought selectively in the mass media, and they cannot really prove it. The relationships are often weak, the formulations are not really tight, alternative explanations have not been ruled out, and the prevailing norms governing exposure are typically overlooked. These shortcomings are exacerbated by the fact that the kind of selective exposure in evidence in these studies is associated with the second, and least interesting, of the three hypotheses listed at the head of this section. In other words, the studies deal primarily with the observed correspondence between a person's attitudes and the communications to which he exposes himself and are virtually silent on whether individuals actively avoid communications that negate their beliefs, and whether the search for reinforcement is accelerated under conditions of dissonance. But the situation need not remain this way. The methodological possibilities of the panel (repeated interviews with the same respondents) or the field experiment, both of which add a time dimension to mass communications research, would certainly lend themselves to the design of more conclusive research in this area.

## UTILITY AS A BASIS OF SELECTIVITY

Even if the hypothesis of supportive selectivity stands up to genuine testing, as I suspect it will, it is very likely that other factors will prove more important as bases for selectivity in exposure to mass communications. Freedman and Sears are correct in calling for more serious attention to some of these other factors and to the psychological dynamics implicit in them.

Thus, Freedman and Sears emphasize the motive of "utility," suggesting that people want information when it answers a felt need or serves a practical purpose. When nonsupportive information is useful, the authors suggest, people will prefer it to less useful information that is supportive.

Freedman and Sears appear to mean by utility any piece of information that helps in the performance of a role or the successful completion of a task. In other words, the notion of utility in this broader sense is nothing short of a functional approach to mass media exposure. It asks, "What do people do with the media?" or, more exactly, "What patterns of communications behavior can be predicted from a knowledge of the needs of different kinds of people?"

Thus, Feldman (1965), for example, indicates that women are more exposed than men to health information—particularly the sort of information that has to do with symptoms of disease—and this despite the lower interest of women in many other substantive areas. Indeed, the difference in the degree of health knowledge between women and men is already evident in the ninth grade. Feldman suggests that these differences in knowledge, interest, and exposure have to do with the fulfillment of role expectations: Health information is "useful" to women in anticipating and carrying out their roles. The same sorts of expectations are directed to educated people and constitute one of the explanations why education is so consistently related to high levels of exposure to all sorts of information, particularly in the realm of public affairs. It also explains why opinion leaders selectively attend to those media which bring information in their own spheres of influence but not to others (Katz, 1958).

Some kinds of exposure, however, are "useful" precisely because they are "useless" in that they permit people to avoid, or escape, the performance of a task or a role (cf. Katz & Foulkes, 1962). For example, the less one has of whatever it is that one's schoolmates happen to value (grades, athletic prowess, money), the more heavily one is exposed to the media, particularly to popular expressions of adolescent protest and alienation (Johnstone, 1961).

But "useful" information can also be rejected—even when it seems to answer an objectively defined need—if one perceives oneself as useless. Thus, in an extremely interesting series of studies, Seeman (1966) has demonstrated that individuals who rank themselves near the "powerlessness" end of a scale manage to avoid learning information which would be of use to them in their specific situations (reformatory, hospital, workers' organizations) although they do not differ from others on the learning of information unrelated to the exercise of control in their environments. These are studies of selective learning rather than selective exposure, but their import seems very much the same. Indeed, they are very closely related to the finding (Schramm, Lyle, & Parker, 1961) that the greater the disparity between a child's own aspirations and the perceived aspirations for him of parents and peers (where the latter are higher than the former), the greater the exposure to "fantasy-oriented" media and the lower the exposure to "reality-oriented" media. In other words, it appears as if beliefs can sometimes override utility as a selective factor in exposure, bringing the argument full circle.

INTEREST AS A BASIS OF SELECTIVITY

Apart from the quest for support and for utility, mere interest would seem to be an important factor in selectivity. The desire to see one's self-reflection is part of this. So is the desire to keep watch over things in which one has invested one's ego. Thus, moviegoers identify with screen stars of similar age and sex (Handel, 1950; Maccoby & Wilson, 1957); one reads in the newspaper about an event in which one personally participated; one reads advertisements for the product one purchased (Ehrlich et al., 1957; Mills, 1965); political partisans immerse themselves in political communications regardless of its source; smokers choose to read material supporting the smoking-lung cancer relationship no less than material disclaiming the relationship, and much more avidly than nonsmokers (Feather, 1963); after one has been introduced to a celebrity one notices (or "follows") his name in print even more frequently.

But while the examples just cited suggest that "interest" as a basis of selective exposure is a different sort of thing than exposure on the basis of seeking support (interest leads to exposure to *both* sides of the argument), it is not as easy as it sounds to separate interest from utility and support-seeking. Indeed, some of the examples themselves are used as arguments for supportive selectivity. The problem of distinguishing between the two processes arises as soon as one postulates that interest is, or leads to, ego-involvement. And, if one then hypothesizes—in the spirit of dissonance theory— a continual quest for assurance that one's ego is worthy or well-cathected, the seeing of oneself or one's interests reflected and validated in the mass media is a kind of supportive selectivity—even when such communications are negative.[2] The famous public relations slogan sums this up very well: "Don't mind what they say about you, just as long as they mention your name." Narcissism, in other words, may have some built-in dissonance, and the consequent quest for external validation may not be easily distinguishable from ego-involvement. But this, of course, is simply another example of the overall problem of isolating the supportive motive in selective exposure. In principle, however, the distinction is clear: Interest, or investment of the ego, may be followed by the desire for validation, and either or both of these may lead to selective exposure.

There is another aspect to the relationship between interest and support as bases of selectivity. We tend to think of opinions as consisting of a component of general interest in a subject, and a component of specific partisanship. Thus, we think of political partisans as having interest in politics in general and a specific partisan commitment. But many opinions or commitments do not work this way. It may well be, for example, that individuals do not have much interest in religion in general, but only in their own denominations. Or, to take another example, it may well be that general interest in a subject—Franco Spain, for example, to hark back to the Hyman-Sheatsley (1947) example—is manifested only by those who are on one side (opponents of the regime, in this case) and that there simply is no "other side" among those who are interested. There are many issues which have enthusiasts on only one side, while all the rest are disinterested (and, by definition, nonpartisan). Studies of selective exposure on a given issue should take account of the empirical relationship between interest and partisanship. Thus, the pro-Franco respondents who had missed the anti-Franco message, according to Hyman and Sheatsley, may have missed the message not because they disagreed but because they were uninterested. And the anti-Franco people, for their part, may have caught the message because they were interested rather than because they were partisan, and would have been equally aware of a pro-Franco communiqué. Methodologically, this argument is exactly analogous to Freedman and Sears' call for holding educational level constant in tests of the supportiveness hypothesis. Interest and utility must be added to the list of factors to control. In any given case, however, it may turn out that selective exposure on the basis of interest and selective exposure on the basis of seeking support may be indistinguishable because interest in a subject may be identical with partisanship.

## ADDITIONAL NOTES AND CONCLUSIONS
The hypothesis that individuals seek information that will support their beliefs and practices and avoid information that challenges them still seems viable from the vantage point of mass communications research. Reexamination of the evidence in the wake of the objections raised by Freedman and Sears, however, reveals how little evidence is required for an hypothesis to be accepted as "proven."

Studies are cited from the fields of public affairs, voting, religion, etc., in support of the hypothesis, though none of them can be considered conclusive or a really strict test. Echoing Freedman and Sears, we have been underlining the importance of holding certain other factors constant before concluding that partisanship is the motivating factor in selective exposure.

But it is not easy to test the hypothesis, especially in a field situation. An ideal test requires (a) the taking account of time, in order to demonstrate that partisanship causes selective exposure rather than vice versa; and (b) a situation in which communications are available on both sides of an issue, and where there is a corresponding division of opinion. But this does not solve the problem of how to demonstrate in the field that people avoid uncongenial information, independent of their preference for congenial information. Some adaptation of the Hyman-Sheatsley (1947) method to include "neutral" communications might prove effective here, in much the way that Mills (1965) compares the degree of interest expressed by respondents in reading about accepted and rejected products and other products which are neither accepted nor rejected.

Further thought must also be given to field-testing the hypothesized relationship between the extent of support-seeking and the magnitude of dissonance. An attempt in this direction was made by Troldahl (1963) in a field experiment which predicted, among other things, that there would be greater advice-giving and greater advice-seeking in interpersonal communication under conditions of inconsistency between a message and previous beliefs. Unfortunately, however, the experimental message, "planted" in an agricultural bulletin directed to suburban farmers, failed to arouse much interest, and consequently there was hardly enough interpersonal communication to test the hypothesis.

An even more basic methodological problem to which attention must be given in field studies has to do with the operational definition of selective exposure itself. What are the mechanisms by means of which individuals recognize that they are in the presence of supportive or discrepant information: Do they scan headlines? Do they anticipate what the content of a communication is likely to be from its source? How, in other words, does an individual select among communications according to the supportiveness principle without being exposed to them? In the laboratory, the subject is asked, typically, whether he would like to read a pamphlet or an advertisement taking a stand for or against his opinion or behavior, or he is shown a list of titles from which to choose. Intuitively, this would seem to be the rough equivalent of headline-reading as a means of selectivity, but is it? And how does this work in the case of TV programs? Or conversation?

Altogether, this paper argues that the supportive selectivity hypothesis is, in part, a special case of an approach to the problem of exposure in terms of "uses" or "gratifications," i.e., in functional terms. Some of the evidence for selective exposure on the basis of utility is reviewed, and the concept of "use" is considerably broadened. It is suggested that a conflict over whether to attend to a communication which includes both nonsupportive and useful elements may be resolved either way. Interest, or ego-involvement, is also discussed as a basis for selective exposure.

The discussion of utility and interest, and to a certain extent, the discussion of supportiveness itself, indicates that the problem of selectivity is not limited to the sphere of mass media information. It relates equally to entertainment and other forms of mass media content, and, indeed, to exposure to the mass media per se (regardless of content). Concern with the notion of utility reflects the overall shift in mass media research away from studies of short-run changes of information and attitude as a result of mass media campaigns to studies of different ways in which mass media messages serve the social and psychological needs of their audiences.

## NOTES

I should like to thank Miss Mady Wechsler for research assistance in this project, and the Social Science Research Committee of the University of Chicago for financial aid.

1. The Catholic programs were not all explicitly such; content analysis confirmed the arbitrary assignment to categories (i.e., the programs designated Catholic had more Catholic content). Although the local audience for Protestant programs was quite small, there were a large number of such programs on the air.
2. I assume here that we are dealing with persons who have high self-esteem (highly positive self concepts) in the area under discussion.

This would exclude situations such as those in the Aronson and Carlsmith (1962) study where subjects were purportedly behaving so as to obtain information confirming their low opinions of themselves (see also McGuire, 1966, 498-500).

## REFERENCES

Aronson, E., and Carlsmith, J. M., "Performance Expectancy as a Determinant of Actual Performance," *Journal of Abnormal and Social Psychology*, 1962, **65**, 178-182.

Berelson, B. R., Lazarsfeld, P. F., and McPhee, W. N., *Voting*, Chicago: University of Chicago Press, 1954.

Cartwright, D., "Some Principles of Mass Persuasion," *Human Relations*, 1949, **2**, 253-267.

Deutschmann, P., "Viewing, Conversation, and Voting Intentions," in S. Kraus (ed.), *The Great Debates*, Bloomington: University of Indiana Press, 1962.

Ehrlich, D., Guttman, I., Schonbach, P., and Mills, J., "Post-Decision Exposure to Relevant Information," *Journal of Abnormal and Social Psychology*, 1957, **54**, 98-102.

Feather, N. T., "Cognitive Dissonance, Sensitivity, and Evaluation," *Journal of Abnormal and Social Psychology*, 1963, **66**, 157-163.

Feldman, J. J., "The Dissemination of Health Information: A Case Study of Adult Learning," unpublished doctoral dissertation, University of Chicago, 1965.

Festinger, L., *A Theory of Cognitive Dissonance*, New York: Harper & Row, 1957.

Freedman, J. L., and Sears, D. O., "Selective Exposure," in L. Berkowitz (ed.), *Advances in Experimental Social Psychology*, vol. 2, New York: Academic, 1965, 58-98.

Handel, Leo, *Hollywood Looks at Its Audience*, Urbana: University of Illinois Press, 1950.

Hyman, H., and Sheatsley, P. B., "Some Reasons Why Information Campaigns Fail," *Public Opinion Quarterly*, 1947, **11**, 412-423.

Johnstone, J. W. C., "Social Structure and Patterns of Mass Media Consumption," unpublished doctoral dissertation, University of Chicago, 1961.

Katz, E., "The Two-Step Flow of Communication: An Up-to-date Report on an Hypothesis," *Public Opinion Quarterly*, 1958, **21**, 61-78.

Katz, E., and Feldman, J. J., "The Kennedy-Nixon Debates: A Survey of Surveys," in S. Kraus (ed.), *The Great Debates*, Bloomington: University of Indiana Press, 1962.

Katz, E., and Foulkes, D., "On the Use of the Mass Media as 'Escape': Clarification of a Concept," *Public Opinion Quarterly*, 1962, **26**, 377-388.

Lazarsfeld, P., Berelson, B., Gaudet, H., *The People's Choice*, New York: Columbia University Press, 1948.

Maccoby, E. E., and Wilson, W. C., "Identification and Observational Learning from Films," *Journal of Abnormal and Social Psychology*, 1957, **55**, 76-87.

McGuire, W. J., "Attitudes and Opinions," *Annual Review of Psychology*, 1966, **17**, 475-514.

Mills, J., "Avoidance of Dissonant Information," *Journal of Personality and Social Psychology*, 1965, **2**, 589-593.

Parker, E. C., Barry, D. W., and Smythe, D. W., *The Television-Radio Audience and Religion*, New York: Harper & Row, 1955.

Schramm, W., Lyle, J., and Parker, E. B., *Television in the Lives of Our Children*, Stanford, Calif.: Stanford University Press, 1961.

Seeman, M., "Alienation, Membership, and Political Knowledge," *Public Opinion Quarterly*, 1966, **30**, 353-367.

Trenaman, J., and McQuail, D., *Television and the Political Image*, London: Methuen, 1961.

Troldahl, V. C., "Mediated Communication and Personal Influence," unpublished doctoral dissertation, University of Minnesota, 1963.

Warner, W. L., "The Radio Daytime Serial: A Symbolic Analysis," *Genetic Psychology Monographs*, No. 37, 1948.

# COMMUNICATION: THE FLOW OF INFORMATION
## Daniel Katz and Robert L. Kahn

The world we live in is basically a world of people. Most of our actions toward others and their actions toward us are communicative acts in whole or in part, whether or not they reach verbal expression. This is as true of behavior in organizations as in other contexts. We have said that human organizations are informational as well as energic systems, and that every organization must take in and utilize information. The intake and distribution of information are also energic processes, of course; acts of sending and receiving information demand energy for their accomplishment. Their energic demands, however, are negligible in comparison with their significance and implications as symbolic acts—as acts of communication and control.

When one walks from a factory to the adjoining head-house or office, the contrast is conspicuous. One goes from noise to quiet, from heavy electrical cables and steam pipes to slim telephone lines, from a machine-dominated to a people-dominated environment. One goes, in short, from a sector of the organization in which energic exchange is primary and information exchange secondary, to a sector where the priorities are reversed. The closer one gets to the organizational center of control and decision-making, the more pronounced is the emphasis on information exchange.

In this sense, communication—the exchange of information and the transmission of meaning—is the very essence of a social system or an organization. The input of physical energy is dependent upon information about it, and the input of human energy is made possible through communicative acts. Similarly the transformation of energy (the accomplishment of work) depends upon communication between people in each organizational subsystem and upon communication be-

Reprinted by permission from *The Social Psychology of Organizations* by Daniel Katz and Robert L. Kahn, New York: Wiley, pp. 223-229. Copyright © 1966 by John Wiley & Sons, Inc. The quotation from *Public Opinion* by Walter Lippmann is reprinted by permission of The Macmillan Company, New York. Copyright 1950 by Walter Lippmann.

tween subsystems. The product exported carries meaning as it meets needs and wants, and its use is further influenced by the advertising or public relations material about it. The amount of support which an organization receives from its social environment is also affected by the information which elite groups and wider publics have acquired about its goals, activities, and accomplishments.

Communication is thus a social process of the broadest relevance in the functioning of any group, organization, or society. It is possible to subsume under it such forms of social interaction as the exertion of influence, cooperation, social contagion or imitation, and leadership. We shall consider communication in this broad sense, with emphasis upon the structural aspects of the information process in organizations, but with attention also to the motivational basis for transmitting and receiving messages.

It is a common assumption that many of our problems, individual and social, are the result of inadequate and faulty communication. As Newcomb (1947) points out, autistic hostility decreases communication and in turn decreased communication enhances autistic hostility. If we can only increase the flow of information, we are told, we can solve these problems. This assumption is found in our doctrine of universal education. It is fundamental in most campaigns of public relations and public enlightenment. Our democratic institutions, with their concern for freedom of speech and assembly, their rejection of censorship, and their acceptance of the principle of equal time for the arguments of opposing political parties, have extended the notion of competition in the market place to a free market for ideas. Truth will prevail if there is ready access to all the relevant information.

The glorification of a full and free information flow is a healthy step forward in intraorganizational problems as well as in the relations of an organization to the larger social system. It is, however, a gross oversimplification. Communication may reveal problems as well as eliminate them. A conflict in values, for example, may go unnoticed until communication is attempted. Communication may also have the effect, intended or unintended, of obscuring and confusing existing problems. The vogue enjoyed by the word *image* in recent years reflects in part an unattractive preoccupation with communication as a means of changing the perception of things without the expense and inconvenience of changing the things themselves. The television commercials, with their incessant and spurious assertion of new products and properties are the worst of numberless examples. In short, the advocacy of communication needs to be qualified with respect to the kind of information relevant to the solution of given problems and with respect to the nature of the communication process between individuals, between groups, and between subsystems.

Communication needs to be seen not as a process occurring between any sender of messages and any potential recipient, but in relation to the social system in which it occurs and the particular function it performs in that system. General principles of communication as a social-psychological process are fine; they set the limits within which we must operate. But they need to be supplemented by an analysis of the social system, so that they can be applied correctly to given situations.

The discovery of the crucial role of communication led to an enthusiastic advocacy of increased information as the solution to many organizational problems. More and better communication (especially, more) was the slogan. Information to rank-and-file employees about company goals and policies was the doctrine; the means too often were stylized programs and house organs homogenized by the Flesch formula for basic English. Communication up the line to give top echelons a more accurate picture of the lower levels was a complementary emphasis.

## SOCIAL SYSTEMS AS RESTRICTED
## COMMUNICATION NETWORKS

Though there were and are good outcomes of this simplistic approach, there are also weak, negligible, and negative outcomes. The blanket emphasis upon more communication fails to take into account the functioning of an organization as a social system and the specific needs of the subsystems.

In the first place, as Thelen (1960b) points out, an organized state of affairs, a social system, implies the restriction of communication among its members. If we take an unorganized group, say 60 people milling around at random in a large room, the number of potential channels of communication is $n(n-1)/2$ or 1770. If, however, they are organized into a network of twelve combinations of five such that each person on a five-man team has one clearly defined role and is interdependent with four other people, the number of channels within the work group is reduced to *ten* in a completely interdependent condition or to *four* in a serial dependent position.

Without going into such complexities as task-relevant communication, the major point is clear. To move from an unorganized state to an organized state requires the introduction of constraints and restrictions to reduce diffuse and random communication to channels appropriate for the accomplishment of organizational objectives. It may require also the introduction of incentives to use those channels and use them appropriately, rather than leave them silent or use them for organizationally irrelevant purposes. Organizational development sometimes demands the creation of new communication channels. The very nature of a social system, however, implies a selectivity of channels and communicative acts—a mandate to avoid some and to utilize others.

In terms of information theory, unrestricted communication produces noise in the system. Without patterning, without pauses, without precision, there is sound but there is no music. Without structure, without spacing, without specifications, there is a Babel of tongues but there is no meaning.

The same basic problem of selectivity in communications can be considered in terms of Ashby's (1952) conceptual model. Thelen (1960a) summarizes the Ashby contribution in these terms.

*Any living system* is an infinitely complex association of subsystems. The complex suprasystem has all the properties of a subsystem plus communication across the boundaries of subsystems. Ashby's brilliant treatment (1952) shows that stability of the suprasystem would take infinitely long to achieve *if* there were "full and rich communication" among the subsystems (because in effect all the variables of all the subsystems would have to be satisfied at once—a most unlikely event). If communication among subsystems is restricted or if they are temporarily isolated, then each subsystem achieves its own stability with minimum interference by the changing environment of other systems seeking *their* stability. With restricted communication, success can accumulate (from successive trials, for example), whereas in the single suprasystem, success is all-or-none. . . . Thus the way an overall system moves toward its equilibrium depends very much on the functional connectedness of its parts. Adaptation of the whole system makes use of two conditions: Enough connectedness that operation of one subsystem can activate another so that the contributions of all can contribute to the whole; and enough separation of subsystems that some specialization of function is possible and such that "equilibrium" can be approached in the system as a whole. But no complex suprasystem would ever have equilibrium in all its subsystems at the same time. Each subsystem has the "power of veto" over equilibria in other subsystems, and under a variety of conditions one subsystem can dominate another.

Our loosely organized political system reflects the system requirements of restriction of full and free communication. Chaos in national decision-making is avoided by the device of the two-party system. Instead of representing in clear fashion in Congress all the factional groups and subsystems within the nation, we go through a quadrennial process of successive agreements within the major parties, culminating in the nomination of a presidential candidate by each of them. This is in effect a restriction and channeling of the communication process. Once candidates are selected, the factional groups within each party tend to unite behind one ticket, and the amount of communication to the candidates is restricted. The rank-and-file voter neither communicates up the line nor receives much in the way of communication down the line except for the projected image of the candidate and the general image of the party.

In fact, the average voter is woefully ignorant of the stand of his party on most political issues. On 16 major issues of the 1956 presidential election, the proportion of people who had an opinion, knew what the government was doing, and saw some differences between the parties never exceeded 36 percent and for some issues was as low as 18 percent (Campbell, et al., 1960). This is one price we pay for the organizational restrictions of a two-party system and the communication distance between the voters and political leaders. Nevertheless, the two-party system has the advantage of overall political stability and facilitation of national decision-making. If all interested groups and ideological factions had their own parties and their own representatives in Congress, we would have more complete communication between the people and their elected leaders but we would have terrific problems of attaining system stability. We would have many possibilities of veto by coalition of minority groups, of legislative stale-mates, and of national indecision. Some European countries with multiple-party systems, with more communication, and perhaps better-informed electorates have had such problems.

## THE CODING PROCESS

Individuals, groups, and organizations share a general charac-teristic which must be recognized as a major determinant of communication: The coding process. Any system which is the recipient of information, whether it be an individual or an organization, has a characteristic coding process, a limited set of coding categories to which it assimilates the information received. The nature of the system imposes omission, selec-tion, refinement, elaboration, distortion, and transformation upon the incoming communications. Just as the human eye selects and transforms light waves to which it is attuned to give perceptions of color and objects, so too does any system convert stimulation according to its own properties. It has been demonstrated that human beings bring with them into most situations sets of categories for judging the facts before them. Walter Lippmann (1922) called attention to the coding process years ago in the following famous passages. Even then he was merely putting into dramatic form what had been recognized by the ancient philosophers.

For the most part we do not first see, and then define, we define first and then see. In the great blooming, buzzing confusion of the outer world, we pick out what our culture has already defined for us, and we tend to perceive that which we have picked out in the form stereotyped for us by our culture. (p. 31)

What matters is the character of the stereotypes and the gullibility with which we employ them. And these in the end depend upon those inclusive patterns which constitute our philosophy of life. If in that philosophy we assume that the world is codified according to a code we possess, we are likely to make our reports of what is going on describe a world run by our code. (p. 90)

Most of us would deal with affairs through a rather haphazard and shifting assortment of stereotypes, if a comparatively few men in each generation were not constantly engaged in arranging, standardizing, and improving them into logical systems, known as the Laws of Political Economy, the Principles of Politics, and the like. (pp. 104-105)

Organizations, too, have their own coding systems which determine the amount and type of information they receive from the external world and the transformation of it according to their own systemic properties. The most general limitation is that the position people occupy in organizational space will determine their perception and interpretation of incoming information and their search for additional information. In other words, the structure and functions of a given subsystem will be reflected in the frame of reference and way of thinking of the role incumbents of that sector of organizational space.

All members of an organization are affected by the fact that they occupy a common organizational space in contrast to those who are not members. By passing the boundary and becoming a functioning member of the organization, the person takes on some of the coding system of the organization since he accepts some of its norms and values, absorbs some of its subculture, and develops shared expectations and values with other members. The boundary condition is thus responsible for the dilemma that the person within the system cannot perceive things and communicate about them in the same way that an outsider would. If a person is within a system, he sees its operations differently than if he were on the outside looking in. It is extremely difficult to occupy different positions in social space without a resulting differential perception. Where boundary conditions are fluid and organizational members are very loosely confined within the system (as with people sent abroad to live among foreign nationals for some governmental agency) there will be limited tours of duty, alternation between foreign and domestic service, and careful debriefing sessions to insure that life outside the physical boundaries of the country has not imparted too much of the point of view of the outsider.

## THE PROBLEM OF TRANSLATION ACROSS
## SUBSYSTEM BOUNDARIES

Within an organization there are problems of clear communication across subsystems. The messages emanating in one part of the organization need translation if they are to be fully effective in other parts. In an earlier chapter, reference was made to Parsons' (1960) specific application of this principle to the chain of command. Instead of a unitary chain from the top to the bottom of an organization, Parsons pointed out that there are significant breaks between the institutional and managerial levels and again between the managerial and technical levels. Communications, then, must be transmitted in general enough terms to permit modification within each of these levels. The same type of translation problem occurs between any pair of substructures having their own functions and their own coding schema. Without adequate translation across subsystem boundaries, communications can add to the noise in the system.

## REFERENCES

Ashby, W. R., *Design for a Brain*, New York: Wiley, 1952.

Campbell, A., Converse, P. E., Miller, W. E., and Stokes, D. E., *The American Voter*, New York: Wiley, 1960.

Lippmann, W., *Public Opinion*, New York: Harcourt Brace Jovanovich, 1922.

Newcomb, T. M., "Autistic Hostility and Social Reality," *Human Relations*, 1, 69-86.

Parsons, T., *Structure and Process in Modern Societies*, New York: Free Press, 1960.

Thelen, H. A., "Exploration of a Growth Model for Psychic, Biological, and Social Systems," mimeographed paper, 1960(a).

Thelen, H. A., personal communication to authors, 1960(b).

# THE SOCIAL EFFECTS OF MASS COMMUNICATION
## Joseph T. Klapper

The title of this paper is extremely broad. Almost any effect which mass communication might have upon large numbers of people could legitimately be called a social effect, for people make up society, and whatever affects large numbers of people thus inevitably affects society.

We might therefore consider any of a thousand different social effects of mass communication—for example, how mass communication affects people's political opinions and voting behavior, or how it affects its audience's purchases of consumer goods. We might also consider somewhat more abstract topics, such as the ways in which mass communication has changed the social structure as a whole and the relationships of the people within it. . . .

It is difficult to deal with so immense a topic in the limited space available here. Perhaps I might best begin by citing some broad general principles which are, I believe, applicable to the effects of mass communication within a vast number of specific topical areas. I will then illustrate these principles by reference to two such specific areas of effect: First, the effect of mass communication upon the esthetic and intellectual tastes of its audiences and, second, the question of how these audiences are affected by the crime and violence that is depicted in mass communication. I have selected these two topics because they seem to me matters of social importance as well as popular concern, . . . and because a good deal of information pertinent to these topics has been provided by high-quality communications research. I would like to recall, however, that the principles which I will first develop can be applied to many other types of effect as well. And although we may talk today primarily of levels of public taste and of the effects of crime and violence, I believe that the same principles will be helpful guidelines in considering the probable nature of other social effects of mass communication.

The first point I wish to make is rather obvious, but its implications are often overlooked. I would like to point out that the audience for mass communication consists of people, and that these people live among other people and amid social institutions. Each of these people has been subject and continues to be subject to numerous influences besides mass communication. All but the infants have attended schools and churches and have listened to and conversed with teachers and preachers and with friends and colleagues. They have read books or magazines. All of them, including the infants, have been members of a family group. As a result of these influences, they have developed opinions on a great variety of topics, a set of values, and a set of behavioral tendencies. These predispositions are part of the person, and he carries them with him when he serves as a member of the audience for mass communication. The person who hears a radio address urging him to vote for a particular political candidate probably had some political opinion of his own before he turned on the set. The housewife who casually switches on the radio and hears the announcer state that a classical music program is to follow is probably already aware that she does or does not like classical music. The man who sees a crime play on television almost surely felt, before seeing the play, that a life of crime was or was not his dish.

It is obvious that a single movie or radio or television program is not very likely to change the existing attitudes of audience members, particularly if these attitudes are relatively deep-seated. What is not so obvious is that these attitudes, these predispositions, are at work before and during exposure to mass communications, and that they in fact largely determine the communications to which the individual is exposed, what he remembers of such communications, how he interprets their contents, and the effect which mass communications have upon him.

Communications research has consistently revealed, for example, that people tend in the main to read, watch, or listen to communications which present points of view with which they are themselves in sympathy and tend to avoid communications of a different hue. During pre-election campaigns in the United States, for example, Republicans have been found to listen to more Republican-sponsored speeches than Democratic-sponsored programs, while Democrats do precisely the opposite. Persons who smoke have been found to be less likely to read newspaper articles about smoking and cancer than those who do not smoke. Dozens of other research findings show that people expose themselves to mass communication selectively. They select material which is in accord with their existing views and interests, and they largely avoid material which is not in accord with those views and interests.

Research has also shown that people *remember* material which supports their own point of view much better than they remember material which attacks that point of view. Put another way, retention, as well as exposure, is largely selective.

Finally, and in some senses most importantly, perception, or interpretation, is also selective. By this I mean that people who are exposed to communications with which they are unsympathetic not uncommonly distort the contents so that they end up perceiving the message as though it supported their own point of view. Communications condemning racial discrimination, for example, have been interpreted by prejudiced persons as favoring such discrimination. Persons who smoke cigarettes, to take another example, were found to be not only less likely than nonsmokers to read articles about smoking and cancer, but also to be much less likely to become convinced that smoking actually caused cancer.

Now it is obvious that if people tend to expose themselves mainly to mass communications in accord with their existing views and interests and to avoid other material, and if, in addition, they tend to forget such other material as they see, and if, finally, they tend to distort such other material as they remember, then clearly mass communication is not very likely to change their views. It is far, far more likely to support and reinforce their existing views.

There are other factors, besides the selective processes, which tend to render mass communication a more likely agent of reinforcement than of change. One of these is the groups and the norms of groups to which the audience member belongs. Another is the workings of interpersonal influence. A third involves the economic aspects of mass media in free enterprise societies. Limitations of space do not permit me to discuss these factors here, but those who are sufficiently interested in this topic will find them all discussed in the literature of communication research.

It will of course be understood that, again because of space limitations, I am writing in terms of general tendencies, and that I cannot here discuss all the exceptions to these general tendencies. I can only say that there are exceptions and that these, too, are discussed in the literature. But the exceptions are, at least in my opinion, precisely that—exceptions. And I have in fact gone so far as to assert, in some writings of my own, and on the basis of the findings of numerous studies performed by numerous people, that the typical effect of mass communication is reinforcive. I have also stated, as I have tried to show in this paper, that this tendency derives from the fact that mass communication seldom works directly upon its audience. The audience members do not present themselves to the radio or the television set or the newspaper in a state of psychological nudity; they are, instead, clothed and protected by existing predispositions, by the selective processes, and by other factors. I have proposed that these factors serve to mediate the effect of mass communication, and that it is because of this mediation that mass communication usually serves as an agent of reinforcement.

Now this does not mean that mass communication can *never* produce changes in the ideas or the tastes or the values or the behavior of its audience. In the first place, as I have already mentioned, the factors which promote reinforcive effects do not function with 100 percent efficiency. In the second place, and more importantly, the very same factors sometimes maximize the likelihood of mass communications serving in the interest of change. This process occurs when the audience member is *predisposed* toward change. For example, a person may, for one reason or another, find his previous beliefs, his previous attitudes, and his accustomed mode of behavior to be no longer psychologically satisfying. He might, for example, become disillusioned with his political party, or his church, or—on another level—he might become bored with the kind of music to which he ordinarily listens. Such a person is likely to seek new faiths, or to experiment with new kinds of music. He has become, as it were, *predisposed to change*. And just as his previous loyalties protected him from mass communications which were out of accord with those loyalties, so his new predispositions will make him susceptible to the influence of those same communications from which he was previously effectively guarded.

Let us now pause for a moment and look back over the way we have come. I have cited what I believe to be three basic principles about the effects of mass communication. I have stated, first, that the influence of mass communication is mediated by such factors as predispositions, selective processes, group memberships, and the like. I have proposed, secondly, that these factors usually render mass communication an agent of reinforcement. Finally, I have said that these very same factors may under some conditions make mass communication an agent of change. All of this has been said in a rather abstract context. Let us now see how these principles apply in reference to such specific topics as the effect of mass communication on levels of public taste, and the effect of depictions of crime and violence.

We would all agree, I believe, that a great proportion of the material on the mass media is on a rather low esthetic and intellectual level. The media do, of course, provide classical music, readings and dramatizations of great books, public affairs programs, and other high-level material. But the lesser material greatly predominates. And we are all familiar with the frequently expressed fear that this heavy diet of light fare will debase or has already debased the esthetic and intellectual tastes of society as a whole. What has communications research discovered in reference to this matter?

Communications research long ago established that the principle of selective exposure held in reference to matters of taste. Persons who habitually read good books were found to listen to good radio programs, and persons who read light books or no books were found to listen to light radio programs. Recent research has indicated that children and young people who like light fiction will tend to seek light entertainment at the television set, and that people who read books on public affairs will find and witness television discussions on public affairs.

Increasing the amount of high-level material on the air has been found to serve very little purpose. There is already a good deal of fine material available on radio and television. Those who like it find it. Those who don't like it turn to other programs which, at least in this country, are almost always available. In short, and in accord with the basic principles I previously mentioned, mass communication generally serves to feed and to reinforce its audience's existing tastes,* rather than to debase or to improve them.

But this is by no means to say that mass media are never involved in changing the tastes of their audience. Our third principle, it will be recalled, states that mass communication will change people if they are already predisposed to change. Let me give an example of this principle at work in reference to levels of taste.

Some years ago a student of communication research made a study of persons who listened to certain serious music programs on the radio. He found that the overwhelming majority had long been lovers of serious music, although some of them, for various reasons, had been unable to hear as much of it as they would have liked until radio made it so easily accessible. About 15 percent of the group, however, considered that the radio had initiated their liking for classical music. But—and here is the essential point—closer analysis revealed that most of these people were predisposed to develop a liking for such music before they began listening to the programs. Some of them, for example, wanted to emulate friends who were serious music lovers. Others had attained a social or occupational status such that they felt they *ought* to be interested in serious music. With these predispositions, they found or sought out the serious music programs, and grew to like that kind of music. Their tastes had indeed been changed by the programs, but they had come to the programs already predisposed to change their tastes. Mass media had simply provided the means for the change.

Findings of this sort inevitably inspire the question of whether it would be possible deliberately to create in people predispositions to enlarge their intellectual and esthetic horizons, and so nurture a widespread rise in levels of taste. Such hypothetical developments are somewhat beyond the scope of this paper, but I would venture the guess that such a development would be possible if it were sufficiently carefully planned and executed. Children seem to me particularly good subjects for such an attempt, since children are naturally "changers." As they grow older, they naturally change in various physical and psychological ways. Their habits of media usage change too, if only in the sense that they progress from material designed for children to material designed for adults. The problem is, then, to so predispose them that they advance not merely to material designed for adults but continue on to progressively better adult material.

I cannot here go into the findings of research pertinent to this problem, but I will say, by way of summary, that this research indicates that even among children mass media do not so much determine levels of taste, but are, rather, used by the child in accordance with his already existing tastes. These tastes appear to be a product of such extra-media factors as the tastes of the child's parents and peer group members, the nature of his relationship with these people, and the child's own level of intelligence and degree of emotional adjustment. Insofar as these conditions are manipulable by parents, by schools, and by social programs, it would appear possible to develop predispositions for high-quality media material, which predispositions could then be served and reinforced by mass media themselves. I would point out, however, that in such a process the media would be functioning in their usual adjunctive manner. They would not be serving, in and of themselves, to elevate standards of public taste. They would rather be serving to supply a channel of change for which their audience had already been predisposed.

Let us now turn to the question of the effect of crime and violence in mass communication. Everyone will agree, I think, that depictions of crime and violence abound in the media. And we are all familiar with the widely expressed fear that these portrayals will adversely affect the values and behavior of the media audiences, possibly to the point of individuals actually committing criminal violence. Communications research, for all its attention to this matter, has not yet provided wholly definitive conclusions. The accumulating findings, however, seem to indicate that the same old principles apply.

A large number of studies have compared children who are heavy consumers of crime and violence material with children who consume little or none of it. Many of these studies have found no differences between the two groups: Heavy users were found, for example, to be no more likely than light users or nonusers to engage in delinquent behavior, or to be absent from school, or to achieve less in school. Other studies, which inquired more deeply into the psychological characteristics of heavy and light consumers, have found differences between the two groups. Heavy users have been found, for example, in one or another study, to be more likely to have problems relative to their relationships with their families and friends, to place blame for difficulties on others rather than themselves, to be somewhat more aggressive, and to have somewhat lower I.Q.s. Children who did not have satisfactory relations with their peers were found in one study not only to be particularly drawn to such material but also to employ it as a stimulant for asocial fantasies. The children with good peer relations, on the other hand, employed the same material as a basis for group games.

Let us now draw some implications from these findings. First of all, since both delinquent and nondelinquent children are found among heavy users of crime and violence material, we may assume that the material is not in and of itself a prime cause of delinquent tendencies. Secondly, such differences as have been found between heavy and light users consist of personality and emotional factors which seem unlikely to have been the *product* of exposure to the media. Finally, the uses to which the material is put appears to be dependent upon these same personality factors. Here again, then, our old principles seem to be at work: Children appear to interpret and react to such material in accordance with their existing needs and values, and the material thus serves to reinforce their existing attitudes, regardless of whether these existing attitudes are socially wholesome or socially unwholesome. The media, as usual, seem to be not a prime determinant of behavioral tendencies but rather a reinforcing agent for such tendencies.

Our basic principles would, however, lead us to expect that the media might play a role in changing the values and behavioral tendencies of audience members who were, for one reason or another, predisposed to change. Unfortunately, I know of no research which throws any light on this topic in relation to tendencies to criminal or violent behavior. Several such studies are now in progress, but none has yet reached the reporting stage.[1]

Here again, as in the case of the discussion of levels of taste, one must inevitably wonder how the undesirable effects might be minimized. And here again the nature of existing research findings suggests that the road cannot involve the media alone. Remedies, if they can be defined at all, seem likely to involve the family, the schools, and all of those forces which create the values and the personality which the child, or the adult, brings to the media experience.

So much, then, for the effects of depictions of crime and violence, and so much for the effects of mass communication on levels of public taste. In the brief space available to me I have not, of course, presented all aspects of the story, but I have tried to present a general picture which I believe is valid for other types of social effects as well. Research strongly suggests, for example, that the media do not engender passive orientations toward life, nor do they stimulate passively oriented persons to activity. They seem to provide a passive activity for the already passive and to stimulate new interests among persons who are intellectually curious, but they rarely change one type of person to another. In general, mass communication reinforces the existing attitudes, tastes, predispositions, and behavioral tendencies of its audience members, including tendencies toward change. Rarely, if ever, does it serve alone to create metamorphoses.

This is, of course, not to say that mass communication is either impotent or harmless. Its reinforcement effect is potent and socially important, and it reinforces, with fine disinterest, both socially desirable and socially undesirable predispositions. Which are desirable and which undesirable is, of course, often a matter of opinion. I have tried to show, however, that reducing such effects as may be considered undesirable, or increasing those which are considered desirable, is not likely to be achieved merely by modifying the content of mass communication. Mass communication will reinforce the tendencies which its audience possesses. Its social effects will therefore depend primarily on how the society as a whole—and in particular such institutions as the family, schools, and churches—fashions the audience members whom mass communication serves.

I would like to mention briefly a few other points. The first and most important of these is long-range effects. I have concentrated largely on short-term effects in this paper, for these are the effects with which research has been concerned. Next to nothing is known as yet regarding the social effects of mass communication over periods of, let us say, two or three decades. A second topic I have omitted is the power of mass communication in creating opinions on new issues—that is, issues on which its audience has no predispositions to reinforce. In related vein, I must mention that the media are quite effective in changing attitudes to which audience members are not particularly committed, a fact which explains much of the media's effectiveness in advertising. All of these topics are discussed in the appended list of books and articles.

## NOTES

1. Dr. Klapper's expectations have recently been borne out by a group of studies which have shown that children with aggressive tendencies are more likely than less aggressive children to imitate violent behavior they see in films and television.

## SUGGESTIONS FOR FURTHER READING

Himmelweit, Hilde T., Oppenheim, A. N., and Vince, Pamela, *Television and the Child*, published for the Nuffield Foundation, London and New York: Oxford University Press, 1958.

Katz, Elihu, and Lazarsfeld, Paul F., *Personal Influence: The Part Played by People in the Flow of Mass Communications*, New York: Free Press, 1955.

Klapper, Joseph T., *The Effects of Mass Communication*, New York: Free Press, 1960.

Lazarsfeld, Paul F., Berelson, Bernard, and Gaudet, Hazel, *The People's Choice*, New York: Columbia University Press, 1948.

Lazarsfeld, Paul F., and Stanton, Frank N. (eds.), *Communications Research, 1948-1949*, New York: Harper & Row, 1949.

Lazarsfeld, Paul F., and Stanton, Frank N. (eds.), *Radio Research, 1941*, New York: Duell, Sloan & Pearce, 1941.

Schramm, Wilbur (ed.), *The Process and Effects of Mass Communication*, Urbana: University of Illinois Press, 1954.

Schramm, Wilbur, Lyle, Jack, and Parker, Edwin B., *Television in the Lives of Our Children*, Stanford, Calif.: Stanford University Press, 1961.

# PART IV
# Intrapersonal
# Dimensions

Among the most fascinating and elusive of messages are those we create privately for ourselves. The notion of *intra*personal activity refers to messages created and sustained mainly *within* rather than *between* individuals. This inner dialogue does not operate in a random or sporadic way, nor is it dependent on the number of persons who are present. It is not limited by the nature of the setting nor the form of deliberation, whether public or private. Each man, in ways consistent with his own inner chemistry, determines what messages are to be self-directed and what is to be shared.

The concept of self has a major bearing on the type of private messages we create for ourselves. No one judges personal experience apart from some form of self-image or self-awareness. The concept of self embraces nothing less than the ideas and attitudes we have about who we are and what we become in the presence of others. In the essay "Encounters with the Self" Don Hamachek explores the concept of self, its origin and leading characteristics, and the impact of roles, expectations, and social interaction on the crucial matter of self-definition.

Closely related to the problem of self-image is the complex matter of self-esteem. The notion of self-esteem is the evaluative counterpart of self-description; impressions of self never occur independent of judgments and evaluation—favorable or unfavorable—of who we are. Hence, persons who rank high in self-esteem tend to evaluate themselves positively whereas those who lack esteem tend to struggle more persistently with feelings of inadequacy, self-doubt, and uncertainty over their identity and intrinsic worth. In the essay "Self-Image and Self-Esteem" Michael Argyle discusses these two dimensions of self and traces some of their implications in interactive situations.

The study of self owes much to the writings of a school known as symbolic interactionism which views the origin and growth of self as mainly social. John Kinch, in "A Formalized Theory of the Self-Concept," surveys leading ideas from the interactionist point of view and shows that an "individual's conception of himself emerges from social interaction and, in turn, governs or influences the behavior of that individual." Kinch also indicates how the communication process evolves along lines that are consistent with the views expressed by respective parties toward themselves and each other.

If there is one underlying principle which best accounts for the nature of self, it is the idea of "psycho-logic." Daryl Bem in "The Cognitive Foundations of Beliefs" discusses the inner logic used to maintain a more-or-less coherent view of the physical world. The use of psycho-logic helps to integrate self-directed ideas, not in random fashion, but in a consistent internal network of beliefs, values, attitudes, and overt action. The foundations of psycho-logic stem from the very acceptance of our sensory experience. This most basic of all beliefs, the impulse to trust our senses, is known as Zero-Order Beliefs. Closely related are other primitive beliefs that arise from the very acceptance of external authority, which in turn makes possible other higher level beliefs grounded in the generalizations and stereotypes formed from communication with others. In his engaging description of the structure of human beliefs, Bem adds an important dimension to our understanding of the nature of intrapersonal messages.

# ENCOUNTERS WITH THE SELF
## Don E. Hamachek

WHAT IS THE SELF?

Interest in the self, what it is and how it develops, is not a
recent phenomenon. As a theoretical concept, the self has
ebbed and flowed with the currents of philosophical and psychological pondering since the seventeenth century when the
French mathematician and philosopher, René Descartes, first
discussed the "cognito," or self, as a thinking substance. With
Descartes pointing the way, the self was subjected to the vigorous philosophical examinations of such thinkers as Leib-
nitz, Locke, Hume, and Berkeley. As psychology evolved
from philosophy as a separate entity, the self, as a related
construct, moved along with it. However, as the tides of be-
haviorism swept the shores of psychological thinking during
the first 40 years of this century, the self all but disappeared
as a theoretical or empirical construct of any stature. Study
of the self was not something which could be easily investigated under rigidly controlled laboratory conditions. As a
consequence, the subject was not considered an appropriate
one for scientific pursuit. Nonetheless, the concept was kept
alive during the early part of the twentieth century, by such
men as Cooley,[1] Mead,[2] Dewey,[3] and James.[4] During the period
since World War II, the concept of self has been revived and has
exhibited remarkable vitality. For example, Allport writes:

> In very recent years the tide has turned. Perhaps without being fully
> aware of the historical situation, many psychologists have commenced
> to embrace what two decades ago would have been considered a heresy.
> They have re-introduced self and ego unashamedly and, as if to make
> up for lost time, have employed ancillary concepts such as self-image,
> self-actualization, self-affirmation, phenomenal ego, ego-involvement,
> ego-striving, and many other hyphenated elaborations which to experi-
> mental positivism still have a slight flavor of scientific obscenity.[5]

### The Ego

Although there is no single, universally accepted definition of
the self, many psychologists accept a distinction between two

aspects of the self—one inferred by an external observer and one of which the person himself is aware. The *inferred self*, that is, the personality structure that represents the core of decision-making, planning, and defensiveness, can be understood best by an external observer (who in fact, may detect unconscious features of which the individual is unaware). This dimension of the self is commonly called the *ego*, a term borrowed from Freud, though not adhering exactly to the Freudian definition. The ego, specifically, is a construction from behavior, a hypothetical construct that, though it cannot be directly observed, can be *inferred* from one's behavior. For example, we speak of a person as having a weak or a strong ego based on how we have observed that person behave under given conditions. The ego is the primary agent of personality which is inferred on the basis of certain observed effects. In a sense, our concept of ego is similar to our concept of electricity, i.e., even though we cannot see electricity we can still know what it does by defining it in terms of its functions and effects. Just as we can assess electric current as weak or strong, in terms of its effects on fuses, gauges, or light bulbs, so we can estimate one's ego as being strong or weak in terms of certain behavioral consequences.

In the language of psychoanalytic psychology, personality is usually thought of as having three distinct components: The *id*, the *ego*, and the *superego*. The id is unconscious and is the source of basic urges and impulses. The id, according to Freud, "has no organization and unified will, only an impulsion to obtain satisfaction for the instinctual needs in accordance with the pleasure principle . . . the id knows no value, no good and evil, no morality."[6] In a manner of speaking, it is that part of each of us that demands vengeance if we are hurt or immediate gratification if we are in need. The superego is synonymous with conscience and is at the other extreme of what has been termed the id. Freud has defined the superego as "the representative of all moral restrictions, the advocate of the impulse toward perfection; in short, it is as much as we have been able to apprehend psychologically of what people call the 'higher' things in human life."[7] It is that part of each of us which may say, "No, you shouldn't," if vengeance is our goal or "No, you mustn't," if immediate gratification of an impulse is our objective. This is where one's ego comes into play. The ego is that part of personality which is in contact with external reality. It is responsible for perceiving inner and outer reality, for regulating behavior, and for controlling our impulses. Think of it this way: The ego is the personality's executive secretary whose job it is to screen and temper the demands and impulses of the id and superego prior to those demands and impulses being expressed in behavior. When we say that a person has a weak ego, we are also saying that he finds it difficult to check his impulses, or he has low frustration tolerance, or he has a hard time postponing gratification, or he can be easily hurt, or any combination of these possibilities. In other words, a strong ego can more successfully hold id-superego demands in check in order to achieve a healthy balance between what one wants and what one can have. In short, the ego perceives, reality-tests, selects, and rejects behavior patterns. It is responsible for learning and for the control and suppression of basic impulses.[8]

### The Self

Whereas the ego is constructed from behavior and inferred by others, the self, as we will use it here, is that part of each of us of which we are consciously aware. Acquiring a self-concept involves a slow process of differentiation as a person gradually emerges into focus out of his total world of awareness and defines progressively more clearly just who and what he is. Jersild is probably as clear as anyone about what the self is when he says:

A person's self is the sum total of all he can call his. The self includes, among other things, a system of ideas, attitudes, values, and commitments. The self is a person's total subjective environment; it is the distinctive center of experience and significance. The self constitutes a person's inner world as distinguished from the outer world consisting of all other people and things.[9]

As the *self* has evolved in psychological literature, it has come to have two distinct meanings. From one point of view it is defined as a person's attitudes and feelings about himself, and from another it is regarded as a group of psychological processes which influence behavior and adjustment. The first meaning can be looked at as a *self-as-object* definition, as it conveys a person's attitudes, feelings, and perceptions of himself as an object. That is, it is as if one could stand outside of himself and evaluate what he sees from a more or less detached point of view. In this sense, the self is what a person thinks of himself. The second meaning may be called the *self-as-process* definition. In other words, the self is a doer, in the sense that it includes an active group of processes such as thinking, remembering, and perceiving.

It is through the door of the self that one's personality is expressed. How the self is expressed is a complex phenomena meaning different things to different people. It is one person's brashness and another person's shyness; it is one person's sympathetic giving and another person's selfish hoarding; it is one person's trusting nature and another person's suspiciousness. An individual's image of himself is constructed from his conception of the "sort of person I am." All of us have beliefs about our relative value and our ultimate worth. We feel superior to some persons but inferior to others. We may or may not feel as worthy or as able as most other individuals, and much of our energy is spent trying to maintain or modify our beliefs about how adequate we are (or would like to be).

William James, a psychologist both of and beyond his time, has observed that how a person feels about himself depends entirely on what he *backs* himself to be and do. For example, in a famous passage James wrote:

I am not often confronted by the necessity of standing by one of my empirical selves and relinquishing the rest. Not that I would not, if I could, be both handsome and fat and well-dressed, and a great athlete, and make a million a year, be a wit, a bon-vivant, and lady-killer, as well as a philosopher, a philanthropist, statesman, warrior, and African explorer, as well as a "tone-poet" and saint. But the thing is simply impossible. The millionaire's work would run counter to the saint's; the bon-vivant and the philanthropist would trip each other up; the philosopher and lady-killer could not keep house in the same tenement of clay . . . to make any one of them actual, the rest must more or less be suppressed. . . . So the seeker of his truest, strongest, deepest self must review the list carefully, and pick out the one on which to stake his salvation. All other selves thereupon become unreal, but the fortunes of this self are real. Its failures are real failures, its triumphs real triumphs, carrying shame and gladness with them. . . .
I, who for the time have staked my all on being a psychologist, am mortified if others know more psychology than I. But I am contented to wallow in the grossest ignorance of Greek. My deficiencies there give me no sense of personal humiliation at all.[10]

I think it is clear from the above quotation that how James felt about himself depended, in large measure, on how he saw himself ranking in comparison to others *who also backed themselves to be psychologists.* In other words, we might generalize that our feelings of self-worth and self-esteem grow in part from our perceptions of where we see ourselves standing in relation to persons whose skills, abilities, talents, and aptitudes are similar to our own. For example, if a math major "backs" himself to be an excellent math student, but can get only C's or if an athlete "backs" himself to be an excellent athlete, but can make only the third team, then each will either have to rationalize their sub-par performances or lower their expectations for themselves or go on to something else in which greater success is more possible. As soon as one's performance in what he backs himself to be is less than his minimum level of self-imposed expectations, then the loss of self-esteem will be greater than its gain. As high self-esteem usually comes from being able to do one or two things at least as good as, if not a trifle better than most other people it would be difficult to maintain, not to mention enhance, self-esteem if one saw himself consistently finishing somewhere behind the group with which he was comparing himself.

Self-imposed expectations refer to our personal levels of aspirations and these expectations are very much connected to our feelings of self-esteem because they help establish what we regard as either success or failure. What is a success or enhancing experience for one can be a failure or deflating experience for another. For example, I remember a C I received in an undergraduate course which I regarded as particularly difficult. That C, however, was quite consistent with my expectations and level of aspiration for performance and I felt it was a minor, if not a major, success. On the other hand, a friend of mine who also received a C in that course viewed this as a total failure, because his expectations and level of aspiration were not lower than a B. In other words, by getting that C I maintained my self-esteem, because it was an even money return on my personal investment in the course. My friend lost a measure of self-esteem, *because the return was less than his personal investment.* By starting out with different amounts of personal investment, we had different expectations for a personal return in order to maintain our original investments. In a similar vein, both of us could have enhanced our self-esteem if we had received a grade which *exceeded* our original levels of aspiration.

Although each person's level of aspiration determines to a large extent what he interprets as failure or success, and hence what either adds to or takes from his self-esteem, another factor worth considering is one's history of successes and failures. For example, to fail at something is more tolerable and less apt to threaten our self-esteem if we have had a history of success in that particular endeavor. Some cases in point: A girl who has had many boyfriends is not likely to sour on boys if she loses one, but a girl with few boyfriends could; a team with a 10—0 record is not apt to give up after losing the eleventh game, but a 0—10 team might; a .350 baseball player is not particularly discouraged when he strikes out, but a .150 player is; a student with a long string of above average grades is not likely to quit school if he fails his first course, but a below average student who fails his tenth course might. In other words, the impact of falling short of one's personal aspirations stands to be a less self-deflating experience if one's list of successes in that endeavor exceeds his tally of failures.

## HOW DOES THE SELF BECOME KNOWN?

Ever since William James, it has been customary to speak of an infant's consciousness as a "big, blooming, buzzing confusion." Although the accuracy of this description may never be determined, it nonetheless seems pretty certain that the infant's consciousness includes no awareness of himself as an individual. In fact, the newborn infant apparently does not even know where his own body leaves off and his environment begins. Since we cannot directly assess the nature of a child's growing awareness, we must appraise the stages through an inferential process.

### Beginnings of Awareness

Self-awareness develops slowly as the child recognizes the distinction between self and not-self, between his body and the remainder of his visible environment. Only gradually does he learn to recognize and sort out his body parts, name, feelings, and behavior as integral parts of a single *me* and build a cluster of beliefs about himself. His serendipitous discoveries of the various parts of his body and the recognition of his own voice are the beginnings of his growing awareness of personal properties and resources. It seems likely that a child's body-awareness furnishes a common core around which self-reference becomes organized, although later he does learn to distinguish self from the physical body. From his behavior we can reasonably infer that soon after he is born he is flooded with a wave of sensory impressions—sensations that exist in his body when he's hungry, sensations from the surface of his body when it is hot or cold, sensations that reach him through his eyes and ears, and probably also sensations of taste and smell. As near as can be judged from a child's earliest reactions, he is not at first able to make a clear distinction between his early sensory experiences and the stimuli which elicit them. For example, if you touch a hot stove you know what is causing the pain. When something hot touches an infant he probably doesn't know where the pain comes from. The birth of self-awareness very likely occurs when a child begins to make a distinction between his sensations and the conditions which produce them.

As a growing child's experience broadens, his sense of personhood gradually extends to include things outside of himself with which he feels personal involvement. When we think of *me* or *my*, we may include such things as our home, possessions we own, groups we are loyal to, the values we subscribe to, and, most particularly, the people we love. The process of identification is an important part of coming to know and expand one's definition of self. Allport describes this process more fully:

A child . . . who identifies with his parent is definitely extending his sense of self, as he does likewise through his love for pets, dolls, or other possessions, animate or inanimate. . . .

As we grow older we identify with groups, neighbors, and nation as well as with possessions, clothes, and home. They become matters of importance to us in a sense that other people's families, nations, or possessions are not. Later in life the process of extension may go to great lengths, through the development of loyalties and interests focused on abstractions and on moral and religious values.[11]

### Influence of Social Roles and Others' Expectations
To some extent, a person's sense of identity is influenced by other peoples' appraisal of the social roles he happens to be in. For example, if the group regards an individual as a leader,

a solid Joe, a follower, a good athlete, or a social rum-dum, he is likely to regard himself in the same way. In other words, a person tends to adopt the values and attitudes that are expected of one in his position. In so doing, he begins to get a certain kind of feedback; this in turn reinforces how he feels about himself. I recall a student I had some years ago who was elected chairman of a group of about 15 students whose assignment it was to work as a total group on a research paper which the chairman would present to the whole class. The lad chosen was a shy, quiet sort of person, I thought, but he did such a remarkable job of presenting the paper that the entire class broke into spontaneous applause when he concluded. (I think it may be that most students are so prepared to be bored by dull presentations made by their peers that violations of their expectations are welcome reliefs indeed.) After class I expressed to the young man what a great job I thought he had done and he responded with something like this: "You know, I was scared to death. I didn't think I could do it! But then I got to thinking about it and I figured that if they wanted me to be a chairman, I'd *act* like a chairman—even if I had to fake it. And you know, that's what I did—faked it. From our first meeting on I just took charge like I had all the confidence in the world. And you know, a strange thing happened. The other kids in the group began to treat me as if I really *was* confident. They seemed to expect me to have answers and be able to organize and pretty soon I didn't know if I was faking it or if that's the way I really felt." Not only did this student learn that he had potential leadership abilities, which was an important discovery in itself, but *he also learned that how he behaved influenced how others behaved toward him.* Although, in this boy's words, he had to "fake" the initial leadership behavior, it may be important for us to remember that all the faking in the world would not have helped his cause if he did not have leadership potential to begin with. By "faking it" he discovered in himself latent qualities which had always been there.

The idea of a person responding in terms of what he thinks another person expects of him is not a new one, but it is receiving increasing attention as a phenomenon in psychological research. For example, Rosenthal[12] and Friedman,[13] have demonstrated that at least one very important variable which has not been controlled in past psychological experimentation is the variable of *what the experimenter expects to happen.* In other words, the result the scientist *expects* to get is more likely to occur than any other. Haimowitz, has extended the "expectation for behavior" idea to an examination of how criminals are "made" and writes:

Gradually, over the years, if he (the Criminal) comes to expect of himself what his neighbors expect of him, he becomes a professional criminal. . . . As a professional criminal, he has standards to live up to, friends who will help him when in trouble, . . . tell him where the police are lax and where strict. . . . At 12, 14, 16, or 18 he has come to a conclusion about his career that ordinary boys may not make until they are 20 or even 40. And he could not have drifted into this career without the help of his family and neighbors who sought a scapegoat and unwittingly suggested to him that he become an outlaw.[14]

The basic unit of interaction that concerns us here is a simple one. One person acts and in so doing intentionally or unintentionally expresses a part of his self, something of what he is, or thinks he is, or hopes he is. A second person responds to the first person's behavior. Very frequently the second person's reactions convey approval or disapproval, acceptance or rejection. The effects of these different responses to behavior soon become quite apparent. Behavior that results in attention or approval or affection tends to be repeated more and more frequently. Behavior that leads to withdrawal or indifference or rejection occurs less and less frequently. There are, of course, exceptions to this general tendency as, for example, when a person behaves in order to obtain a response, any response, in order to bring attention to himself or take it away from someone else.

However, because of the human capacity for self-consciousness the process of developing a sense of self is not a matter of simple reinforcement. That is, an individual's behavioral patterns arouse responses within himself leading to perceptions of himself which become stable. As an illustration, if a student has had reasonably good success in school and has high personal expectations for maintaining a high achievement level, he is not likely to respond to the expectations that his less achievement-oriented buddies may have for him to study less often. On the other hand, if it is more important for a student to be socially accepted than it is to get high grades, then that student may, in fact, be more susceptible to the shifting whims of others' expectations. Riesman[15] has described these different modes of responding to either internal or external expectations as *inner-directedness* or *other-directedness*.

An important first step along the road of self-understanding is the ability to be able to discriminate between those expectations which come from inside the self and those which come from outside the self. Rogers,[16] for example, speaking from his many years of experience as a psychotherapist, has noted that when an individual moves away from compulsively "meeting others' expectations," he becomes free to listen to his own expectations and to become the person he *feels* he wants to be.

Sometimes it is difficult *not* to listen to others' expectations.

Just as it is likely that a certain behavior can arouse certain expectations in the minds of others for future behavior of a similar sort, it is also possible that perceived expectations may trigger behavior which may not have been produced if those expectations had not been there in the first place. Let's untangle this with a few examples. A ninth-grade girl I counseled some years ago told me of an incident with her mother which may help make this idea of expectations clearer. She brought home her first ninth-grade report card with three Cs and a D in math. Her mother looked at it and said something like, "The way you think when numbers are involved it's no wonder you got a D. Besides, I was never any good in math so I'm not surprised you're not either. You'll probably be lucky to pass." The girl received a somewhat similar response from her father and the matter was dropped. As a consequence of this feedback (and other feedback like it), the girl nurtured the impression that she was expected to do poorly. That is, her mother and father did not *expect* her to do well in math. In other words, her behavior (a D in math) evoked certain expectations ("You'll be lucky to pass.") for this girl's future behavior, which she began to believe as being true.

Let's take another example. During an interview I had with a 17-year-old delinquent boy who had just been returned to the reformatory, I asked him why he had gotten into so much trouble while he was back home for three weeks. He screwed up his face and replied, "Man, what did you expect. The whole neighborhood knew I was at this place for nine months. Man, I wanted to do good—I tried, but even my grandfather wouldn't hardly talk to me. Some of the parents in the neighborhood—some with kids in more trouble than me—wouldn't even let their kids talk to me. They would say something like there goes that kid from the vocational school, watch out for him. They had their minds made up before they even looked to see if I had changed. Hell with them. They want me to be bad—I'll *be* bad." In other words, it was clear to this boy that people in his neighborhood *expected* him to play the role of the delinquent boy and he ended up behaving in terms of what he perceived their expectations to be for him. True, his delinquency history determined their expectations, but their expectations facilitated the very behavior they were opposed to in the first place. This doesn't excuse the boy's behavior, but it does help us understand it. Expectations for behavior have a strong influence on what kind of behavior is expressed.

### Influence of Social Interaction

The self grows within a social framework. If, for example, you were to make a list of as many personality characteristics you could think of, you would find that each is influenced in some way or other by social interaction. Some, like friendliness or shyness are social by definition; that is, one cannot be friendly or shy except in relation to other people. Other characteristics, like creativeness or independence, are less social by definition. Although one can be creative or independent in solitude, it is difficult to see how one could acquire such traits apart from social interaction.

Mead, in describing the social interaction processes involved in the development of the self writes:

> The self arises in conduct, when the individual becomes a social object in experience to himself. This takes place when the individual assumes the attitude or uses the gesture which another individual would use and responds to it himself or tends to so respond. . . . The child gradually becomes a social being in his own experience, and he acts toward himself in a manner analogous to that in which he acts toward others.[17]

This description may be made clear by a single example. Let's say that a child play-acts being mother or father. In his play, he talks to himself as his mother and father have talked to him, and he responds to this imaginary talk of his mother and father. Eventually, the end result of speaking to himself as others have spoken to him is that he comes to perceive himself as a social object to which other people respond. He learns to conceive of himself as having characteristics which are perceived and encouraged by others. For example, as a young child grows he learns that words such as cute, good, bad, intelligent, dumb, heavy, lazy, shy, etc., are attributed to him as a person; it is through his long immersion in an interpersonal stream of continual reflected appraisals from other people (particularly people who *matter* to him) that he gradually develops a picture of himself which he then strives to maintain.

Perhaps we can appreciate the importance of social interaction if we look at an example in which there was virtually no interaction at all. Davis[18] reported the case of Anna, a five-year-old child, who was found tied to a chair in a secluded room. She had apparently been kept there for several years by her grandfather who found her unbearable because she was a second illegitimate child. When found she was unable to move or talk. Her leg muscles had atrophied to the point that her flaccid feet fell forward. She was malnourished and showed no response to sound or sight. Within three days of being taken out of this isolated environment she was able to sit up if placed in a sitting position and could move her arms and hands. She was massaged, placed on a high vitamin diet, and given lots of attention. At first she neither smiled nor cried and was almost expressionless, although later she began to smile if coaxed and showed signs of temper if physically restrained. Ten days after the first visit, the examiners found the child more alert and able to fix her attention. She showed taste and visual discrimination, smiled more often, and began to display ritualistic motions with her hands and a series of tricks that any infant performs. Two months after being found, Anna ceased to improve. In nine months she had learned little. She could not chew or drink from a glass or control her bodily processes, and she could barely stand even when holding on to some support.

At this time Anna was placed in a foster home in the keeping of a warm, supporting foster mother. Within a month of this placement she had learned to eat, hold a glass, and feed herself. Improvement continued until she understood many instructions and babbled, although she could not use words. Motor ability increased, but her initiative was low. Again she seemed to hit a plateau and was placed in a home for retarded children. In 1942 she was speaking at about the level of a two-year-old. She reflected signs of being socialized, used a spoon, conformed to toilet habits, loved her dolls, and spoke a few simple sentences. She died shortly thereafter at an estimated age of ten and one-half.

Records revealed that as a baby she had appeared normal, indeed attractive. The matter of hereditary endowment is open to speculation, for the mother was dull mentally, and there was doubt as to her father's identity. Nonetheless, there is little doubt but that Anna's lack of social interaction and environmental stimulation contributed heavily to her retarded growth as a total human being.

Social interaction is the medium of exchange through which one hones his perceptions of the outside world, develops his interpersonal skills, extends his intelligence, and acquires attitudes about himself. As Tenenbaum[19] and Deutsch and Brown,[20] among others, have demonstrated in their research with the disadvantaged, impoverished children who grow up with restricted cultural and social opportunities suffer both intellectually and emotionally. Suffice it to say, interaction with others is an important social vitamin in one's daily nourishment of an expanding self-awareness.

## REFERENCES

1. Cooley, Charles H., *Human Nature and Social Order*, New York: Scribner's, 1902.
2. Mead, G. H., *Mind, Self and Society*, Chicago: University of Chicago Press, 1934.
3. Dewey, John, *Democracy and Education*, New York: Macmillan, 1916.
4. James, W., *Principles of Psychology, I*, New York: Holt, Rinehart and Winston, 1890.
5. Allport, G. W., *Becoming*, New Haven, Conn.: Yale University Press, 1955, 104-105.
6. Freud, Sigmund, *New Introductory Lectures on Psycho Analysis*, trans. W. J. H. Sprott, New York: Norton, 1933, 104-105.
7. Freud, *op. cit.*, 95.
8. Hartmann, H., "Comments on the Psychoanalytic Study of the Child," in Anna Freud and others (eds.), *The Psychoanalytic Study of the Child*, vol. I, New York: International Universities Press, 1947, 11-38.
9. Jersild, Arthur T., *In Search of Self*, New York: Teachers College Press, Columbia University, 1952.
10. James, *op. cit.*, 91.
11. Allport, *op. cit.*, 45.
12. Rosenthal, Robert, *Experimenter Effects in Behavioral Research*, New York: Appleton-Century-Crofts, 1966.
13. Friedman, Neil, *The Social Nature of Psychological Research: The Psychological Experiment as a Social Interaction*, New York: Basic Books, 1967.
14. Haimowitz, Morris L., "Criminals Are Made, Not Born," in M. L. Haimowitz and N. R. Haimowitz (eds.), *Human Development, Selected Readings*, New York: Crowell, 1960, 374.
15. Riesman, David, *Faces in the Crowd*, New Haven, Conn.: Yale University Press, 1952.
16. Rogers, C. R., *On Becoming a Person*, Boston: Houghton Mifflin, 1961, 163-198.
17. Mead, *op. cit.*, 48.
18. Davis, Kingsley, "Extreme Social Isolation of a Child," *American Journal of Sociology*, 1940, 45, 554-565.
19. Tenenbaum, S., "The Teacher, the Middle Class, the Lower Class," *Phi Delta Kappan*, 1963, 45, 82-86.
20. Deutsch, M., and Brown, B., "Social Influences in Negro-White Intelligence Differences," *Journal of Social Issues*, 1964, 20, 24-35.

# SELF-IMAGE AND SELF-ESTEEM
## Michael Argyle

THE DIMENSIONS OF SELF AND THEIR MEASUREMENT

1. *The Self-image*, or "ego-identity," refers to how a person
consciously perceives himself. The central core usually consists of his name, his bodily feelings, body-image, sex, and
age. For a man the job will also be central—unless he is suffering from "job alienation," like the hero of *Saturday Night and
Sunday Morning.* For a woman her family and her husband's
job may also be central. The core will contain other qualities
that may be particularly salient, such as social class, religion,
particular achievements of note, or anything that makes a
person different from others. In addition to the core, there
are a series of subidentities which an individual holds in relation to particular activities or groups. The same person may
be a lecturer, a father, and a member of various committees
and clubs. He plays each role in a characteristic style; the way
he sees himself in each role is a part of his ego-identity. He
may perceive himself vaguely or clearly. The more he has discussed his personal problems with others the more clearly he
is likely to see himself. During psychotherapy, the therapist
may provide the concepts which the patient can use to talk
about himself. Some aspects of the self-image are more important to a person than others: It is more upsetting if these are
challenged.

The ego-identity can be assessed by verbal methods, and
various special kinds of questionnaire have been used for the
purpose. One such method is the "Semantic Differential," in
which subjects can be asked to describe "the kind of person I
actually am" along a series of seven-point scales such as:

strong  — — — — — — —  weak
kind  — — — — — — —  cruel

The answers are affected by the tendency to give a favorable
impression, although that does not necessarily matter since it

Reprinted by permission from *The Psychology of Interpersonal Behavior* by Michael Argyle, Harmondsworth, Middlesex, England: Penguin
Books Ltd., pp. 117-132. Copyright © 1967 by Michael Argyle.

**209**

is important to know how favorably a person views himself. A method which is free from this difficulty is the so-called "Q-sort" in which subjects are asked to place a series of statements on cards in order, with the cards which apply most to themselves at the top. If all the cards have equally desirable (or undesirable) descriptive phrases on them, a purely descriptive and nonevaluative account of the ego-identity can be obtained.

How far does a person's self-image correspond with the way he is seen by others? As will be seen, people present a somewhat improved, idealized and censored version of themselves for public inspection, so that there is likely to be some discrepancy. Also some people succeed in insulating themselves from the views of others so that they are simply unaware of how they are regarded.

2. *The ego-ideal* is the kind of person one would most like to be. This may be based on particular individuals who are taken as admired models, and who may be parents, teachers, film stars, or characters from literature. It may consist of a fusion of desired characteristics drawn from various sources. Of particular interest is the amount of discrepancy between the self and the ego-ideal. This can be assessed by means of the measures described already. The Semantic Differential can be filled in to describe "the kind of person I actually am," and "the kind of person I would most like to be." The average discrepancy between scale scores is then worked out thus:

$$\text{(ego-ideal) (self)}$$
$$\text{X} \quad \text{X}$$
$$\text{kind} \; - \; - \; - \; - \; - \; - \; \text{cruel}$$

A number of studies have found that neurotics have greater self/ego-ideal conflict than normals, and that the discrepancy gets smaller during psychotherapy. However there are some groups of people, by no means well-adjusted, who show very little such conflict—because they perceive themselves so inaccurately.

When there is much conflict, it contributes to low self-esteem. It may also lead to efforts to attain the ego-ideal: When there is actually movement in this direction there is said to be "self-realization." Such efforts may take two rather different directions. One way is to make intensified efforts to project a certain self-image, in ways which will be discussed below. If the appearance is in conflict with the reality, this strategy will be a source of inner conflict and stress. The other way is not to bother so much about external appearances, but to be concerned with the actual attainment of certain standards, ideals, or results. This may be unsatisfactory for those people who are greatly dependent on public confirmation. A curious feature of the ego-ideal is that a person who attains it does not necessarily rest on his laurels enjoying the self-esteem, but may revise his goals upwards—as if the very entertainment of the fantasies, and the anticipation of the quest are a source of satisfaction.

3. *The organization of the self.* We have just described one kind of conflict between ego-identity and ego-ideal. There may also be conflicts within each of these. As has been seen, the ego-identity contains a series of sub-identities referring to relations with particular groups: The same is true of the ego-ideal. A child may admire saints and soldiers, poets and financiers, but eventually he has to decide which is the direction in which he really wants to go. The degree of integration or diffusion of ego-identity is an important aspect of personality. At one extreme are the completely dedicated, single-minded fanatics, at the other are those adolescents who do not yet know "who they are or where they are going." The more integrated the self-image, the more consistent a person's behavior will be: One effect of the self-image on behavior is the suppression of behavior that is out of line. This "consistency" may take various forms, depending on whether the self-image is based on the attributes of some person, on a set of ethical or ideological rules of conduct, or on an occupational or social-class role. Another aspect of the self-image is the extent to which a person sees himself as unique and different from others. The child in the family, a soldier in the Army, a member of a crowd—they may simply see themselves as members of a group, not differing notably from the others. Most adolescents try to separate themselves from the corporate family identity; many kinds of eccentric, deviant, and even delinquent behavior have the same motivation. On the other hand, people also belong to groups, and part of their identity is based on group memberships. Some psychologists believe that there is constant tension between individual identity and group identity, or between "autonomy and mutuality." The synthesis

may be in terms of taking a role in a group where all members share common ways of behavior but recognize and accept the individual contributions and idiosyncrasies of each person. There are probably wide variations in the extent to which uniqueness is stressed. It seems to be a strong tendency among middle-class intellectuals, but is less strong for working-class youth, who cling to group identities such as "mod" or "rocker."

4. *Self-esteem* is the extent to which a person approves of and accepts himself, and regards himself as praiseworthy, either absolutely or in comparison with others. Like ego-identity, self-esteem has a stable core, together with a series of peripheral esteems based on relationships with different groups of people. One complication about self-esteem is that some people develop an exaggerated self-regard in compensation for basic feelings of inferiority. In these cases it is difficult to decide whether they "really" have high or low self-esteem—it would depend on whether this was measured by direct or indirect measures.

Self-esteem can be assessed by the same sort of questionnaire methods which were described for ego-identity—e.g., some of the scales in the Semantic Differential give a score for "evaluation" (e.g., good—bad). Rosenberg (1965) constructed an attitude scale for measuring self-esteem that was found to agree well with free self-descriptions, and in the case of hospital patients with ratings by nurses. It is also possible to find out the basic, unconscious degree of self-acceptance. The method is to ask the subject to make ratings of samples of recorded speech, handwriting, etc., including specimens from the subject himself. It is found that subjects often give very favorable self-evaluations, but a number give very unfavorable judgments; few give neutral ratings (Huntley, 1940).

## THE ORIGINS OF THE SELF
*The origins of the self-image.* There are three of these, the first being the reactions of other people. It is difficult to get direct feedback on one's own behavior; however from childhood onwards we become aware of how others see us, and this becomes part of the ego-identity. This has been called the theory of the "looking-glass self"—to see ourselves we look to see how we are reflected in the reactions of others.

The writer has formulated this as a process of *introjection*, whereby children adopt the perceptions, attitudes, and reactions to themselves of parents and others. If parents tell a child he is clever, or treat him as if he is untrustworthy, these attributes may become part of the ego-identity. The whole pattern of reaction is important here, the spoken and the unspoken. A group of students once played a joke on a rather dull, unattractive female student, by treating her as if she was tremendously attractive and popular. "Before the year was over, she had developed an easy manner and a confident assumption that she was popular" (Guthrie, 1938). Adults and teachers do not hesitate to give full descriptive feedback to children, but amongst older people there is something of a taboo on such direct verbal feedback, especially in its negative aspects. It is reported that those who go on leadership training courses ask to be told point-blank how others perceive them (Bennis et al., 1964), and it has been suggested that it would be helpful to provide people with rather more of such information than is currently regarded as polite. On the other hand, it can be very traumatic to find this out, and it should be done with tact, or indirectly by subtle cues, hints, and nonverbal reactions.

A second source of the self-image is the comparison of oneself with brothers, sisters, friends, or others who are constantly present and are sufficiently similar to invite comparison. If other families in the neighborhood are wealthier, a child will regard himself as "poor"; if his brothers and sisters are cleverer, he will see himself as not clever, and so on. It is possible to change a child's self-image completely, and quite rapidly, by sending him to a different school, where the other children are, for example, more athletic, or of a lower social class. When a person belongs to a group, and does not deviate much from the group norms, he will perceive himself as a member of that group, and as possessing the group characteristics. If a person does not belong to any group, he will feel alienated; he belongs nowhere, and has no norms to obey.

The third source of the self-image is simply the roles a person has played in the past, or is playing in the present. A child plays at many parts, and the adolescent crisis of identity which commonly occurs in Western society is brought about by the need to choose which of these parts to emphasize.

Adults often see themselves primarily in terms of the job they do, although roles of particular importance or excitement in their past may be even more salient. Roles provide an easy solution to the problem of ego-identity—there is a clear public identity to adopt. On the other hand they can be burdensome, since so much of the self cannot be fitted into a particular role. A solution to this is to maintain a certain role distance, i.e., to take the role in a slightly deviant way, laughing a little at it, as when a child rides on a roundabout in a funny way. This is to indicate that there is more to oneself than can be seen in just this role.

These three sources of self-image operate right through childhood. Children do not need to work out a consistent self-image—teddy-bears and Greek, dolls and trigonometry, are not experienced as incongruous. During adolescence, and during student life, there is still no need to decide on a particular identity, and young people are allowed to experiment with and play at various identities, before they finally commit themselves. For the adult however there is a strong drive towards consistency: Somewhere between the ages of 16 and 22 there is often an identity crisis when he is forced to make up his mind which of all these bits and pieces of identity to hang on to, which to suppress (Erikson, 1956). The basis of this is partly the necessity of adopting one occupational role rather than another, partly the need to choose between conflicting action-tendencies.

*The origins of self-esteem.* Self-esteem is partly a function of the self-image, and its development is partly due to very similar processes. Children introject their parents' love and admiration of themselves. If they are never loved they will come to reject themselves and suffer from low self-esteem in later life. If they are sometimes loved and sometimes not, they will learn to present those aspects of themselves which were greeted most favorably. As with the self-image, self-esteem is partly based on comparisons with members of available peer groups. In a study of a large number of adolescents in New York State, Rosenberg (1965) found that those with the highest self-esteem tended to be of higher social class, to have done better at school, and to have been leaders in clubs—all of which could be bases for favorable comparisons of self and others. Thirdly, self-esteem may be affected by roles which have been played, especially when these were very prestigeful—or particularly disgraceful.

When the self-image becomes unified in late adolescence, an overall level of self-esteem develops. The desire behind ego-identity is to make it consistent, and for many people to make it unique. The drive behind self-esteem is for it to be as favorable as possible. In each case wishes are limited by reality: Otherwise behavior becomes absurd and preposterous, and there is continual lack of confirmation by others. This happens in the case of paranoia. In fact people vary widely in their feelings of esteem, from conceit to inferiority. Both extremes usually reflect failure to perceive accurately the present responses of others, and can be regarded as failures of adjustment. A mythical psychotherapist is said to have told a patient who suffered from feelings of inferiority, "But you really are inferior." The real reason that people feel inferior is generally that they have been unduly rejected by their parents, or have chosen too elevated a comparison group.

It is quite possible to select prestigeful items out of the long list of self-attributes and roles once played, and such items often become a favorite item of conversation. However, the total self-esteem is greatly affected by the ego-ideal. Thus self-esteem depends jointly on a person's position on a series of evaluative dimensions, and upon the value placed on each of these dimensions. Values depend on the group, so self-esteem depends on whether the group values a person's attributes—but a group will have been joined because it does value them. When a person has deeply rooted values, or is strongly attached to a group, this may contribute to low self-esteem if he does not possess the right attributes; he would then be in a state of self ego-ideal conflict. When a person has low self-esteem either for this reason or because of rejections in the past, he will be unhappy and more likely to suffer from mental illness.

## THE EFFECTS OF THE SELF-IMAGE ON BEHAVIOR
Certain aspects of behavior during social encounters can be looked at as consequences of the participants having self-images. They present themselves in a certain way, adopt a particular "face," and try to get others to accept this picture of themselves. Various strategies are adopted to do so; if un-

successful there will be embarrassment and a breakdown of interaction.

*Projecting a self-image.* People want to project a self-image for several reasons. To begin with, for interaction to occur at all it is necessary for the participants to be able to categorize one another—they need guidance on how to respond to each other. It was shown before that different styles of behavior are used depending on the social class, occupation, nationality, etc., of the other. If it is not clear where a person falls on such dimensions, or if the important things about him are concealed, people do not know how to interact with him, and will be very perplexed. It is essential that all interactors should present themselves clearly in *some* way. Sometimes the self-presentation includes a definition of the situation—as when a social-survey interviewer stops someone in the street.

A person may not present himself in quite the same way in all situations and may adopt a face which is not warranted: Interaction can still proceed, but there will be embarrassment if face is lost, and the concealing or suppressing of large sectors of the self-image is a source of tension. Much social behavior has an element of acting, role-playing, "impression-management," or "face-work" as Goffman calls it (1955). When a person first becomes a waiter, undertaker, or model, for example, this will be accentuated; when the identity has been assimilated the behavior becomes quite natural. People do not work at their image-projection all the time; there is a difference between being "on-stage" and "off-stage"; in the former, people feel under observation and are very concerned about the image they are projecting.

An individual may be concerned about his face for professional purposes. Butlers, Lord Mayors, and film stars, as well as teachers, psychotherapists, and salesmen, all need to project a certain image of professional competence. There is a good reason for this: Clients are more likely to respond in the desired way if they have confidence in the expertise of the practitioner. Another reason a person may need confirmation of his self-image or self-esteem is that he may be "insecure"—i.e., be in constant need of reassurance from others that he is what he hopes he is. If the self-image has not been firmly established in the past, more time has to be spent looking in the mirror of others' reactions in the present. Adolescents, who have only just formed a tentative self-image, are particularly sensitive to the reactions of others, and are "insecure" in this sense. People who have changed their social class, their job, or their nationality are often in a similar position.

How do people project an identity? The most obvious way would be simply to tell the others present, but it is not socially acceptable to do this except with intimate friends and relations; in England particularly, only the most modest of claims is acceptable. It is possible to dress in clothes that portray the man, and indeed a person's clothes are one of the best clues to his self-image. People can drop indirect hints, though this is liable to be unpopular if esteem is also claimed too overtly, as in "name-dropping." Stephen Potter has given a satirical account of indirect ways of claiming a prestigeful identity in his book *One-Upmanship* (1952). For example:

Layman: Thank you, Doctor. I was coming home rather late last night from the House of Commons . . .

M.D.—Man: Thank you . . . now if you'll just let me put these . . . hair brushes and things off the bed for you . . . that's right . . .

Layman: I was coming home rather late. Army Act, really . . .

M.D.—Man: Now just undo the top button of your shirt or whatever it is you're wearing . . .

Layman: I say I was coming . . .

M.D.—Man: Now if you've got some hot water—really hot—and a clean towel.

Layman: Yes, just outside. The Postmaster-General . . .

M.D.—Man: Open your mouth, please.

The most effective way of projecting a self-image is to behave in accordance with it—"actions speak louder than words." Thus people suppress behavior which they would like to engage in, but which is not part of their adopted role. A working-class person who has adopted a middle-class identity will strive to adopt the appropriate ways of behaving, including the way he speaks and the way he votes. If a young person comes to look on himself as a juvenile delinquent, and as one who is alienated from society, he will be more likely to act out this part by further law-breaking. Part of the success of Chinese thought reform is due to bringing about a different self-perception of the "students" as a result of a lengthy process of confession-writing.

*Seeking esteem.* People like to be admired, mainly it is believed in order to confirm their feelings of self-esteem. That is why they only really care about being admired by particular people or groups, for things which they have actually done, or can do, and which are important to them. For example, it is doubtful if anyone gets much satisfaction from being cheered by a crowd that believes he is someone else.

Again, insecure people have an unusually strong need for reassurance from others. There is, as might be expected, a general tendency for secure people to have high self-esteem, but there are many exceptions to this, as Maslow (1945) has shown. People with *high* self-esteem but *low* security need continual admiration from others, feel hostile and dependent on them, and may behave in a very ruthless manner. People who have *low* self-esteem and *high* security are quiet, dependent, and undemanding. Those with *low* esteem and *low* security want their inferiority to be confirmed in a masochistic kind of way.

The strategies which are used for projecting a self-image apply here too. In addition there are certain techniques which particularly apply to the praiseworthy aspects of behavior. One is concealment: People are careful not to reveal aspects of themselves which are likely to lead to disapproval. Jourard (1964) surveyed large numbers of students, using a questionnaire asking how much they had revealed about themselves to other people. There were big differences of content: More was revealed about opinions and attitudes than about sexual behavior or money for instance. People will reveal most to people who they can trust not to reject them—to their mothers, close friends, people who are similar to themselves, and (we may add) to psychiatrists and clergymen. Rather similar to concealment is the cautious, ritualized and conventional behavior which people display on first meeting strangers. Disclosure is a risk, as there is a danger of the other person disapproving. Jourard has found that if an interviewer makes some self-disclosures, the other is more likely to do the same.

As in the case of the self-image, real behavior is the most effective way of promoting self-esteem. It is thought that people enter for examinations, races, and competitions of all kinds in order to "evaluate themselves." It is interesting that most people do not feel they are good, at tennis for example, because they have beaten someone who has never played before; nor do they feel they have failed if a Wimbledon champion defeats them. What they want to do is to beat others of about their own ability—to justify their feelings of self-esteem or of small increases in them. As was said above, there is no end-goal for dimensions of achievement: People always want to do a little better. People may also try to demonstrate their superiority by competing in the social situation itself—by trying to outdo the others in being clever, funny, holy, or in some other way.

*Disconfirmation of self-image or self-esteem.* When this occurs there is embarrassment and disruption of interaction. If A presents himself as an upper-class person but B reacts to him as a working-class person, interaction will not proceed smoothly. There must be some degree of acceptance of the self-definitions offered, and in some cases these must be a complementary role—a "teacher" requires a "pupil" in order to act out his identity. Disconfirmation or "loss of face" may come about in a number of ways; the effect is always embarrassment, partly because people are sorry for the person who has lost face, but also because the assumptions on which interaction were based have been destroyed. A person may present a self-image which simply is not accepted by the others—as in the case of a lunatic who claims to be Napoleon. Or a person's face may be invalidated by events, as when his job or qualifications turn out to be less impressive than were claimed. There may be deliberate attacks on someone's face, as in practical jokes intended to tease, test, or train in poise.

Embarrassment can be looked at as a failure in skilled performance—like an accident for a manual-skill performer. It can also be seen as a failure of meshing, brought about when people disagree, not about facts but about the nature of the situation or about their roles in it. Garfinkel (1963) has carried out some intriguing "demonstrations" in which investigators behaved in their own homes like lodgers, treated other customers in shops as salesmen, or flagrantly broke the rules of games—such as by moving the opponent's pieces. This produced embarrassment, consternation and anger. Gross and Stone (1964) collected reports of 1,000 instances of embarrassment. These included cases, like those above, where self-images were discredited or mistaken; there were also cases where things went wrong on formal occasions like weddings, including an extraordinary case of a man who got the tablecloth caught in his trouser buttons. These instances can be included in the earlier notion—someone has made a fool of himself and is therefore discredited; it is worse at a formal occasion since he is to some extent putting on a performance and implicitly making greater claims of competence.

When these things happen, some people are able to "carry off" the situation by remaining poised and managing to cope in one of the ways described below. It is more likely that people will become "embarrassed"—they blush, fumble, sweat, stutter, and in more severe cases burst into tears, flee from the situation, even (mainly in the Far East) commit suicide. Face is a very valuable possession, and it can be extremely painful to lose it. Embarrassment is contagious, it spreads rapidly to the others present. Once a person has lost control this makes the situation worse, as he is now ashamed also of his lack of poise. He is temporarily incapable of interacting. He will avoid eye-contact with the others, perhaps to withdraw from interaction, or just to avoid seeing their expressions of disapproval.

Some of the possible causes of embarrassment can be avoided by presenting a face which cannot be invalidated, and it is less likely to happen to those who are not dependent on external confirmation of their self-image and self-esteem. Breakdown of interaction may still occur, however, as a result of accidental errors, as in social *gaffes*. Rules of etiquette and skills of tact help to avoid such breakdowns. An example of etiquette is the rule not to send invitations too long before the event, because it is difficult to refuse them. An example of tact is knocking on doors or coughing when a couple may be making love on the other side of it. (Etiquette can become a positive source of embarrassment, on the other hand, when the rules become so complex or so strictly enforced that people are terrified of breaking them.) Friends, relations and colleagues always have plenty of material which could be used to embarrass each other. However, they want interaction to proceed smoothly, so on the whole they do not make use of this information.

When A's face has been disbelieved or discredited there are various strategies open to him. One is simply to ignore what has happened or to laugh it off as unimportant. It is certainly important to retain poise as far as possible. It would be expected . . . that a person who had failed to project an image would try alternative ways of doing so. If he is rattled he may fall back on less subtle techniques of the kind "Look here, young man, I've written more books about this subject than you've read," "Do you realize that I . . . ," etc. This may succeed in modifying the other's perceptions, but it will almost certainly cause embarrassment and make the speaker look ridiculous. A milder technique might be a quiet "Well, as a matter of fact I have taken some interest in that subject. . . ."

If these methods fail it may be necessary to alter the face that has been presented, at any rate to the individuals or group in question. This is painful, both because of the shock to self-image and self-esteem, and because it entails working out a new pattern of interaction which is compatible with the changed assumptions. When it is mainly esteem which has been withheld by the group, it is possible to alter behavior in a way that will produce the desired response from others. It is found that insecure people are more affected by social influences and pressures of all kinds. In small social groups, for example, one of the main causes of conformity is the avoidance of being rejected, as deviates tend to be. Those who conform most are those who feel inferior, lack self-confidence, and are dependent on others (Krech, Crutchfield, & Ballachey, 1962). People may embark on all kinds of self-improvement, either apparent or real, in response to negative reactions from others, including the modification of styles of interaction as in operant verbal conditioning.

The remaining responses can really be regarded as "defense mechanisms," in that their main object is the avoidance of anxiety, while no realistic adjustment of self-image or behavior is involved. One of these is rationalization. It has been found that salesgirls in shops preserve their image of competence, in the face of customers whom they can't please, by categorizing them as "nasty," or in some similar way (Lombard, 1955). If a low opinion is formed of B, it doesn't matter whether B confirms the girl's self-image of competence or not. Another defense is self-deception in its various forms. A person may distort the reactions of others in a favorable direction, or simply not perceive them at all. The extreme of this is psychotic withdrawal from the difficulties of interpersonal relations into a private world of fantasies which cannot be disturbed by outside events. It is possible to withdraw from the people or groups who react in the wrong way; studies of friendship show that people are more attracted to those who confirm their self-image.

When a person is embarrassed, the others present usually want to prevent the collapse of social interaction, and will help in various ways. To begin with, they will try to prevent loss of face by being tactful in the ways described. They may pretend that nothing has happened, make excuses for the offender—he was only joking, was off form, etc., or in some other way "rescue the situation." Finally, if face is irrevocably lost they may help the injured party to rehabilitate himself in the group in a new guise (Goffman, 1955; Gross & Stone, 1964).

*Audience anxiety*, or *"stage fright."* This is not quite the same as embarrassment. Here the performer is aroused and anxious because his esteem and image are exposed to the risk of being damaged. The arousal will be greater the larger and the more important the audience: Performance will be most effective at intermediate degrees of such arousal—if the audience is too small he may be too bored to bother with it; if too large his performance becomes disrupted by anxiety. Although stage fright usually becomes less with experience, it declines very slowly.

When someone addresses any kind of audience it is no good his speaking in the informal "familial" style—he won't be heard properly: It is inevitable that he must put on some kind of "performance." Once he does so he is accepting a certain definition of the situation and presenting a certain face: He is someone who is able to perform before this audience and is worth attending to. It is this implicit claim which creates the risk of loss of face.

How can audience anxiety be reduced? If the performer is fairly confident of a favorable reception, as a result of past experience, he will not be so anxious; emotional arousal may now take the form of excitement. If he does not claim a self-image which cannot be sustained he is less vulnerable; while he must put on a performance, he can do it in a modest way. If he concentrates on his immediate goal of teaching, persuading or amusing the audience, he will be less concerned with the confirmation of his image. Experiments were reported which showed that audience anxiety is reduced if the speaker stands behind the audience, or at some distance from them. With less eye-contact and greater distance, the reactions of the audience have a weaker impact—but there is a danger of losing much-needed audience feedback.

## REFERENCES

Bennis, W. G., et al., *Interpersonal Dynamics,* Homewood, Ill.: Dorsey, 1964.

Erikson, E. H., "The Problem of Ego Identity," *American Journal of Psychoanalysis,* 1956, 4, 56-121.

Garfinkel, H., "Trust and Stable Actions," in O. J. Harvey, *Motivation and Social Interaction,* New York: Ronald, 1963.

Goffman, E., "On Face-Work: An Analysis of Ritual Elements in Social Interaction," *Psychiatry,* 1955, 18, 213-231.

Gross, E., and Stone, G. P., "Embarrassment and the analysis of role requirements," *American Journal of Sociology,* 1964, 70, 1-15.

Guthrie, E. R., *The Psychology of Human Conflict,* New York: Harper & Row, 1938.

Huntley, C. W., "Judgments of Self Based upon Records of Expressive Behavior," *Journal of Abnormal and Social Psychology,* 1940, 35, 398-427.

Jourard, S. M., *The Transparent Self,* New York: Van Nostrand Reinhold, 1964.

Krech, D., Crutchfield, R. S., and Ballachey, E. L., *Individual in Society,* New York: McGraw-Hill, 1962.

Lombard, G. G. F., *Behavior in a Selling Group,* Cambridge, Mass.: Harvard University Press, 1955.

Maslow, A. H., et al., "A Clinically-Derived Test for Measuring Psychological Security-Insecurity," *Journal of General Psychology,* 33, 24-41.

Potter, S., *One-Upmanship,* London: Hart-Davis, 1952.

# A FORMALIZED THEORY OF THE SELF-CONCEPT
## John W. Kinch

### THE SELF-CONCEPT

The interactionist notions about the self-concept, based on the writings of G. Mead, Cooley, and several others, are well known to social psychologists. The theory attempts to explain the conception that the individual has of himself in terms of his interaction with those about him.

Although there have been a variety of words used in describing what is meant by an individual's conception of himself, it appears that general agreement could be reached on the following definition: *The self-concept is that organization of qualities that the individual attributes to himself.* It should be understood that the word "qualities" is used in a broad sense to include both *attributes* that the individual might express in terms of adjectives (ambitious, intelligent) and also the *roles* he sees himself in (father, doctor, etc.).

*The general theory.* In very general terms the basic notions of the theory can be stated in one sentence: *The individual's conception of himself emerges from social interaction and, in turn, guides or influences the behavior of that individual.*

### BASIC PROPOSITIONS OF FORMALIZED
### THEORY OF SELF-CONCEPT

The following statements are at least implicit in most treatments of the self-concept using this tradition and will be used as the basic postulates of our formalized theory.

1. The individual's self-concept is based on his perception of the way others are responding to him.
2. The individual's self-concept functions to direct his behavior.
3. The individual's perception of the responses of others toward him reflects the actual responses of others toward him.

Reprinted by permission of the University of Chicago Press and John W. Kinch from "A Formalized Theory of the Self-Concept," by John W. Kinch in *The American Journal of Sociology*, LXVIII, Jan. 1963, pp. 481–483.

Intrapersonal Dimensions

(These postulates are not expected to hold under all conditions: The formalization procedure described below allows us to consider under what conditions they will hold.)
These three statements make up the postulates of the theory. The reason for this selection will become apparent later. Within these propositions there are four basic concepts or variables:

1. The individual's self-concept (S). (Defined above.)
2. His perception of the responses of others toward him (P). (The response of the individual to those behaviors of others that he perceives as directed toward him.)
3. The actual responses of others toward him (A). (The actual behavior of the others, that is, in response to the individual.)
4. His behavior (B). (The activity of the individual relevant to the social situation.)

At this point it is possible to see the first advantage from our formalized theory. By the use of simple logic we may take the three basic propositions and deduce from them three more. For example, from postulates 1 and 2 we can conclude that the way an individual perceives the response of others toward him will influence his behavior, for if his perception determines his self-concept and his self-concept guides his behavior, then his perception will determine his behavior. In symbolic form,

$$\begin{array}{ll} \text{if } P \to S & \text{postulate 1} \\ \text{and } S \to B & \text{postulate 2} \\ \hline \text{then } P \to B & \text{proposition 4} \end{array}$$

Therefore, the fourth proposition of the theory (call it a derived proposition) is:

5. The way the individual perceives the responses of others toward him will influence his behavior.

In like manner from postulates 1 and 3 we deduce a fifth proposition:

6. The actual responses of others to the individual will determine the way he sees himself (his self-concept).

And, finally, by combining either propositions 5 and 2, or 3 and 4 we get the sixth proposition:

7. The actual responses of others toward the individual will affect the behavior of the individual.

Our theory so far can be summarized in the following statement: The actual responses of others to the individual will be important in determining how the individual will perceive himself; this perception will influence his self-conception which, in turn, will guide his behavior. Symbolically,

$$A \rightarrow P \rightarrow S \rightarrow B \longrightarrow = \text{``leads to''}$$

Before proceeding further into the analysis of the theory let us consider a short anecdote to clarify what we have said so far. The following story is alleged by some to be true; however, the present author has no confirmation of this and the story is presented only as a helpful device to make a point.

A group of graduate students in a seminar in social psychology became interested in the notions implied in the interactionist approach. One evening after the seminar five of the male members of the group were discussing some of the implications of the theory and came to the realization that it might be possible to invent a situation where the "others" systematically manipulated their responses to another person, thereby changing that person's self-concept and in turn his behavior. They thought of an experiment to test the notions they were dealing with. They chose as their subject (victim) the one girl in the seminar. The subject can be described as, at best, a very plain girl who seemed to fit the stereotype (usually erroneous) that many have of graduate student females. The boys' plan was to begin in concert to respond to the girl as if she were the best-looking girl on campus. They agreed to work into it naturally so that she would not be aware of what they were up to. They drew lots to see who would be the first to date her. The loser, under the pressure of the others, asked her to go out. Although he found the situation quite unpleasant, he was a good actor and by continually saying to himself "she's beautiful, she's beautiful . . ." he got through the evening. According to the agreement it was now the second man's turn and so it went. The dates were reinforced by the similar responses in all contacts the men had with the girl. In a matter of a few short weeks the results began to show. At first it was simply a matter of more care in her appearance; her hair was combed more often and her dresses were more neatly pressed, but before long she had been to the beauty parlor to have her hair styled, and was spending her hard-earned money on the latest fashions in women's campus wear. By the time the fourth man was taking his turn dating the young lady, the job that had once been undesirable was now quite a pleasant task. And when the last man in the conspiracy asked her out, he was informed that she was pretty well booked up for some time in the future. It seems there were more desirable males around than those "plain" graduate students.

Our story suggests that the girl perceived the actual response of others (the men) in such a way as to require a change in her self-concept which in turn eventually changed her behavior. So their behavior influenced hers. However, the story brings to light another proposition that has so far been overlooked. At the end of the experiment we saw that the men's responses to the girl's behavior had changed, and they were now reacting to her as a desirable young lady. A new postulate then would be:

7. The behavior that the individual manifests influences the actual responses of others toward that individual.

We are not dealing with any new variables but rather with a new combination of the old ones. The theory at this point becomes circular:

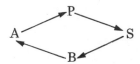

It will be noted that with the addition of this new postulate a whole new set of derived propositions emerge. There are now 16 interrelated propositions in our simple theory which has only four variables. Rather than laboriously listing these propositions, let us now consider some of the factors which modify one of the propositions.

It is apparent that as the theory now stands it has not gone far enough in explaining the phenomena under consideration, and it might prove misleading if left as is. The major problem lies in the fact that the propositions are presented as if there was a one-to-one relationship between the variables dealt with. It is obvious that in reality these propositions hold only in varying degrees under certain conditions. To illustrate the type of thing that might be done, we will briefly consider the conditions under which we would expect proposition 3 to hold

This postulate states that the individual's perception of the responses of others toward him reflects the actual responses of others. We have a rather generous supply of evidence relating to the accuracy of this postulate: Studies of role-taking ability have, almost without exception, operationally defined role-taking ability in terms of the relationship between the individual's perception of the responses of others and the actual responses. *The evidence seems to suggest that the accuracy of postulate 3 varies with (1) the individual's familiarity with the others, (2) his familiarity with the situation, (3) the social visibility of the situation, (4) the individual's past experience in interpersonal situations, and (5) other factors which relate to all types of perception (conditions of body, immediate past, etc.).* Briefly, what this proposition says is that the more familiar the individual is with the situation and the others in the situation, the more socially visible the situation is, the more experience the individual has had in interpersonal situations and the less interference there is from irrelevant conditions, the more likely it is that postulate 3 will hold.

# THE COGNITIVE FOUNDATIONS OF BELIEFS
## Daryl J. Bem

Certain opinions seem to go together. For example: I support strong civil rights legislation; I was always a "dove" on Vietnam; I am more afraid of fascism than of communism in our country; I worry less about the size of our national debt than about the unequal distribution of our national wealth; I believe that college women should no more be subjected to curfews than college men; and I think the Black Power movement is a good thing. On their surface, these diverse opinions do not seem to follow logically from one another—there are even some implied inconsistencies among them—and yet, if you knew only one of my opinions, you could probably guess the others with pretty fair accuracy. Certain opinions do seem to go together.

Of course, there does seem to be a kind of logic involved here. The opinions given above all appear to follow more or less from a common set of underlying values (such as equality, for example). This can be true of "conservative" opinions as well. For example, my neighbor says that his major value is individual freedom and that therefore he is opposed to open-housing laws and to legislation which regulates the possession of firearms. I may disagree with his opinions, but I can appreciate the logic involved. Curiously, however, my freedom-loving neighbor also advocates stiffer penalties for the use of marijuana, feels that women belong in the home, and believes that consenting adults who engage in homosexual behavior should get long prison terms. Here the logic involved is less than clear, yet these opinions too seem strangely predictable. Indeed, my neighbor and I both profess to hold individual freedom as a basic value, and we both claim that our opinions are consistent with our values. Yet we find each other's opinions highly disagreeable.

In short, beliefs, attitudes, and values do seem to be logi-

From Daryl J. Bem, *Beliefs, Attitudes, and Human Affairs*, pp. 4-13. Copyright © 1970 by Wadsworth Publishing Company, Inc. Reprinted by permission of the publisher, Brooks/Cole Publishing Company, Monterey, California.

cally connected, but in some instances the logic seems more Freudian than Aristotelian. It is this mixture of logic and psycho-logic that concerns us. It is this mixture of logic and psycho-logic that constitutes the cognitive foundations of beliefs and attitudes.

## PRIMITIVE BELIEFS

If a man perceives some relationship between two things or between some thing and a characteristic of it, he is said to hold a belief. For example, he might suppose asteroids and oranges to be round, the dean of women to be square, God to be dead, men to love freedom, himself to dislike spinach, and Republicans to promote progress. Collectively, a man's beliefs compose his understanding of himself and his environment.

Many beliefs are the product of direct experience. If you ask your friends why they believe oranges are round, they will most likely reply that they have seen oranges, felt oranges, and that oranges are, indeed, round. And that would seem to end the matter. You could, of course, ask them why they trust their senses, but that would be impolite.

Consider a more complicated belief. If you ask your friends why they believe the asteroids are round (that is, spherical), the more sophisticated among them might be able to show how such a conclusion is derived from physical principles and astronomical observations. You could press them further by asking them to justify their belief in physical principles and astronomical observations: Whence comes their knowledge of such things? When they answer that question—perhaps by citing the *New York Times*—you can continue to probe: Why do they believe everything they read in the *Times*? If they then refer to previous experience with the accuracy of the *Times* or recall that their teachers always had kind words for its journalistic integrity, challenge the validity of their previous experience or the credibility of their teachers.

What you will discover by such questioning—besides a noticeable decline in the number of your friends—is that every belief can be pushed back until it is seen to rest ultimately upon a basic belief in the credibility of one's own sensory experience or upon a basic belief in the credibility of some external authority. Other beliefs may derive from these basic beliefs, but the basic beliefs themselves are accepted as givens. Accordingly, we shall call them "primitive beliefs."[1]

### Zero-Order Beliefs

Our most fundamental primitive beliefs are so taken for granted that we are apt not to notice that we hold them at all; we remain unaware of them until they are called to our attention or are brought into question by some bizarre circumstance in which they appear to be violated. For example, we believe that an object continues to exist even when we are not looking at it; we believe that objects remain the same size and shape as we move away from them even though their visual images change; and, more generally, we believe that our perceptual and conceptual worlds have a degree of orderliness and stability over time. Our faith in the validity of our sensory experience is the most important primitive belief of all.

These are among the first beliefs that a child learns as he interacts with his environment, and in a psychological sense, they are continuously validated by experience. As a result, we are usually unaware of the fact that alternatives to these beliefs *could* exist, and it is precisely for this reason that we remain unaware of the beliefs themselves. Only a very unparochial and intellectual fish is aware that his environment is wet. What else could it be? We shall call primitive beliefs of this fundamental kind "zero-order" beliefs. They are the "nonconscious" axioms upon which our other beliefs are built.[2]

### First-Order Beliefs

Because we implicitly hold these zero-order beliefs about the trustworthiness of our senses, particular beliefs that are based upon direct sensory experiences seem to carry their own justification. When a man justifies his belief in the roundness of oranges by citing his experiences with oranges, that in fact usually does end the matter. He does not run through a syllogistic argument of the form:

1st Premise: My senses tell me that oranges are round.
2nd Premise: My senses tell me true.
Conclusion: Therefore, oranges are round.

There is no such inferential process involved in going from the first premise to the conclusion, as far as the individual himself is concerned, because he takes the second premise for granted: It is a zero-order belief. Accordingly, the first premise ("My senses tell me that oranges are round") is psychologically synonymous with the conclusion ("Oranges are round"). We shall call such conclusions "first-order" beliefs. Unlike zero-order beliefs, an individual is usually aware of his first-order beliefs because he can readily imagine alternatives to them (oranges could be square), but he is usually *not* aware of any inferential process by which they derive from zero-order beliefs. Like zero-order beliefs, then, first-order beliefs are still appropriately called primitive beliefs—that is, beliefs which demand no independent formal or empirical confirmation and which require no justification beyond a brief citation of direct experience.

### Primitive Beliefs Based on External Authority

We not only experience our world directly, we are told about it as well. It is in this way that notions about such intangibles as God, absent grandmothers, and threatened tooth decay first enter a child's system of beliefs. And to the child, such beliefs may seem as direct, as palpable, and as assuredly valid as any beliefs based on direct sensory encounter. When mommy says that not brushing after every meal causes tooth decay, that is synonymous with the *fact* that not brushing after every meal causes tooth decay. Such a belief is a primitive first-order belief for the child because the intervening premise, "Mommy says only true things," is nonconscious; the possibility that mommy sometimes says false things is not a conceivable alternative. First-order beliefs based upon a zero-order belief in the credibility of an external authority, then, are functionally no different from first-order beliefs based upon an axiomatic belief in the credibility of our senses. As sources of information, mommy and our senses are equally reliable. Our implicit faiths in them are zero-order beliefs.

This emphasis upon the innocence of childhood should not obscure the fact that we all hold primitive beliefs. It is an epistemological and psychological necessity, not a flaw of intellect or a surplus of naïveté. We all share the fundamental zero-order beliefs about our senses, and most of us hold similar sorts of first-order beliefs. For example, we rarely question beliefs such as "This woman is my mother" and "I am a human being." Most of us even treat arbitrary social-linguistic conventions like "This is my left hand" and "Today is Tuesday" as if they were physical bits of knowledge handed down by some authority who "really knows." Finally, most religious and quasi-religious beliefs are first-order beliefs based upon an unquestioned zero-order faith in some internal or external source of knowledge. The child who sings "Jesus loves me—this I know,/For the Bible tells me so" is actually being less evasive about the metaphysical—and hence noncomfirmable—nature of his belief than our founding fathers were when they presumed to interpret reality for King George III: "We hold these truths to be self-evident. . . ."

### Generalizations and Stereotypes

Very few of our primitive beliefs rest directly upon a single experience. Most of them are abstractions or generalizations from several experiences over time. Thus an individual may believe life in the city to be hectic, John to be generous, freedom to be wonderful, and modern art to be hard to understand. Each such belief arises out of several separate situations, but because the individual still relates such beliefs to direct experience, they are properly classified as primitive beliefs. As far as the individual is concerned, they still spring directly from a source whose credibility is axiomatic and self-evident: His senses.

But life in the city is not always hectic; John has been stingy on occasion; freedom is sometimes not so wonderful; and modern art is frequently comprehensible. Generalizations, in short, are not always true for all instances beyond the set of experiences upon which they are based. And when an individual treats such generalizations as if they were universally true, we usually call them stereotypes. For a number of reasons, most of us have learned to regard stereotypes as undesirable. Sometimes, for example, stereotypes are based upon no valid experience at all but are picked up as hearsay or are formed to rationalize our prejudices. Then, too, stereotypes are frequently used to justify shabby treatment of individuals on the basis of assumed group characteristics which neither they nor the group, in fact, possess.

But it is important to realize that the process by which most stereotypes arise is not itself evil or pathological. Generalizing from a limited set of experiences and treating individuals as members of a group are not only common cognitive acts but necessary ones. They are "thinking devices" which enable us to avoid conceptual chaos by "packaging" our world into a manageable number of categories. It is simply not possible to deal with every situation or person as if it or he were unique, and the formation of "working stereotypes" is inevitable until further experiences either refine or discredit them. For example, many freshmen from rural areas of the country spend the first few weeks of college thinking all New Yorkers are Jews and all Jews are New Yorkers. There is not necessarily any malice or ill will behind such a stereotype; the freshman has simply not yet seen the distinguishing characteristics of Jews and New Yorkers uncorrelated—if there are such characteristics. But when his "obviously-New-York-Jewish" roommate turns out to be a Christian Scientist from New Jersey named Murphy, and the Texan with cowboy boots allows as how his father is a rabbi in Houston, the freshman soon begins to sort his social environment into more finely differentiated categories. I suspect that most of our stereotypes are of this benign variety and that we learn to discard the irrelevant characteristics from our social categories as our experiences broaden and multiply.

The most important word here, however, is "broaden." The new experiences must be the kind which does, in fact, separate the relevant characteristics from the irrelevant ones, not the kind which serves to reinforce the stereotypes. For example, it is often suggested that increased contact between ethnic groups will automatically cause the disappearance of stereotypes. But nobody has more interracial contact than black ghetto residents and white policemen. Yet these interracial contacts are not particularly noted for producing spectacular interracial tolerance. The point, of course, is that the white policemen deal primarily with the criminal element within the ghetto and that the black residents see precisely those whites in the ghetto who are cast in authoritarian roles. Such contacts only reinforce the stereotypes on both sides because the racial identification continues to be coupled with the irrelevant characteristics.

The worst failure of such contacts is not that they occur in hostile situations (although that certainly doesn't help) but that the participants are not of equal status (Allport, 1954). Thus, we see similar kinds of stereotypes being maintained on both sides even in the more benign encounters between black ghetto residents and white shop owners or welfare agency employees, where, again, the equal-status requirement is not fulfilled. It is when this requirement is satisfied that the participants are most likely to see each other as sharing common beliefs, attributes, and goals, rather than perceiving each other as participants in the old stereotyped roles.

The kind of vicarious interracial contact supplied by the mass media must operate on this same principle of equal-status representation if it too is to be helpful in eliminating stereotypes. In 1968, after years of pressure from civil rights organizations, the mass media finally began to observe this principle by regularly featuring black faces in other than "Negro" roles. Thus, although television commercials may continue to offend our sensibilities for other reasons, they actually do help Americans lose their stereotypes—if only by demonstrating that any odors black Americans may have are the familiar kinds which can be cured by Dial or Listerine.

But if some stereotypes are vulnerable to new experiences, many others can be remarkably impervious to evidence against them. Even repeated disconfirmations of a stereotype can often fail to alter it because the individual treats them as exceptions. Thus, he notes that there is Sidney Poitier or Supreme Court Justice Thurgood Marshall—but then there are "all the rest of them." And some stereotypes are even more cleverly insulated from reality than this because the individual sees to it that there is no way even for exceptions to occur. He simply never bothers to check the stereotype against an independent criterion. For instance, many people claim they can "spot a homosexual a mile away." They can do no such thing, of course. What they can do is recognize a man who displays slightly effeminate gestures, and when they do, they proclaim that they have "spotted another homosexual," thereby reinforcing their stereotype. But since they decline to ascertain the sexual preferences of the "spotted" individual, their reasoning is purely circular. They thus mistakenly classify as homosexual large numbers of nonhomosexual individuals who display effeminate gestures. The man who lays claim to such "homosexual radar" might be mildly unhappy to learn that he is misclassifying these individuals, but it is a safe bet that he would be considerably more agitated to learn that he is failing to detect all those homosexuals who are so inconsiderate as to mingle in our midst without an identifying "swish." But he is safe: Since evidence plays no valid role in the maintenance of such a stereotype, it is effectively insulated against either kind of disconfirmation, and he will never know.

Stereotypes, then, are overgeneralized beliefs based on too limited a set of experiences. Whether stereotypes are evil or benign in their consequences, they are like other first-order primitive beliefs in that they appear to the individual to be self-evident; they appear to demand no justification beyond a citation either of direct experience or of some external authority whose credibility is taken for granted, whose credibility, in other words, is a zero-order primitive belief. All of us rely upon stereotypes to some extent for "packaging" our perceptual and conceptual worlds.

## HIGHER-ORDER BELIEFS

### The Vertical Structure of Beliefs

Although we all hold primitive beliefs throughout our lives, we learn as we leave childhood behind us to regard our sensory experiences as potentially fallible and similarly learn to be more cautious in believing external authorities. We begin, in short, to insert an explicit and conscious premise about an authority's credibility between his word and our belief:[3]

The Surgeon General says that smoking causes cancer.
The Surgeon General is a trustworthy expert.
Therefore, smoking causes cancer.

In such cases, we no longer treat the first premise as synonymous with the conclusion because the second premise is no longer a nonconscious zero-order belief. We are, for example, explicitly aware of the possibility that the Surgeon General might be in error. Accordingly, the conclusion "Smoking causes cancer" is not a primitive belief but rather a derived, or higher-order, belief. It has a "vertical structure" of beliefs underneath it, beliefs which "generate" it as the product of quasi-logical inference.

We also learn to derive higher-order beliefs by reasoning inductively from our experiences:

My aunt contracted cancer.
She died soon after.
Therefore, cancer can cause death.

And finally, we can derive beliefs of a still higher order by building upon premises which are themselves conclusions of prior syllogisms. For example, we can use as premises the conclusions to the two syllogisms above:

Smoking causes cancer.
Cancer can cause death.
Therefore, smokers die younger than nonsmokers.

Note that it is possible for two men to hold the same surface belief but to have different vertical structures of belief. For example, the Surgeon General believes that smokers die younger on the average than nonsmokers, but so also does the man who believes that:

Smoking is a sin.
The wages of sin is death.
Therefore, smokers die younger than nonsmokers.

But the Surgeon General's belief is a higher-order belief based upon a long chain of careful syllogistic reasoning, whereas, for this man, the same conclusion, or surface belief, is only a second-order belief (based on two first-order primitive beliefs).

When a belief has a deep vertical structure, it is said to be highly elaborated or differentiated; to the extent that it has little or no syllogistic reasoning underneath it, it is said to be unelaborated or undifferentiated. A primitive belief is, by definition, completely undifferentiated.

### The Horizontal Structure of Beliefs
We might expect higher-order beliefs to be quite vulnerable to disconfirmation because any one of the underlying premises could be destroyed. Thus, a higher-order belief would appear to be only as strong as its weakest link. This would be true if most higher-order beliefs were not also bolstered by "horizontal" structures as well. That is, a particular higher-order belief is often the conclusion to more than one syllogistic chain of reasoning. For example, the Surgeon General believes that:

| | | |
|---|---|---|
| Smoking causes cancer. | Smokers drink more heavily than non-smokers. | Statistics show smokers die younger than nonsmokers. |
| Cancer can cause death. | Heavy drinking can lead to early death. | These statistics are reliable. |
| Therefore, smokers die younger. | Therefore, smokers die younger. | Therefore, smokers die younger. |

If a man derives his belief that "smokers die younger" from all three lines of reasoning, then his belief will only be partially weakened if one of the syllogisms is faulty or one of the premises turns out to be false. It seems likely that most of our higher-order beliefs rest not upon a single syllogistic pillar but upon many. They have broad horizontal as well as deep vertical structures.

In the course of time, the vertical and horizontal structures of a higher-order belief can change without disturbing the belief itself. We believe as we did before, but our reasons for believing have altered. For example, all the evidence upon which we once based our trust in the *New York Times* may have faded from memory until now our devotion is a blind article of faith, a zero-order belief. Alternatively, additional support may have been obtained for beliefs that were once primitive beliefs or otherwise lacking in respectable justification.

### The Centrality of Beliefs
A belief which has both a broad horizontal and a deep vertical structure is still not necessarily a very important or central belief in an individual's belief system. For example, my belief that asteroids are spherical is based on several different kinds of evidence, and some of the chains of reasoning behind the belief are quite lengthy. My belief therefore has a broad horizontal and a deep vertical structure; it is broadly based and highly differentiated. But if my belief in round asteroids were to be changed somehow, few of my other beliefs would have to be changed as a consequence. In terms of our syllogistic model, many syllogisms lead up to my belief in round asteroids, but few syllogisms depart from it; it appears as a conclusion to many syllogisms but enters as a premise into a very few. This is what is meant by saying that the belief is not very central in my belief system.

Highly differentiated and broadly based beliefs are not necessarily central; the opposite is also true. For example, primitive beliefs are, by definition, completely undifferentiated; they have neither vertical nor horizontal support. And yet many of our primitive beliefs are very central in our belief systems. In fact, our primitive zero-order belief in the general credibility of our senses is the most central belief of all; nearly all of our other beliefs rest upon it, and to lose our faith in it is to lose our sanity. Also, as noted earlier, most of our religious and philosophical beliefs are primitive first-order beliefs upon which many of our other beliefs are built. They, too, are central.

Beliefs, then, differ from one another in the degree to which they are differentiated (vertical structure), in the extent to which they are broadly based (horizontal structure), and in their underlying importance to other beliefs (centrality). These are some of the major factors that contribute to the complexity and richness of our cognitive belief systems.

## LOGIC VERSUS PSYCHO-LOGIC

Underlying the syllogistic description of beliefs presented in this chapter is the notion that individuals do not merely subscribe to random collections of beliefs but rather they maintain coherent systems of beliefs which are internally consistent. This central theme has been the basis for a number of recent psychological theories, called "cognitive consistency" theories. But it is appropriate to point out that to say that a man is consistent is not necessarily to say that he is logical or rational. Thus, even though we have employed the syllogism as a convenient way of representing the structure of beliefs, many of the examples have shown that we are not dealing with strict deductive logic but rather with a kind of psycho-logic. First of all, an inductive generalization based upon experience is often faulty—as our discussion of stereotypes has indicated. Second, even when the logic itself is impeccably deductive, the conclusions to syllogisms can be wrong if any one of the underlying premises is false. Third, there are often inconsistencies between different higher-order beliefs even though the internal reasoning behind each separate belief is consistent within its own vertical structure. That is, one line of reasoning leads to one conclusion; a second line leads to a contradictory conclusion. Finally, one's attitudes and "ulterior motives" can distort the reasoning process so that the logic itself is subtly illogical. When I mention this final point in class, my students are quick to provide their parents' favorite syllogism as an example:

Most heroin addicts started on marijuana.
You kids are experimenting with marijuana.
Therefore, you will become heroin addicts.

As my students suggest in rebuttal, most heroin addicts started on mother's milk. Therefore . . .

## NOTES

1. I have borrowed and slightly modified the concept of a primitive belief from Rokeach (1968).
2. I have chosen the word "nonconscious" to characterize the kind of unawareness described here. In this book, the term "unconscious" is reserved for beliefs or attitudes that we "repress" or keep out of awareness because we find them too painful to admit to ourselves.
3. I have borrowed the idea of using syllogisms to characterize beliefs and attitudes from Jones and Gerard (1967). They are not, of course, responsible for the modifications I have introduced.

## REFERENCES

Allport, G. W., *The Nature of Prejudice*, Reading, Mass.: Addison-Wesley, 1954.

Jones, E. E., and Gerard, H. B., *Foundations of Social Psychology*, New York: Wiley, 1967.

# PART V
# Interpersonal
# Dimensions

The shift in interest to interpersonal dimensions of communication theory at once enlarges and enriches the nature of our inquiry. The study of interpersonal behavior focuses on the interaction of social forces, as against strictly psychological ones, as they relate to the effect of messages on the parties engaged in communication. Clearly, then, the interpersonal dimensions are reciprocal. They involve mutuality and give-and-take. What one person does alters every other aspect of the interchange, particularly the perceptions each party has of himself, each other, the topic, the relationship, and the salient aspects of the physical surroundings.

It is usually fruitless to try to understand the meaning of a message apart from the significance of relationships. Relationships, after all, impose on the meaning of message content. In the essay on "The Meeting of Personalities" Michael Argyle demonstrates why the outcome of a given relationship depends on forces that begin to operate long before the first word is spoken. Argyle also examines the struggle of new associates to synchronize and coordinate their verbal interchange by adjusting such matters as amount and rate of talk, nonverbal reactions, and numerous other facets of behavior which, taken together, help to stabilize a relationship and reach a state of equilibrium.

It is not always necessary for people to start talking in order to initiate a communicative act. Mutual recognition may be all that is required to convey a sense of anticipation and regard. In the essay on "The Perception of People" Hastorf, Schneider, and Polefka examine the tendency of persons to regard the actions of others in causal terms. It is natural to view the actions of other persons as directed at us personally. Person perception also tends to be organized along lines that are interpreted as personally significant. Hence, the process of person perception does not resemble the neutral and passive image of a TV camera; rather, it occurs in ways that can be described as structured, stable, and meaningful.

The experience of other persons also follows another important psychological principle. In any social experience that is defined as personally satisfying, one can usually identify some tangible psychological payoff for the respectives parties. We tend to avoid social situations that have negative or incidental psychological rewards. Conversely, we gravitate to social settings that optimize the chance to satisfy egocentric needs. In "Rewards Others Provide: Propinquity" Berscheid and Walster examine the link between psychological reward and the psychological and physical aspects of proximity. While proximity seems to favor feelings of attraction and mutual regard, the generalization does not always hold. Much of the explanation, according to the authors, is due to the principle of consistency discussed in earlier readings.

Closely related to the issue of person perception and psychological reward is the complex matter of source credibility. Images of credibility impose on the meaning of relationships and message content. Everything about a person—his style and manner, appearance and actions—may contribute to the impressions others have of him. Yet some matters are far more central in forming personal impressions than others; particularly significant are the dimensions of trustworthiness, authoritativeness, and dynamism. In an essay on "The Influence of Source Credibility on Communication Effectiveness" Zimbardo and Ebbesen show how impressions of credibility influence the impact of persuasive messages.

Implicit in the notion of social interaction is the idea of risk. Communication involves the risk of change and sometimes the change is not pleasant. Hence, persons create inner defenses to ward off the potentially adverse effect of social wounds. In a discussion of "Defensive Communication" Jack Gibb examines the complex interplay between our inner feelings of threat and the process of communication. Defensive behavior diverts energy from common tasks to self-defense; it may also trigger defensive reactions in others or interfere with effective listening and accurate perception. If left unchecked, it may lead to severe losses of efficiency in communication. From data gathered from recordings of various conversations, Gibb offers an insightful view of defensive communication and the requirements necessary to establish a supportive social climate.

# THE MEETING OF PERSONALITIES
## Michael Argyle

### PERCEPTION OF THE OTHER

Subject A will have his own characteristic set of social techniques; but these will vary to some extent according to the age, sex, and personality of the other, of B. A will use one set of techniques for one group of people, and a somewhat different set for another group. Before he can select one style rather than another, A has to perceive and categorize B. And of course while A is categorizing B and preparing to use a particular set of social responses, B is doing exactly the same with regard to A.

Much may happen before they meet at all. We shall not consider questions of previous correspondence, or telephone calls, because these are really forms of interaction. A may know a lot about B by repute, from what he has been told by other people. This can be reproduced in laboratory experiments on "set," in which subjects are given information about one another. As we shall see, it makes a great difference to the subsequent interaction whether the other person is described as "warm" or "cold" for example. It also makes a difference whether the other person is known to be a friend or foe, of higher or lower status, and so on.

The actual occasion of meeting may be accidental, by introduction, or through belonging to the same group. At this point A experiences his first perception of B. An important aspect of this perception is that A will categorize B in terms of social class, race, age, intelligence or whatever dimensions of people are most important to him, and this will activate the appropriate set of social techniques on the part of A. It is found that people vary widely in what they look for first in others. Women (and psychologists) tend to look for personality traits and social techniques; men on the other hand are more interested in status and achievement. People become most accurate at assessing whatever qualities concern them most—anti-Semites are better at identifying Jews for example.

The categorization needs to be made, because an anti-Semitic person will use quite different social techniques with Jews and Gentiles, and he wants to know which to select. Precisely the same is true of a person for whom differences of social class, or of intelligence, are of most importance.

In addition to this categorization, B will be classified as being one "kind of person" or another, i.e., in terms of personality traits. While psychologists use traits such as "introvert ," "neurotic," "authoritarian," nonpsychologists make use of all kinds of private systems for classifying each other. The categories may be extremely weird, and reflect peculiar personal mythologies. Others may be divided simply into the "saved" and the "not-saved," U and non-U, or into finer subgroups. These categorizations are based on B's clothes, accent, facial expression, and other cues: A girl with a lot of lipstick is commonly perperceived as highly sexed; a man with tousled hair is seen as aggressive. This personal classification also affects the selection of appropriate social techniques, and thus has a great effect on behavior, no matter how odd it may be or how unrelated to the latest psychological research on personality dimensions.

In addition to perceiving B's personality, A also keeps a continual watch on B's emotional state, B's attitude to A, and his degree of involvement in the interaction. The cues for this are mainly B's facial expression, direction of gaze, and tone of voice. A keeps a check on the first two by intermittent glances in the region of the eyes.

There are great individual differences in sensitivity to these cues; some kinds of mental patient are very bad at it. Sherlock Holmes was very good at it: He perceived that Watson had returned to his medical practice in this way:

if a gentleman walks into my rooms smelling of iodoform, with a black nitrate of silver upon his right forefinger, and a bulge on the side of his top hat to show where he has secreted his stethoscope, I must be dull indeed if I do not pronounce him to be an active member of the medical profession [A Scandal in Bohemia].

Sensitivity is a result of past experience; anyone who goes to Africa or Asia has to learn a new set of cues even to judge age; the cues for social class, personality, and emotion are much more difficult. Sensitivity can be increased by special training; this is useful in training for professional skills and may also prove to be useful in therapy.

## THE SELECTION OF SOCIAL TECHNIQUES

While there are as many private category systems as there are people, the most common factors determining social style are the other's sex, age, social class, and "warmth" or "coldness." It may be that B arouses particular motivations, or A may have learnt from past experience that different types of persons need to be handled in different ways, so that appropriate social techniques must be used from the outset.

Some people behave so differently towards men and women that they seem to undergo a personality change when moving from one kind of encounter to the other. A young man may be very relaxed with men, but terrified of women, or aggressive and competitive towards men and very amorous and at ease with women. Such differences of techniques are learnt in the course of relations with parents, and later with male and female members of the peer group during adolescence. The effect of both sex and age are shown in a study by Block (1953). The nine members of a laboratory were asked to describe their manner of interaction with every other member, by placing a set of cards in order, with the cards best describing the interaction on top. The senior members of the department were reacted to as shown by the following cards. "I am sarcastic to him," "I try to deceive him," "I am ill at ease," and others indicating the erection of a self-protective shell in the presence of people of higher status. On the other hand, behavior towards the female secretaries shows an easy "acquaintanceship without intimacy." Some of the middle-ranking members were reacted to as follows: "I confide in him," "I am sympathetic and warm to him," "I get angry at him."

Age is a more differentiated variable than sex: Some people have different ways of behaving towards young children, older children, teenagers, young adults, etc., with any number of fine variations; others may use broader divisions, e.g., between those who are older or younger than themselves.

Social class, especially in Britain, is an important dimension for the classification of others for most people. Authoritarians in particular treat those of greater or less status and power quite differently—deferring to the one, and dominating the other. It is found that salesgirls in retail stores categorize the customers in terms of class, and feel nervous and apprehensive about the upper-middle-class ones, because of the haughty manner they are felt to adopt (Woodward, 1960). Social class, like age, is a dimension which can be subdivided many times.

Social class and age each have two separate effects on the social techniques adopted. Firstly there is the question of whether the other person is higher or lower, secondly of how great the social distance. There may be certain age or class groups for which a person virtually has no social techniques at all—he is simply unable to interact with members of them. This can be observed for some adults in relation to children, some upper-middle-class and working-class people to each other, some adolescents in relation to adults, and most children in relation to adults outside the family circle. This no doubt reflects a lack of experience with the groups in question, combined with the discovery that the familiar social techniques are completely useless.

The warmth or coldness of another person can be seen from his manner, or it can be introduced experimentally in the experimental instructions. Kelley (1950) did this and found that the subjects' behavior was markedly affected. When led to expect that the other person would be warm they were more eager to interact with him, and behaved in a more friendly way. If a person is seen as cold, not only is less affiliative behavior shown towards him, but usually the whole style of behavior is changed, in the direction of greater formality.

But do different people need to be handled differently? The evidence above shows that people act as if this is so, but they may not be right. The interesting point is that while people vary their behavior according to demographic variables—age, sex, and class, a lot of research suggests that social techniques really need to be adjusted with respect to the *personality* of the other. It may still be the case that demographic distinctions are important; there is little evidence, and we may conclude that people have found out from experience that they are, and vary their techniques accordingly. However, it looks as if they are failing to modify their techniques with personality dimensions—probably because these are less easily perceived. It follows that most people could improve the effectiveness of their social performance if they learnt to modify it in this way. We now turn to some of the evidence in this area.

Introverts and extroverts need to be handled differently. Experiments with schoolchildren show that introverts respond better to praise, while extroverts respond better to blame: It may be felt that it would be unethical to use blame for extroverts on the strength of this finding, but at least it should be realized that blame is ineffective with introverts. Variation of motivation in others means that they will strive for different goals in social situations and can be rewarded in different ways. One may need a strong leader, another a submissive follower, a third needs acceptance of his self-image and so on. For those very low in affiliative needs the usual social rewards will not be rewarding, and this will be true if the other person has no wish for affiliative relations with the actor.

Variations in anxiety, or neuroticism, mean that some people will be very ill at ease in social situations. When with them it is important to adopt social techniques which will reduce their anxiety. Experienced interviewers may spend up to half an interview doing just this. Some methods of persuasion involve arousing anxiety and then suggesting ways of relieving it: For those who are anxious already this creates so much anxiety that they simply want to forget the whole affair.

Attitudes to authority and to the peer group are important. Juvenile delinquents are often very hostile to authority but behave quite differently with members of their peer group. Those in authority can only handle such boys if they adopt the manner of an older member of the peer group, and make special efforts to win the confidence of the boys, such as taking them into their confidence, or granting special privileges. On the other hand, some children, and a few students, have a great reverence for authority, being strong in dependency: For them the mildest suggestion is enough to influence their behavior.

## SOCIAL TECHNIQUES AND SOCIAL INTERACTION

Two people may meet, each with his own social drives and his own social techniques, but there will be no proper interaction unless the two sets of techniques mesh together in a synchronized and coordinated manner. If both talk all the time, if both shout orders or ask questions, to give three obvious cases, there cannot be said to be social interaction at all. Between such extreme cases, and a well-conducted interview or a conversation between friends, there are degrees of coordination of techniques. Rather low on the scale for example would be conversation with a schizophrenic, with long pauses, irrelevant remarks, and inappropriate emotions being expressed.

If A wants to use his favored social techniques, it is necessary for B to adopt a synchronizing set. This may involve behaving in a similar way to A, such as sharing his emotional state, or in a complementary way, such as being dominant while A is dependent. If A and B both produce their preferred techniques, they will not find in general that there is a perfect fit: One or both therefore will have to change their techniques so that there is better coordination. When they know each other well there will be excellent coordination, and getting to know a person better involves such improved coordination.

If A's and B's techniques are not coordinated, neither set of techniques will be successful; particularly in relation to affiliative needs the experience of clashing techniques is felt immediately to be jarring and unpleasant. People usually attempt to correct this state of affairs at once by modifying their techniques. If they cannot do so as a result of having a limited repertoire, or through being unwilling to depart too far from their preferred techniques, they will find the situation unrewarding, and leave it if they can. It is possible for a person to restrict his social contacts to people with whom he interacts perfectly. Two people may come to synchronize their social techniques by a period of gradual adjustment to one another, and may be helped by the existence of rules governing interaction, and in particular by rules of politeness and etiquette. Synchronization is necessary along a number of different dimensions for smooth and motivationally satisfying interaction to take place.

1. *Amount of speech.* Two people should speak enough for nearly all of the time to be filled with speech, for the duration of the encounter. If they speak more than this, there will be interruption and double-speaking; if they speak less than this, there will be periods of silence. When A has finished speaking, B should reply. The period of silence which can be tolerated before it is experienced as embarrassing depends on the situation and the general tempo of interaction. If interaction is smooth, then A speaks X percent of the time, and B a little under 100 minus X percent of the time. As they will usually

alternate, if A speaks more than B this is because his speeches are longer than B's. The length and frequency of encounters is a quite different matter and, as will be seen below, is mainly a function of how rewarding each party finds them. However, this too is something on which they would have to synchronize their behavior, as it takes two to make an encounter.

2. *The speed or tempo of interaction* consists of a number of variables, which are found to go together—the actual rate of speaking in words per second, the shortness of the interval before replying, and the rate of movements of eyes, facial expression and other parts of the body. If A has a much faster rate than B, A may feel bored, and regard B as slow and dull, while B may feel rattled and ill at ease, and regard A as jumpy and nervous. Each would find the interaction dissatisfying, if not intolerable.

3. *Dominance* is partly a matter of who speaks most, partly of the degrees of deference with which A and B treat each other, of whose ideas are to be taken most seriously, and of who shall for purposes of the encounter be regarded as the more important person. If A and B each wish to consider themselves to be the dominant member, there is incompatibility of styles—both may give orders, but none are obeyed. If A is really senior to B, but is not treated with sufficient deference, again there is disharmony: B is not playing the necessary complementary role for A. "If everyone is somebody, no one is anybody"; for one person to have high status it is necessary to have enough people playing the supporting roles properly. Schutz (1958) set up experimental groups whose members were incompatible in that more than one was high in dominance—thus creating a struggle for dominance and an initial failure of meshing. These groups were found to be very ineffective in the performance of cooperative tasks.

There may be failure of meshing in another way. Haythorn (1956) created groups of four, where one member was designated the leader, and where different combinations of authoritarian and nonauthoritarian leaders and followers were compared. The groups ran most smoothly, with least conflict between leader and followers, when both leader and followers were authoritarian, or where both were nonauthoritarian. In each case leader and followers were using social techniques which fitted in a complementary way.

4. *Intimacy* we have discussed previously and shown to be a function of physical closeness, eye-contact, conversation on personal topics, and so on. If A uses techniques corresponding to greater intimacy than B, A will feel that B is cold, formal, and standoffish. B will feel that A is intrusive and overfamiliar. This immediate incongruity can only be overcome by the adoption of an intermediate position on the dimensions of intimacy, such as agreeing to an intermediate amount of spatial proximity and eye-contact. This will involve motivational costs to both A and B. Again, when we say that A adopts affiliative techniques, this means that he is seeking a certain pattern of response from the other. It is not enough to look B in the eye—B must look back with a friendly expression.

5. *Cooperation and competition.* It is no good trying to run a race against someone if they don't try to win too—it takes two to have a competition and the other must play his part. Similarly A may want B to cooperate in some task, which means trusting B not to take advantage of him. Many situations have elements of both cooperation and competition, so that it is necessary for A and B to work out just how far and over what areas they are going to compete. This is a common situation in professional life, when two friends may both be candidates for the same job.

6. *Emotional tone.* If A is elated and euphoric while B is anxious or depressed, there is incongruity. To everything that happens A and B are likely to react in quite different ways, involving incompatible reactions and remarks.

7. *Task, topic, and procedure.* Two children may want to play different games, two research workers may want to set about the work differently, psychotherapist and patient may want to talk about different topics. These are all cases of disharmony, which must be resolved before smooth interaction, and efficient task performance can take place. Any small group of people who work together develop standardized, even "ritualized," procedures for situations that commonly occur.

Meshing involves a smooth sequence of verbal utterances, or whatever the social behavior consists of. In an experiment by the writer and some of his colleagues it was found that subjects, particularly male ones, did not need to see the person they were talking to if they were invisible themselves. The explanation of this may be that normally interactors are engaged in a kind of "kinesic dance" in which their visible bodily movements are closely coordinated with those of their partners. When a person is invisible no coordination is necessary.

Once a pair of people, or a small social group, has developed synchronized social techniques which meet to some extent the social needs of all, there is then a resistance to any change from this state of affairs. It is often described as a condition of "equilibrium" in that any change is met with forces to restore the status quo. If A behaves in a more aggressive or less friendly way than usual this leads to negative reactions from the others, and anxiety on the part of A that he will be rejected and not able to take part in future encounters. As a result he is liable to make up for his behavior by a period of unusually pleasant and friendly behavior. If B talks more than usual, this will be met by interruptions, and negative reactions on the part of the others, resulting in a period of silence by B. If C talks less than usual, others will address questions to him, and in other ways prompt him to talk more. Lennard and Bernstein (1960) studied interactions between therapists and patients over a long series of sessions for each pair. They found that after the initial sessions each pair settled down to a characteristic, equilibrium style of interaction. For example the proportion of conversation due to the therapist was remarkably constant, rarely deviating by more than 6½ percent from his average. In some sessions equilibrium was disturbed by the occurrence of long silences, giving rise to discomfort and anxiety. It was found that the therapist usually restored the equilibrium in the session immediately following by making statements containing more specific information (which reduce anxiety) while the patient asked for evaluation, e.g., "Do you think we are getting anywhere, Doctor?"

Goffman (1955) has made some very acute observations on how equilibrium is restored after loss of face by a participant. If a person behaves unpleasantly, or in some other way fails to live up to the image he has projected, equilibrium is disturbed. The usual sequence for restoring equilibrium is as follows: (a) The offending member is challenged, calling attention to what has happened; (b) he is offered a chance to correct things—it was only a joke, it was unintentional, he was not a free agent; otherwise his image must be corrected, he

251

makes penance for his offence, and gives compensation to the injured parties; (c) the offender accepts this situation, and (d) shows gratitude to the others.

Once an equilibrium condition has been reached, can it ever be changed? It probably can, provided that this is a very gradual process, and provided that the others gain rather than lose in the satisfactions which they get from the relationship. Suppose that A talks 30 percent of the time, B 65 percent of the time, and that A wants to talk more. He can gradually increase the length of his speeches, or interrupt B, provided that what he says is sufficiently interesting, flattering, or otherwise rewarding for B. Suppose that A is dominated by B, and would like to turn the tables. He can gradually put forward stronger suggestions, and become more resistant to accepting B's, provided that the content of his suggestions is acceptable to B, or that he thinks of schemes which are to B's advantage.

## PREDICTION OF OUTCOME
If two people, A and B, are introduced, is it possible to predict what kind of social relationship or pattern of interaction will be set up? In one sense this should be easy—the whole study of personality suggests that people are fairly consistent in the extent to which they are anxious, aggressive, extroverted, and so on. However someone who is for example dominant, is not equally dominant on all occasions, while on some he may be positively submissive. In fact, it is found that only a rather poor general prediction can be made of how A will behave with any particular B. Everyone has a number of "subpersonalities," $A_1$, $A_2$, etc.—cases of multiple personality are an extreme of what is universal. Which of these subpersonalities will appear for B's benefit will depend on how B is categorized, as we saw above—whether B is seen as warm or cold, or of a particular social class. These subpersonalities are not of course completely independent, like a series of different people. Take anxiety as an example: A has an average level of anxiety, but he may be much more anxious than usual ($A_1$, say) in a really frightening situation, and rather less anxious than usual ($A_2$) in a particularly safe and relaxing situation. Another person, C, who is generally less anxious than A will be less anxious than A in each of these situations.

Anxiety is partly a matter of the person, partly of the situation. Precisely the same is true of dominance, affiliation, amount of speech, etc.—A has an average level of each, but the amount on a particular occasion depends on the other person, B. The whole situation is now complicated by the fact that B has a series of subpersonalities too, so that we have to predict whether the final outcome will be $A_1 B_2$, $A_5 B_3$, etc.

It follows from this that it is possible to make some prediction about how A will behave simply from knowledge of A's personality—how strong his affiliative and dominance needs are, how talkative he is, and so on. However, a better prediction can be made by taking account of B's personality too. For example it is possible to predict the dividing up of the time: That is, the percentage of the time that A will speak. Borgatta and Bales (1953) observed 126 men in 14 groups of 9, and recorded the interaction rate of each. The men were classified as high, medium, or low interactors, and placed in new groups of three in various combinations. It was found that a subject's rate of interaction in the new group was positively related to his previously observed level. It was also *inversely* related to the previous interaction rates of the other two group members—i.e., a subject talked more when placed with low interactors, and vice versa. Thus A's new rate of interaction was both a consistent manifestation of his personality, i.e., his general interaction style, and a function of the others present.

In another study, the dominant and submissive relations between each pair of people in groups of five were predicted from previous measures of the individuals concerned. An ascendance index for each person was computed on the assumption that subjects of higher age, social class, and intelligence, and males as opposed to females, would be more dominant. There was also a questionnaire measure of dominance. A's dominance of B could be predicted from A's dominance index, or (inversely) from B's, but the best prediction came from subtracting B's index from A's (Breer, 1960).

In another experiment, pairs of subjects differing in extroversion and intelligence were asked to discuss a topic on which it was known from previous testing that they disagreed. When a highly intelligent person confronted a less intelligent person, the more intelligent person usually managed to persuade the less intelligent person to change his mind. Extroverts were able to dominate introverts in a similar way. The experimenters believed that one person can dominate another if he speaks first and talks more than the other; this was confirmed, since the intelligent and extroverted subjects behaved in this way (Carment, Miles, & Cervin, 1965).

When the prediction of detailed sequences of social responses is considered, the problem becomes far more difficult. Each response of A's is not only a product of A's motivation and style, but also of B's behavior, and in particular his most recent social acts. The internal dynamics of this series are fascinating and will be pursued in later chapters.

How can we tell which person will have to adjust most in a situation where the interaction styles of the two people are initially incompatible? For example, if at first both are talking too much, who will have to give way? Although wanting to outtalk or to dominate the other is a common example, we are concerned with a much wider problem. There may be conflicts about the amount of intimacy that is desired, about what is done or talked about, or one person may want the other to act as a strong leader on whom he can be dependent. There are a number of ways in which a person may acquire the power to control the way in which the interaction proceeds. (1) A may have formal power over B, so that he is able to deliver major rewards and punishments, as in the case of foremen and parents. (2) A may be less attracted towards the situation, and therefore less dependent on it, than B. This is the reason that the most effective performers in some situations avoid close friendships with those they have to deal with. (3) A can provide large rewards for B in that he can help B to attain some goal, whether social or otherwise. (4) If A for some reason is able to initiate the interaction, as in the case of waiters or salesmen, this gives him the chance to control the course of interaction. (5) If A is less sensitive than B to minor negative reactions from the other, or is less concerned about them, he will adjust his behavior less. However, if he goes too far in ignoring B's responses and does not provide large enough rewards for B in compensation, B may simply withdraw.

It has been seen how everyone has a profile of motivation,

so that certain drives are particularly strong, and certain goals will be sought in social situations. The more a person can succeed in establishing the pattern of behavior which meets his needs, the more he will enjoy the situation; the more he has to move away from his preferred interaction pattern the less he will like it. On the other hand there may be other compensatory rewards provided by a particular situation or person, in which case he will on balance still be drawn towards it or him, but in a conflictful way, generating internal tension.

## THE GROWTH OF RELATIONSHIPS
Between the first encounter and the formation of a stable relationship several things happen. Such relationships include friendship between peers, dominant-dependent or sexual relationships, and other more complex ones.

When A and B first meet and experience a sample of the other's social performance, the sample which they experience will not necessarily be a representative one, since it has been selected as described above on the basis of the initial perceptions made by the other. A Jew who has been correctly identified by an anti-Semitic Gentile, or a working-class person who has been correctly placed by a middle-class snob, will not receive a typical sample of the other's social techniques. What he gets is lower in affiliation, and higher in aggression or dominance than is usual for that person. However, this is all that A has to go on, and he will use these early samples of behavior to decide whether the relationship is sufficiently rewarding for it to be continued any further.

When two people first meet they do not at once reveal their innermost secrets, their deepest beliefs or their highest aspirations. Nor do they reveal much about themselves as social persons: Their social techniques are restrained and subdued, so that a very poor sample of their behavior is shown to each other. The reason is similar—if too much is revealed, there is a risk that the other may not like it; if too much of the social person is shown there is a danger that it may not be possible to synchronize with the other. More intimate information is revealed when it is felt that the other will not reject. There are certain standard, and safe, topics of conversation—the weather, cricket scores—for which the conversation is virtually scripted, and very little is revealed about the speakers—at any rate by the verbal aspects of the encounter. At first meeting people fall back on these safe topics and behave with an unusual degree of politeness and formality—indeed, one function of codes of manners is to make such encounters easy. The American and British versions of this have sometimes been contrasted. At first meeting the Englishman is often shy and reserved and has difficulty in making contact at all. The American is much more at ease, and produces a lot of easy small talk, which reveals as little as the Englishman's performance reveals about him.

There is an interesting exception to this restraint at first meeting, and that is when it is known that the other person will never be seen again. People may tell their life story to strangers on trains, but not to their next-door neighbors; intimate relationships may suddenly develop between people who meet on holiday. Sometimes interviewers can capitalize on their "stranger value." These are different from other social encounters since there is no question of continuing relationships, in which synchronizing and acceptance by the other are important.

The longer the period over which two people interact, the more they will disclose about themselves to each other. Taylor (1965) studied pairs of students who shared rooms at college. The amount of self-disclosure increased during the first nine weeks and then leveled off—but at quite different degrees of intimacy for different pairs (see Figure 1). The main increase was at the most superficial level; there was not much increase of disclosure about intimate matters and basic values. Other studies show that intimate disclosure is increased when two people are isolated, and that if A discloses to B, B will disclose to A.

In the early stages of interaction between two people, the relationship is highly unstable—it has not reached a state of equilibrium—so that small disturbances may become magnified in their effects. In an experiment by Back (1951) pairs of subjects were introduced in order to carry out a joint task. Members of some pairs were told that they would find the other person agreeable and easy to get on with, while in other pairs the reverse was indicated. If A is told that B is friendly this causes him to behave in a friendly way towards B; this (and his instructions) in turn elicits friendly responses from

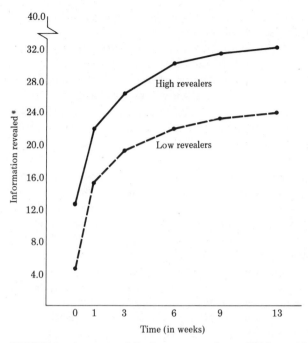

**FIGURE 1.** Amount of disclosure over time of high- and low-revelation between groups of two (Taylor, 1965).

B, confirming A's instructions, and so on. This has been described as a state of "autistic friendship," though in fact it can develop into real friendship. When the negative set is induced, each partner becomes progressively more cautious and suspicious, until eventually interaction ceases and a state of "autistic hostility" ensues—autistic because the partners cannot now find out what the other is really like. Such unstable sequences are known as cases of "positive feedback" (unstable vicious circles) and can be contrasted with self-correcting "negative feedback," which is also a common feature of social performance.

Another positive feedback sequence leading to friendship is that in which frequent interaction leads to liking, and liking leads to more frequent interaction. A number of studies show that frequent interaction leads to interpersonal sentiments becoming more definite, and changing in the direction of increased liking.

In a study of students at Sheffield University, Warr (1965) investigated the effect of living in the same hostel on friendship choices. He found that frequencies of both liking and of disliking were increased by such physical proximity (and hence more frequent interaction), though liking was considerably more common than disliking. The explanation probably is that if two people succeed in establishing a mutually satisfying system of interaction further meetings are rewarding, if not they are punishing. The more the meetings, the greater the chance of adjusting to one another. This raises the problem of why such a positive feedback system should ever stop; whenever two people like rather than dislike each other this should set up increasing circles of interaction and liking until the two people are inseparable. This does sometimes happen, but in most cases the process stops short of the limit. The explanation probably is that as intimacy and frequency of interaction increase, this places greater demands on the synchronizing of social techniques—as is discovered by acquaintances who go on camping holidays together for example. Lovers' quarrels are probably due to stresses produced by the increased difficulties of synchronizing in this increasingly intimate situation. In addition, the amount of time people can spend together is limited by the fact that they have other things to do; i.e., they are affected by other motivations as well.

A second process which takes place in a developing relationship is that the two partners come to find the relationship increasingly rewarding, and therefore find that they are very dependent on the other person. Waller and Hill (1951) have described how this takes place during courtship. Each partner may try to hide his dependence from the other and each may try to test the other's degree of dependence by temporary withdrawal, and feel suicidal himself if the other withdraws. Perhaps the sudden process of "falling in love" corresponds to the interaction-liking cycle, with the attendant sudden increase in dependence.

There is a strong social norm of "reciprocity"—if A helps B, B should do something equivalent for A (Gouldner, 1960). This perhaps helps in the growth of mutual trust. A would not let B down, and assumes that B would act likewise. Similarly A feels able to reveal more intimate and discreditable things about himself to B, without fearing that B will reject him.

Another cyclical process is that between interaction and similarity of attitudes and interests. The more people interact, the more similar their attitudes, beliefs, opinions, and interests become—simply because they influence each other during interaction. However, people also interact more with those who hold similar attitudes—because this gives them social support, and with those who have similar interests—because they can pursue them or talk about them together. Again we might expect interaction and similarity to increase indefinitely once started—but usually they do not. The limiting factor in this case is the rootedness of interests and attitudes in the personality and in other groups. Attitudes and beliefs are often linked to basic motivation, and so cannot be changed without loss; they may also be shared with other groups whose approval is valued. For both these reasons there is often a limit on how far attitudes can be changed as a result of interaction, and consequently a limit on how far intimacy can develop. During adolescence attitudes are more pliable, and there is intense conformity among groups of teenagers and students. This may explain why intimacy develops so readily at this period of life and why friendships formed then are so long-lasting.

## THE DETERMINANTS OF FRIENDSHIP
Much of the research which has been carried out into friendship has used the method known as "sociometry." Subjects are asked which two people out of a given group they would most like to be with in some joint activity, such as being in the same seminar group, or living in the same tent. The choices should be made in private, and the choices should lead to these groupings actually being made. The choices can be plotted in a "sociogram," showing who chooses whom. Figure 2 is part of one.

This example illustrates several patterns often found in sociograms—(1) a cleavage between two subgroups; (2) cliques of people who choose each other (A B G); (3) popular people (E); (4) unpopular people, or "isolates" (D).

The question of immediate interest is why, for example, A should choose B and not C. A may say that B is nicer than C, but D does not agree. People are liked not so much because of their intrinsically "nice" personality traits, but because of something about the relation between A's personality and B's.

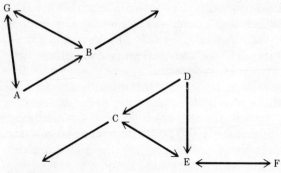

FIGURE 2. Sample sociogram.

The first factor, without which other factors cannot operate, is that A and B must meet, and the more frequently they meet, the more they will like one another, as was shown above.

The next general principle governing liking is the extent to which one person satisfies the needs of another. This was shown in a study by Jennings of 400 girls in a reformatory (1950). She found that girls were chosen if they helped other girls, encouraged them, cheered them up or simply made them feel accepted and wanted. The girls who were not chosen did not provide rewards in these ways, but tried to extract rewards for themselves, by demanding attention, or trying to dominate others or make them do things. Homans (1961) has suggested that all social relationships are like economic bargains, or an exchange of gifts. If A finds he is not receiving enough rewards from B he will become bored, uncooperative, or angry, thus showing B that some adjustment must be made. Or A may start withdrawing from the situation, or cease to provide whatever rewards B expects from the situation. However, although neither A nor B will stay in a relationship unless they find it rewarding, it is not the case that they will receive equal rewards. One person may simply have less attractive alternatives open to him, and so be forced to accept the rather unsatisfactory terms offered by B. Nor is it always the case that when A's rewards fall he will react in a way to cut B's rewards. Very often he will do so, by becoming cold or aggressive, but he may change his social techniques in quite different ways, even becoming warmer and less aggressive, in the hope of influencing B more effectively.

As was shown above, people of similar values and interests

will like one another. Another person with the same beliefs provides social support for one's own. Friendship choices also tend to be directed towards those of similar personality traits. There is another hypothesis—that opposites attract each other. Several studies show that dominant and submissive people may choose one another, but on other traits it is similars rather than opposites who attract. Another related process occurs when the other confirms A's role and ego-identity by taking the complementary role, e.g., pupil to teacher, patient to doctor. B can also confirm A's ego-identity without adopting complementary behavior, as in a "mutual admiration society." This is an example of exchange of gifts, as well as of similar personalities attracting.

A will like B if he sees that B likes him. It is rewarding to be liked, so this is a good basis for liking. The actual proportion of choices that are reciprocated is greater in smaller groups, and where the members know one another well. In some studies people are asked not only for friendship or companionship choices, but also about whom they dislike or reject. It is not found that rejections are reciprocated more than would be expected by chance. The reason is probably that in our society people do not express hostility, while they do express liking, so that it is not known who one's rejectors are.

Lastly, people may choose others who can help them in a particular enterprise, which they cannot carry out so well alone. They are not, in the first place at least, attracted to the other's personality or because any social needs are satisfied. People come to like other members of cooperative groups—because the other members help them to attain their own goals, as when African villagers help each other with house-building, or in catching wild animals. They also combine together in interesting ways to form coalitions against others who are more powerful. When people have been drawn together in any of these ways in order to solve external problems, this establishes a rewarding interpersonal system, sets off a cycle of interaction leading to liking, and may end in genuine friendship choices.

How far does the same person tend to be chosen by many others? To put it another way, is popularity a function of personality? As was said earlier, friendship is due to compatibility between pairs of people, rather than to the "niceness" of the chosen one, but it could still be the case that some people can make themselves agreeable to a larger number of those around them. In fact, there is a small statistical tendency for people high in the following traits to be more popular than those who are low: Extroversion, emotional adjustment, social sensitivity, and intelligence. Rather more important is the extent to which a person conforms to the group norms, manifests the ideals of the group, or contributes to the group's activities. This explains why a person can be highly popular in one group or social setting, but completely rejected in another.

## REFERENCES

Back, K. W., "Influence Through Social Communication," *Journal of Abnormal and Social Psychology*, 1951, **46**, 9-23.

Block, J., "The Assessment of Communication; Role Variation as a Function of Interactional Content," *Journal of Personality*, 1953, **21**, 272-286.

Borgatta, E. F., and Bales, R. F., "Interaction of Individuals in Reconstituted Groups," *Sociometry*, 1953, **16**, 302-320.

Breer, P. E., "Predicting Interpersonal Behavior from Personality and Role," Harvard Ph.D., 1960.

Carment, D. W., Miles, C. G., and Cervin, V. B., "Persuasiveness and Persuasibility as Related to Intelligence and Extroversion," *British Journal of Social and Clinical Psychology*, 1965, **4**, 1-7.

Goffman, E., "On Face-Work: An Analysis of Ritual Elements in Social Interaction," *Psychiatry*, 1955, **18**, 213-231.

Gouldner, A. W., "The Norm of Reciprocity: A Preliminary Statement," *American Sociological Review*, 1960, **25**, 161-178.

Haythorn, W., "The Effects of Varying Combinations of Authoritarian and Egalitarian Leaders and Followers," *Journal of Abnormal and Social Psychology*, 1956, **52**, 210-219.

Homans, G. C., *Social Behavior: Its Elementary Forms*, New York: Harcourt Brace Jovanovich, 1961.

Jennings, H. H., *Leadership and Isolation*, New York: McKay, 1950.

Kelley, H. H., "The Warm-Cold Variable in First Impressions of Persons," *Journal of Personality*, 1950, **18**, 431-439.

Lennard, H. L., and Bernstein, A., *The Anatomy of Psychotherapy*, New York: Columbia University Press, 1960.

Schutz, W. C., *FIRO: A Three-Dimensional Theory of Interpersonal Behavior*, New York: Holt, Rinehart and Winston, 1958.

Taylor, D. A., "Some aspects of the development of interpersonal relationship: social penetration processes," Naval Medical Research Institute, Washington, 1965.

Waller, W. W., and Hill, R., *The Family, a Dynamic Interpretation*, New York: Holt, Rinehart and Winston, 1951.

Warr, P. B., "Proximity as a Determinant of Positive and Negative Sociometric Choice," *British Journal of Social and Clinical Psychology*, 1965, 4, 104-109.

Woodward, J., *The Saleswoman*, New York: Pitman, 1960.

# THE PERCEPTION OF PEOPLE
## Albert H. Hastorf, David J.
## Schneider, and Judith Polefka

Let us now turn our attention more explicitly to the perception of other people. The characteristics of the world of experience in general should hold for our experiences of people, but are there special facets to our experience when we perceive other human beings? Is there not more to our experience of other people than their size, color, and shape? The answer is certainly "Yes."

As an aid in our discussion of person perception, let us consider an example of one person describing another. In *Eminent Victorians*, Lytton Strachey describes Dr. Thomas Arnold, Headmaster of Rugby School:

Such was the man who, at the age of thirty-three, became headmaster of Rugby. His outward appearance was the index of his inward character: everything about him denoted energy, earnestness, and the best intentions. His legs, perhaps, were shorter than they should have been; but the sturdy athletic frame, especially when it was swathed (as it usually was) in the flowing robes of a Doctor of Divinity, was full of an imposing vigour; and his head, set decisively upon the collar, stock, and bands of ecclesiastical tradition, clearly belonged to a person of eminence. The thick, dark clusters of his hair, his bushy eyebrows and curling whiskers, his straight nose and bulky chin, his firm and upward-curving lower lip—all these revealed a temperament of ardour and determination. His eyes were bright and large; they were also obviously honest. And yet—why was it?—Was it in the lines of the mouth or the frown on the forehead?—it was hard to say, but it was unmistakable—there was a slightly puzzled look upon the face of Dr. Arnold.[1]

First of all, this description is a special example of person perception in that it is more organized than many of our experiences in everyday life, partly, no doubt, because the author is attempting to communicate explicitly his perceptions to others. The author also goes well beyond just providing us with a description of Dr. Arnold's physical characteristics and behavior. Many of the characteristics listed are the result of inferences by the author, and yet they are cast as if

Reprinted by permission from *Person Perception* by Albert H. Hastorf, David J. Schneider, and Judith Polefka, Addison-Wesley, Reading, Mass., 1970, pp. 10-15. The excerpt by Red Smith from *The New York Herald Tribune* is reprinted by permission of W. C. C. Publishing Co., Inc.

they were just as clear and as given in experience as is the individual's physical height. The leap from describing such characteristics as hair color and eyebrows to inferences about "energy" and "ardour and determination" is made with considerable agility. The author also includes statements about Dr. Arnold's intentions; he appeared, at least to Mr. Strachey, as having "the best intentions." This tendency not only to perceive others as having intentions but also to make a value judgment about the intentions is, as we shall see, often apparent in our perception of others. The description also includes inferences (stated as perceptual facts) about enduring personality characteristics, such as "honesty" and "eminence." Finally, although the author cannot specify the cues, he infers that Dr. Arnold felt puzzled; he perceives the other's feelings. We can use the characteristics of this description to point out some of the special features of our perception of other people and the ways in which the perception of people differs from the perception of objects. As we noted earlier in our discussion of the constancies, the stimuli produced by objects vary as a function of the conditions under which they are perceived. This is also true of people as stimuli. Furthermore, people behave and behavior is a dynamic rather than a static thing; it is ever-changing and must be carved up into units in order that we may define the stimulus. One of the major ways we separate our ongoing behavior into distinct units is by taking into account behavioral effects. The individual does something and we observe its effect. In essence, the first level of coding in person perception consists of grouping together acts and effects to create manageable perceptual units.

Let us now turn our attention to two very crucial facets of our experience of other people. The first is that we perceive them as *causal agents*. They are potential causes of their behavior. They may intend to do certain things, such as attempting to cause certain effects; and because we see them as one source of their actions, we consider them capable of varying their behavior to achieve their intended effects. This position was formulated by Heider (1944, 1958). Our perception of others' intentionality leads us next to organize the behavior of other people into intent-act-effect segments which form perceptual units. We infer the intentions of another; but we go further. If we perceive a particular intent on several occasions, we are prone to perceive the other as having an enduring personality characteristic. A person who seems to intend to hurt others much of the time will be quickly labeled as hostile. Our verbal label now becomes more abstract because we are categorizing the person according to a characteristic which endures over time.

Second, we perceive other people as similar to ourselves. Hence we are pushed to infer that they possess attributes which, unlike size and behavior, we cannot observe directly but which we are aware of in ourselves. In particular, we perceive others to possess emotional states; we see them as feeling angry, happy, or sad. On some occasions these experiences are of fleeting or temporary states; however, if we perceive them often enough in a person, we code or label that person as having that state as an enduring characteristic; e.g., chronically sad people are depressed.

We can now take a brief look at how our three attributes of experience (structure, stability, and meaning) relate to the perception of people.

*Our experiences of other people are structured.* Just as we create structure in the inanimate world by categorizing stimuli into objects and their attributes, so we create order in the world of people by categorizing them and their behavior. The number of ways that we can categorize people is overwhelmingly large; we can go well beyond any of the possible schemata for inanimate objects. The dictionary, for example, contains thousands of trait names describing ways in which we can perceive people as different. Often we use categories which have been functional in the past. The football coach will employ very different categories for perceiving members of the freshman class than will the Dean of Students or a professor of physics. You may remember that the description of Dr. Arnold by Mr. Strachey was heavily couched in "good Victorian" words like "vigour," "eminence," and "determination" rather than those we might be more likely to use today, such as "warm," "happy," or even (given Dr. Arnold's position) "intellectual."

Dornbush et al. (1965) demonstrated that our past experiences and our present motives affect the categories we use when they explored the categorizing activities of ten- and eleven-year-old children at a summer camp. Children who had lived together in the same tent for two or three weeks were requested in an interview situation to describe their tent mates. The interviewer carefully avoided stipulating any categories; he asked the children to "tell me about ———." The interviews were then coded in order to classify the categories the children had employed in describing one another. An example of a category is "neatness." A statement was classified in this category if it described the other person as being either neat or sloppy. The authors were primarily interested in category usage, not in where the person was placed within the category.

Especially pertinent to our thesis is a comparison of the categorization employed by a common perceiver of different stimuli with the categorization by two different perceivers of a common-stimulus person. The category overlap was greatest when one perceiver described two different children (57%); the overlap for two different perceivers describing the same stimulus person was smaller (45%) and not very different from the overlap obtained (38%) when the descriptions of two different perceivers, each describing a different person, were compared. The last figure was interpreted as the amount of overlap created by a common culture. These data imply that the perceiver plays a dominant role in selecting the characteristics of other people to be observed (and described). He does not passively record the attributes of the other person, but selects and organizes his perceptions in terms of categories which are particularly useful to him.

However, we should be very cautious in designating an individual described by two perceivers as "a common-stimulus person." It is highly likely that when one person interacts with different people on different occasions, he is really not the same stimulus person. His behavior will vary as a function of the situation, which includes the nature of the other participants. This fact is an example of the complexity of both social interaction and person perception. How you categorize and perceive me will influence how you behave toward me, and your behavior, in turn, will influence how I behave. Our point, for the moment, is to stress the role the selecting and categorizing activities of the perceiver play in *creating* his perceptions of the other and in producing structure in his world of other people.

*Our experiences of other people have stability*. The behaviors engaged in by another person vary widely over even brief periods of time; thus the interpersonal acts of another provide as continually varying a stimulus as the size of his body provides the retina when he walks across a room. Were we to perceive as discrete all the acts of another person, our experiential world would be as rapidly changing and unstable as our experience of his size if that were dependent merely on the size of the retinal image. The stability in our experience of other people seems to be produced by processes analogous to those involved in the constancies in perception. We search to perceive the invariant properties of other people.

In perceiving attributes of another person, we focus not on his behavior, which is ever-changing, but on more invariant characteristics, namely, his intents and purposes. Since these invariant properties cannot be perceived directly, our search for invariance is centered on discovering functional relationships between behavior-effect sequences, which are observable, and intentions, which are not. For example, suppose that another person shoves you in the hall, verbally abuses you in a class, and criticizes your friends in private. The behaviors and the contexts in which they are expressed differ, but the same end is achieved: The other person hurts you. Yet the effect is an invariant function of the behavior and the context, just as proximal size is an invariant function of object size and distance. In the attribution to him of the intent to hurt you, an invariance will have been achieved. Whenever we can assume that the person had the ability to produce the behaviors and hence the effects, when we can assume that he was the cause of what occurred, we tend to attribute to him the intent of producing the effect. This attribution of intent provides us with knowledge which will make our future interactions with the person more predictable.

Should we observe the same person behaving in a similar manner toward others, we go further and attribute to him the dispositional property of desiring to hurt other people; we consider him hostile or aggressive. This attribution of a dispositional property to another results again from the search for invariance. If we can classify a person according to certain traits or concepts, we can increase the predictability of our interpersonal world. An aggressive person will act to hurt not only us but others as well. We can predict his behavior in a wide variety of situations. It is also possible that such inferences about enduring dispostions will lead us into dramatic misperceptions. It is very disruptive for us to perceive as failing a person we "know" to be capable and to be trying hard. This is especially true if we have some strong loyalty to or identification with him. That our dispositional inferences can lead us astray was amusingly pointed out by the sports columnist, Red Smith:

You see, Steve Ellis is the proprietor of Chico Vejar, who is a highly desirable tract of Stamford, Connecticut, welterweight. Steve is also a radio announcer. Ordinarily, there is no conflict between Ellis the Brain and Ellis the Voice because Steve is an uncommonly substantial lump of meat who can support both halves of a split personality and give away weight on each end without missing it.

This time, though, the two Ellises met head-on, with a sickening, rending crash. Steve the Manager sat at ringside in the guise of Steve the Announcer broadcasting a dispassionate, unbiased, objective report of Chico's adventures in the ring. . . .

Clear as mountain water his words came through, winning big for Chico. Winning? Hell, Steve was slaughtering poor Fiore.

Watching and listening, you could see what a valiant effort the reporter was making to remain cool and detached. At the same time you had an illustration of the old, established truth that when anybody with a preference watches a fight, he sees only what he prefers to see.

That is always so. That is why, after any fight that doesn't end in a clean knockout, there always are at least a few hoots when the decision is announced. A guy from, say, Billy Graham's neighborhood goes to see Billy fight and he watches Graham all the time. He sees all the punches Billy throws, and hardly any of the punches Billy catches. So it was with Steve.

"Fiore feints with a left," he would say, honestly believing that Fiore hadn't caught Chico full on the chops. "Fiore's knees buckle," he said, "and Chico backs away." Steve didn't see the hook that had driven Chico back. . . .[2]

*Our experiences of other persons are meaningful.* We see other people as organized entities, and nearly always their behavior makes sense. Nonetheless, the behavior of others does confuse and puzzle us on occasion. It is probably a good guess that if a person is consistently puzzling to us, our inability to make sense of him leads us to avoid further interactions with him. No wonder the behavior of most of the people we "know" makes sense!

What are the processes by which we develop these organized

perceptions of others as meaningful entities? First, as already pointed out, we organize their behavior into intent-act-effect units, and that procedure not only enables us to develop some behavioral organization but also permits and even pushes us to develop some hypotheses covering the enduring intents and dispositions or personality traits. Second, meaning derives from the fact that other people are similar to one another and to ourselves. We all share a certain number of important characteristics; we all behave, think, and feel; and some of the structured meanings we experience derive from the assumption that other people are like us. The assumption of similarity—"That's the way I would feel"—can lead to assumed relationships between both behaviors and intents. Even though the process may not be conscious, we often operate as follows: "I engage in behavior $A$ and also in behavior $B$;" therefore, "if he engages in behavior $A$, then he must also engage in behavior $B$." The same operation would apply to intents and feelings. This process is one of the sources of what we shall later call *implicit personality theory*; it produces assumptions about relationships between personality traits in other people, so that knowing some things about a person permits us to infer other things. The process does not imply that the inferences are necessarily correct, however.

NOTES
1. Strachey, Lytton, *Eminent Victorians*, New York: Modern Library, 1933, 193-194. Quoted by permission of Harcourt, Brace and World; Mrs. A. S. Strachey; and Chatto and Windus.
2. Smith, Red, *New York Herald Tribune*, December 21, 1951.

REFERENCES
Dornbusch, S. M., Hastorf, A. H., Richardson, S. A., Muzzy, R. E., and Vreeland, Rebecca S., "The Perceiver and Perceived: Their Relative Influence on Categories of Interpersonal Perception," *Journal of Personality and Social Psychology*, 1965, 1, 434-440.
Heider, F., "Social Perception and Phenomenal Causality," *Psychological Review*, 1944, 51, 358-374.
Heider, F., *The Psychology of Interpersonal Relations*, New York: Wiley, 1958.

Interpersonal Dimensions

# REWARDS OTHERS PROVIDE: PROPINQUITY
# Ellen Berscheid and
# Elaine Hatfield Walster

## PROXIMITY AS AN INTENSIFIER OF SENTIMENT

A frequently advanced and commonly accepted notion is that propinquity, or proximity, has a strong influence on one's friendship choices. Stated in its simplest form, the proposition is as follows: Other things being equal, the closer two individuals are located geographically, the more likely it is that they will be attracted to each other. Studies demonstrating the impact of proximity on friendship choices are so numerous that we will mention only a few.

Several investigators have collected data which indicate that students tend to develop stronger friendships with those students who share their classes, or their dormitory or apartment building, or who sit near them, than with those who are geographically located only slightly farther away (Maisonneuve, Palmade, & Fourment, 1952; Willerman & Swanson, 1952; Festinger, 1953; Byrne & Buehler, 1955, Byrne, 1961). Clerks in a large department store and members of a bomber crew have been found to develop closer relations with those who happen to work next to them than with co-workers a few feet away (Gullahorn, 1952; Kipnis, 1957; Zander & Havelin, 1960).

One of the more interesting studies demonstrating the relationship between proximity and friendship choice was conducted by Festinger, Schachter, and Back (1950). These investigators examined the development of friendships in a new housing project for married students. The housing development studied consisted of small houses arranged in U-shaped courts, such that all except the end houses faced onto a grassy area. The two end houses in each court faced onto the street. Festinger (1951) arrived at the intriguing conclusion that to a great extent architects can determine the social life of the residents of their projects. According to Festinger:

Reprinted by permission from *Interpersonal Attraction* by Ellen Berscheid and Elaine H. Walster, Addison-Wesley, Reading, Mass., 1969, pp. 46-51.

It is a fair summary to say that the two major factors affecting the friendships which developed were (1) sheer distance between houses and (2) the direction in which a house faced. Friendships developed more frequently between next-door neighbors, less frequently between people whose houses were separated by another house, and so on. As the distance between houses increased, the number of friendships fell off so rapidly that it was rare to find a friendship between persons who lived in houses that were separated by more than four or five other houses . . .

There were instances in which the site plan of the project had more profound effects than merely to determine with whom one associated. Indeed, on occasion the arrangements of the houses severely limited the social life of their occupants . . . In order to have the street appear "lived on," ten of the houses near the street had been turned so that they faced the street rather than the court area as did the other houses. This apparently small change in the direction in which a house faced had a considerable effect on the lives of the people who, by accident, happened to occupy these end houses. They had less than half as many friends in the project as did those whose houses faced the court area. The consistency of this finding left no doubt that the turning of these houses toward the street had made involuntary social isolates out of the persons who lived in them.[1]

There were still other architectural features which were found by Festinger, Schachter, and Back to have important effects on the social life of the residents. Any architectural feature which brought an individual into proximity with other residents tended to increase his popularity. It was found, for example, that the positions of the stairways enabled the residents of the apartments near the entrances and exits of the stairways to make more friends than other residents. Similarly, the position of the mailboxes in each building improved the social life of the residents of the apartment near which they were located.

Many of the studies which have demonstrated the potency of proximity upon friendship formation have important social implications. It has been found, for example, that white persons who experience increased contact with Negroes become less prejudiced subsequent to that contact. This finding has been secured in such varied settings as in a meat packing plant (Palmore, 1955), a housing project (Deutsch & Collins, 1958), and in a university classroom (Mann, 1959). It is interesting that this finding, that integrated housing may produce increased racial harmony, has been the ammunition with which both integrationists and segragationists have defended their disparate points of view. Deutsch and Collins (1958), for example, concluded on the basis of these data that integrated housing should be encouraged since such integration helps eradicate racial prejudice. Segregationists, however, have concluded that since the evidence suggests that integration would lead to interracial friendships and "race mixing," segregation should be preserved at all costs.

Propinquity also has been found to be an important factor in mate selection. Several studies have demonstrated that there is an inverse relationship between the distance separating potential marriage partners and the number of marriages. One such study was conducted by Bossard (1932) who examined 5,000 marriage licenses in which one or both applicants were residents of Philadelphia. He found that 12 percent of the couples were already living at the same address at the time they applied for their license; one third of them lived within five or less blocks of each other. The percentage of marriages decreased steadily and markedly as the distance between the residences of the engaged couples increased. Corroboration of the importance of propinquity in mate selection comes from Abrams (1943), Kennedy (1943), and Katz and Hill (1958).

All of these data are compatible with the hypothesis that the less physical distance there is between two individuals, the more likely it is that they will become attracted to each other. But since these studies have focused upon friendship formation rather than "enemy formation," their findings do not disconfirm the equally plausible, but contrary, proposition that the less physical distance there is between two individuals, the more likely it is that they will dislike each other.

Evidence that close proximity to another may be likely to produce interpersonal hostility as well as interpersonal attraction comes primarily from police records, rather than from the social scientist's notebook. The Detroit Police Department's 1967 Annual Report, for example, indicates that in the majority of robberies the perpetrator was either related to, or acquainted with, the victim. It is somewhat surprising to find that thieves are much more likely to rob an intimate than a stranger. It would seem that if a thief had common sense, he would be careful to steal from someone who could not easily identify him. The evidence, however, indicates that individuals are most likely to victimize those in close proximity. Perhaps those ladies who fear the intrusion of "thieving maniacs" into their homes may be able to take some comfort from the fact that the intruder is likely to be a friend.

Aggravated assault, like thievery, appears also to be directed toward intimates. According to J. Edgar Hoover, "Most aggravated assaults occur within the family unit or among neighbors and acquaintances. The victim and offender relationship as well as the very nature of the attack make this crime similar to murders" (1966, p. 9). With respect to homicide, Hoover's statistics reveal that killings within the family make up almost a third of all murders. If one adds to this those which occur between "romantic lovers," the figure is even higher.

It seems logically clear, then, that distance per se does not have the strong consequences for positive attraction which the friendship-formation data suggest. While propinquity may be a necessary condition for attraction, it appears that it also may be a necessary condition for hatred.

## INCREASED PROBABILITY OF ACQUIRING INFORMATION

What underlies the often obtained relationship between proximity and sentiment? Obviously something is made possible, or more likely, with decreasing distance. It seems apparent that what is made possible is an increased probability of receiving information about another person and an increased probability of receiving rewards or punishments from the other. Sentiments such as liking or disliking, and especially the strong sentiments of love and hate, are not likely to be felt for people about whom we have minimal information and with whom we have had little experience. What proximity appears to allow, and what distance prevents, is an opportunity to obtain information and accumulate experience regarding the rewards or punishments we are likely to receive from the other person.

Can we conclude, then, that if we know the degree of proximity between two people, and do not have knowledge of the content of the information exchange such proximity has made possible, we cannot make a prediction concerning whether a positive sentiment or a negative sentiment will develop? There appear to be a number of factors which may make such a conclusion erroneous: It appears that there is a somewhat greater tendency for proximity to breed attraction than hostility.

Newcomb has advanced the hypothesis that proximity should produce positive rather than negative attraction. He argues that ". . . when persons interact, the reward-punishment ratio is more often such as to be reinforcing than extinguishing . . ." (1956, p. 576). Thus, he reasons that the information which proximity permits is more likely to be favorable than unfavorable and that liking, therefore, will more often result from proximity than disliking. There is little direct evidence to support this proposition. Nevertheless, Newcomb's arguments do seem plausible. Since people are to a great extent dependent upon one another for the satisfaction of their needs, it seems probable that individuals generally take care to reward others as much as possible in interaction with them. In addition, social canons of courtesy often prohibit dealing out punishments to others even when one is so inclined.

### Heider's Balance Theory

There is yet another reason why close proximity with another may favor the development of positive rather than negative affect. The prediction that proximity will more often lead to liking than disliking can be derived from a number of the cognitive-consistency theories. It can perhaps be most easily derived from Heider's (1958) balance theory. The basic tenet of Heider's theory is that people strive to make their sentiment relationships harmonious with their perception of the unit relationships existent between objects.

What does Heider mean by the phrase *"sentiment relationships"*? A "sentiment" is simply a positive or negative attitude toward someone or something. What does Heider mean by the phrase *"unit relationships"*? Separate entities are said to have a unit relationship when they are perceived as belonging together. The members of a family, for example, are usually perceived of as a unit, as are a person and his clothing, and so on. In his discussion of the conditions which facilitate unit formation, Heider draws upon the principles of perceptual organization which were formulated by the Gestalt psychologists. The Gestaltists discovered that one relationship between objects which is especially likely to lead to unit formation is proximity: Objects which are close together spatially tend to be perceived as a unit. According to Heider s theory, then, if one perceives that a unit relationship with another exists (e.g., the other is in close proximity), this perception should induce a harmonious sentiment relationship (e.g., liking).

To test whether or not unit formation produced by the anticipation of interacting intimately with another would increase attraction, Darley and Berscheid (1967) led college women to expect that they were going to discuss their sexual standards and behavior with another girl, ostensibly participating in the same study. After the expectation of further interaction had been induced, each girl was given two folders. One folder was said to contain personality information about her partner, the girl with whom she would converse and exchange information. The other folder was said to contain information about another girl, who would also participate in the study but whom she would never meet. The personality information contained in both folders was designed to produce as ambiguous a picture as possible of the girl described.

Half of the subjects believed that the girl described in folder A was their "randomly selected" discussion partner; the other half believed that the girl described in folder B was their partner. Subjects were instructed to read through both folders, form a general impression of both girls, and then rate each of them along a number of dimensions, including liking.

The results of this study clearly indicated that the subjects expressed more liking for the girl who had been designated as their discussion partner than they did for the girl who was not.

This study suggests, then, that the factor of proximity, uncontaminated by the specific information which proximity often permits to be exchanged, may produce a feeling of unit formation between two people. This feeling of being in a unit relationship with another may then induce feelings of liking for that other. Knowledge that one will be in close proximity with another may result, then, in an individual's going *into* an interaction situation with increased liking for the other person prior to the actual interaction and prior to actual knowledge of possible rewards which may be obtained in the interaction.

It is interesting that the liking produced by the anticipation of being in close proximity with another may lead a person to voluntarily choose to associate with the other person, even though the original interaction which was anticipated has been canceled. Berscheid, Boye, and Darley (1968) found that even when a subject anticipated interacting with an objectively undesirable person, the attraction induced by the anticipation of close interaction caused subjects to choose voluntarily to interact with that negative person more readily than did people who had not previously anticipated association with him.

In conclusion, then, actual proximity is probably correlated with attraction (or repulsion) because proximity allows one to obtain an increased amount of information about the other person and to experience rewards or punishments from the other. There is some suggestive evidence that proximity in and of itself, apart from any information it may provide about another and apart from any rewards or punishments which the other may administer, may facilitate attraction as a by-product of the individual's desire for cognitive consistency.

NOTE

1. Festinger, L., "Architecture and Group Membership," *Journal of Social Issues*, 1951, 1, 156-157.

REFERENCES

Abrams, R. H., "Residential Propinquity as a Factor in Marriage Selection," *American Sociological Review*, 1943, 8, 288-294.

Berscheid, E., Boye, D., and Darley, J. M., "Effects of Forced Association upon Voluntary Choice to Associate," *Journal of Personality and Social Psychology*, 1968, 8, 13-19.

Bossard, J. H. S., "Residential Propinquity as a Factor in Mate Selection," *American Journal of Sociology*, 1932, 38, 219-224.

Byrne, D., "The Influence of Propinquity and Opportunities for Interaction on Classroom Relationships," *Human Relations*, 1961, 14, 63-70.

Byrne, D., and Buehler, J. A., "A Note on the Influence of Propinquity upon Acquaintanceships," *Journal of Abnormal and Social Psychology*, 1955, 51, 147-148.

Darley, J. M., and Berscheid, E., "Increased Liking as a Result of the Anticipation of Personal Contact," *Human Relations*, 1967, 20, 29-40.

Deutsch, M., and Collins, M. E., "The Effect of Public Policy in Housing Projects upon Interracial Attitudes," in Eleanor Maccoby, T. M. Newcomb, and E. L. Hartley (eds.), *Readings in Social Psychology*, 3rd ed., New York: Holt, Rinehart and Winston, 1958, 612-623.

Festinger, L., "Architecture and Group Membership," *Journal of Social Issues*, 1951, 1, 152-163.

Festinger, L., "Group Attraction and Membership," in D. Cartwright and A. Zander (eds.), *Group Dynamics: Research and Theory*, New York: Harper & Row, 1953.

Festinger, L., Schachter, S., and Back, K., *Social Pressures in Informal Groups: A Study of Human Factors in Housing*, New York: Harper & Row, 1950.

Gullahorn, J., "Distance and Friendship as Factors in the Gross Interaction Matrix, *Sociometry*, 1952, **15**, 123-134.

Heider, F., *The Psychology of Interpersonal Relations*, New York: Wiley, 1958.

Hoover, J. E., "Crime in the United States," *Uniform Crime Reports*, August, 1966, U.S. Dept. of Justice, Washington, D.C.

Kennedy, R., "Premarital Residential Propinquity," *American Journal of Sociology*, 1943, **48**, 580-584.

Katz, A. M., and Hill, R., "Residential Propinquity and Marital Selection: A Review of Theory, Method, and Fact," *Journal of Marriage and the Family*, 1958, **20**, 327-335.

Kipnis, D. M., "Interaction Between Members of Bomber Crews as a Determinant of Sociometric Choice," *Human Relations*, 1957, **10**, 263-270.

Maisonneuve, J., Palmade, G., and Fourment, C., "Selective Choices and Propinquity," *Sociometry*, 1952, **15**, 135-140.

Mann, J. H., "The Effect of Interracial Contact on Sociometric Choices and Perceptions," *Journal of Social Psychology*, 1959, **50**, 143-152.

Newcomb, T. M., "The Prediction of Interpersonal Attraction," *American Psychologist*, 1956, **11**, 575-586.

Palmore, E. B., "The Introduction of Negroes into White Departments," *Human Organization*, 1955, **14**, 27-28.

Willerman, B., and Swanson, L., "An Ecological Determinant of Differential Amounts of Sociometric Choices Within College Sororities," *Sociometry*, 1952, **15**, 326-329.

Zander, A., and Havelin, A., "Social Comparison and Interpersonal Attraction," *Human Relations*, 1960, **13**, 21-32.

Interpersonal Dimensions

# THE INFLUENCE OF SOURCE CREDIBILITY ON COMMUNICATION EFFECTIVENESS
## Philip Zimbardo and Ebbe B. Ebbesen

The question of how to produce a large amount of change in the attitudes of an audience has been studied quite extensively. To rephrase the problem, let us suppose that we have decided to use a formal communication (a speech or persuasive verbal message) as our main method of producing attitude change. How can we, without changing the structure or content of the communication, increase the amount of this change? It may actually be that the only thing which affects the amount of attitude change is the communication itself. But if not, what extra-communication variables are likely to increase such change, and why? One variable which we intuitively feel should affect attitude change is the source of the communication.

It seems likely that a trustworthy source, giving the same persuasive message as an untrustworthy source, would produce more attitude change. Although it does appear intuitively obvious, we can still ask how much *more* change a trustworthy source produces than an untrustworthy source. Another interesting question is whether or not untrustworthy sources produce attitude change in the opposite direction from the communication. To adequately and accurately answer these and any other questions on the effect of source credibility, it is necessary to conduct an experiment. Hovland and Weiss (1951) conducted a study which was intended to answer just such questions.

The design of the study was quite simple. The subjects, undergraduate college students at Yale University who were in an advanced history course, filled out an opinion questionnaire a week before receiving persuasive communications. For

Reprinted by permission from *Influencing Attitudes and Changing Behavior* by Philip Zimbardo and Ebbe B. Ebbesen, Addison-Wesley, Reading, Mass., 1969, pp. 27-30.

some subjects, the communicators associated with particular communications were trustworthy, while for others they were untrustworthy. Immediately after the communications were presented, another opinion questionnaire was administered. Finally, a third opinion questionnaire was filled out one month later.

Keeping the overall design in mind, the details of the study were as follows. Five days after the administration of the first opinion questionnaire (designed to be a general opinion survey conducted by the "National Opinion Survey Council"), one of the experimenters entered the history class as a guest lecturer. The fact that he was a guest lecturer, who had never come to class before, was meant to dissociate his activities from the previous opinion questionnaire. He stated that he had been asked by the regular professor to discuss the psychology of communications with the class, since so many of their attitudes and opinions were determined by what they heard and read. He then added that before he talked with the class, he wished to have "live data" from a survey which attempted to assess the role of newspaper and magazine reading as a vehicle of communication. After obtaining these data, he would discuss them with the class at a later session. The lecturer continued by summarizing what he wished the class to do: Namely, read a few newspaper and magazine articles on controversial topics, which were based on the best available information. After reading the articles, the students would be expected to fill out a short questionnaire on their reactions to them.

Each student was then handed a booklet of four readings on four different controversial issues:

A. Should the anti-histamine drugs continue to be sold without a doctor's prescription?
B. Can a practicable atomic-powered submarine be built at the present time (1949-1950)?
C. Is the steel industry to blame for the current shortage of steel?
D. As a result of TV, will there be a decrease in the number of movie theaters in operation by 1955?

For each topic, respectively, the high and low "credibility" sources were:

|              High              |              Low              |
| :----------------------------- | :---------------------------- |
| A. *New England Journal of Biology and Medicine* | Magazine *A* (a mass circulation, monthly pictorial magazine) |
| B. J. Robert Oppenheimer       | *Pravda*                      |
| C. *Bulletin of National Resources Planning Board* | Writer *A* (a widely syndicated, anti-labor, anti-New Deal, "rightist" newspaper columnist) |
| D. *Fortune*                   | Writer *B* (an extensively syndicated, woman movie-gossip columnist) |

For each topic there were both pro and con versions of the communication. Each booklet contained two pro and two con communications, one on each topic, and one pro communication and one con communication attributed to a low-credibility source. The other two communications were attributed to high-credibility sources. All the communications on a topic were identical, differing only in the attributed source. There was a total of 24 different booklets, with different combinations of topic, source, and advocated position.

After the subjects had read the booklets, they were given a second questionnaire which differed in format from the previous opinion survey. This questionnaire first asked general questions about the subjects' reactions to the articles and then asked for their own opinions. At the end of the questionnaire, there was a multiple-choice, fact quiz. The final questionnaire, given one month later, was identical to the second one (in order to assess delayed effects). However, the very first questionnaire, in addition to asking opinion questions, asked the subjects to rate many sources for trustworthiness. Included among these sources were the ones actually used in the experiment.

In considering the results of the experiment, we would first want to know how trustworthy the subjects judged the various sources. Did they indeed see the high-credibility sources as more trustworthy than the low-credibility sources? To answer this question, the ratings from the very first opinion survey can be used. The results can be seen in Table 1. A cursory glance at these results overwhelmingly confirms the hope that the high-credibility sources were seen as more trustworthy than the low-credibility sources.

**TABLE 1.** Percent of Subjects Rating Source as Trustworthy (Adapted from Hovland and Weiss, 1951)

| Topic | High credibility | Low credibility |
|-------|------------------|-----------------|
| A | 95 | 6 |
| B | 94 | 1 |
| C | 81 | 17 |
| D | 89 | 21 |

What about attitude change? In order to consider the amount of attitude change produced, we have to be able to summarize the data. The summary technique used in this experiment was to take the percent of subjects who changed their attitude (from questionnaire 1 to questionnaire 2) in the direction of the communication and subtract from that the percent of subjects who changed in the opposite direction from the communication. Thus, if the communication were pro, the percent changing in the pro direction minus the percent changing in the con direction would be our measure (net change) of the amount of attitude change produced. The net changes of opinion in the direction of the communication for sources judged to be trustworthy or untrustworthy are presented in Table 2.

These results show that the *difference* between the average (across topics) net change for the trustworthy sources and the untrustworthy sources was 14.1 percent. The probability

**TABLE 2.** Net Changes of Opinion in Direction of Communication for Sources Judged Trustworthy or Untrustworthy by Individual Subjects (Adapted from Hovland and Weiss, 1951)

| | Net change (percentage) | |
|-------|-------------------------|-------------------------|
| Topic | Sources judged trustworthy | Sources judged untrustworthy |
| A | 25.5 | 11.1 |
| B | 36.0 | 0.6 |
| C | 18.2 | 7.4 |
| D | 12.9 | 17.2 |
| Average change | 22.5% | 8.4% |

of this difference being caused by change is .03 (i.e., it would occur by chance only 3 times in 100); thus this difference appears to be a real one. That is, subjects are more likely to change their attitudes in the direction of a communication if they think that it came from a trustworthy source, than if they think it came from an untrustworthy one.

But why does a trustworthy source produce more change? Do the subjects pay more attention to him and thus learn the arguments better? Data from the fact quiz in the second questionnaire indicated that there was no difference between the trustworthy and untrustworthy source conditions in the amount of information recalled about the communications.

In conclusion, it seems that intuition proved to be correct. An experiment demonstrated that more attitude change was produced by a persuasive message if the message were attributed to high-credibility sources than if it were attributed to low-credibility sources. The magnitude of the difference in attitude change produced by the different communicators was fairly large. In addition, the low-credibility sources seemed to produce a low net percent of attitude change (8.4%). To summarize, more attitude change follows from a formal communication if the source is trustworthy than if the source is untrustworthy. Further, untrustworthy sources seem to produce little, if any, attitude change.

REFERENCES

Hovland, C. I., and Weiss, W., "The Influence of Source Credibility on Communication Effectiveness," *Public Opinion Quarterly*, 1951, 15, 635-650.

# DEFENSIVE COMMUNICATION
## Jack R. Gibb

One way to understand communication is to view it as a people process rather than as a language process. If one is to make fundamental improvement in communication, he must make changes in interpersonal relationships. One possible type of alteration—and the one with which this paper is concerned—is that of reducing the degree of defensiveness.

## DEFINITION AND SIGNIFICANCE

Defensive behavior is defined as that behavior which occurs when an individual perceives threat or anticipates threat in the group. The person who behaves defensively, even though he also gives some attention to the common task, devotes an appreciable portion of his energy to defending himself. Besides talking about the topic, he thinks about how he appears to others, how he may be seen more favorably, how he may win, dominate, impress, or escape punishment, and/or how he may avoid or mitigate a perceived or an anticipated attack.

Such inner feelings and outward acts tend to create similarly defensive postures in others; and, if unchecked, the ensuing circular response becomes increasingly destructive. Defensive behavior, in short, engenders defensive listening, and this in turn produces postural, facial, and verbal cues which raise the defense level of the original communicator.

Defense arousal prevents the listener from concentrating upon the message. Not only do defensive communicators send off multiple value, motive, and affect cues, but also defensive recipients distort what they receive. As a person becomes more and more defensive, he becomes less and less able to perceive accurately the motives, the values, and the emotions of the sender. The writer's analyses of tape recorded discussions revealed that increases in defensive behavior were correlated positively with losses in efficiency in communication.[1] Specifically, distortions became greater when defensive states existed in the groups.

Reprinted by permission of Jack R. Gibb and International Communication Association from "Defensive Communication" by Jack R. Gibb in the *Journal of Communication*, Vol. II, Sept. 1961, pp. 141-148.

The converse, moreover, also is true. The more "supportive" or defense reductive the climate, the less the receiver reads into the communication distorted loadings which arise from projections of his own anxieties, motives, and concerns. As defenses are reduced, the receivers become better able to concentrate upon the structure, the content, and the cognitive meanings of the message.

## CATEGORIES OF DEFENSIVE AND SUPPORTIVE COMMUNICATION

In working over an eight-year period with recordings of discussions occurring in varied settings, the writer developed the six pairs of defensive and supportive categories presented in Table 1. Behavior which a listener perceives as possessing any of the characteristics listed in the left-hand column arouses defensiveness, whereas that which he interprets as having any of the qualities designated as supportive reduces defensive feelings. The degree to which these reactions occur depends upon the personal level of defensiveness and upon the general climate in the group at the time.[2]

### Evaluation and Description

Speech or other behavior which appears evaluative increases defensiveness. If by expression, manner of speech, tone of voice, or verbal content the sender seems to be evaluating or judging the listener, then the receiver goes on guard. Of course, other factors may inhibit the reaction. If the listener thought that the speaker regarded him as an equal and was being open and spontaneous, for example, the evaluativeness in a message would be neutralized and perhaps not even per-

TABLE 1. Categories of Behavior Characteristic of Supportive and Defensive Climates in Small Groups

| Defensive Climates | Supportive Climates |
| --- | --- |
| 1. Evaluation | 1. Description |
| 2. Control | 2. Problem orientation |
| 3. Strategy | 3. Spontaneity |
| 4. Neutrality | 4. Empathy |
| 5. Superiority | 5. Equality |
| 6. Certainty | 6. Provisionalism |

ceived. This same principle applies equally to the other five categories of potentially defense-producing climates. The six sets are interactive.

Because our attitudes toward other persons are frequently, and often necessarily, evaluative, expressions which the defensive person will regard as nonjudgmental are hard to frame. Even the simplest question usually conveys the answer that the sender wishes or implies the response that would fit into his value system. A mother, for example, immediately following an earth tremor that shook the house, sought for her small son with the question: "Bobby, where are you?" The timid and plaintive "Mommy, I didn't do it" indicated how Bobby's chronic mild defensiveness predisposed him to react with a projection of his own guilt and in the context of his chronic assumption that questions are full of accusation.

Anyone who has attempted to train professionals to use information-seeking speech with neutral affect appreciates how difficult it is to teach a person to say even the simple "who did that?" without being seen as accusing. Speech is so frequently judgmental that there is a reality base for the defensive interpretations which are so common.

When insecure, group members are particularly likely to place blame, to see others as fitting into categories of good or bad, to make moral judgments of their colleagues, and to question the value, motive, and affect loadings of the speech which they hear. Since value loadings imply a judgment of others, a belief that the standards of the speaker differ from his own causes the listener to become defensive.

Descriptive speech, in contrast to that which is evaluative, tends to arouse a minimum of uneasiness. Speech acts which the listener perceives as genuine requests for information or as material with neutral loadings is descriptive. Specifically, presentations of feelings, events, perceptions, or processes which do not ask or imply that the receiver change behavior or attitude are minimally defense producing. The difficulty in avoiding overtone is illustrated by the problems of news reporters in writing stories about unions, communists, Negroes, and religious activities without tipping off the "party" line of the newspaper. One can often tell from the opening words in a news article which side the newspaper's editorial policy favors.

## Control and Problem Orientation

Speech which is used to control the listener evokes resistance. In most of our social intercourse someone is trying to do something to someone else—to change an attitude, to influence behavior, or to restrict the field of activity. The degree to which attempts to control produce defensiveness depends upon the openness of the effort, for a suspicion that hidden motives exist heightens resistance. For this reason attempts of nondirective therapists and progressive educators to refrain from imposing a set of values, a point of view, or a problem solution upon the receivers meet with many barriers. Since the norm is control, noncontrollers must earn the perceptions that their efforts have no hidden motives. A bombardment of persuasive "messages" in the fields of politics, education, special causes, advertising, religion, medicine, industrial relations, and guidance has bred cynical and paranoidal responses in listeners.

Implicit in all attempts to alter another person is the assumption by the change agent that the person to be altered is inadequate. That the speaker secretly views the listener as ignorant, unable to make his own decisions, uninformed, immature, unwise, or possessed of wrong or inadequate attitudes is a subconscious perception which gives the latter a valid base for defensive reactions.

Methods of control are many and varied. Legalistic insistence on detail, restrictive regulations and policies, conformity norms, and all laws are among the methods. Gestures, facial expressions, other forms of nonverbal communication, and even such simple acts as holding a door open in a particular manner are means of imposing one's will upon another and hence are potential sources of resistance.

Problem orientation, on the other hand, is the antithesis of persuasion. When the sender communicates a desire to collaborate in defining a mutual problem and in seeking its solution, he tends to create the same problem orientation in the listener; and, of greater importance, he implies that he has no predetermined solution, attitude, or method to impose. Such behavior is permissive in that it allows the receiver to set his own goals, make his own decisions, and evaluate his own progress—or to share with the sender in doing so. The exact methods of attaining permissiveness are not known, but they must involve a constellation of cues and they certainly go beyond mere verbal assurances that the communicator has no hidden desires to exercise control.

## Strategy and Spontaneity

When the sender is perceived as engaged in a stratagem involving ambiguous and multiple motivations, the receiver becomes defensive. No one wishes to be a guinea pig, a role player, or an impressed actor, and no one likes to be the victim of some hidden motivation. That which is concealed, also, may appear larger than it really is with the degree of defensiveness of the listener determining the perceived size of the suppressed element. The intense reaction of the reading audience to the material in the *Hidden Persuaders* indicates the prevalence of defensive reactions to multiple motivations behind strategy. Group members who are seen as "taking a role," as feigning emotion, as toying with their colleagues, as withholding information, or as having special sources of data are especially resented. One participant once complained that another was "using a listening technique" on him!

A large part of the adverse reaction to much of the so-called human relations training is a feeling against what are perceived as gimmicks and tricks to fool or to "involve" people, to make a person think he is making his own decision, or to make the listener feel that the sender is genuinely interested in him as a person. Particularly violent reactions occur when it appears that someone is trying to make a stratagem appear spontaneous. One person has reported a boss who incurred resentment by habitually using the gimmick of "spontaneously" looking at his watch and saying, "My gosh, look at the time—I must run to an appointment." The belief was that the boss would create less irritation by honestly asking to be excused.

Similarly, the deliberate assumption of guilelessness and natural simplicity is especially resented. Monitoring the tapes of feedback and evaluation sessions in training groups indicates the surprising extent to which members perceive the strategies of their colleagues. This perceptual clarity may be quite shocking to the strategist, who usually feels that he has cleverly hidden the motivational aura around the "gimmick."

This aversion to deceit may account for one's resistance to politicians who are suspected of behind-the-scenes planning to get his vote, to psychologists whose listening apparently is motivated by more than the manifest or content-level interest in his behavior, or to the sophisticated, smooth, or clever person whose "one-upmanship" is marked with guile. In training groups the role-flexible person frequently is resented because his changes in behavior are perceived as strategic maneuvers.

In contrast, behavior which appears to be spontaneous and free of deception is defense reductive. If the communicator is seen as having a clean id, as having uncomplicated motivations, as being straightforward and honest, and as behaving spontaneously in response to the situation, he is likely to arouse minimal defense.

### Neutrality and Empathy

When neutrality in speech appears to the listener to indicate a lack of concern for his welfare, he becomes defensive. Group members usually desire to be perceived as valued persons, as individuals of special worth, and as objects of concern and affection. The clinical, detached, person-is-an-object-of-study attitude on the part of many psychologist-trainers is resented by group members. Speech with low affect that communicates little warmth or caring is in such contrast with the affect-laden speech in social situations that it sometimes communicates rejection.

Communication that conveys empathy for the feelings and respect for the worth of the listener, however, is particularly supportive and defense reductive. Reassurance results when a message indicates that the speaker identifies himself with the listener's problems, shares his feelings, and accepts his emotional reactions at face value. Abortive efforts to deny the legitimacy of the receiver's emotions by assuring the receiver that he need not feel bad, that he should not feel rejected, or that he is overly anxious, though often intended as support giving, may impress the listener as lack of acceptance. The combination of understanding and empathizing with the other person's emotions with no accompanying effort to change him apparently is supportive at a high level.

The importance of gestural behavioral cues in communicating empathy should be mentioned. Apparently spontaneous facial and bodily evidences of concern are often interpreted as especially valid evidence of deep-level acceptance.

## Superiority and Equality

When a person communicates to another that he feels superior in position, power, wealth, intellectual ability, physical characteristics, or other ways, he arouses defensiveness. Here, as with the other sources of disturbance, whatever arouses feelings of inadequacy causes the listener to center upon the affect loading of the statement rather than upon the cognitive elements. The receiver then reacts by not hearing the message, by forgetting it, by competing with the sender, or by becoming jealous of him.

The person who is perceived as feeling superior communicates that he is not willing to enter into a shared problem-solving relationship, that he probably does not desire feedback, that he does not require help, and/or that he will be likely to try to reduce the power, the status, or the worth of the receiver.

Many ways exist for creating the atmosphere that the sender feels himself equal to the listener. Defenses are reduced when one perceives the sender as being willing to enter into participative planning with mutual trust and respect. Differences in talent, ability, worth, appearance, status, and power often exist, but the low defense communicator seems to attach little importance to these distinctions.

## Certainty and Provisionalism

The effects of dogmatism in producing defensiveness are well known. Those who seem to know the answers, to require no additional data, and to regard themselves as teachers rather than as co-workers tend to put others on guard. Moreover, in the writer's experiment, listeners often perceived manifest expressions of certainty as connoting inward feelings of inferiority. They saw the dogmatic individual as needing to be right, as wanting to win an argument rather than solve a problem, and as seeing his ideas as truths to be defended. This kind of behavior often was associated with acts which others regarded as attempts to exercise control. People who were right seemed to have low tolerance for members who were "wrong"—i.e., who did not agree with the sender.

One reduces the defensiveness of the listener when he communicates that he is willing to experiment with his own behavior, attitudes, and ideas. The person who appears to be taking provisional attitudes, to be investigating issues rather than taking sides on them, to be problem solving rather than debating, and to be willing to experiment and explore tends to communicate that the listener may have some control over the shared quest or the investigation of the ideas. If a person is genuinely searching for information and data, he does not resent help or company along the way.

## CONCLUSION
The implications of the above material for the parent, the teacher, the manager, the administrator, or the therapist are fairly obvious. (Arousing defensiveness interferes with communication and thus makes it difficult—and sometimes impossible—for anyone to convey ideas clearly and to move effectively toward the solution of therapeutic, educational, or managerial problems.)

## NOTES
1. Gibb, J. R., "Defense Level and Influence Potential in Small Groups," in L. Petrullo and B. M. Bass (eds.), *Leadership and Interpersonal Behavior*, New York: Holt, Rinehart and Winston, 1961, 66-81.
2. Gibb, J. R., "Sociopsychological Processes of Group Instruction," in N. B. Henry (ed.), *The Dynamics of Instructional Groups*, Fifty-ninth Yearbook of the National Society for the Study of Education, Part II, 1960, 115-135.

# PART VI
# Cultural
# Dimensions

One fundamental tenet of communication asserts that communication must be interpreted only in its proper context. Ordinarily we think of context in physical terms—location, occasion, seating arrangement, background, atmosphere, mood, and other aspects of our immediate physical surroundings. And still we all know that persons engaged in communication share far more than common physical context. There is a social context; persons who live in a given setting also share patterns of behavior, common ideas and expectations, tastes and values, social conventions, and comparable ways of looking at reality. What links all of these and countless other commonalities of experience is nothing less than a common cultural context. And within each culture is to be found a web of subcultures bound by shared habit, work, friendship, resources, and affiliations.

The essays in this section afford four different perspectives on the role of culture in communication. In "Intercultural Communication" Edward Hall and William Whyte examine the impact of culture on a diverse range of social behaviors: Styles and patterns of talk, interpretations of language, semantic considerations, modes of expression, norms of physical contact, variations in scheduling and timing of social contacts, reactions to physical settings, and interpretations of social class and role.

In the second essay, "Proxemics in a Cross-Cultural Context: Germans, English, and French," Edward T. Hall explores some common cultural pitfalls associated with the problem of physical and social distance. Few other aspects of culture so dramatically testify to the subtle and pervasive ways in which culture imposes its assumption on the process of communication. Included in the survey is a discussion of different uses of the senses, the disparate interpretations of proxemic factors, intonation, eye-contact, and numerous other hidden dimensions of cultural experience.

In the third perspective, "Adumbration as a Feature of Intercultural Communication," Hall analyzes some of the profound consequences of adumbration on what might be termed the metacommunication or subtext of messages. Adumbration consists of any sign or cue which "enables organisms to engage in the mutual exchange and evaluation of covert information or what each can expect from the other. . . . [and] foreshadow what organisms will do, perform corrective functions, and help set the directions a given communication will take, as well as the actions resulting from it."

Finally, in "The Reverse Transmission of Culture," Richard Farson examines the impact of the flow of information from one generation to another in a given culture. In the traditional pattern of culture, the older persons defined for the young what was to be considered appropriate rules of conduct; but now, Farson contends, "the direction is changing." Culture is now transmitted in reverse, from the young to the old. At issue are a number of conflicting forces: The accelerated rate of change, diverse modes of communication among old and young, differences in models of social change, role differences, values, patterns of social influence, and, most important, differences in sensory experiences that, taken together, call into question traditional notions about "intergenerational communication." Though his position is surely controversial, Farson offers a unique way of looking at the problem of communication within cultures.

# INTERCULTURAL COMMUNICATION
# Edward T. Hall and
# William Foote Whyte

How can anthropological knowledge help the man of action in dealing with people of another culture? We shall seek to answer that question by examining the process of intercultural communication.

Anthropologists have long claimed that a knowledge of culture is valuable to the administrator. More and more people in business and government are willing to take this claim seriously, but they ask that we put culture to them in terms they can understand and act upon.

When the layman thinks of culture, he is likely to think in terms of (1) the way people dress, (2) the beliefs they hold, and (3) the customs they practice—with an accent upon the esoteric. Without undertaking any comprehensive definition, we can concede that all three are aspects of culture, and yet point out that they do not get us very far, either theoretically or practically.

Dress is misleading, if we assume that differences in dress indicate differences in belief and behavior. If that were the case, then we should expect to find people dressed like ourselves to be thinking and acting like ourselves. While there are still peoples wearing "colorful" apparel quite different from ours, we find in many industrializing societies that the people with whom we deal dress much as we do—and yet think and act quite differently.

Knowledge of beliefs may leave us up in the air because the connections between beliefs and behavior are seldom obvious. In the case of religious beliefs, we may know, for example, that the Mohammedan must pray to Allah a certain number of times a day and that therefore the working day must provide for praying time. This is important, to be sure, but the point is so obvious that it is unlikely to be overlooked by anyone. The administrator must also grasp the less dramatic

Reproduced by the permission of the Society for Applied Anthropology from Vol. 19, No. 1, 1960, *Human Organization*. Footnotes are omitted.

aspects of everyday behavior, and here a knowledge of beliefs is a very imperfect guide.

Customs provide more guidance, providing we do not limit ourselves to the esoteric and also search for the pattern of behavior into which a given custom fits. The anthropologist, in dealing with customary behavior, is not content with identifying individual items. To him, these items are not miscellaneous. They have meaning only as they are fitted together into a pattern.

But even assuming that the pattern can be communicated to the administrator, there is still something important lacking. The pattern shows how the people act—when among themselves. The administrator is not directly concerned with that situation. Whatever background information he has, he needs to interpret to himself how the people act *in relation to himself*. He is dealing with a cross-cultural situation. The link between the two cultures is provided by acts of communication between the administrator, representing one culture, and people representing another. If communication is effective, then understanding grows with collaborative action. If communication is faulty, then no book knowledge of culture can assure effective action.

This is not to devalue the knowledge of culture that can be provided by the anthropologist. It is only to suggest that the point of implementation of the knowledge must be in the communication process. Let us therefore examine the process of intercultural communication. By so doing we can accomplish two things: (a) Broaden knowledge of ourselves by revealing some of our own unconscious communicative acts; (b) clear away heretofore almost insurmountable obstacles to understanding in the cross-cultural process. We also learn that communication, as it is used here, goes far beyond words and includes many other acts upon which judgments are based of what is transpiring and from which we draw conclusions as to what has occurred in the past.

Culture affects communication in various ways. It determines the time and timing of interpersonal events, the places where it is appropriate to discuss particular topics, the physical distance separating one speaker from another, the tone of voice that is appropriate to the subject matter. Culture, in this sense, delineates the amount and type of physical contact, if any, which convention permits or demands, and the intensity of emotion which goes with it. Culture includes the relationship of *what is said to what is meant*—as when "no" means "maybe" and "tomorrow" means "never." Culture, too, determines whether a given matter—say, a business contract—should be initially discussed between two persons or hacked out in a day-long conference which includes four or five senior officials from each side, with perhaps an assist from the little man who brings in the coffee.

These are important matters which the businessman who hopes to trade abroad ignores at his peril. They are also elusive, for every man takes his own culture for granted. Even a well-informed national of another country is hard put to explain why, in his own land, the custom is thus-and-so rather than so-and-thus; as hard put, indeed, as you would probably be if asked what is the "rule" which governs the precise time in a relationship that you begin using another man's first name. One "just knows." In other words, you do not know and cannot explain satisfactorily because you learn this sort of thing unconsciously in your upbringing, in your culture, and you take such knowledge for granted. Yet the impact of culture on communication can be observed and the lessons taught.

Since the most obvious form of communication is by language, we will first consider words, meanings, voice tones, emotions, and physical contact; then take up, in turn, the cultural impact of time, place, and social class relations on business situations in various lands. Finally, we will suggest what the individual administrator may do to increase his effectiveness abroad, and what students of culture may do to advance this application of anthropology.

## BEYOND LANGUAGE

Americans are often accused of not being very good at language, or at least not very much interested in learning foreign languages. There is little evidence that any people are inherently "better" at languages than any other, given the opportunity and incentive to learn. The West and Central European who has since childhood been in daily contact with two or three languages learns to speak them all, and frequently to read and write them as well. Under similar conditions, American children do the same. Indeed, a not uncommon sight on the backroads of Western Europe is a mute, red-faced American military family lost on a Sunday drive while the youngest child, barely able to lisp his own English, leans from the window to interpret the directions of some gnarled farmer whose dialect is largely unintelligible to most of his own countrymen.

We should not underestimate the damage our lack of language facility as a nation has done to our relations all over the world. Obviously, if you cannot speak a man's language, you are terribly handicapped in communicating with him.

But languages can be learned and yet most, if not all, of the disabling errors described in this article could still be made. Vocabulary, grammar, even verbal facility are not enough. Unless a man understands the subtle cues that are implicit in language, tone, gestures, and expression, he will not only consistently misinterpret what is said to him, but he may offend irretrievably without knowing how or why.

## DO THEY MEAN WHAT THEY SAY?

Can't you believe what a man says? We all recognize that the basic honesty of the speaker is involved. What we often fail to recognize, however, is that the question involves cultural influences that have nothing to do with the honesty or dependability of the individual.

In the United States we put a premium on direct expression. The "good" American is supposed to say what he means and to mean what he says. If, on important matters, we discover that someone spoke deviously or evasively, we would be inclined to regard him thereafter as unreliable if not out-and-out dishonest.

In some other cultures, the words and their meanings do not have such a direct connection. People may be more concerned with the emotional context of the situation than with the meaning of particular words. This leads them to give an agreeable and pleasant answer to a question when a literal, factual answer might be unpleasant or embarrassing.

This situation is not unknown in our culture, of course. How many times have you muttered your delighted appreciation for a boring evening? We term this simple politeness and understand each other perfectly.

On the other hand, analogous "polite" behavior on a matter

of factory production would be incomprehensible. An American businessman would be most unlikely to question another businessman's word if he were technically qualified and said that his plant could produce 1,000 gross of widgets a month. We are "taught" that it is none of our business to inquire too deeply into the details of his production system. This would be prying and might be considered an attempt to steal his operational plans.

Yet this cultural pattern has trapped many an American into believing that when a Japanese manufacturer answered a direct question with the reply that he could produce 1,000 gross of widgets, he meant what he said. If the American had been escorted through the factory and saw quite clearly that its capacity was, at the most, perhaps 500 gross of widgets per month, he would be likely to say to himself:

Well, this fellow probably has a brother-in-law who has a factory who can make up the difference. He isn't telling the whole story because he's afraid I might try to make a better deal with the brother-in-law. Besides, what business is it of mine, so long as he meets the schedule?

The cables begin to burn after the American returns home and only 500 gross of widgets arrive each month.

What the American did not know was that in Japanese culture one avoids the direct question unless the questioner is absolutely certain that the answer will not embarrass the Japanese businessman in any way whatsoever. In Japan for one to admit being unable to perform a given operation or measure up to a given standard means a bitter loss of face. Given a foreigner who is so stupid, ignorant, or insensitive as to ask an embarrassing question, the Japanese is likely to choose what appears to him the lesser of two evils.

Americans caught in this cross-cultural communications trap are apt to feel doubly deceived because the Japanese manufacturer may well be an established and respected member of the business community.

### EXCITABLE PEOPLE?
Man communicates not by words alone. His tone of voice, his facial expressions, his gestures all contribute to the infinitely varied calculus of meaning. But the confusion of tongues is more than matched by the confusion of gesture and other culture cues. One man's nod is another man's negative. Each

culture has its own rich array of meaningful signs, symbols, gestures, emotional connotations, historical references, traditional responses and—equally significant—pointed silences. These have been built up over the millennia as (who can say?) snarls, growls, and love murmurs gathered meaning and dignity with long use, to end up perhaps as the worn coinage of trite expression.

Consider the Anglo-Saxon tradition of preserving one's calm. The American is taught by his culture to suppress his feelings. He is conditioned to regard emotion as generally bad (except in weak women who can't help themselves) and a stern self-control as good. The more important a matter, the more solemn and outwardly dispassionate he is likely to be. A cool head, granite visage, dispassionate logic—it is no accident that the Western story hero consistently displays these characteristics.

In the Middle East it is otherwise. From childhood, the Arab is permitted, even encouraged, to express his feelings without inhibition. Grown men can weep, shout, gesture expressively and violently, jump up and down—and be admired as sincere.

The modulated, controlled Anglo-Saxon is likely to be regarded with suspicion—he must be hiding something, practicing to deceive.

The exuberant and emotional Arab is likely to disturb the Anglo-Saxon, cause him to writhe inwardly with embarrassment—for isn't this childish behavior? And aren't things getting rather out of hand?

Then, again, there is the matter of how loudly one should talk.

In the Arab world, in discussions among equals, the men attain a decibel level that would be considered aggressive, objectionable, and obnoxious in the United States. Loudness connotes strength and sincerity among Arabs; a soft tone implies weakness, deviousness. This is so "right" in the Arab culture that several Arabs have told us they discounted anything heard over the "Voice of America" because the signal was so weak!

Personal status modulates voice tone, however, even in Arab society. The Saudi Arab shows respect to his superior—to a sheik, say—by lowering his voice and mumbling. The affluent American may also be addressed in this fashion, making almost impossible an already difficult situation. Since in the American culture one unconsciously "asks" another to raise his voice by raising one's own, the American speaks louder. This lowers the Arab's tone more and increases the mumble. This triggers a shouting response in the American—which cues the Arab into a frightened "I'm not being respectful enough" tone well below audibility.

They are not likely to part with much respect for each other.

## TO TOUCH OR NOT TO TOUCH?
How much physical contact should appropriately accompany social or business conversation?

In the United States we discourage physical contact, particularly between adult males. The most common physical contact is the handshake and, compared to Europeans, we use it sparingly.

The handshake is the most detached and impersonal form of greeting or farewell in Latin America. Somewhat more friendly is the left hand placed on another man's shoulder during a handshake. Definitely more intimate and warm is the *"doble abrazo"* in which two men embrace by placing their arms around each other's shoulders.

These are not difficult conventions to live with, particularly since the North American can easily permit the Latin American to take the initiative in any form of contact more intimate than the handshake. Far more difficult for the North American to learn to live with comfortably are the less stylized forms of physical contact such as the hand on one's arm during conversation. To the North American this is edging toward what in his culture is an uncomfortable something—possibly sexual—which inhibits his own communication.

Yet there are cultures which restrict physical contact far more than we do. An American at a cocktail party in Java tripped over the invisible cultural ropes which mark the boundaries of acceptable behavior. He was seeking to develop a business relationship with a prominent Javanese and seemed to be doing very well. Yet, when the cocktail party ended, so apparently did a promising beginning. For the North American spent nearly six months trying to arrange a second meeting. He finally learned, through pitying intermediaries, that at the cocktail party he had momentarily placed his arm on the shoulder of the Javanese—and in the presence of other people. Humiliating! Almost unpardonable in traditional Javanese etiquette.

In this particular case, the unwitting breach was mended by a graceful apology. It is worth noting, however, that a truly cordial business relationship never did develop.

## THE FIVE DIMENSIONS OF TIME

If we peel away a few layers of cultural clothing, we begin to reach almost totally unconscious reactions. Our ideas of time, for example, are deeply instilled in us when we are children. If they are contradicted by another's behavior, we react with anger, not knowing exactly why. For the businessman, five important temporal concepts are: Appointment time, discussion time, acquaintance time, visiting time, and time schedules.

Anyone who has traveled abroad or dealt at all extensively with non-Americans learns that punctuality is variously interpreted. It is one thing to recognize this with the mind; to adjust to a different kind of *appointment time* is quite another.

In Latin America, you should expect to spend hours waiting in outer offices. If you bring your American interpretation of what constitutes punctuality to a Latin American office, you will fray your temper and elevate your blood pressure. For a 45-minute wait is not unusual—no more unusual than a five-minute wait would be in the United States. No insult is intended, no arbitrary pecking order is being established. If, in the United States, you would not be outraged by a five-minute wait, you should not be outraged by the Latin-American's 45-minute delay in seeing you. The time pie is differently cut, that's all.

Further, the Latin American doesn't usually schedule individual appointments to the exclusion of other appointments. The informal clock of his upbringing ticks more slowly and he rather enjoys seeing several people on different matters at the same time. The three-ring circus atmosphere which results, if interpreted in the American's scale of time and propriety, seems to signal him to go away, to tell him that he is not being properly treated, to indicate that his dignity is under attack. Not so. The clock on the wall may look the same but it tells a different sort of time.

The cultural error may be compounded by a further miscalculation. In the United States, a consistently tardy man is likely to be considered undependable, and by our cultural clock this is a reasonable conclusion. For you to judge a Latin American by your scale of time values is to risk a major error.

Suppose you have waited 45 minutes and there is a man in his office, by some miracle alone in the room with you. Do you now get down to business and stop "wasting time"?

If you are not forewarned by experience or a friendly advisor, you may try to do this. And it would usually be a mistake. For, in the American culture, *discussion* is a means to an end: The deal. You try to make your point quickly, efficiently, neatly. If your purpose is to arrange some major affairs, your instinct is probably to settle the major issues first, leave the details for later, possibly for the technical people to work out.

For the Latin American, the discussion is a part of the spice of life. Just as he tends not to be overly concerned about reserving you your specific segment of time, he tends not as rigidly to separate business from nonbusiness. He runs it all together and wants to make something of a social event out of what you, in your culture, regard as strictly business.

The Latin American is not alone in this. The Greek businessman, partly for the same and partly for different reasons, does not lean toward the "hit-and-run" school of business behavior, either. The Greek businessman adds to the social element, however, a feeling about what length of discussion time constitutes good faith. In America, we show good faith by ignoring the details. "Let's agree on the main points. The details will take care of themselves."

Not so the Greek. He signifies good will and good faith by what may seem to you an interminable discussion which includes every conceivable detail. Otherwise, you see, he cannot help but feel that the other man might be trying to pull the wool over his eyes. Our habit, in what we feel to be our relaxed and friendly way, of postponing details until later smacks the Greek between the eyes as a maneuver to flank him. Even if you can somehow convince him that this is not the case, the meeting must still go on a certain indefinite—but, by our standards, long—time or he will feel disquieted.

The American desire to get down to business and on with other things works to our disadvantage in other parts of the world, too; and not only in business. The head of a large, successful Japanese firm commented: "You Americans have a terrible weakness. We Japanese know about it and exploit it every chance we get. You are impatient. We have learned that if we just make you wait long enough, you'll agree to anything."

Whether this is literally true or not, the Japanese executive singled out a trait of American culture which most of us share and which, one may assume from the newspapers, the Russians have not overlooked, either.

By *acquaintance time* we mean how long you must know a man before you are willing to do business with him.

In the United States, if we know that a salesman represents a well-known, reputable company, and if we need his product, he may walk away from the first meeting with an order in his pocket. A few minutes conversation to decide matters of price, delivery, payment, model of product—nothing more is involved. In Central America, local custom does not permit a salesman to land in town, call on the customer and walk away with an order, no matter how badly your prospect wants and needs your product. It is traditional there that you must see your man at least three times before you can discuss the nature of your business.

Does this mean that the South American businessman does not recognize the merits of one product over another? Of course it doesn't. It is just that the weight of tradition presses him to do business within a circle of friends. If a product he needs is not available within his circle, he does not go outside it so much as he enlarges the circle itself to include a new friend who can supply the want. Apart from his cultural need to "feel right" about a new relationship, there is the logic of his business system. One of the realities of his life is that it is dangerous to enter into business with someone over whom you have no more than formal, legal "control." In the past decades, his legal system has not always been as firm as ours and he has learned through experience that he needs the sanctions implicit in the informal system of friendship.

*Visiting time* involves the question of who sets the time for a visit. George Coelho, a social psychologist from India, gives an illustrative case. A U.S. businessman received this invitation

Cultural Dimensions

from an Indian businessman: "Won't you and your family come and see us? Come anytime." Several weeks later, the Indian repeated the invitation in the same words. Each time the American replied that he would certainly like to drop in— but he never did. The reason is obvious in terms of our culture. Here "come any time" is just an expression of friendliness. You are not really expected to show up unless your host proposes a specific time. In India, on the contrary, the words are meant literally—that the host is putting himself at the disposal of his guest and really expects him to come. It is the essence of politeness to leave it to the guest to set a time at his convenience. If the guest never comes, the Indian naturally assumes that he does not want to come. Such a misunderstanding can lead to a serious rift between men who are trying to do business with each other.

*Time schedules* present Americans with another problem in many parts of the world. Without schedules, deadlines, priorities, and time-tables, we tend to feel that our country could not run at all. Not only are they essential to getting work done, but they also play an important role in the informal communication process. Deadlines indicate priorities and priorities signal the relative importance of people and the processes they control. These are all so much a part of our lives that a day hardly passes without some reference to them. "I have to be there by 6:30." "If I don't have these plans out by 5:00 they'll be useless." "I told J. B. I'd be finished by noon tomorrow and now he tells me to drop everything and get hot on the McDermott account. What do I do now?"

In our system, there are severe penalties for not completing work on time and important rewards for holding to schedules. One's integrity and reputation are at stake.

You can imagine the fundamental conflicts that arise when we attempt to do business with people who are just as strongly oriented away from time schedules as we are toward them.

The Middle Eastern peoples are a case in point. Not only is our idea of time schedules no part of Arab life but the mere mention of a deadline to an Arab is like waving a red flag in front of a bull. In his culture, your emphasis on a deadline has the emotional effect on him that his backing you into a corner and threatening you with a club would have on you.

One effect of this conflict of unconscious habit patterns is that hundreds of American-owned radio sets are lying on the shelves of Arab radio repair shops, untouched. The Americans made the serious cross-cultural error of asking to have the repair completed by a certain time.

How do you cope with this? How does the Arab get another Arab to do anything? Every culture has its own ways of bringing pressure to get results. The usual Arab way is one which Americans avoid as "bad manners." It is needling.

An Arab businessman whose car broke down explained it this way:

First, I go to the garage and tell the mechanic what is wrong with my car. I wouldn't want to give him the idea that I didn't know. After that, I leave the car and walk around the block. When I come back to the garage, I ask him if he has started to work yet. On my way home from lunch I stop in and ask him how things are going. When I go back to the office I stop by again. In the evening I return and peer over his shoulder for a while. If I didn't keep this up, he'd be off working on someone else's car.

If you haven't been needled by an Arab, you just haven't been needled.

### A PLACE FOR EVERYTHING

We say that there is a time and place for everything, but compared to other countries and cultures we give very little emphasis to place distinctions. Business is almost a universal value with us; it can be discussed almost anywhere, except perhaps in church. One can even talk business on the church steps going to and from the service. Politics is only slightly more restricted in the places appropriate for its discussion.

In other parts of the world, there are decided place restrictions on the discussion of business and politics. The American who is not conscious of the unwritten laws will offend if he abides by his own rather than by the local rules.

In India, you should not talk business when visiting a man's home. If you do, you prejudice your chances of ever working out a satisfactory business relationship.

In Latin America, although university students take an active interest in politics, tradition decrees that a politician should avoid political subjects when speaking on university grounds. A Latin American politician commented to anthropologist Allan Holmberg that neither he nor his fellow politicians would have dared attempt a political speech on the grounds of the University of San Marcos in Peru—as did Vice President Nixon.

To complicate matters further, the student body of San Marcos, anticipating the visit, had voted that Mr. Nixon would not be welcome. The University Rector had issued no invitation, presumably because he expected what did, in fact, happen.

As a final touch, Mr. Nixon's interpreter was a man in full military uniform. In Latin American countries, some of which had recently overthrown military dictators, the symbolism of the military uniform could hardly contribute to a cordial atmosphere. Latin Americans need no reminder that the United States is a great military power.

Mr. Nixon's efforts were planned in the best traditions of our own culture: He hoped to improve relations through a direct, frank, and face-to-face discussion with students—the future leaders of their country. Unfortunately, this approach did not fit in at all with the culture of the host country. Of course, elements hostile to the United States did their best to capitalize upon this cross-cultural misunderstanding. However, even Latin Americans friendly to us, while admiring the Vice President's courage, found themselves acutely embarrassed by the behavior of their people and ours in the ensuing difficulties.

## BEING COMFORTABLE IN SPACE

Like time and place, differing ideas of space hide traps for the uninformed. Without realizing it, almost any person raised in the United States is likely to give an unintended snub to a Latin American simply in the way we handle space relationships, particularly during conversations.

In North America, the "proper" distance to stand when talking to another adult male you do not know well is about two feet, at least in a formal business conversation. (Naturally at a cocktail party, the distance shrinks, but anything under eight to ten inches is likely to provoke an apology or an attempt to back up.)

To a Latin American, with his cultural traditions and habits, a distance of two feet seems to him approximately what five feet would to us. To him we seem distant and cold; to us, he gives an impression of pushiness.

As soon as a Latin American moves close enough for him

to feel comfortable, we feel uncomfortable and edge back. We once observed a conversation between a Latin and a North American which began at one end of a 40-foot hall. At intervals we noticed them again, finally at the other end of the hall. This rather amusing displacement had been accomplished by an almost continual series of small backward steps on the part of the American, trying unconsciously to reach a comfortable talking distance, and an equal closing of the gap by the Latin American as he attempted to reach his accustomed conversation space.

Americans in their offices in Latin America tend to keep their native acquaintances at our distance—not the Latin American's distance—by taking up a position behind a desk or typewriter. The barricade approach to communication is practiced even by old hands in Latin America who are completely unaware of its cultural significance. They know only that they are comfortable without realizing that the distance and equipment unconsciously make the Latin American uncomfortable.

## HOW CLASS CHANNELS COMMUNICATION

We would be mistaken to regard the communication patterns which we observe around the world as no more than a miscellaneous collection of customs. The communication pattern of a given society is part of its total culture pattern and can only be understood in that context.

We cannot undertake here to relate many examples of communication behavior to the underlying culture of the country. For the businessman, it might be useful to mention the difficulties in the relationship between social levels and the problem of information feedback from lower to higher levels in industrial organizations abroad.

There is in Latin America a pattern of human relations and union-management relations quite different from that with which we are familiar in the United States. Everett Hagen of MIT has noted the heavier emphasis upon line authority and the lesser development of staff organizations in Latin American plants when compared with North American counterparts. To a much greater extent than in the United States, the government becomes involved in the handling of all kinds of labor problems.

These differences seem to be clearly related to the culture and social organization of Latin America. We find there that society has been much more rigidly stratified than it has with us. As a corollary, we find a greater emphasis upon authority in family and the community.

This emphasis upon status and class distinction makes it very difficult for people of different status levels to express themselves freely and frankly in discussion and argument. In the past, the pattern has been for the man of lower status to express deference to his superior in any face-to-face contact. This is so even when everyone knows that the subordinate dislikes the superior. The culture of Latin America places a great premium upon keeping personal relations harmonious on the surface.

In the United States, we feel that it is not only desirable but natural to speak up to your superior, to tell the boss exactly what you think, even when you disagree with him. Of course, we do not always do this, but we think that we should, and we feel guilty if we fail to speak our minds frankly. When workers in our factories first get elected to local union office, they may find themselves quite self-conscious about speaking up to the boss and arguing grievances. Many of them, however, quickly learn to do it and enjoy the experience. American culture emphasizes the thrashing-out of differences in face-to-face contacts. It deemphasizes the importance of status. As a result, we have built institutions for handling industrial disputes on the basis of the local situation, and we rely on direct discussion by the parties immediately involved.

In Latin America, where it is exceedingly difficult for people to express their differences face-to-face and where status differences and authority are much more strongly emphasized than here, the workers tend to look to a third party—the government—to take care of their problems. Though the workers have great difficulty in thrashing out their problems with management, they find no difficulty in telling government representatives their problems. And it is to their government that they look for an authority to settle their grievances with management.

Status and class also decide whether business will be done on an individual or a group basis.

In the United States, we are growing more and more accustomed to working as members of large organizations. Despite this, we still assume that there is no need to send a delegation to do a job that one capable man might well handle.

In some other parts of the world, the individual cannot expect to gain the respect necessary to accomplish this purpose, no matter how capable he is, unless he brings along an appropriate number of associates.

In the United States, we would rarely think it necessary or proper to call on a customer in a group. He might well be antagonized by the hard sell. In Japan—as an example—the importance of the occasion and of the man is measured by whom he takes along.

This practice goes far down in the business and government hierarchies. Even a university professor is likely to bring one or two retainers along on academic business. Otherwise people might think that he was a nobody and that his affairs were of little moment.

Even when a group is involved in the U.S., the head man is the spokesman and sets the tone. This is not always the case in Japan. Two young Japanese once requested an older American widely respected in Tokyo to accompany them so that they could "stand on his face." He was not expected to enter into the negotiation; his function was simply to be present as an indication that their intentions were serious.

## ADJUSTMENT GOES BOTH WAYS
One need not have devoted his life to a study of various cultures to see that none of them is static. All are constantly changing and one element of change is the very fact that U.S. enterprise enters a foreign field. This is inevitable and may be constructive if we know how to utilize our knowledge. The problem is for us to be aware of our impact and to learn how to induce changes skillfully.

Rather than try to answer the general question of how two cultures interact, we will consider the key problem of personnel selection and development in two particular intercultural situations, both in Latin cultures.

One U.S. company had totally different experiences with "Smith" and "Jones" in the handling of its labor relations. The local union leaders were bitterly hostile to Smith, whereas they could not praise Jones enough. These were puzzling reactions to higher management. Smith seemed a fair-minded and understanding man; it was difficult to fathom how anyone could be bitter against him. At the same time, Jones did not appear to be currying favor by his generosity in giving away the firm's assets. To management, he seemed to be just as firm a negotiator as Smith.

The explanation was found in the two men's communication characteristics. When the union leaders came in to negotiate with Smith, he would let them state their case fully and freely—without interruption, but also without comment. When they had finished, he would say, "I'm sorry. We can't do it." He would follow this blunt statement with a brief and entirely cogent explanation of his reasons for refusal. If the union leaders persisted in their arguments, Smith would paraphrase his first statement, calmly and succinctly. In either case, the discussion was over in a few minutes. The union leaders would storm out of Smith's office complaining bitterly about the cold and heartless man with whom they had to deal.

Jones handled the situation differently. His final conclusion was the same as Smith's—but he would state it only after two or three hours of discussion. Furthermore, Jones participated actively in these discussions, questioning the union leaders for more information, relating the case in question to previous cases, philosophizing about labor relations and human rights and exchanging stories about work experience. When the discussion came to an end, the union leaders would leave the office, commenting on how warmhearted and understanding he was, and how confident they were that he would help them when it was possible for him to do so. They actually seemed more satisfied with a negative decision from Jones than they did with a hard-won concession with Smith.

This was clearly a case where the personality of Jones happened to match certain discernible requirements of the Latin American culture. It was happenstance in this case that Jones worked out and Smith did not, for by American standards both were top-flight men. Since a talent for the kind of negotiation that the Latin American considers graceful and acceptable can hardly be developed in a grown man (or perhaps even in a young one), the basic problem is one of personnel selection in terms of the culture where the candidate is to work.

The second case is more complicated because it involves much deeper intercultural adjustments. The management of the parent U.S. company concerned had learned—as have the directors of most large firms with good-sized installations overseas—that one cannot afford to have all of the top and middle-management positions manned by North Americans. It is necessary to advance nationals up the overseas-management ladder as rapidly as their abilities permit. So the nationals have to learn not only the technical aspects of their jobs but also how to function at higher levels in the organization.

Latin culture emphasizes authority in the home, church, and community. Within the organization this produces a built-in hesitancy about speaking up to one's superiors. The initiative, the acceptance of responsibility which we value in our organizations had to be stimulated. How could it be done?

We observed one management man who had done a remarkable job of building up these very qualities in his general foremen and foremen. To begin with, he stimulated informal contacts between himself and these men through social events to which the men and their wives came. He saw to it that his senior North American assistants and their wives were also present. Knowing the language, he mixed freely with all. At the plant, he circulated about, dropped in not to inspect or check up, but to joke and to break down the great barrier that existed in the local traditions between authority and the subordinates.

Next, he developed a pattern of three-level meetings. At the top, he himself, the superintendents, and the general foreman. At the middle level, the superintendents, general foremen, and foremen. Then the general foremen, foremen, and workers.

At the top level meeting, the American management chief set the pattern of encouraging his subordinates to challenge his own ideas, to come up with original thoughts. When his superintendents (also North Americans) disagreed with him, he made it clear that they were to state their objections fully. At first, the general foreman looked surprised and uneasy. They noted, however, that the senior men who argued with the boss were encouraged and praised. Timorously, with great hesitation, they began to add their own suggestions. As time went on, they more and more accepted the new convention and pitched in without inhibition.

The idea of challenging the boss with constructive
ideas gradually filtered down to the second and third
meetings. It took a lot of time and gentle handling, but out
of this approach grew an extraordinary morale. The native
general foremen and foremen developed new pride in themselves, accepted new responsibilities, even reached out for
more. They began to work to improve their capacities and to
look forward to moving up in the hierarchy.

## CONFORMITY OR ADJUSTMENT?

To work with people, must we be just like them? Obviously
not. If we try to conform completely, the Arab, the Latin
American, the Italian, whoever he might be, finds our behavior confusing and insincere. He suspects our motive. We are
expected to be different. But we are also expected to respect
and accept the other people as they are. And we may, without
doing violence to our own personalities, learn to communicate with them by observing the unwritten patterns they are
accustomed to.

To be aware that there are pitfalls in cross-cultural dealings
is the first big step forward. And to accept the fact that our
convictions are in no respect more eternally "right" than
someone else's is another constructive step. . . .

# PROXEMICS IN A CROSS-CULTURAL CONTEXT: GERMANS, ENGLISH, AND FRENCH
## Edward T. Hall

The Germans, the English, the Americans, and the French share significant portions of each other's cultures, but at many points their cultures clash. Consequently, the misunderstandings that arise are all the more serious because sophisticated Americans and Europeans take pride in correctly interpreting each other's behavior. Cultural differences which are out of awareness are, as a consequence, usually chalked up to ineptness, boorishness, or lack of interest on the part of the other person.

### THE GERMANS

Whenever people from different countries come into repeated contact they begin to generalize about each other's behavior. The Germans and the German Swiss are no exception. Most of the intellectual and professional people I have talked to from these two countries eventually get around to commenting on American use of time and space. Both the Germans and the German Swiss have made consistent observations about how Americans structure time very tightly and are sticklers for schedules. They also note that Americans don't leave any free time for themselves (a point which has been made by Sebastian de Grazia in *Of Time, Work, and Leisure*).

Since neither the Germans nor the Swiss (particularly the German Swiss) could be regarded as completely causal about time, I have made it a point to question them further about their view of the American approach to time. They will say that Europeans will schedule fewer events in the same time than Americans do and they usually add that Europeans allow more time for virtually everything involving important human relationships. Many of my European subjects observed that in Europe human relationships are important whereas in the

From *The Hidden Dimension* by Edward T. Hall, pp. 57-59, 123-138. Copyright © 1966 by Edward T. Hall. Reprinted by permission of Doubleday & Company, Inc.

Cultural Dimensions

United States the schedule is important. Several of my subjects then took the next logical step and connected the handling of time with attitudes toward space, which Americans treat with incredible casualness. According to European standards, Americans use space in a wasteful way and seldom plan adequately for public needs. In fact, it would seem that Americans feel that people have no needs associated with space at all. By overemphasizing the schedule Americans tend to underemphasize individual space needs. I should mention at this point that all Europeans are not this perceptive. Many of them go no further than to say that in the United States they themselves feel pressured by time and they often complain that our cities lack variety. Nevertheless, given these observations made by Europeans one would expect that the Germans would be more upset by violations of spatial mores than the Americans.

## GERMANS AND INTRUSIONS

I shall never forget my first experience with German proxemic patterns, which occurred when I was an undergraduate. My manners, my status, and my ego were attacked and crushed by a German in an instance where 30 years' residence in this country and an excellent command of English had not attenuated German definitions of what constitutes an intrusion. In order to understand the various issues that were at stake, it is necessary to refer back to two basic American patterns that are taken for granted in this country and which Americans therefore tend to treat as universal.

First, in the United States there is a commonly accepted, invisible boundary around any two or three people in conversation which separates them from others. Distance alone serves to isolate any such group and to endow it with a protective wall of privacy. Normally, voices are kept low to avoid intruding on others and if voices are heard, people will act as though they had not heard. In this way, privacy is granted whether it is actually present or not. The second pattern is somewhat more subtle and has to do with the exact point at which a person is experienced as actually having crossed a boundary and entered a room. Talking through a screen door while standing outside a house is not considered by most Americans as being inside the house or room in any sense of the word. If one is standing on the threshold holding the door

open and talking to someone inside, it is still defined infor-
mally and experienced as being *outside*. If one is in an office
building and just "pokes his head in the door" of an office
he's still outside the office. Just holding on to the doorjamb
when one's body is inside the room still means a person has
one foot "on base" as it were so that he is not quite inside
the other fellow's territory. None of these American spatial
definitions is valid in northern Germany. In every instance
where the American would consider himself *outside* he has
already entered the German's territory and by definition
would become involved with him. The following experience
brought the conflict between these two patterns into focus.

It was a warm spring day of the type one finds only in the
high, clean, clear air of Colorado, the kind of day that makes
you glad you are alive. I was standing on the doorstep of a
converted carriage house talking to a young woman who
lived in an apartment upstairs. The first floor had been made
into an artist's studio. The arrangement, however, was peculiar because the same entrance served both tenants. The occupants of the apartment used a small entryway and walked
along one wall of the studio to reach the stairs to the apartment. You might say that they had an "easement" through
the artist's territory. As I stood talking on the doorstep, I
glanced to the left and noticed that some 50 to 60 feet away,
inside the studio, the Prussian artist and two of his friends
were also in conversation. He was facing so that if he glanced
to one side he could just see me. I had noted his presence, but
not wanting to appear presumptuous or to interrupt his conversation, I unconsciously applied the American rule and
assumed that the two activities—my quiet conversation and
his conversation—were not involved with each other. As I was
soon to learn, this was a mistake, because in less time than it
takes to tell, the artist had detached himself from his friends,
crossed the intervening space, pushed my friend aside, and
with eyes flashing, started shouting at me. By what right had
I entered his studio without greeting him? Who had given me
permission?

I felt bullied and humiliated, and even after almost 30
years, I can still feel my anger. Later study has given me
greater understanding of the German pattern and I have
learned that in the German's eyes I really had been intolerably

rude. I was already "inside" the building and I intruded when I could *see* inside. For the German, there is no such thing as being inside the room without being inside the zone of intrusion, particularly if one looks at the other party, no matter how far away.

Recently, I obtained an independent check on how Germans feel about visual intrusion while investigating what people look at when they are in intimate, personal, social, and public situations. In the course of my research, I instructed subjects to photograph separately both a man and a woman in each of the above contexts. One of my assistants, who also happened to be German, photographed his subjects out of focus at public distance because, as he said, "You are not really supposed to look at other people at public distances *because it's intruding.*" This may explain the informal custom behind the German laws against photographing strangers in public without their permission.

### The "Private Sphere"

Germans sense their own space as an extension of the ego. One sees a clue to this feeling in the term "Lebensraum," which is impossible to translate because it summarizes so much. Hitler used it as an effective psychological lever to move the Germans to conquest.

In contrast to the Arab, as we shall see later, the German's ego is extraordinarily exposed, and he will go to almost any length to preserve his "private sphere." This was observed during World War II when American soldiers were offered opportunities to observe German prisoners under a variety of circumstances. In one instance in the Midwest, German P.W.s were housed four to a small hut. As soon as materials were available, each prisoner built a partition so that he could have *his own space.* In a less favorable setting in Germany when the *Wehrmacht* was collapsing, it was necessary to use open stockades because German prisoners were arriving faster than they could be accommodated. In this situation each soldier who could find the materials built his own tiny dwelling unit, sometimes no larger than a foxhole. It puzzled the Americans that the Germans did not pool their efforts and their scarce materials to create a larger, more efficient space, particularly in view of the very cold spring nights. Since that time I have observed frequent instances of the use of architectural extensions of this need to screen the ego. German houses with balconies are arranged so that there is visual privacy. Yards tend to be well fenced; but fenced or not, they are sacred.

The American view that space should be shared is particularly troublesome to the German. I cannot document the account of the early days of World War II occupation when Berlin was in ruins but the following situation was reported by an observer and it has the nightmarish quality that is often associated with inadvertent cross-cultural blunders. In Berlin at that time the housing shortage was indescribably acute. To provide relief, occupation authorities in the American zone ordered those Berliners who still had kitchens and baths intact to share them with their neighbors. The order finally had to be rescinded when the already overstressed Germans started killing each other over the shared facilities.

Public and private buildings in Germany often have double doors for soundproofing, as do many hotel rooms. In addition, the door is taken very seriously by Germans. Those Germans who come to America feel that our doors are flimsy and light. The meanings of the open door and the closed door are quite different in the two countries. In offices, Americans keep doors open; Germans keep doors closed. In Germany, the closed door does not mean that the man behind it wants to be alone or undisturbed, or that he is doing something he doesn't want someone else to see. It's simply that Germans think that open doors are sloppy and disorderly. To close the door preserves the integrity of the room and provides a protective boundary between people. Otherwise, they get too involved with each other. One of my German subjects commented, "If our family hadn't had doors, we would have had to change our way of life. Without doors we would have had many, many more fights. . . . When you can't talk, you retreat behind a door. . . . If there hadn't been doors, I would always have been within reach of my mother."

Whenever a German warms up to the subject of American enclosed space, he can be counted on to comment on the noise that is transmitted through walls and doors. To many Germans, our doors epitomize American life. They are thin and cheap; they seldom fit; and they lack the substantial quality of German doors. When they close they don't sound and feel solid. The click of the lock is indistinct, it rattles and indeed it may even be absent.

The open-door policy of American business and the closed-door patterns of German business culture cause clashes in the branches and subsidiaries of American firms in Germany. The point seems to be quite simple, yet failure to grasp it has caused considerable friction and misunderstanding between American and German managers overseas. I was once called in to advise a firm that has operations all over the world. One of the first questions asked was, "How do you get the Germans to keep their doors open?" In this company the open doors were making the Germans feel exposed and gave the whole operation an unusually relaxed and unbusinesslike air. Closed doors, on the other hand, gave the Americans the feeling that there was a conspiratorial air about the place and that they were being left out. The point is that whether the door is open or shut, it is not going to mean the same thing in the two countries.

### Order in Space

The orderliness and hierarchical quality of German culture are communicated in their handling of space. Germans want to know where they stand and object strenuously to people crashing queues or people who "get out of line" or who do not obey signs such as "Keep out," "Authorized personnel only," and the like. Some of the German attitudes toward ourselves are traceable to our informal attitudes toward boundaries and to authority in general.

However, German anxiety due to American violations of order is nothing compared to that engendered in Germans by the Poles, who see no harm in a little disorder. To them lines and queues stand for regimentation and blind authority. I once saw a Pole crash a cafeteria line just "to stir up those sheep."

Germans get very technical about intrusion distance, as I mentioned earlier. When I once asked my students to describe the distance at which a third party would intrude on two people who were talking, there were no answers from the Americans. Each student knew that he could tell when he was being intruded on but he couldn't define intrusion or tell how he knew when it had occurred. However, a German and an Italian who had worked in Germany were both members of my class and they answered without any hesitation. Both stated that a third party would intrude on two people if he came within seven feet!

Many Americans feel that Germans are overly rigid in their behavior, unbending and formal. Some of this impression is created by differences in the handling of chairs while seated. The American doesn't seem to mind if people hitch their chairs up to adjust the distance to the situation—those that do mind would not think of saying anything, for to comment on the manners of others would be impolite. In Germany, however, it is a violation of the mores to change the position of your chair. An added deterrent for those who don't know better is the weight of most German furniture. Even the great architect Mies van der Rohe, who often rebelled against German tradition in his buildings, made his handsome chairs so heavy that anyone but a strong man would have difficulty in adjusting his seating position. To a German, light furniture is anathema, not only because it seems flimsy but because people move it and thereby destroy the order of things, including intrusions on the "private sphere." In one instance reported to me, a German newspaper editor who had moved to the United States had his visitor's chair bolted to the floor "at the proper distance" because he couldn't tolerate the American habit of adjusting the chair to the situation.

## THE ENGLISH

It has been said that the English and the Americans are two great people separated by one language. The differences for which language gets blamed may not be due so much to words as to communications on other levels beginning with English intonation (which sounds affected to many Americans) and continuing to ego-linked ways of handling time, space, and materials. If there ever were two cultures in which differences of the proxemic details are marked it is in the educated (public school) English and the middle-class Americans. One of the basic reasons for this wide disparity is that in the United States we use space as a way of classifying people and activities, whereas in England it is the social system that determines who you are. In the United States, your address is an important cue to status (this applies not only to one's home but to the business address as well). The Joneses from Brooklyn and Miami are not as "in" as the Joneses from Newport and Palm Beach. Greenwich and Cape Cod are worlds apart from Newark and Miami. Businesses located on Madison and Park avenues have more tone than those on Seventh and Eighth avenues. A corner office is more prestigious than one next to the elevator or at the end of a long hall. The Englishman, however, is born and brought up in a social system. He is still Lord—no matter where you find him, even if it is behind the counter in a fishmonger's stall. In addition to class distinctions, there are differences between the English and ourselves in how space is allotted.

The middle-class American growing up in the United States feels he has a right to have his own room, or at least part of a room. My American subjects, when asked to draw an ideal room or office, invariably drew it for themselves and no one else. When asked to draw their present room or office, they drew only their own part of a shared room and then drew a line down the middle. Both male and female subjects identified the kitchen and the master bedroom as belonging to the mother or the wife, whereas Father's territory was a study or a den, if one was available; otherwise, it was "the shop," "the basement," or sometimes only a workbench or the garage. American women who want to be alone can go to the bedroom and close the door. The closed door is the sign meaning "Do not disturb" or "I'm angry." An American is available if his door is open at home or at his office. He is expected not to shut himself off but to maintain himself in a state of constant readiness to answer the demands of others. Closed doors are for conferences, private conversations, and business, work that requires concentration, study, resting, sleeping, dressing, and sex.

The middle- and upper-class Englishman, on the other hand, is brought up in a nursery shared with brothers and sisters. The oldest occupies a room by himself which he vacates when he leaves for boarding school, possibly even at the age of nine or ten. The difference between a room of one's own and early conditioning to shared space, while seeming inconsequential, has an important effect on the Englishman's attitude toward his own space. He may never have a permanent "room of his own" and seldom expects one or feels he is entitled to one.

Even Members of Parliament have no offices and often conduct their business on the terrace overlooking the Thames. As a consequence, the English are puzzled by the American need for a secure place in which to work, an office. Americans working in England may become annoyed if they are not provided with what they consider appropriate enclosed work space. In regard to the need for walls as a screen for the ego, this places the Americans somewhere between the Germans and the English.

The contrasting English and American patterns have some remarkable implications, particularly if we assume that man, like other animals, has a built-in need to shut himself off from others from time to time. An English student in one of my seminars typified what happens when hidden patterns clash. He was quite obviously experiencing strain in his relationships with Americans. Nothing seemed to go right and it was quite clear from his remarks that we did not know how to behave. An analysis of his complaints showed that a major source of irritation was that no American seemed to be able to pick up the subtle clues that there were times when he didn't want his thoughts intruded on. As he stated it, "I'm walking around the apartment and it seems that whenever I want to be alone my roommate starts talking to me. Pretty soon he's asking 'What's the matter?' and wants to know if I'm angry. By then I am angry and say something."

It took some time but finally we were able to identify most of the contrasting features of the American and British problems that were in conflict in this case. When the American wants to be alone he goes into a room and shuts the door—he depends on architectural features for screening. For an American to refuse to talk to someone else present in the same room, to give them the "silent treatment," is the ultimate form of rejection and a sure sign of great displeasure. The English, on the other hand, lacking rooms of their own since childhood, never developed the practice of using space as a refuge from others. They have in effect internalized a set of barriers, which they erect and which others are supposed to recognize. Therefore, the more the Englishman shuts himself off when he is with an American the more likely the American is to break in to assure himself that all is well. Tension lasts until the two get to know each other. The important point is that the spatial and architectural needs of each are not the same at all.

## Using the Telephone

English internalized privacy mechanisms and the American privacy screen result in very different customs regarding the telephone. There is no wall or door against the telephone. Since it is impossible to tell from the ring who is on the other end of the line, or how urgent his business is, people feel compelled to answer the phone. As one would anticipate, the English when they feel the need to be with their thoughts treat the phone as an intrusion by someone who doesn't know any better. Since it is impossible to tell how preoccupied the other party will be they hesitate to use the phone; instead, they write notes. To phone is to be "pushy" and rude. A letter or telegram may be slower, but it is much less disrupting. Phones are for actual business and emergencies.

I used this system myself for several years when I lived in Santa Fe, New Mexico, during the depression. I dispensed with a phone because it cost money. Besides, I cherished the quiet of my tiny mountainside retreat and didn't want to be disturbed. This idiosyncrasy on my part produced a shocked reaction in others. People really didn't know what to do with me. You could see the consternation on their faces when, in answer to the question, "How do I get in touch with you?" I would reply, "Write me a post card. I come to the post office every day."

Having provided most of our middle-class citizens with private rooms and escape from the city to the suburbs, we have then proceeded to penetrate their most private spaces in their home with a most public device, the telephone. Anyone can reach us at any time. We are, in fact, so available that elaborate devices have to be devised so that busy people can function. The greatest skill and tact must be exercised in the message-screening process so that others will not be offended. So far our technology has not kept up with the needs of people to be alone with either their families or their thoughts. The problem stems from the fact that it is impossible to tell from the phone's ring who is calling and how urgent his business is. Some people have unlisted phones but then that makes it hard on friends who come to town who want to get in touch with them. The government solution is to have special phones for important people (traditionally red). The red line bypasses secretaries, coffee breaks, busy signals, and teenagers, and is connected to White House, State Department, and Pentagon switchboards.

### Neighbors
Americans living in England are remarkably consistent in their reactions to the English. Most of them are hurt and puzzled because they were brought up on American neighboring patterns and don't interpret the English ones correctly. In England propinquity means nothing. The fact that you live next door to a family does not entitle you to visit, borrow from, or socialize with them, or your children to play with theirs. Accurate figures on the number of Americans who adjust well to the English are difficult to obtain. The basic attitude of the English toward the Americans is tinged by our ex-colonial status. This attitude is much more in awareness and therefore more likely to be expressed than the unspoken right of the Englishman to maintain his privacy against the world. To the best of my knowledge, those who have tried to relate to the English purely on the basis of propinquity seldom if ever succeed. They may get to know and even like their neighbors, but it won't be because they live next door, because English relationships are patterned not according to space but according to social status.

### Whose Room Is the Bedroom?
In upper middle-class English homes, it is the man, not the woman, who has the privacy of the bedroom, presumably as protection from children who haven't yet internalized the English patterns of privacy. The man, not the woman, has a dressing room; the man also has a study which affords privacy. The Englishman is fastidious about his clothes and expects to spend a great deal of time and attention in their purchase. In contrast, English women approach the buying of clothes in a manner reminiscent of the American male.

### Talking Loud and Soft
Proper spacing between people is maintained in many ways. Loudness of the voice is one of the mechanisms which also

varies from culture to culture. In England and in Europe generally, Americans are continually accused of loud talking, which is a function of two forms of vocal control: (a) Loudness, and (b) modulation for direction. Americans increase the volume as a function of distance, using several levels (whisper, normal voice, loud shout, etc.). In many situations, the more gregarious Americans do not care if they can be overheard. In fact, it is part of their openness showing that we have nothing to hide. The English do care, for to get along without private offices and not intrude they have developed skills in beaming the voice toward the person they are talking to, carefully adjusting it so that it just barely overrides the background noise and distance. For the English to be overheard is to intrude on others, a failure in manners and a sign of socially inferior behavior. However, because of the way they modulate their voices the English in an American setting may sound and look conspiratorial to Americans, which can result in their being branded as troublemakers.

### Eye Behavior
A study of eye behavior reveals some interesting contrasts between the two cultures. Englishmen in this country have trouble not only when they want to be alone and shut themselves off but also when they want to interact. They never know for sure whether an American is listening. We, on the other hand, are equally unsure as to whether the English have understood us. Many of these ambiguities in communication center on differences in the use of the eyes. The Englishman is taught to pay strict attention, to listen carefully, which he must do if he is polite and there are not protective walls to screen out sound. He doesn't bob his head or grunt to let you know he understands. He blinks his eyes to let you know that he has heard you. Americans, on the other hand, are taught not to stare. We look the other person straight in the eye without wavering only when we want to be particularly certain that we are getting through to him.

The gaze of the American directed toward his conversational partner often wanders from one eye to the other and even leaves the face for long periods. Proper English listening behavior includes immobilization of the eyes at social distance, so that whichever eye one looks at gives the appearance of looking straight at you. In order to accomplish this feat, the Englishman must be eight or more feet away. He is too close when the 12-degree horizontal span of the macula won't permit a steady gaze. At less than eight feet, one *must* look at either one eye or the other.

## THE FRENCH

The French who live south and east of Paris belong generally to that complex of cultures which border the Mediterranean. Members of this group pack together more closely than do northern Europeans, English, and Americans. Mediterranean use of space can be seen in the crowded trains, buses, automobiles, sidewalk cafés, and in the homes of the people. The exceptions are, of course, in the châteaus and villas of the rich. Crowded living normally means high sensory involvement. Evidence of French emphasis on the senses appears not only in the way the French eat, entertain, talk, write, crowd together in cafés, but can even be seen in the way they make their maps. These maps are extraordinarily well thought out and so designed that the traveler can find the most detailed information. One can tell from using these maps that the French employ all their senses. These maps make it possible for you to get around and they also tell you where you can enjoy a view; where you'll find picturesque drives, and, in some instances, places to rest, refresh yourself, take a walk, and even eat a pleasant meal. They inform the traveler which senses he can expect to use and at what points in his journey.

### Home and Family

One possible reason why the French love the outdoors is the rather crowded conditions under which many of them live. The French entertain at restaurants and cafes. The home is for the family and the outdoors for recreation and socializing. Yet all the homes I have visited, as well as everything I have been able to learn about French homes, indicate that they are often quite crowded. The working class and the petite bourgeoisie are particularly crowded, which means that the French are sensually much involved with each other. The layout of their offices, homes, towns, cities, and countryside is such as to keep them involved.

In interpersonal encounters this involvement runs high; when a Frenchman talks to you, he really looks at you and there is no mistaking this fact. On the streets of Paris he looks at the woman he sees very directly. American women returning to their own country after living in France often go through a period of sensory deprivation. Several have told me that because they have grown accustomed to being looked at, the American habit of *not* looking makes them feel as if they didn't exist.

Not only are the French sensually involved with each other, they have become accustomed to what are to us greatly stepped-up sensory inputs. The French automobile is designed in response to French needs. Its small size used to be attributed to a lower standard of living and higher costs of materials; and while there can be no doubt but that cost is a factor, it would be naïve to assume that it was the major factor. The automobile is just as much an expression of the culture as is the language and, therefore, has its characteristic niche in the cultural biotope. Changes in the car will reflect and be reflected in changes elsewhere. If the French drove American cars, they would be forced to give up many ways of dealing with space which they hold quite dear. The traffic along the Champs-Elysées and around the Arc de Triomphe is a cross between the New Jersey Turnpike on a sunny Sunday afternoon and the Indianapolis Speedway. With American-size autos, it would be mass suicide. Even the occasional "compact" American cars in the stream of Parisian traffic look like sharks among minnows. In the United States, the same cars look normal because everything else is in scale. In the foreign setting where they stand out, Detroit iron can be seen for what it is. The American behemoths give bulk to the ego and prevent overlapping of personal spheres inside the car so that each passenger is only marginally involved with the others. I do not mean by this that all Americans are alike and have been forced into the Detroit mold. But since Detroit won't produce what is wanted, many Americans prefer the smaller, more maneuverable European cars which fit their personalities and needs more closely. Nevertheless, if one simply looks at the styles of the French cars, one sees greater emphasis on individuality than in the United States. Compare the Peugeot, the Citroen, the Renault and the Dauphine and the little

2 C.V. shoebox. It would take years and years of style changes to produce such differences in the United States.

### French Use of Open Spaces

Because total space needs must be maintained in balance, the urban French have learned to make the most of the parks and the outdoors. To them, the city is something from which to derive satisfaction and so are the people in it. Reasonably clean air, sidewalks up to 70 feet wide, automobiles that will not dwarf humans as they pass on the boulevards make it possible to have outdoor cafés and open areas where people congregate and enjoy each other. Since the French savor and participate in the city itself—its varied sights, sounds, and smells; its wide sidewalks and avenues and parks—the need for insulating space in the automobile may be somewhat less than it is in the United States where humans are dwarfed by sky-scrapers and the products of Detroit, visually assaulted by filth and rubbish, and poisoned by smog and carbon dioxide.

### The Star and the Grid

There are two major European systems for patterning space. One of these, "the radiating star" which occurs in France and Spain, is sociopetal. The other, the "grid," originated in Asia Minor, adopted by the Romans and carried to England at the time of Caesar, is sociofugal. The French-Spanish system connects all points and functions. In the French subway system, different lines repeatedly come together at places of interest like the Place de la Concorde, the Opéra, and the Madeleine. The grid system separates activities by stringing them out. Both systems have advantages, but a person familiar with one has difficulty using the other.

For example, a mistake in direction in the radiating center-point system becomes more serious the farther one travels. Any error, therefore, is roughly equivalent to taking off in the wrong direction. In the grid system, baseline errors are of the 90-degree or the 180-degree variety and are usually obvious enough to make themselves felt even by those with a poor sense of direction. If you are traveling in the right direction, even though you are one or two blocks off your course, the error is easily rectified at any time. Nevertheless, there are certain inherent advantages in the center-point system. Once one learns to use it, it is easier for example to locate objects or events in space by naming a point on a line. Thus it is possible, even in strange territory, to tell someone to meet you at the 50 KM mark on National Route 20 south of Paris; that is all the information he needs. In contrast, the grid system of co-ordinates involves at least two lines and a point to locate something in space (often many more lines and points, depending on how many turns one has to make). In the star system, it is also possible to integrate a number of different activities in centers in less space than with the grid system. Thus, residential, shopping, marketing, commercial, and recreation areas can both meet and be reached from central points.

It is incredible how many facets of French life the radiating star pattern touches. It is almost as though the whole culture were set up on a model in which power, influence, and control flowed in and out from a series of interlocking centers. There are 16 major highways running into Paris, 12 into Caen (near Omaha Beach), 12 into Amiens, 11 for Le Mans, and 10 for Rennes. Even the figures don't begin to convey the picture of what this arrangement really means, for France is a series of radiating networks that build up into larger and larger centers. Each small center has its own channel, as it were, to the next higher level. As a general rule, the roads between centers do not go through other towns, because each town is connected to others by its own roads. This is in contrast to the American pattern of stringing small towns out like beads on a necklace along the routes that connect principal centers.

In *The Silent Language* I have described how the man in charge of a French office can often be found in the middle—with his minions placed like satellites on strings radiating outward from him. I once had occasion to deal with such a "central figure" when the French member of a team of scientists under my direction wanted a raise because his desk was in the middle! Even de Gaulle bases his international policy on France's central location. There are those, of course, who will say that the fact that the French school system also follows a highly centralized pattern couldn't possibly have any relationship to the layout of offices, subway systems, road networks, and, in fact, the entire nation, but I could not agree with them. Long experience with different patterns of culture has taught me that the basic threads tend to be woven throughout the entire fabric of a society.

The reason for the review of the three European cultures to which the middle class of the United States is most closely linked (historically and culturally) is as much as anything else a means of providing contrast to highlight some of our own implicit patterns. In this review it was shown that different use of the senses leads to very different needs regarding space no matter on what level one cares to consider it. Everything from an office to a town or city will reflect the sense modalities of its builders and occupants. In considering solutions to problems such as urban renewal and city sinks it is essential to know how the populations involved perceive space and how they use their senses.

# ADUMBRATION AS A FEATURE OF INTERCULTURAL COMMUNICATION
## Edward T. Hall

More than two decades of observing Americans working with other cultures lead me to believe that the majority fall into two groups. One group—mostly professional linguists and anthropologists—is convinced that it is a waste of time to send a man abroad until he is thoroughly conversant with the language and culture on all levels. The other group, appalled by the cost of implementing such a policy and drawing from naïve experience, sees language and culture only as screens that have to be penetrated in order to find the *real* man or people underneath. This second group believes that there is a dichotomy between man and his language-culture and also that good will is the primary material needed to pave the road to understanding.

Intuitively, the specialist in intercultural communications has known for a long time that neither of these positions is appropriate as a matter of policy. There are many times when all the good will in the world would not reach the mind of, say, a Japanese. On the other hand, knowledge of the language and culture will not enable one to "get through" to the other fellow in every instance, even if he is a member of one's own culture.

Anyone who has lived and worked abroad knows that the overseas world is full of surprises, not all of them pleasant, which are due to accumulated slippage in reading subtle signs of which we are often unaware. The surprises that characterize life abroad, as well as at home, are due not so much to ignorance of overt culture as to changes or shifts in the signs that we read to penetrate peoples' facades, signs that tell us what's going on underneath. Goffman (1957, 1959) refers to this process as "going backstage," Ability to read these signs enables us to be "sensitive," to know how the other person is reacting to what we are saying and doing.

To do this, one must be able to read and interpret correctly

Reprinted by permission of the American Anthropological Association from *American Anthropologist*, Vol. 66, No. 6, Pt. 2, 1964.

what I have termed "adumbrations": Those indications preceding or surrounding formal communications which enable organisms to engage in the mutual exchange and evaluation of covert information on what each can expect from the other. Adumbrations are the feedback mechanisms that enable us to steer a smooth course through life or to prepare for attack when combat cannot be avoided. They foreshadow what organisms will do, perform corrective functions, and help set the directions a given communication will take, as well as the actions resulting from it. As we shall see, absence of the adumbrative feature can have catastrophic consequences. In addition, adumbrations are often closely linked with territory, or personal space, occur on different levels, and have proxemic implications (Hall, 1955, 1959, 1963a, 1963b).

Most, if not all, of the conceptual models I have examined have implicit in them the concept that the events referred to occur at different levels in depth. Thinking in the fields of depth psychology, ethnography, and descriptive linguistics has from the very beginning been intermingled on the matter of levels. Freud made the original contribution. Since then, recognition of the need to distinguish between different analytic levels has become fairly widespread, owing to work of Boas (1911), Linton (1936), Kluckhohn (1943), Sapir (1921, 1925, 1927), Sullivan (1947), and others.

Recently, there has been a shift to another dimension. Goffman's frontstage-backstage model implies a horizontal rather than a vertical dimension. Recent studies in ethology suggest that a temporal dimension should be added to our ever-growing inventory.

A LINGUISTIC MODEL FOR ANALYSIS OF CULTURE
In 1953, Trager and I introduced the notion that cultural events occur not on two but on three levels: The formal, the informal, and the technical. We described how these different levels function and can be identified. My own description (Hall, 1959) does not deviate in any significant degree from the joint version. However, I have come to feel that it was somewhat oversimplified and this I shall attempt to correct.

Originally, Trager and I had collected microtexts of references to time as they occurred in the context of conversations in natural settings. After a while (an informal reference) we noted that the items we were collecting were not at all of the same degree of specificity but were in fact quite different. This observation suggested a three-part classification that we later called formal, informal, and technical. Brief examples will suffice here: *Technical:* "Resolving time is 1 $\mu$ sec"; *Formal:* "We always start services promptly at 11"; *Informal:* "I'll see you later." In English we have not only a word for time but an extensive formal vocabulary devoted to it. Whorf's description of linguistic events (see papers in Carroll, 1956) is based on *formal* differences between languages, and this is one reason why they are so difficult to grasp, a generalization which still holds. (On technical, formal, and informal, see Hall, 1959, Ch. IV, for extended discussion.)

To use a spatial metaphor, the formal-informal-technical concept is like a river: The readily perceived main current is the technical, surrounded by the informal back eddies and quiet pools, all of which are contained in a formal channel. Like all analogies, this one has limitations, yet it did help in the organization of our data and in talking to outsiders about what we were doing. When we were developing it, we suggested (Hall & Trager, 1953; Hall, 1959) that a linguistic model was an excellent one for the analysis of culture; that, in fact, all culture could be viewed as communication and all cultural events could be analyzed with the methods of linguistics.

The linguistic model has served us well and will continue to do so, but it requires some broadening, as noted by several linguists (Hockett, 1958; Sebeok, 1962). The great strengths of linguistics are that it has distinguished between *etic* and *emic* events (Hymes, 1962; Greenberg, 1959a, 1959b) and has been able to handle greater and greater complexity. Descriptive linguistic models break down, however, when it is necessary to deal with feedback or teleology. The ability to handle the complexity necessary for discourse analysis has not proceeded with any degree of sophistication, with one exception (Joos, 1962).

Recent advances in isolating the relationship of biochemistry to the environment (Christian, 1961; Deevey, 1960), however, explain population control as the result of a series of interlocking and interdependent servomechanisms that conform to information theory principles as laid down by Wiener

(1948), Shannon and Weaver (1949), Pierce (1956), and their followers. Gilliard (1962) has shown how display behavior also fits this pattern and is also an important process in evolution. Hockett (1958) defined communication so generally as to comprise any event that triggers a response in another organism.

It would seem then that the time is ripe to take the first (even though faltering) steps towards the integration of linguistic models with the communication models of wider scope recently developed in the fields referred to above.

It is suggested that interpersonal communication occurs as a hierarchy of formally determined cybernetic responses. Two processes to which adumbrative behavior is particularly important are those beginning with the informal and becoming increasingly technical, in stages, whenever an inappropriate response is met on either side, and, conversely, those beginning with the technical, and becoming increasingly informal, as appropriate responses are met. Courtship and business negotiation offer many examples of such processes. When the parties know each other well and have enough in common, there is very little need for technical statements. The greater the distance (and the greater the investment), the more necessary it becomes to spell things out, even to the point of specifying which language version, say English or Spanish, of a contract will hold in case of litigation. In other words, the degree of explicit information content of a communication is a function of the degree to which the other party is already appropriately programed. Less explicit means serve the ends of economy, and often avoid the commitment of organisms beyond a point of no return if things don't seem to be going well. On the other hand, some things can be accomplished only if the less explicit means can be successfully employed. Much interaction is under constraints like those set by the girl who wants to be kissed but not to be asked.

These same processes hold true to a lesser degree within a primarily technical sphere, such as conversations between scientists on scientific topics, in the laboratory, as contrasted to publication in a scientific journal.

All this represents a redefinition of the formal, the informal, and the technical levels and is a first attempt to bring these concepts into line with the general principles (but not the details) of information theory.[1] This change in definition is made possible by recognition of constant feedback in man and in animals on every level, from the biochemical to the international (Hall, 1959).

## IMPORTANCE OF ADUMBRATION IN COMMUNICATION

This paper focuses on the informal adumbrative process. It advances the hypothesis that the formal or technical message is more often understood than the informal, but, since the latter influences the meaning of the former, there is always a parataxic element (noise) present in any conversation and this element becomes greater as cultural distance increases.

In essence, every communication appears to comprise three interrelated parts or phases: A beginning phase, a peak phase, and a terminating phase, analogous to a sine wave on an oscilloscope. Musicians refer to the first and last as the attack and decay phase of a musical note.

What happens in one phase apparently influences the other two very considerably. That is, communications have an adumbrative phase (the part that indicates what is coming), the message itself, and a terminal or transition phase that signals how things went or the nature of reply expected. It is my hypothesis that the greatest confusion in intercultural communication can often be traced to failures in catching the true significance of the adumbrative and/or the terminal-transition phase, while, as a general rule, the message itself is often understood. Since the communication is taken as a whole in which the parts are interrelated, however, distortion of or failure to grasp the beginning or end can result in *total* distortion, or what Sullivan (1947) called parataxic communication. (For intracultural consequences as within a family, of contradiction between the message and its context, including the temporal phases dealt with here, see Bateson [1960, 1963] and cf. Ruesch [1961, passim].)

I am going to dwell chiefly on nonverbal communication of which there are many varieties (Hall, 1959; Hymes, 1962), drawing chiefly on my work in time and space as communication. One can begin with the setting which is a form of communication; changes in the setting foreshadow other changes. One might assume that we are talking about the cues, but this is not so. The cue is a short message of minimal redundancy in full awareness from A to B that indicates what A wants B to do. The adumbration, on the other hand, is a perceivable manifestation of A's feelings of which he may not even be aware: His tone of voice (paralinguistic behavior), facial expression, even his dress, posture, and handling of appointments "in time." While most of us are familiar with cues as a special type of communication, adumbrations are less well understood. They were first described under a different name by ecologists studying the behavior of other life forms (ranging from lizards to birds), courting, fighting, socializing, and caring for their young.

## PRE-HUMAN ADUMBRATIVE BEHAVIOR

Adumbration can be observed in all vertebrates, although it is easier for man to recognize it in some forms than in others. Display is the principal vehicle of adumbration among animals. Gilliard (1962) lists four types of display: Vocal, mechanical, mobile, and static-terrestrial. Most, if not all, bird calls can be classified as vocal display. Various mechanical means are also used to produce display by sound. The peacock's tail feathers rustle as he spreads them in display. The bowerbird snaps his bill, the gorilla thumps his chest (Schaller, 1963), and the rattlesnake vibrates his tail to produce a threatening buzz. Movement displays are varied; their most familiar form is the strutting of male pigeons, the neck-stretching and head-bobbing of the gulls. Almost anyone familiar with chickens will recognize the static-terrestrial posturing of the barnyard cock as a display.

Recently display has received more and more attention from the ethologist and the animal psychologist and is seen as an active agent in evolution. It also performs a number of extraordinarily important and vital functions, many of them associated with language in man. Correct interpretation of the significance of given displays is normally limited to within the species, sometimes to within genera.

Display behavior is not limited to a single act but is a sequence of events that combine in different ways with different results. Anyone who has observed gulls will have noted a good deal of posturing and head-bobbing. Tinbergen (1954) gives an excellent description of the significance of this behavior, which appears so bizarre at first glance.

During the mating season, a male blackheaded gull lays claim to a territory, a small plot of land that he defends against his own kind, particularly other males. Whenever another gull lands on his turf, the gull responds with a "long call" (vocal display) and postures his body obliquely (static-terrestrial display). This is the first in a series of "threat displays." During the second step, the two gulls draw closer together, lean forward, and often perform movements of the head and neck (movement displays) that look as if they were choking each other. Then they assume "upright posture" (static-terrestrial display). The third step in the sequence is "head flogging." Performed by only *one* of two males, it signals submission and serves to suppress further aggression. During courtship, head flogging is performed by *both* the male and the female to signal appeasement. This three-step scene (approach, threat, appeasement) is played over and over again until the two gulls apparently get to know each other (are mutually programed) and learn that in this instance *both* can be counted on to end the aggressive exchange sequence by giving the appeasement display. *Repetition* and the ability to *recognize individuals* are important elements in communication sequences such as these.

In still another context, male sea lizards on the Galapagos Islands, defending their territories during mating, engage in mutual display and nobody gets hurt. The ethologist Eibl-Eibesfeldt (1961), recognizing and wishing to test the function of display in suppressing aggression, put male sea lizards in other lizards' territories, thereby short-circuiting the normal display sequence. As soon as this happened, terrible fighting broke out.[2]

Those who have studied display are generally agreed that it performs several important communicative functions both within a species and between species. It reduces the amount of actual combat and limits serious fighting to interspecies. During courtship it synchronizes the behavior of the sexes, gets attention, suppresses nonsexual responses, and releases the submissive posture in the female. On the other hand, lack of participation in a given display pattern isolates even closely related species from each other, thus acting as an evolutionary force in the maintenance of reproductive isolation.

In encounters between species, ability to interpret correctly at least part of the display sequence is of critical importance. Hediger (1955), the animal psychologist, has stressed the necessity for men to be able to identify the adumbration behavior of other species. Pandas, bears, and snakes are dangerous to man because it is difficult to know how they are feeling from moment to moment.[3]

The hypothesis can be advanced that: *Unless the adumbrative sequence is known, two species or societies or two individuals cannot interact in any way towards each other except in a parataxic manner and with ultimate aggression.* Within species, short-circuiting the adumbrative sequence leads to serious fighting.[4]

### THE ADUMBRATIVE FUNCTION IN MAN

As we have seen, some of the functions of adumbration are: To protect organisms (including man) from becoming overcommitted, to give them some control over their encounters with others, to protect egos, and to provide an automatic buffer or means of transition from one segment of a communication sequence to another; adumbration may also serve to establish intimacy. In many cultures, there are intermediaries who act in an adumbrative role, relative to the focal messages of a relationship. They may serve as buffers to save face and prevent over-commitment, on the one hand, to establish the necessary or desired closeness on the other. In our own culture, time, space, and materials communicate on many levels including the adumbrative level.

The examples I shall use are drawn from my studies of proxemics, the human use of microspace (Hall, 1963a, 1963b). There are three different types of microspace (Hall, 1963a, 1963b): Fixed-feature space (including the setting); semifixed-feature space (components that are part of the setting and can be moved); and dynamic space (man's informal repertoire for handling space). The desirability of choosing a proper setting for a communication is so well known that there would be no need to mention it, if it were not for the fact the choice of setting differs from culture to culture, often for the same act.

This is one reason why Americans in foreign lands who become ill often suffer from anxiety as soon as they go to the doctor. Sivadon (ms.) has stressed the importance, even for the indigenous population, of recognizing the adumbrative side of the setting. He states that hospital waiting rooms and doctors' offices should emphasize the familiar and be as free as possible of the unknown, such as glass cases full of chromium instruments which are familiar to the physician but not to the patient.

In the international political arena, adumbrative space has proved to be significant indeed. All other things being equal, and given a willingness to negotiate in the first place, there is little adumbrative significance for Americans regarding the choice of the place of a negotiation. Our approach is to get on with negotiations and "not hold up the show." Allowing the other party to choose or move a negotiation site, once it has been established, signifies only that we intend to be "reasonable." However, when the American negotiators readily agreed to move the setting of the Korean truce negotiations from the Swedish peace ship in Seoul harbor to Panmunjom, the Chinese Communists apparently assumed that this represented an "appeasement" display. As most Americans will remember, it took a while to disabuse them of this misconception.

In the international business context, there are numerous examples of how familiarity with the differences in the adumbrative significance of the setting helped negotiations, while ignorance hindered them. Some of our more adept American firms have learned that they do better if they create settings with design features which enable their Latin American counterparts to progress, like Tinbergen's gulls, through known stages in the business courtship. One very successful Wall Street executive specializing in Latin America chooses a club that features dark, oak-paneled walls, heavy, leather-covered chairs, high ceilings, and stained-glass windows, a setting that is impressive and at the same time "simpatico" to his clients. A little settee with a low table in front permits the necessary closeness to begin a relationship. As many American business men have discovered, the home is *not* the setting that a Latin American chooses to consummate a business deal. The home is for the family and not for business.

In Japan, business men often take the preliminary steps in a negotiation on the golf course. As one oil executive put it, "We soon learned, from the number of golf games involved, how to compute the size of the contract we were going to negotiate."

Even on familiar home ground in the United States, there are instances when inferences drawn from spatial behavior have proved to be in error. This type of mistake can be due either to socioeconomic or regional differences in the background of the two individuals. Courting provides us with some excellent examples of breakdown in the adumbrative phase that is often serious enough to kill a budding romance. Difficulties of this type have been fully described in our printed folk literature. I would like, however, to use one of my own examples because it seems quite appropriate.

In the early thirties, when automobiles were just beginning to be commonly used for courting, where the girl sat when she entered the car foreshadowed what kind of evening the couple was going to have. This was particularly true of the first date. The convention in my part of the country was for a "nice" girl to sit as far away from the driver as she could get (which wasn't very far). There was, however, a category of female, a member of a particular subculture, for whom it was not only permissible but customary to "snuggle up" to her date, even on a first night out, without the slightest intention of putting ideas into his head about what kind of a girl she was. Undoubtedly there were boys who were sufficiently motivated to surmount this particular source of adumbrative interference in communication when they faced it for the first time, and who eventually pieced together successfully the foreshadowing features of each successive stage in the courtship. In most instances, however, reproductive isolation was successfully maintained. Those I have talked to who ran afoul of this difference in pattern were so frustrated by it that they gathered up what was left of their wounded egos, said goodnight, and quickly shifted their attention to women in whom there was a more predictable connection between what one observed and what was going on inside.

Some of the most familiar instances of adumbrations in which the feelings are at variance with the overt behavior pattern are those having to do with where people stand and sit in relation to each other and whether they touch each other. There is, first of all, a large group in which touching is important, even with strangers. An equally numerous group of people avoids touching. Those who are not used to being approached closely are made uncomfortable by the laying-on of hands and take it as preliminary to either a fight or a sexual "pass."

Stated this way, there seems to be nothing mysterious about adumbrative communication and, *in fact, the idea is deceptively simple.* My hypothesis is that the specific technical communication on the overt level is seldom seriously misinterpreted, even in cross-cultural contexts, if the adumbrative part is read correctly. What is most often misinterpreted is the adumbration. In some instances, this can be serious enough to prevent the real communication from ever emerging or even to result in a fight.

In the course of this discussion, nothing has been said about transitions or juncture phenomena in transcultural encounters, mostly because virtually nothing is known about it. Our own version of Western culture seems to emphasize the build-up or attack phase and to pay little attention to the equivalent of terminal junctures and transitions. Yet I recall numerous instances when I was forced to look back on a sequence of events that seemed to be going well at the time and reappraise what I thought was going on because of an ending that appeared abrupt. In most instances it was impossible to judge whether things went well or badly until someone familiar with the local dialect of behavior could be consulted.

## SUMMARY

In this article there has been no attempt to be definitive, and only broad outlines have been sketched. In summary, the view seems to be gaining currency that communication occurs simultaneously on several levels in depth, as well as proceeding sequentially according to quite rigid but unstated rules. How a given communication sequence develops can be seen as a function of the strength of motivations of the two parties, their knowledge of the system, and how they respond to each other's adumbrations. All communication in this sense can be viewed as a discourse, even though different styles (Joos, 1962) are used, while ability to participate in the discourse is a function of programing.

In the display sequences of animals, we find simple models

of behavior that may have relevance to man within cultures and across cultures. The study of animal behavior is relevant because man does not experience as much difficulty with speech (even if the language is different) as he does with these older, more primitive, and possibly more basic communications which are currently in the early stages of examination. In the larger sense, display is seen to perform important functions in evolution and in population control which may also be of some relevance to man.

148 C

## NOTES

1. See also Sebeok (1962) for integration of ethological data with information theory; Reusch and Kees (1956) use an information theory model but not a linguistic one as a point of departure.
2. For a more detailed treatment of display, the reader is referred to Hinde and Tinbergen (1958).
3. It is also a distortion, or absence, of normal adumbrative functions that makes the assaultive psychotic so dangerous. Personnel treating such patients are in constant danger until they learn to pick up the subtle signs that foretell impending aggression.
4. One of the consequences of overcrowding may be that there is not enough room for proper display.

## REFERENCES

Boas, Franz, "Introduction," in *Handbook of American Indian Languages*, F. Boas (ed.), *Bulletin of the Bureau of American Ethnology*, 1911, 40, part I, Washington, D.C.

Bateson, G., "Minimal Requirements for a Theory of Schizophrenia," *A.M.A. Archives of General Psychiatry*, 1960, 2, 477-491.

Bateson, G., "Exchange of Information About Patterns of Human Behavior," in *Information Storage and Neural Control*, W. Fields and W. Abbott (eds.), Springfield, Ill.: Thomas, 1963, 1-12.

Carroll, John B., *Language, Thought and Reality. Selected Writings of Benjamin Lee Whorf*, New York, Wiley, 1956.

Christian, John J., "Phenomena Associated with Population Density," *Proceedings National Academy of Sciences* 1961, 47, (April), 428-449.

Deevey, E. S., "The Hare and the Haruspex: A Cautionary Tale," *American Scientist*, 1960, 48(3), 415.

Eibl-Eibesfeldt, I., "The Fighting Behavior of Animals," *Scientific American*, 1961, 207 (December), 112-122.

Gilliard, E., "On the Breeding Behavior of the Cock-of-the-Rock (*aves, rupicola rupicola*)," *Bulletin of the American Museum of Natural History*, 1962, 124, article 2, New York.

Cultural Dimensions